Bashful Billionaire

Bashful Billionaire

The story of Howard Hughes

by Albert B. Gerber

LYLE STUART, INC. ★ NEW YORK

To Rhona

my editor, critic and whip-cracker

CONTENTS

Bashful Billionaire

A Mysterious Train Ride

SUNDAY, JULY 17, 1966

SUPREME COURT Justice William O. Douglas, sixty-seven, and Cathleen Curran Heffernan, twenty-three, were married last night at a friend's home in Encino, a suburb of Los Angeles. Justice Douglas and his bride were considering a visit to Red China as part of their honeymoon trip.

Musicals were having a field day in New York with *Fiddler on the Roof* at the Imperial, *Wait a Minim* at the Golden, *Sweet Charity* at the Palace, and *Mame* at the Winter Garden.

The movie houses featured *The Blue Max*, Elizabeth Taylor and Richard Burton in *Who's Afraid of Virginia Woolf*, Sidney Poitier in *A Patch of Blue*, and a Swedish import, *Dear John*.

Number one on the fiction best-seller list was *Valley of the Dolls*, followed by *The Adventurers* and *The Source*. The latter book, by James A. Michener, still going strong after sixty weeks on the list, was on its way to a new record.

Howard Hughes was sixty years old.

1

The sun was just setting outside the grimy Santa Fe Terminal in Los Angeles that hot Sunday evening in July. The workmen coupling the pair of luxury private Pullmans to the Chicago-bound Super Chief had little interest in their purpose or in the passengers they would receive. One, troubled by thirst, remarked to his partner, "I bet there's cold water inside. I'm going to take a look."

As he approached the car door, a natty young man with a crew-cut greeted him pleasantly. "Anything I can do for you?"

Puzzled, the railroad man replied, "I don't think so. I'm just going inside for something."

Crew-cut stopped smiling. "I'm afraid you can't come in here."

The railroad worker, annoyed by the rapidly receding vision of the anticipated drink, replied belligerently, "Who are you to tell me what to do!"

"These cars are private and no one is allowed inside," was the firm answer.

The railroad man went back to his hose connections and a few minutes later four men approached the cars, dragging a hand truck piled high with an unorthodox assortment of baggage. There were office files, a small refrigerator, medical supplies, hospital-type oxygen equipment, and other unusual items.

The men escorting and pulling the baggage truck were even more unexpected. They were dressed in neat business suits, white shirts and conservative ties. Any one of them would have been at home in a bank or board room. As soon as they pulled up alongside the two cars they began to move the equipment from the baggage car into the Pullmans. Silently and efficiently they worked.

Not a word passed between them, until one muttered "damn" when a large overstuffed parlor chair would not go through the doorway. All four men joined in the effort to get the chair through the aperture but to no avail. Their faces showed the first sign of emotion as they regretfully carried the chair back to the truck.

Quickly the remainder of the contents of the truck was transferred to the two cars. The men now ranged themselves about the platform, attempting inconspicuously but unsuccessfully to melt into the background. It was obvious to the most casual observer that the train was under surveillance.

One of the men pulled a newspaper out of his pocket, but his eyes made it apparent that he was watching from behind the concealing sheets. Occasionally he glanced down at the date, Sunday, July 17, 1966, but his vigilance remained constant.

All along the platform, passengers were boarding the train and visitors were alighting from it; cheerful commands of "take care of yourself" and "have a good time" floated freely through the air. The train was more crowded than usual because a current airline strike had forced many who would normally zoom through the skies to use this now-nearly-outmoded method of long distance transportation. The final moment came and the old familiar cry of "all aboard" could be heard. Doors clanged shut and the guards jumped aboard the two private Pullman cars. The Super Chief was on its way.

No more than ten minutes passed before the crack train began to reduce speed as it approached the Pomona station. Trainmen and passengers buzzed to each other speculatively. It was a long time since the Chief had stopped at Pomona. As the train ground to its unscheduled halt, a shabby black limousine pulled up and discharged a tall, gangly man clad in pajamas, a topcoat draped over his shoulders. With him were several more of the crewcut young men, bearing luggage and briefcases. The party boarded the private cars and the train resumed its journey.

The next day rumors circulated freely through the train.

"The President is on the train."

"President Johnson?"

"No, the President of the Santa Fe Railroad."

"No, you're wrong. I heard it's the President's two daughters."

Included in the speculation were the names of the Vice President of the United States, the Governor of California, the Governor of almost every other state of the United States, famous men of the world: J. Paul Getty, Harold Wilson, Rothschild. The identity of the mysterious passenger, however, remained a secret. Several curiosity seekers, both railroad employees and passengers, tried craftily to gain admittance to the Pullman. All were politely but firmly halted. All inquiries were left unanswered.

Tuesday evening the two cars were dropped from the train in Chicago and later attached to a New York Central train which arrived in Boston on the following day. Many of the people on board, determined to solve the puzzle, waited around to see who left the two closely guarded, mystery-shrouded Pullman cars.

The watchers were doomed to disappointment. A polished limousine, empty except for the driver, pulled up to a side door and a crew-cut man about 40 years of age, undistinguished in appearance and unknown to anyone in the crowd, left the Pullman, went directly to the side exit where the limousine waited, entered the car and was driven away.

The crowds, frustrated and disappointed, finally melted away. It had not been Lyndon Johnson or his two daughters; it had not been Barry Goldwater. The traveler appeared to be a man nobody knew.

But the incident was not yet closed. After all the passengers, the baggage, the mail and everything else consigned to Boston had been unloaded, the train, with the Pullmans still attached, began an unscheduled ride northward. After traveling a distance of about six miles it stopped at a little way station where the tall, lean man, followed by the other members of his party, disembarked and entered a waiting limousine, which drove back into Boston and pulled up at the service entrance of the Ritz-Carlton Hotel.

Other guards were waiting with the service elevator, commandeered and held in readiness for the arrival of the mystery man. Silently it whisked him to the fifth floor, reserved in its entirety for the unknown man and his party.

The next morning the unidentified guest left the same way he had entered, was taken to the Peter Bent Brigham Hospital and installed in the three private rooms that had been reserved in his name. Shortly after his arrival he was seen by Dr. George Stowen, Chief of Medicine at the hospital and a renowned endocrinologist, world-famous for his knowledge of hormones and hormone therapy. He had treated his nameless patient before, but a return visit had become necessary.

This is not the beginning of a spy story or a novel of intrigue. It is a first glimpse of Howard Hughes—the bashful billionaire.

Howard Hughes vs.
the United States Army

AUGUST, 1947

THE *New York Times* reported that the highest military authorities had been thrown into "concern and apprehension" when civilian officials granted the Kaiser-Hughes experimental Flying Boat contract at the most critical period in the war. The *Times* attributed its information to Robert A. Lovett, Under Secretary of State.

Senator Homer Ferguson, Republican of Michigan, chairman of the Senate subcommittee investigating defense contracts, issued a subpoena for Howard Hughes to appear before the committee "forthwith."

The millionaire aircraft designer told reporters he would appear before the committee on Wednesday, August 6, 1947.

The United States offered to mediate the undeclared war between the Netherlands and the Republic of Indonesia.

Princess Elizabeth and Lieutenant Philip Mountbatten announced that they would be married in Westminster Abbey on November 20, 1947. King George read to a special privy council meeting in Buckingham Palace his formal declaration of consent to the marriage.

The Dow-Jones average of thirty industrials closed at 183.18. The stock exchange leaders in trading included Studebaker at $22, United Corporation at $3.50, Baltimore and Ohio Railroad at $13.50, and United States Steel at $74.25.

The leading movies were Humphrey Bogart and Barbara Stanwyck in *The Two Mrs. Carrolls,* James Mason in *The Secret of Stambul,* and Esther Williams in *Fiesta.*

Howard Hughes was forty-one years old.

2

THE CAUCUS ROOM of the Senate Office Building was enveloped in the humid heat of a Washington summer day. Howard Hughes sat quietly listening to the proceedings of a subcommittee investigating the National Defense Program. He had been carefully following the daily transcripts of the testimony to the committee and he was annoyed, recognizing that this was a political persecution rather than an honest investigation.

Senator Owen Brewster, instigator of the inquiry, was doing his utmost to make it the springboard to the Republican Vice-Presidential, or even hopefully the Presidential, nomination. Furthermore, Brewster had a secondary but equally significant purpose in this investigation of Howard Hughes—the Senator, sometimes called Juan Trippe's boy in the Senate, had tried for years to force Hughes to sell out his TWA holdings to Pan American Airways and thereby give Trippe's Pan Am a monopoly on American aviation overseas.

Hughes contemplated these bureaucrats who had contributed nothing but words to the war effort, yet now dared to impugn his patriotism. He knew if all the facts were examined honestly, the true patriot would be revealed to all. He could hardly be held responsible for the bias of the Army aviation people. He had tried his best, but they didn't like him and so they turned their backs on his ideas, and his remarkable talent. The armed forces were obviously not prepared to greet his inventions and technical improvements with loud hosannas and congratulations.

His first venture into aircraft development had been almost accidental and, he believed, providential. A skilled aviator, having learned to fly when still a boy, he became interested in a hydroplane he saw in California one day, and he bought it. He ordered the flying boat hauled to a repair shop in Burbank, California, where he could have some modifications made. The shop assigned a young

aviation enthusiast, Glen Odekirk, to work with Hughes. The two
men got along well together. One day Odekirk, who was also a
pilot, learned that Hughes planned to fly the plane east and needed
a mechanic to go with him. Eagerly Odekirk applied for the job.

"But you're married and this job will take at least three months,"
Hughes objected.

Odekirk argued, "That doesn't matter, I'll go with you anyway.
My wife won't care."

Hughes, saying he would think about it, turned and walked away,
but after taking a few steps tossed back over his shoulder to Odekirk, "We'll leave in the morning."

The trip stretched out for many months and included participation in the All-American Air Meet in which Hughes won an amateur
pilot event. During that year of 1934, the skilled French pilot
Raymond Delmotte, in a plane developed by the Government of
France at a purported cost in excess of one million dollars, captured
the land speed record from the American, James Wedell. The new
record was 314.219 miles per hour and it was part personal pride
and part patriotism that decided Howard to recapture the record
for the United States. More, he would do it in a plane of his own
manufacture.

He sent Odekirk back to California to locate and equip a hangar,
and to get ready to design and build a plane. Odekirk found a suitable location at the Glendale, California, Airport and began to lay
in a stock of needed tools and equipment. Hughes returned shortly
thereafter and hired Richard Palmer, a recent graduate of the California Institute of Technology, and meteorologist W.C. Rockefeller,
together with another dozen men, all skilled workers.

With Hughes as task-master the group soon learned what it
meant to work beyond human endurance. For days without rest,
Hughes would work around the clock, sustaining himself on sandwiches and milk. If he did become overwhelmed with the need for
sleep, he would slip away for a few hours in the middle of the day.
Then he would return completely refreshed and ready for another
extended siege of hard work.

Occasionally Hughes would disappear without a word to anyone,
and return days later, offering no explanation for his absence. The
careful observer, however, might have noted that when he returned
he had new information on a problem that had been plaguing
them. He might have been to an Army installation in Virginia where

he would discuss the question with the Army's best aeronautical engineers; he might visit one of the important universities to pick the brains of the appropriate professors; but wherever he went he returned full of vital information and new ideas on how to solve the currently vexing problem.

Word of Hughes' purpose and plan leaked out and the newspapers and magazines sent reporters to get the story. Hughes, however, suspected them of being from rival manufacturers, evincing for the first time what would become a fetish for privacy and secrecy. He hired guards to keep all visitors away, and this naturally stirred even more curiosity. Instead of stemming the publicity he succeeded only in spurring it on. An aviation magazine printed an article in which it said, "Hughes' ship is still a mystery. No dope on its design, construction or performance has been released. The wings are of combined wood and metal construction. The rest of the ship is all metal. Both the landing gear and the tail wheel are retractable. Wind-tunnel tests are supposed to have indicated possible speed of 365 m.p.h."

Part of the magazine writer's information was correct but much of it was not. The retractable landing gear was the first of Hughes' great innovations. Although the idea was not new, it had never actually been applied in flight. This was a period of striving to "streamline" aircraft and designers well knew that the greater the size and number of surfaces a plane presented against the wind, the more resistance it would create and the less speed the plane would develop.

In flight, of course, the landing gear was unnecessary and if it could somehow be brought up and concealed in the fuselage there would be comparably less wind resistance. In Delmotte's plane the French designers sheathed the landing gear in smooth metal, thereby cutting down somewhat on its resistance. Hughes, on the other hand, put the landing equipment on a pivot and worked out a system for bringing it up into the fuselage.

A second innovation in the H-1 was a completely smooth surface. Despite their knowledge of streamlining, no aeronautical engineers had as yet paid attention to exposed nuts or bolts. From a word dropped by a professor, Hughes realized that each uneven surface added to the problem of increasing his speed and consequently he and his men designed the plane so that every nut, bolt and rivet was countersunk in such fashion as to present to the wind an absolutely smooth surface.

Finally, Hughes designed the wing spread to the smallest point consistent with sound aeronautical principles that would allow the plane to rise in the air and to stay there. The wings presented another point of resistance to the speed of flight—they were essential for the plane to be able to rise and remain in the air, but they served no speed function. Up until that time planes were designed with a wing span sufficient to allow the plane to rise and fly, and with enough extra span to provide a margin of safety. This margin Hughes was willing to sacrifice to gain additional speed.

By August, 1935, the plane was ready for flight testing and a heated discussion arose about who the test pilot would be. Over the protests of Odekirk, Rockefeller and the others, Hughes announced, "This is my plane and I intend to test it!"

Further argument was useless—Hughes was not a man to change his mind. Throughout his life as a builder of planes, Hughes continued to insist on performing the test flights himself. His obstinacy on this point later almost cost him his life, but he never changed. The challenge of the air called strongly to him and it could be met only by his personal handling of the controls.

At last the H-1 was moved by ground transport to the Municipal Airport in Los Angeles and on August 18, 1935, Hughes made his first test flight. Word of the unveiling of the mystery ship had gotten out and workers and enthusiasts from company presidents down to grease monkeys flocked to the field to watch. Howard climbed into the cockpit and sat there quietly waiting for the temperature gauge to indicate that the carburetors were hot and the engine ready for flight. Satisfied at last, he taxied out on the runway as he saw the flashing green light from the tower signaling permission for take-off.

A last check of gauges and magneto assured him that the plane was ready to go. Now with the throttle on full, and the stick pulled back almost into his stomach, he felt the plane move forward. As it gathered speed, he gently eased the stick forward to cut down wind resistance, then gradually pulled it back again. He could see the end of the runway rushing up to meet him, but he fought the temptation to pull back sharply, although the rough grass and uneven ground beyond the end of the runway would certainly wreck the plane if he did not lift off in time. For one panic-stricken moment

he may have wondered if he had overdone the short wing span—
with a foot or two more of wing surface the plane would have already risen into the air. Odekirk's words rang in his ears, "If I had
known you were going to fly this test I would definitely have
made some changes in the plans." Now, just as it seemed certain
that the aircraft would use up the remaining runway too soon, it
rose gently into the air and continued its upward flight. Hughes did
not try to test for speed. He circled the field for fifteen minutes, and
then brought the plane in for a smooth, perfect landing.

The flight test revealed the need for certain changes which he
and his mechanics began to make at once. He also decided to use
a field with a longer take-off strip for the next flight. On September
12, he towed the plane to Martin Field in Santa Ana, California,
where he would endeavor to break the Frenchman's speed record.
Since he wanted his efforts to be official, he had to comply with the
established requirements of the American National Aeronautics Association and the Air Nationale Federation Aeronautique.

The rules of both associations specified four measured course
flights on the same day in order to qualify as an official record. In
addition, all flights had to be from a level position, timed and wit-
nessed by official judges. The world's outstanding female aviatrix—
Amelia Earhart Putnam—watched the flight aloft in her own plane,
accompanied by Paul Mantz, the famous American flyer, and Lawrence Therkelson representing the American association.

It was late afternoon before all of the timing devices and photographic equipment were ready and those involved in the flight
thought it might be wise to wait for the following day. However,
the impatient Hughes was not one to accept delay of his plans with
equanimity. In spite of official objections, he took off. He made his
first pass into the measured mile-and-three-quarters at a speed of
346 miles per hour, but unfortunately he entered the course in a
descending flight path in violation of the rules, so the judges had
to disqualify the flight.

He returned to his starting position and this time hit the course
on a completely level pattern, being clocked at a speed of 352 miles
per hour; the return flight showed 339 miles per hour. It appeared
that Hughes was well on his way to setting a new world record
when the judges were forced to end the trial because impending
darkness made it impossible to see and photograph the tests.

Hughes, frustrated and unable to rest until the tests were over, spent the night inspecting, adjusting and readjusting various parts of the plane to bring it to a peak of perfection.

On Friday morning, September 13, 1935, the unsuperstitious Howard Hughes took off once again in his H-1 and made four perfect runs over the course. Unofficially he apparently had achieved a record 350 miles per hour, considerably in excess of the existing official record of 314 miles per hour.

However, the speed achieved on some of the runs did not satisfy the demanding perfectionist, so he decided to essay a few more trials. On the sixth pass the engine died and Hughes, believing that the fuel supply was gone, switched to his extra tank, but the engine failed to restart. Spotting a likely location, he lowered the landing gear and glided down onto a deep patch of grass. When the observers raced up to Hughes, they found him sitting on the ground making notes.

Hughes responded to the congratulations on breaking the world's record in typical fashion: "That plane can do 385 miles per hour and might well have done it at this time if the cockpit shield hadn't blown off." Then he added in typical Hughesian fashion: "I only got a chance to use 900 of the 1100 horsepower available."

Later a thorough examination of the plane revealed that a wad of steel wool was jammed into the main gas line. In spite of much muttering about sabotage, no proof could be obtained that the plane had been tampered with.

The two aviation associations agreed on an official record time of 352.388 miles per hour. American aviation prestige took a major stride forward. In addition, the record-breaking H-1 added another dimension in economy: the plane had cost only $120,000.

Hughes was interested in long distance flying both on a personal basis—he liked to speed through the air—and also for the purpose of carrying passengers. He watched as speed flight after speed flight gradually lowered the record time for the California-to-New York flight until finally Roscoe Turner made the coast-to-coast run in a a few minutes over ten hours during the Bendix Air Race in September, 1934. It was then that Hughes determined to seek a new record. He considered carefully and at last decided not to use the H-1 but instead to fly a Northrop Gamma mail plane, modified with extra tanks.

Hughes had the Northrop installed in his hangar at Glendale and proceeded to turn it into a totally new model. From the Army

Air Corps he borrowed the latest Cyclone engine and a Hamilton variable pitch propeller. During that fall of 1935 Hughes forgot everything but the plane as he drove himself and his crew to complete the modifications that would make the Northrop the fastest long distance plane in the world.

Late one night, while Hughes and his men labored on in total disregard of the clock, Odekirk asked Howard, "Do you know what day this is?"

Hughes looked at him blankly, then smiled, remembering. "Yes, it's my birthday," he answered, pleased at Odekirk's reminder.

"Howard, that's not exactly what I meant," replied Odekirk quietly. "It's Christmas Eve and I think we should let the men leave."

Howard acquiesced, but the following day and for the next two weeks, they made up in long, hard hours for the short time off.

At noon on January 13, 1936, Hughes climbed into the plane, taxied to the beginning of the airstrip and received his clearance for take-off. The hands of the clock stood at exactly 12:15 P.M. Pacific Standard Time as he climbed up and away from the Los Angeles Union Air Terminal in a plane carrying a record load for its type—in excess of 10,000 pounds.

From the beginning, the flight to New York was plagued with troubles. On take-off, the radio antenna snapped off, leaving Hughes with no method of communicating with the ground. As soon as he reached his assigned 15,000 feet altitude, the weather closed in, forcing him to fly blind. He studied his fuel consumption, made a few rapid calculations, and decided that the only way to conserve fuel was to fly higher. Unable to notify the ground of his decision, he took it upon himself to increase his altitude to 18,000 feet.

Over Wichita, Kansas, the plane encountered rough air and bounced around so severely that the dial dropped off the compass. Hughes, with neither radio guidance nor compass bearing, still refused to quit. Fortunately, the moon rose and it, together with the stars and the familiar patterns made by occasional city lights, provided him with navigation aids. He sped on through the night.

Now the rarefied atmosphere at 18,000 feet began to produce anoxia and he had to fight against lethargic drowsiness. Fortunately, he had equipped the plane with an oxygen tank from which he could take whiffs to revive himself. When he recognized Indianapolis below him, he advanced the throttle to increase his speed from 275 to 300 miles per hour. At midnight he wheeled over Pittsburgh and headed for the Newark Airport where he touched down at 12:42:10 A.M. Eastern Standard Time, having completed the distance, coast-to-coast, in a total of 9 hours, 27 minutes, 10 seconds. He had bettered the old record by more than half an hour!

As always with anything Hughes did, the trip had been clothed in secrecy. Aside from the official timers who were alerted both in Los Angeles and in New York, no one, including the press, had been notified. Word of the record-breaking flight spread rapidly after his landing and alert reporters quickly tracked Hughes to his suite in the Waldorf-Astoria. Later in his career, he learned to protect his privacy by not making use of the better-known hotels. Now, however, awakened by the newsmen, he favored them with a series of honest comments which somehow earned him an unanticipated amount of publicity.

In reply to questions, he stated laconically, "I wanted to go to New York so I tried to see how fast I could get there."

"No," he replied to one reporter, "I did not eat anything on the flight. I had too much to do and no time to eat."

For the first time the reporters, forced to repeat their questions several times, began to suspect a hearing problem which the *New York Times* commented on in a report of the flight. The general belief was that he had been deafened by his flight, but in truth he was gradually losing his hearing.

When asked to speculate on how long he thought his new record would last, Hughes replied, "There is no record that can't be beaten."

After listening to a reporter marvel at the ability to travel from Los Angeles to New York in less than ten hours, Hughes predicted, "That's not much. Regular passenger ships will be making the trip in ten hours or less soon."

In response to questions on how he accounted for the remarkable success of his mission he gave full credit to the Army Air Corps Cyclone engine as the major factor.

The ice and snow, and the leaden sky of New York in January were not to Hughes' liking so he returned to his plane and flew down to Miami for rest and relaxation. While there he learned that speed pilot James Wedell had a short time earlier broken the Miami-New York record by completing the flight in slightly over five hours. Hughes regarded this as a personal challenge.

On April 21, 1936, at about noon, he left Miami in his modified Northrop Gamma and traveled the 1200 miles to New York in 4 hours, 21 minutes, 32 seconds. Now the newspapers had a field day. They labeled Hughes the hottest pilot of all time and predicted that he would break all the existing speed records. Annoyed by this unwelcome attention, Howard began to develop the innumerable disguises he would use for the rest of his life. He coined pseudonyms for hotel registers, grew beards and shaved them off, and adopted unusual dress habits, all with the single purpose of evading the reporters and the curiosity-seekers.

Hughes' next stop in his now world-famous plane was Chicago, where he met a friend with whom he discussed the present speed of the Northrop and the possibilities for increased speed in the future. Howard said that it would not be too long before a person could have lunch in Chicago and dinner in Los Angeles. Commercial aircraft in 1936 flew the 1,800 miles in twelve to thirteen hours. Howard's friend offered to bet him $50 that Hughes could not have his lunch in Chicago and arrive in Los Angeles in time for dinner —even including the two hours gained by virtue of the different time zones. Hughes accepted the wager and on May 14, 1936 at 1:05 P.M. Chicago time (11:05 A.M. Los Angeles time) he lifted his heavily loaded Northrop out of the Chicago airport.

To compensate for the initial weight of a full load of gasoline the flight plan provided for flying the first thousand miles at 3,000 feet and the balance of the trip at 16,000 feet. This meant that during the second half of the trip he would have to use oxygen. As so often happened to him, on this flight too the fates seemed to conspire against him.

Shortly out of Chicago he met headwinds of 40 miles per hour and had to climb to 20,000 feet to get over the gale and avoid loss of his forward speed. The thinner air at this altitude forced him to use oxygen but a defect in the tank blocked the flow. Drawing deep breaths of the thin air into his straining lungs, he fought off the onset of anoxia. Struggling to remain conscious he held his altitude until he passed over Kansas City, after which he descended to a lower level only to encounter dense fog. With no radio—it had failed —he had to fly blind and isolated from the earth below. And now nature flung down her final challenge—ice began to form on the wings!

A lesser pilot would have given up, but not Howard Hughes. Not the wager but the challenge drove him on. He could not admit defeat. Against all odds, he doggedly flew on and at 7:15:25 P.M. Pacific Coast time, he brought his plane down safely on the strip at the Los Angeles Municipal Airport, exactly 8 hours, 10 minutes, 25 seconds after he had left Chicago. He went at once to the lunch counter in the Grand Central Air Terminal and ordered dinner, thus winning his bet!

"I have learned more in eight hours," he said to questioners, "than in the last ten years."

Novelist Rupert Hughes, commenting on his nephew's exploits in the air, remarked, "Born without wings, man has made them for himself. He out-climbs the eagle, leaves the hawk behind, out-plays the swallow in the air." In his bold attacks on space and time, Howard had done all of this.

The H-1 gave Hughes a world speed record. The Northrop Gamma gave him distance speed records. Together they gave him knowledge and experience which sparked a series of brilliant ideas for military planes. He went immediately to the installation at the Glendale Airport, which he now called Hughes Aircraft Company, and instructed General Manager J. B. Alexander to offer to build a new model plane for the Army.

Hughes had the design completely outlined in his mind. At that time almost all aircraft were biplanes: two-wing planes resembling an ice-cream sandwich with the fuselage neatly nestled between the wings. These aircraft flew more like kites than the powered gliders that Hughes envisioned. He visualized a single-wing plane driven by two or more motors. The clean, sleek lines would be balanced and enhanced by a cantilevered wing, constructed with such strength that external bracing (which caused additional wind resistance) would be unnecessary.

Hughes outlined his idea for the monoplane pursuit ship to Alexander. He would build the fastest plane in the military world. It would cruise at approximately 400 miles per hour and it would outfly every military aircraft in existence. Equipped with highpowered machine guns it would out-shoot and out-maneuver anything that could be put into the air against it. The United States would be guaranteed air supremacy for many years to come. Excited and eager to start construction, Hughes ordered Alexander to make immediate contact with the military at Wright Field to work out arrangements for full scale construction on the new plane.

The Army was unimpressed with Hughes' idea. It countered with objections and argued the lack of money to build new airplanes in 1936. To Hughes, they sounded just like what they really were—excuses for doing nothing.

After long and fruitless efforts to obtain approval of his idea, Hughes got word that the Army was interested in having him design an interceptor. This was a new type of plane for the United States, although England had already built one, and it was slightly different in design from a pursuit ship. He went to work on it at once.

The more he thought about it the more he realized that in order to get the real speed, maneuverability, and other characteristics needed by a military plane, it would be necessary not only to make a cantilever monoplane but also to equip it with at least two engines to provide the world's greatest power plant. He devoted himself completely and enthusiastically to this dream and designed a plane which would guarantee America's supremacy in the air. He kept the blueprint shop busy around the clock.

When the design was finished and ready to submit, the Army informed him that it would be necessary for him to hold up and wait until other aircraft companies, particularly Lockheed, could also furnish designs. Hughes was forced to sit back and do nothing. Waiting did not come easily to him. He became bitter and restive. Some of his engineers, with little to do while they waited, left their jobs and went to work for Lockheed. By a not so strange coincidence, when Lockheed unveiled its newly designed military interceptor plane, it too was a two-engine cantilever monoplane. The Army awarded the contract to Lockheed to build the plane which later was designated as the P-38. This aircraft caused its maker to become one of the largest airplane manufacturing companies in the world.

Howard Hughes was deeply embittered by this experience. He was convinced that the Army, instead of judging solely on the merits of the design for the new aircraft, had been influenced by social contacts. Lockheed representatives had wined and dined the Army Air Corps officers at Wright Field. (This was standard operating procedure for contractors trying to get government orders.) Hughes, on the other hand, had been too busy designing the best possible planes to have time for superficial social entertaining.

Hughes was brought out of his reverie by the sound of his name. Senator Homer Ferguson of Michigan, chairman of the subcommittee, told him to raise his right hand. "Do you solemnly swear that in the matter now pending before this committee you will tell the truth, the whole truth, and nothing but the truth, so help you God?"

Howard replied, "I do."

Now came the routine questions.

Ferguson: "What is your full name?"

Hughes: "Howard R. Hughes."

Ferguson: "And what is your address?"

Hughes: "Business or residence?"

Ferguson: "Give us both."

Hughes: "Well, I have several business addresses: In Houston, in care of the Hughes Tool Company; and in California at 7000 Romaine Street."

Half-listening, he replied automatically to the questions as his mind considered this problem of address. He had many business addresses and many home addresses too. He rarely went to the Hughes Tool Company plant in Texas and hardly ever stepped into the beige stucco two-story building at the corner of Romaine Street. For him, these were merely mail and telephone headquarters. The lucky individual might theoretically reach him there. At odd intervals he called in to get messages and to leave orders.

The simplicity of the questions being asked required the attention of only one small corner of his mind, leaving the remainder free to respond to the thoughts being suggested and stirred by them. He snorted silently when he was asked if Hughes Tool Company was a closed corporation or if the stock was available on the market. Absurd! Anyone who knew anything about corporate affairs in general, or his affairs specifically, knew that he owned 100% of this very important American industrial unit. Imagine having anyone else own one share of it! Howard Hughes did not share anything with others. He retained full ownership and full control!

Movie camera men, kleig lights, still photographers and reporters buzzed about, sounding to him like a swarm of bees. In spite of the special acoustical hearing device his engineers had set up for him, he had trouble hearing what was being said. The contrivance was efficient, but it had not been designed to separate official conversation from the extraneous hum of news reporters and photographers. Finally he was forced to speak out.

"Senator, with all the noise and these cameras I have trouble hearing you. Can we take the pictures first and then go on with the testimony?"

The chairman of the subcommittee was shamed into taking action. Reluctantly he halted all proceedings while the pictures were taken and then said, "Now, all cameras will cease and we will get down to the testimony."

Hughes reminded him, "Can we turn out the lights, please?"

Senator Ferguson ordered the lights to be turned out, called a halt to all picture taking and commanded silence in the hearing room. The questioning resumed in a more orderly and dignified atmosphere.

The interrogation dragged on for days, impertinent, irrelevant, rarely significant. During the course of the hearing Hughes had indicated several times his displeasure with the Army. Now, finally, one of his inquisitors asked the reason for this unseemly quarrel with the military. Howard's thoughts drifted back to the second occasion when he had tried to interest the Army in a Hughes plane.

It was about the middle of 1936 when Hughes ordered Odekirk and his mechanics to bring the H-1 into the Hughes Aircraft plant for remodeling. The old engine was removed and replaced with a new 14-cylinder Wasp which generated 1000 horsepower. He had designed a new wing and installed new oxygen equipment. Hughes planned to fly the modified H-1 at a high altitude in order to take advantage of the prevailing easterly jet stream.

Howard, not satisfied with his Los Angeles to New York record, intended to better it before someone else did it. On January 19, 1937, shortly after 2:00 P.M. Pacific Standard Time, Hughes took off in the rebuilt H-1, determined to set a new record. True to past performances, nothing went smoothly with the flight. His new oxygen equipment failed to function properly, giving him too much thin air and too little oxygen, so that over the high Sierras he almost lost consciousness. The radio failed to function also, forcing him to fly by dead reckoning. He finally managed to repair his oxygen supply so that he could resume high altitude flight but by the time he reached Indiana, the oxygen was exhausted.

Faced with a choice between anoxia and reducing his speed by descending to a lower altitude, he elected to gamble everything in a drive to set a new record. Using his old trick of gulping air to fill his straining lungs, he concentrated on staying conscious. The fates were kind. Seven hours, twenty-eight minutes, twenty-five seconds after take-off, he arrived at Newark Airport, having achieved an average speed of 332 miles per hour for the 2490 miles traveled.

The press hailed this new speed record, but focused its major attention on the fact that Hughes wore the same double-breasted gray suit he had worn on his first transcontinental flight.

When a reporter asked him if he regarded this suit as a lucky piece, Hughes drawled, "No. I guess I better get rid of it and get a new one."

Now seated in the Senate caucus room, Hughes' mind busied itself with thoughts of the efforts he had made to sell that remarkable plane to the Army. Certainly the craft was far ahead of its time— no one had anything even close to it. Well, it was nothing new for the Hughes family to have problems with the Armed Forces. As a lad young Howard had often heard the story about how his father, Howard Hughes, Sr., had read about the slow, painful work involved in drilling to plant mines and establish trenches in Europe.

When World War I broke out, Howard, Sr., developed a revolutionary new drilling instrument which he offered to the American Army Engineers. They marveled over it but maintained the United States had no money to develop it, and in any case the war in Europe was far away and of no concern to the American military.

The Chief of Ordnance in Washington suggested that Mr. Hughes offer it to the British. The British appointed a commission which tested it and reported enthusiastically on its efficiency. However, a British colonel in France examined the blueprints and commented briefly, "Very pretty, but it won't work in the chalky soil of France."

Howard R. Hughes, Sr., grunted disgustedly when he received the report, "Chalky soil would be the favorite food of this bit."

In spite of the shortsighted predictions of the American Army, the United States did enter the war and American soldiers joined the British in the trenches of France. Howard, Sr., believing that British red tape and conservatism would no longer hold back acceptance of his invention, offered his machine again to the American War Department. Aggravated by the delay in receiving a reply, he

Hughes Aircraft's "dress rehearsal for mobilization." Not long after, the Korean fighting broke out, and orders for military equipment flooded the industry. Hughes Aircraft became the sole source of supply for the fire-control systems of all interceptors—North American Aviation's F-86, Northrop's F-89 and F-94, and even the Navy's McDonnell Aircraft F-2H4.

Up to the Korean conflict most of the industrial giants of America had left this type of electronics manufacturing to small outfits like Hughes Aircraft. However, in 1950 the Air Force sponsored a design competition for an electronic fire-and-navigational control system to be used in the F-102 Supersonic Interceptor. This newly developed fighter plane would become a mainstay of the American defensive and offensive systems, and production of its electronic firing and navigational systems would involve millions of dollars.

More than twenty companies competed for the design award, including General Electric, Westinghouse, and organizations new to the field who were seeking to diversify. Hughes Aircraft exhibited remarkable ingenuity in winning this competition and shutting out the major American corporations. The company acquired a near-monopoly on the Air Force's sophisticated electronics requirements, especially in the fire and navigational control fields.

Delivery figures indicate the rapid rise of the company. In 1949 Hughes Aircraft delivered $8,600,000 in equipment. This rose the following year to $151 million and approached $200 million by 1953.

Hughes was delighted with the turn of events. He gave his people at Hughes Aircraft carte blanche in ordering equipment and personnel, with the result that the Culver City establishment in the mid-1950's had one of the finest electronics laboratory facilities in the world and employed some of the best brains in the industry.

Over a thousand physicists, electronics engineers, mathematicians, and other high-grade professional technicians worked for Hughes Aircraft. An incomplete roster would include the names of Dr. Ralph P. Johnson, formerly Deputy Director of Research of the Atomic Energy Commission; Dr. Harper Q. North, who had been one of the outstanding research men at General Electric; Dr. Andrew V. Haess, one of the nation's most talented scientists; Dr. Lester C. VanAtta, previously the foremost expert on antennae for the United States Navy; Dr. Allen E. Puckett, an expert in aerodynamics, and Dr. Burton F. Miller, who had headed the Electrical Engineering Division of the Manhattan Project at the University of California.

Although theoretically the scientists at Hughes Aircraft could have anything they wanted, in practice it did not work so smoothly. Hughes Aircraft was still a division of Hughes Tool Company which meant that major requests had to be approved by Toolco. Unfortunately, Noah Dietrich, who ran Toolco, was not personally enthusiastic about the aircraft company. Dietrich seemed at times to believe that the aircraft company was nothing more than a hobby for Howard Hughes, and as supervising manager, he was not disposed to waste too much money on a hobby. For a while General George managed to get along by calling Hughes in the middle of the night or by leaving word at the Romaine Street headquarters that he wanted Hughes. Usually within a reasonable time he had his answer.

This picture changed abruptly in 1951 when Hughes moved his base of operations from California to Las Vegas, Nevada. Here he rented four suites in four different hotels along the Strip and maintained communication only with certain selected personnel at Romaine Street. This created long delays in the exchange of messages and sometimes weeks went by while George waited for Hughes to return a call.

In the meantime Hughes Aircraft was getting large orders and it needed working capital. In fact, the actual amount of business done by Hughes Aircraft at that time was even larger than that turned out by Hughes Tool Company. Nevertheless Toolco ran the aircraft company, lock, stock and barrel and no one from the aircraft company was ever elected to the Board of Directors of the tool company. The result was that when the Toolco Board met to consider a decision about aircraft company affairs nobody there really understood the problem or had any empathy with the people running the aircraft company.

One of the first serious complaints arose when, in order to meet the Air Force schedule, Wooldridge and Ramo felt it necessary to double the laboratory staff, which would necessitate considerably more space. They sent a request through George to Hughes for additional facilities requiring an expenditure of close to $4 million. Weeks passed before the answer came back that any additional facilities would have to be built at Las Vegas. Hughes at this time had acquired much land on the outskirts of Las Vegas, but he never told General George or anyone else in the aircraft company about his plan to divide the company facilities in this fashion.

George, Wooldridge, and Ramo rejected Hughes' idea to move a major portion of Hughes Aircraft to Las Vegas. They believed that such a separation would injure the operation and they feared their scientists and engineers would refuse to live either in the desert or in the turmoil of Las Vegas.

Without resolving the matter satisfactorily General George began construction of additional facilities at the Culver City plant. Hughes became churlish. Up to this point his major interest had been in the solution of unusual engineering or electronics problems. Suddenly he became interested in all problems in and about the plant, including construction plans for the new facilities. He issued an order that all blueprints had to be submitted to him for approval.

The architect's drawings would be sent to him and would come back, sometimes within a day or two and sometimes within a week or two, with unlikely alterations such as a change in the position of the windows or some rearrangement of corridors and with detailed instructions on the most minor points. At one time he insisted they change the color of paint, commenting, "I favor light colors."

Once while the Hughes Aircraft management breathlessly awaited Hughes' decision on expenditures involving millions of dollars for new laboratory facilities, they received an imperious demand for a detailed breakdown of the disposition of four years' proceeds from the sale of candy bars, milk, and other refreshments, sold in the plant vending machines. In another ukase, Hughes insisted that they change all the procedures for purchasing and cleaning seat covers for company cars!

Hughes and General George became involved in a dispute over the grass runway which was part of the original plant. While this had been satisfactory for light use, it became totally inadequate to handle the hundreds of military planes landing and taking off in tests of the control systems installed at the plant.

The runway was a muddy morass during the rainy season and rough during the dry season. At one point conditions deteriorated so much it became necessary to stop the testing, and George insisted on authorization to pave the runway. It took an unbelievable two and a half years and an official Air Force protest that the runway was damaging its equipment before Hughes agreed to have it paved.

Some of Hughes' decisions infuriated his executives. He owned 1,200 acres at the aircraft company site, but the plant itself used only something under one-tenth of the acreage. Facilities at the plant were highly congested, and excellent use could have been made of the additional land. For example, Dr. Wooldridge required broad areas in which to test his experimental radar antenna. The land was available and it would only be necessary to build antenna towers. The real estate in question was zoned for agricultural use and carried a very low tax rate. Hughes insisted that no change be made because industrial zoning would bring about an increase in taxes. In spite of the fact that the government would have borne the additional expense, Hughes refused to consider any change.

It is possible that the managerial staff of Hughes Aircraft might have survived all of these frustrations and irritations if it had not been for Noah Dietrich. When Hughes Aircraft first began to do business, Dietrich had been amused and treated it as a Hughes plaything. However, when the company thrived, Dietrich launched a campaign to become general manager. In the past, Dietrich had been successful in defeating every aspirant to a major position in the Hughes empire. He originally rid Toolco of Colonel Rudolph C. Kuldell, a retired Army engineer who ran the company until replaced by Dietrich. He superseded Jack Frye, head of TWA until 1947. Now Dietrich wanted to run Hughes Aircraft.

At the beginning of 1950 Dietrich set out to undermine the authority of General George and his assistants. General George and Charles D. Thornton, the assistant general manager, requested bank lines of $35 million for the year 1952 in order to meet an estimated $150 million of anticipated delivery. Dietrich refused their request, cutting the amount to $25 million, which he negotiated with the Delaware National Bank in Pittsburgh.

The reduction in credit forced the management to attempt to induce the Army to make partial payments, to postpone paying bills, and to take other action to try to make $25 million do the work of $35 million. Dietrich finally was forced to raise the amount to that originally requested.

A showdown came when the accountant's 1951 inventory audit showed a shortage of $500,000 in the finished parts inventory. General George immediately instituted an investigation which revealed that four men on the assembly line, trying desperately to meet delivery schedules, had bypassed inventory procedures to take finished parts directly to the assembly line.

This meant that a finished part might have been installed in the *'thinking boys'*

final product for delivery to the Army without being accounted for on the way. Although the practice was irregular, it apparently was necessary and there was no evidence of fraud.

General George explained all this to Noah Dietrich, who refused to accept it and insinuated that the missing parts had gone to the black market.

General George said furiously, "What you have just stated is in fact an accusation of fraud, lack of integrity, and deceit on the part of certain principal executives."

The charge was withdrawn but the bitterness remained. As Dietrich took over more and more control of the affairs of Hughes Aircraft, word drifted down that he was beginning to run the show. The people at Hughes Aircraft were unhappy about this. A fundamental philosophical difference existed between General George and Noah Dietrich. George had established a system where management and staff acted as a team. The "thinking boys," as the general called them, and management personnel worked together on the same problem. This system might or might not work elsewhere but it demonstrably worked at Hughes Aircraft, which seemed to solve its problems more satisfactorily than almost any other electronics group in the country. *work of some public[?]*

Dietrich, on the other hand, felt that these people should have nothing to do with management. At a meeting of the upper echelon of the Culver City operation, the subject turned to sales, expenses, budgets, and other financial matters and Dietrich directed that the scientists and technical personnel leave the room during the discussion. They had nothing to do with that problem, he said. General George refused to accede to Dietrich's request.

By June, 1952, the Culver City management group had had enough of Dietrich's interference, so they prepared a letter headed IMPORTANT COMMUNICATION which they forwarded to Hughes. George, Thornton, Wooldridge, and Ramo signed the statement which accused Dietrich of trying "to seize personal power without regard to the consequences." They made it clear that Dietrich's actions were hurting the company and would interfere with meeting the Air Force schedules. They asked for an immediate audience with Hughes.

Hughes treated this request as a move in a war of nerves. He neither acknowledged receipt of the communication nor scheduled the requested meeting. Shortly thereafter Hughes was seen showing the plant to a group of strangers whom he did not bother to introduce to anyone, but who were identified as Westinghouse executives. It was rumored that Hughes planned to sell the aircraft company and that Westinghouse wanted to buy it. The rumor did not disturb the aircraft company personnel, who were confident they would be welcomed by Westinghouse or any other established American corporation. Their greatest problems arose from working for Hughes.

The Hughes Aircraft executives met to discuss the matter. These people had developed some of the most sophisticated electronics systems in use by the United States Armed Forces. They had revolutionary ideas on the drawing board. They knew they were capable of generating hundreds of millions of dollars in business both with the government and commercially. They were especially eager to become involved in methods of airport flight control. They decided that if the company were to be sold they should help locate a buyer. They learned that Dan Pepper, then head of Penrose Corporation, was interested and had formed a syndicate, which included some of the major Wall Street financial houses, to buy Hughes Aircraft.

Significantly, Pepper's syndicate was prepared to offer the principal executive of Hughes Aircraft the opportunity to become an owner of a part of the equity—a possibility Hughes had never suggested.

Pepper had a number of meetings with Hughes in Los Angeles, but he got nowhere. Hughes would never set an asking price nor would he show any of the company's figures. It soon became apparent that Hughes was not going to sell, so Pepper returned to New York.

Now the company executives realized that Hughes had no intention of selling Hughes Aircraft—apparently he only wanted to know how much buyers would pay for the property. (He had gone through almost the same act a few years before, with Wall Street asking him to name a price for Hughes Tool Company. When he finally received a firm bid of $230 million, he turned it down.)

Company management then took a different tack. They wrote Hughes that they could no longer accept responsibility for meeting the schedules set by the Air Force in their contracts, and that they were prepared to so notify the Air Force.

This ultimatum elicited a response from Hughes. On September 20, 1952, George, Thornton, Wooldridge, and Ramo were directed to present themselves at the Beverly Hills Hotel, where Hughes maintained his hundred-dollar-a-day bungalow.

An affable Howard Hughes greeted them. He wore slacks, and a coat with leather elbow patches over a new white shirt. Hospitably, he provided food and liquor and freely he praised the work the men had been doing. He was very sorry that he could not get down to the aircraft company plant more often, he assured them, but they must understand how busy he was running RKO, refinancing TWA, and handling the purchase of property near Las Vegas. He even joked with them that RKO was "a bad nuisance—it represents about 15 percent of my business and takes 85 percent of my time."

Then he told them that they were allowing their emotions to cloud their judgment—after all, they all had the same goals—there were no real differences between them. In spite of Hughes' attentions to them and his persuasive and confidential manner, General George and his companions remained unconvinced. They made it clear that they required—indeed demanded—complete authority to carry out their responsibilities to the aircraft company.

Hughes retained his equanimity. He remarked that internal quarrels over the control of a company were not unusual in large corporations. They must consider the problem he faced because he relied so completely on Dietrich to take care of his "whole picture." Their insistence on having their own way and their unswerving solidarity and collective action he seriously considered a "Communistic practice."

A few days later Ramo, Wooldridge, and Thornton, with the approval of General George, flew to Washington to tell the Defense Department what was happening and to prepare them for the imminent blowup. The die was cast; all possibility of rapprochement with Hughes was ended. Washington decided that it could do nothing.

At this moment the appearance of a new buyer brought about a temporary truce. Although Hughes had no real interest in selling, Robert Gross of Lockheed made a serious offer to lease the aircraft company's facilities for ten years. Lockheed was prepared to buy the entire inventory, including the work in progress, and to make an additional payment for good will.

Negotiations between Hughes and Gross fell into the accustomed pattern. In battered Chevrolets in the middle of the night they rode around arguing and bargaining. Many of these meetings were held near Las Vegas. Hughes would pick up Gross and they would go for a drive in the fresh desert air. Hughes continually increased his price. He asked $34 million, and after Gross agreed, he wanted $36 million.

from ask When Hughes raised the price to $50 million, Gross gave up and went back to California. The $36 million offer had been generous. Hughes would have ended up with the cash from Hughes Aircraft —about $10 million, the nonelectronics part of the business with a net worth of about $9 million, and the liquidated value of other assets in the amount of $15 million. This made a grand total of close to $35 million, the sum Hughes had invested originally in the Culver City plant. Hughes would have had his investment liquidated plus the $36 million profit paid by Gross. He would have continued to own the physical plant, which would have returned to him at the end of the ten-year lease.

Meanwhile, on the Dietrich front the war continued. Dietrich held up agreed-upon executive bonuses for 1952. He ordered General George to cease negotiating with the Air Force on prices. Ramo and Wooldridge decided to make one more attempt to arrive at a solution with Hughes. In July, 1953, they met with him and spoke directly and sincerely about how much was at stake. They reminded him of the vast potential of Hughes Aircraft and how much they could do with it if he would let them.

Hughes listened politely. He assured them he would never sell the plant, that everything would be all right, that he would straighten out all of their problems.

"You are full of promises," they told him.

Hughes replied, "Be patient, I may have a little trouble making up my mind, but once I do, I move fast."

The two men waited for twenty days and then submitted their resignations. As soon as this news became public the Pentagon called General George to find out what his future plans were.

"I intend to stay so long as I am able to do any good," he replied.

George's good intentions went down the drain when Dietrich fired George's comptroller without consulting George and announced he was moving his own office to the Culver City plant. George immediately notified Hughes that unless the comptroller was reinstated and Dietrich restrained from further interference he would resign.

There was no reply. On September 11, 1953, their month's notice up, Ramo and Wooldridge left the plant. On September 14 George sent in his resignation. A wholesale exodus followed. Dr. Johnson, head of research and development, resigned. Dean Smith, sales manager, resigned. Sixteen senior members of the technical staff handed in resignations.

At last Hughes left Las Vegas for Los Angeles, where he met with George. He made an emotional appeal to the general to stay on, reminding him of all that he had done for him, how important it was to the company, and bringing up any other factors that might influence George.

The general was adamant. He was not going to stay if he was going to be kicked around by Dietrich while he struggled to break through the wall with which Hughes surrounded himself. George had thought a lot about the problem. He wanted a board of directors to run Hughes Aircraft, made up of two directors from Hughes Tool Company, two directors from Hughes Aircraft itself, and one outsider—some nationally known figure who would be satisfactory to him and who would in effect take the role of arbitrator.

Hughes complained, "You are proposing to take from me the rights to manage my own property. I'll burn the plant down first."

"You are accomplishing the same result without matches," George retorted.

The Air Force was by now thoroughly disturbed by developments in the plant which was its sole source for important electronics equipment. They notified Hughes that he must make every effort to hold the staff together.

One night Hughes called a meeting of the scientists at the plant. They probed and questioned him until at last he agreed to offer them a full statement on revised policies for future plant operation. Later they learned that Hughes had told the Air Force that they were going to stay, although they had not yet made such an agreement. They insisted on another meeting, this time with General George and Charles Thornton present.

Charles J. V. Murphy, writing about *The Blowup at Hughes Aircraft* in *Fortune* said, "There ensued another extraordinary gathering, with Hughes listening sternly while the scientists told him that he had all but wrecked a successful management and, even worse, had imperiled a national defense program. Hughes asked for three months to work things out."

By now everyone recognized that Hughes would say anything to keep them but would do nothing afterward. At this crucial point the Secretary for the Air Force and the assistant secretary of matériel arrived from the Pentagon. Secretary Talbott told Hughes, "You have made a hell of a mess of a great property and, by God, as long as I am Secretary of the Air Force you're not going to get another dollar to do business."

Hughes offered a typical reply, "If you mean to tell me that the government is prepared to destroy a business merely on the unfounded charges of a few disgruntled employees, then you are introducing Socialism, if not Communism."

The Air Force asked several key employees to stay on and make sure the contracts were carried out. In addition, they made it known to the rest of the electronics industry that the Air Force would be unhappy if anyone began to steal talent from Hughes Aircraft. In this makeshift manner the company limped along.

Wooldridge and Ramo, after leaving Hughes, started a small electronics company called the Ramo-Wooldridge Corporation, which was spectacularly successful. Hughes brought in a new manager, William C. Jordan, formerly president of Curtiss-Wright; and production schedules continued somehow to be met. The Air Force meanwhile developed a plan by which it awarded a contract to a company and then forced Hughes to sell it his equipment and plans for the fire-control systems.

In the midst of all this turmoil Howard Hughes came up with one of his brainstorms. On January 10, 1954, he announced the formation of a nonprofit institution for medical research. He called it the Howard Hughes Medical Foundation and his first gift to the foundation was the assets of the Hughes Aircraft Company. Dr. Verne Mason, the physician who had attended Hughes when he crashed in 1946, became the first director of the foundation.

The events of 1953 had shocked Howard Hughes out of his customary complacency. He was deeply hurt and disappointed over what he regarded as the defection of General George and scientists Ramo and Wooldridge. He persuaded some of the lower-echelon people to remain under a new system in which a three-man administrative board would make all decisions and operate Hughes Aircraft. The board consisted of William C. Jordan, general manager of

Hughes Aircraft; Howard Hall, one of the Hughes' attorneys; and a third man. Any two of the three could make a policy decision without prior consultation with Hughes. Initially the jurisdictional authority of Dietrich was left unsettled.

Jordan did a good job of placating the men and warding off Dietrich but at the end of six months he left, pleading ill health. His public statements contained nothing but praise for Hughes and the company.

Hughes found himself in the position of the boy who cried "Wolf" too often. This time he did not let matters drift. He quickly put together a new management committee and brought in Laurence Hyland from Bendix Corporation, to act as general manager. Hyland was almost exactly what Hughes needed—a determined, competent individual who would brook no nonsense.

At last Hughes Aircraft Company could soar ahead. All the basic elements of Hughes' original plan for the world's most sophisticated electronics company were there. The organization employed thousands of people familiar with every branch of modern scientific knowledge. The plant contained some of the best electronics laboratory equipment available anywhere. The company had the basic patents and the know-how to make the finest electronic fire-control systems. Already on the drawing board were plans for a missile system, known as the Falcon Missile, which would become part of the American Defense System. The entire enterprise was now too well organized, too well founded, too well stocked with wisdom, ability, and competence to be destroyed by an internecine fight.

During those two years two important events took place. In 1956 Noah Dietrich went on safari during his differences with Hughes and ended the pressure of his drive to control Hughes Aircraft. In 1957 Howard Hughes got married and at least for a time lost his desire to be the active head of the world's finest electronics company. Instead, he permitted those who knew how to do so to run the company.

All of the preparatory work, the skilled complements of personnel, the excellent equipment, the fine reputation, began to pay off in 1958. Beginning in January of that year Hughes Aircraft Company negotiated millions of dollars of contracts for the development of a variety of electronics systems. They acquired a $20 million contract to complete two advanced versions of the Falcon Missile, a $40 million contract for a new aircraft fire-control system, and other multimillion-dollar contracts for various electronics systems. On March 13, 1958, the company announced its plans to hire 2,000 additional scientists and engineers and 1,500 more technical employees.

From this point on there was a steady flow of millions of dollars worth of contracts. Hughes Aircraft Company became the leading contractor in the field of electronics control of weapons firing. It was also the only company manufacturing, and improving, the Falcon Missile. The volume of work made it mandatory to obtain more space. Before the end of 1958 the company had rented another plant with 156,000 square feet of space in Newport Beach, California.

None of the work at Hughes Aircraft consisted of the simple manufacturing of electronic hardware but, in spite of the highly sophisticated and advanced nature of the varied operations, there was always time to accept new challenges. In 1959 the firm accepted a contract without a specified dollar recompense to develop "unorthodox approaches" to deflect and confuse enemy missiles. In July of 1959 the company announced that it was experimenting with a small but highly accurate atomic clock to be fitted into a satellite while a twin clock would be retained on Earth. The purpose was to learn if a clock placed in orbit around the Earth would operate at a different rate from its twin on the ground. This project would explore one aspect of Einstein's theory on relativity.

The seventh decade of the twentieth century saw still more expansion at Hughes Aircraft. A new plant was built at El Segundo, California; a missile plant at Tucson, Arizona; and another plant at Fullerton, California.

In 1960 Hughes Aircraft Company received its first contract with the National Aeronautics and Space Administration (NASA)— a beginning from which would later rise contracts in the multimillion-dollar range for the construction of some of the most unusual space vehicles yet known. The initial contract amounted to less than $1 million for building an experimental engine to power a space ship. The company produced an ingenious and inspired plan which astounded and delighted NASA. (Competitors say it is unlikely that the engine could possibly have been built for the allotted $500,000. However, Hughes Aircraft Company was working under so many contracts that the extra costs could probably have been balanced. It required the talents of a highly skilled government auditor to pass through the labyrinth of accounting involved in these contracts.)

One contract was for $3 million to manufacture high frequency radio receivers for the Air Force. Another was a $10 million Army contract to build a mobile truck-mounted missile-control system. A contract with industry called for development of a narrow light beam—a laser. A $5 million contract with the Army was to build a radar system for the Monitor Missile. This would be followed by a $70 million Army contract to construct defense command posts for the Monitor Missile. An Air Force contract for $65 million called for building Falcon air-to-air guided missiles.

And the really big one was a contract to develop a small satellite capable of receiving telephone and television signals and relaying them back to Earth. This satellite would be placed in a stationary orbit over the equator and would act as a relay point. Hung at a height of 20,300 miles, three such stationary satellites evenly spaced in orbit could provide a complete communications system for all of Earth. This satellite, later called Syncom I, occupied a substantial segment of the Hughes plant when NASA let the first contract.

Concentration on the space program did not keep the company out of other fields. In 1961 Hughes Aircraft accepted a $20 million contract to develop a control system for the Nike-Hercules anti-aircraft missile. A $10 million contract for the Polaris submarine missile control, a contract to develop Project Artemis (the Navy's long-range submarine detection system), and opening talks with NASA for construction of a spacecraft to make a soft landing on the moon—these too became part of Hughes Aircraft Company's participation in the space age.

Before the end of 1961 the Hughes people had demonstrated to NASA a degree of competence on the communications satellite project that earned them a specific contract to build the first Syncom. In addition, they continued to work on the Falcon air-to-air missile and on another $50 million of miscellaneous electronics contracts.

In 1962 business remained in the multimillion-dollar class with work from all branches of the United States Government, foreign governments, and private business. The Swiss government ordered a fire-control system for an amount of money not specified. Boeing gave Hughes a $27 million contract to produce an electronic data analysis system for the Minute Man solid fuel missile. Work was going ahead also on the Falcon Missile and on Syncom I.

As 1962 drew to a close Syncom I neared completion. After a number of dry-run tests, launch was scheduled for February 14, 1963, at Cape Canaveral, Florida. The satellite measured 28 inches long, weighed 150 pounds, and was designed to receive radio signals from specific points on earth and relay them to other points. Tension was high at Hughes as the satellite lifted off and moved toward its orbit. Then something went wrong with radio communications and for ten days the scientists struggled to find out what had happened. Finally on February 24, 1963, the telescopes in a South African observatory located Syncom I. Satellite control found it could turn Syncom's batteries on and off and make it respond to signals. While this first effort at a synchronous orbit was not a complete success, it was far from a failure. One valuable lesson learned from Syncom I was that the plan to have perfect equatorial alignment was too difficult to maintain and was not necessary.

The Hughes scientific staff went back to the drawing board and worked feverishly around the clock. By July 6, 1963, they were back at Cape Canaveral with Syncom II. This time the orbit pattern would be a figure eight in which the satellite would travel slightly north and then swing slightly south of the equator.

Syncom II was shaped like a drum, weighed 86 pounds, and measured 28 inches in diameter and 15½ inches in height. It had 3,840 silicon solar cells to power its battery and was equipped to handle telephone signals, teletype, and even facsimile. It was not yet ready for TV. Shortly after launching it achieved a perfect orbit, then began to drift slightly. NASA scientists used radio signals to start the hydrogen peroxide jets which would move it back into orbit. Everything worked perfectly. It became immediately possible to make telephone calls between the United States and Europe via satellite without using the Atlantic Cable.

Hughes Aircraft now received a contract to build another synchronous orbit satellite. This one, named Olympic Star, would include the capability of relaying television signals. (It received its name because it would be used as the TV relay station for worldwide transmission of the Olympic games.) On August 19, 1964, from the same point, now called Cape Kennedy, the Olympic Star was launched and it, too, worked perfectly. People all over the world watched telecasts of the Olympic games from Tokyo—a new high in television coverage, and a new gem in Hughes Aircraft's crown of accomplishments.

Meanwhile, the government of Japan announced that it was going to adopt what was now known as the Hughes Air Defense System—a complete electronics system which could alert a central command post to approaching aircraft. This would mean uncountable millions of dollars in contracts for the company. Hughes Aircraft was also one of the first firms to get a contract from the new Communication Satellite Corporation, known popularly as Comsat.

The United States Army requested development of an anti-tank missile to be mounted on a truck or tank. The Air Force authorized a $61 million contract to increase the radar sensitivity of its supersonic fighters. There were standard contracts from NASA to build satellites, and unusual contracts such as one to develop a system of launching missiles from helicopters.

In 1964 Hughes negotiated a contract with NASA to develop a moon exploration unit called the Surveyor. On December 11, 1964, a dummy model of Surveyor was orbited but had to be abandoned as unstable and redesigned. Less than a year later, on September 22, 1965, a 2,000-pound model of the new Surveyor was successfully launched from Cape Kennedy. Now all signals were "go" to make the actual landing of the Surveyor on the moon. The unmanned lunar probe was launched on May 30, 1966. Object: soft landing on the moon.

To do so it would travel 231,483 miles in 63 hours and 36 minutes. The complexity of this launch may be glimpsed when it is realized that Surveyor had to be aimed at a point in space where the moon *would be* at a given time in the future and that it had to land in a predetermined area.

Surveyor weighed 620 pounds and was designed to travel at a speed of 6,000 miles per hour. It had to be capable of control throughout the flight, reducing speed while still in space and maneuvering into position to touch down on the moon's surface at a speed of less than eight miles per hour. It arrived exactly five seconds late and landed precisely ten miles from the selected point of impact. At touchdown its three landing legs opened as planned and absorbed the shock of first lunar contact. Immediately after landing, Surveyor began to radio pictures of the moon's surface to the eagerly waiting Earthmen. Both the launching and the accomplishments of Surveyor after the moon landing rank as one of man's most advanced scientific achievements.

Surveyor's pioneering triumphs were appropriately topped by Surveyor III on April 22, 1967, when its tubular arm dug a trench on the moon's surface.

Hughes Aircraft Company was also actively engaged in the construction of communications satellites for Comsat. These "Early Bird" satellites serve as a link for commercial TV, telephone, and telegraph between North America and Europe. On August 14, 1965, Comsat launched the first of the "Early Bird" satellites manufactured by Hughes Aircraft. Pleased with the perfect orbit and successful operation, Comsat went ahead with plans for a complete global communication system to be completed by 1967 and invited all the nations of the world to sign up to use it. Forty-six countries accepted the invitation. Obviously, Hughes Aircraft would make the system.

There is no doubt that by 1967 Hughes Aircraft Company either had completed, or was well on its way to meeting, the visionary goals set for it by Howard Hughes when he first revamped the company to create "the world's finest electronics company."

Howard Hughes and His North-South Airline

THE YEAR 1956

NASSER SEIZED the Suez Canal. The world's tiniest kingdom once described by W. Somerset Maugham as a "sunny spot for shady people" became one of the top spots in the news when its handsome young ruler, His Serene Highness, Prince Rainier III, married Grace Kelly, a Hollywood movie actress.

Communist Party boss Nikita Khrushchev delivered a long denunciation of Stalin, starting an uproar in the Communist world.

John Gunther's *Inside Africa* stayed on the bestseller list an amazingly long time for a specialized type of book. Also making the bestseller list for an unusual length of time was John Schindler's *How to Live 365 Days a Year*. The national book award went to John O'Hara's *Ten North Frederick*. Senator John Kennedy published *Profiles in Courage*. MacKinlay Kantor's *Andersonville* won a Pulitzer Prize.

In the theatre: *The Diary of Anne Frank;* Shelley Winters in *A Hat For Lorraine;* Bert Lahr in *Waiting for Godot*. The Comédie Française after 275 years of existence made its first appearance in the United States with the production of Molière's *Bourgeois Gentilhomme*. In the field of musicals the smash hit was *My Fair Lady* with Rex Harrison and Julie Andrews.

Howard Hughes was fifty.

20

During World War II a large percentage of Howard Hughes' time was devoted to the development of the "Spruce Goose" and his photo-reconnaissance plane, and to the manufacture of war material. What time that was left he used to build up the technical strength of TWA.

With the end of the war his planning paid off. TWA earned worldwide recognition as the most progressive airline in flying equipment, knowhow and procedures. The Civil Aeronautics Board, where route decisions were made, realized this too, and Hughes obtained almost 25,000 miles of new international routes including the "Rich Plum Run" across the North Atlantic from New York to London and Paris.

Hughes thus became the first proprietor of an American airline with both domestic routes and international routes. Pan-American, although well routed and scheduled internationally, had no runs inside the continental limits of the United States. This gave TWA the edge as the first national, as well as international, airline. TWA was completely prepared for around-the-world service when it obtained routes through Egypt and India to the Orient. The final link required a Pacific run and routing through China. The latter was barely defeated when the Chinese Communists took over Shanghai in 1948. Although he never got routing around the world, nevertheless Hughes did realize his goal of having the only American airline offering service both within and without the continental United States.

The American airlines tended, primarily as a result of the "grandfather routes" acquired with the establishment of the Civil Aeronautics Board in 1938, to run either in a north-south direction or in an east-west direction. Eastern and National are examples of primarily north-south runs whereas United and TWA cover basically east-west routes.

This is not, of course, an absolute because there are routes which move diagonally and other routes, basically east-west, which also travel north-south runs. However, a study of the routing of any domestic airline (excluding the regional airlines) will quickly indicate its major character to be either of the north-south variety or of the east-west variety.

Just as Hughes had broken the pattern of national vs. international lines he decided to break the pattern with respect to north-south vs. east-west carriers. The grant of a north-south run to an east-west airline would not be of any real significance unless that particular north-south route was equally significant. Probably the major north-south route in the United States in terms of lucrativeness of traffic is the Boston-New York-Philadelphia-Washington-Miami route.

From October to March this route is unquestionably *Florida* one of the most profitable in the world and as Florida grows in importance as a summer vacation resort the route gradually assumes aspects of an all-year-around gold mine. The question thus becomes—how does an east-west airline like TWA with international commitments get in on an East Coast north-south run coveted by practically every airline in the United States?

The problem seems almost insoluble: A direct application by TWA for such a routing would have no chance of being granted. Despite the complexity and seeming impossibility of accomplishment, the determined Howard Hughes almost carried it off.

Northeast Airlines was born in 1931, controlled by, and as a complement to, two New England railroads. Its major purpose was to assist these railroads in handling passenger traffic throughout their area without necessitating the laying of additional track to handle some of the unprofitable longer hauls. *alpa cap!*

At the time of its establishment Northeast was a stepchild, suffering because it owed its birth to the needs of railroad men rather than the enthusiasms of air travel devotees. When new legislation forced the divorce of airline carriers from rail carriers, the control of Northeast passed into the hands of Atlas Corporation, a holding company controlled by Floyd Odlum. Odlum was not a flyer but his wife was the famous aviatrix, Jacqueline Cochran.

Up to this time Northeast Airlines had functioned as an adjunct to the railroad. Now it began to strike out on its own. In the late 1940's Northeast applied to the Civil Aeronautics Board for permission to fly between Boston and New York. This busy commuter route was then primarily the property of American Airlines. The CAB granted Northeast the route and thus set the stage for the next step.

In the 1950's Odlum was busy acquiring uranium mine holdings for Atlas. He believed that development of atomic energy was the coming field and therefore uranium had to become the most precious mineral. To acquire such holdings Odlum needed cash; he also anticipated great profits from them and wanted to find a tax loss corporation to offset this probability. He found both of these in a company owned by Howard Hughes—RKO Pictures Corporation. This was not the motion picture studio but just a corporate shell with $18 million in cash and a $30 million tax loss carry forward. Odlum made a deal whereby he acquired the corporation from Hughes in exchange for 10% of Atlas Common Stock.

Hughes now became the largest individual holder of Atlas Corporation. But Atlas controlled Northeast Airlines and Hughes controlled TWA. The Civil Aeronautics Act does not permit one man to control more than one airline without consent of the CAB. Therefore Hughes was forced to place his Atlas stock in a trust. Nevertheless, shortly after Hughes entered the Northeast picture that airline applied for a certificate to fly between New York and Miami, making convenient stops in both Philadelphia and Washington.

Northeast Airlines had been losing money and it desperately needed a profitable operation to keep it alive. There is little doubt that the decision to grant the certificate was based on sound economics rather than backstage influence by Hughes. Some airline economists believed that the grant of this temporary certificate in 1956 was made on the theory that traffic on the route in question was going to become heavy enough to outweigh the ability of the two existing airlines then servicing it to keep up.

Naturally, both Eastern and National argued long and vehemently that they would be glad to accommodate all passengers. But there were also cogent arguments based on the predicted increase in passenger traffic between Megalopolis, U.S.A., and Florida vacation lands. There were also other analysts of the situation who believed that the CAB granted the certification simply to help an obviously ailing airline.

Whatever intention CAB had, the fact that the grant was temporary helped to defeat the purpose. Because the new routing was temporary the airline could not arrange any permanent financing and it faced intervals when it could barely meet its bills for food and fuel. Each time this happened Hughes came to the rescue, making loans to keep the airline in operation.

Bad luck dogged the steps of Northeast Airlines. Just when the company received delivery on new equipment for the New York-Florida route, one of its planes crashed on Rikers Island where the survivors could be interviewed by television on the spot—a piece of negative publicity and unfortunate advertising that no other airline has had to face. In addition, in the first five years of flying the Golden Route there were two financial recessions which cut heavily into holiday and vacation traffic between New York and Miami.

Only Hughes proved willing to help Northeast financially. Many airlines tried to take over Northeast primarily for the purpose of acquiring the route but only Hughes actually put in dollars. Despite this the CAB continually rendered decisions adverse to Hughes and when the Eastern finance group forced his TWA stock into a voting trust in 1960 the CAB indicated that it would take a long, hard look at the situation before permitting Hughes to gain control of Northeast.

This was not the only time that the Board demonstrated hostility to Hughes. In 1958 a CAB examiner set up a plan which would permanently bar control by Hughes of Northeast Airlines. Even the first trusteeing of Hughes' stock became a fight between Hughes and CAB. Although Hughes had puchased his 10% control of Atlas Corporation in 1956 it was not until August of 1958 that word leaked out that the CAB was investigating the possible violation of law by Mr. Hughes in his endeavor to control two airlines.

On August 20, 1958 the CAB issued an official pronouncement that it would end its investigation if Hughes would agree to put his holdings of either TWA or NE into a trust. Hughes wrote a short note to CAB Chairman James Durfee that he would set up a trust within 20 days and report to CAB on its operation. Although Hughes accepted the Board ruling he wrote a sharp letter through his attorney, Raymond A. Cook, stating that he disputed the "fairness and necessity" of the divestiture of his stock. He also pointed out that in his opinion the system of ordering a settlement as a substitute for investigation was a dangerous precedent in the field of regulatory law.

Despite the opposition of CAB, in 1960 Northeast Airlines an-

nounced its intention to merge with TWA. The plan called for the
exchange of 1 share of TWA stock for 3 shares of NE stock. Opposition to the merger became immediately manifest. Chairman Emanuel Celler of the House Judiciary Committee announced that he
had requested CAB and the Justice Department to investigate possible violations of law inherent in the proposed merger.

The CAB challenged the merger and indicated that it might well
resort to the cancellation of the certification for the Northeast Airline's New York-Florida route if the two companies persisted in the
merger plans. Recognizing at last the utter futility of a frontal assault on the CAB, Hughes abandoned his merger plans.

Meanwhile NE continued to lose money, possibly a little faster
than before. However, following the Hughesian tradition it was
not only not economizing, it was in fact expanding. In 1961, at
the height of its financial troubles, NE announced that it was going
to build a new passenger terminal at Idlewild Airport (now JFK),
in conjunction with Northwest and Braniff Airlines. Completion
was scheduled for the spring of 1962 and the cost would be about
$10 million.

CAB was experiencing a frantic reaction to its dealings with the
determined and willful Hughes. It could visualize either the bankruptcy of NE on the one hand or complete control by Hughes
on the other. Now the board was driven to take a most unusual step:
behind the scenes the suggestion was made to other airlines that
they might consider merging with NE.

By this time the five year temporary certificate authorizing the
New York to Florida run was about to expire and although application for extension of the temporary certificate and also a request
for permanent certification were pending, it was an open secret
that the CAB was holding up approval, hoping for a merger to
materialize.

Although CAB was working behind the scenes the airlines were
out in the open. Pan American announced publicly that it would
consider a merger provided that the New England local routes
would be transferred to other carriers—this long-haul airline did not
want to become involved with the interesting but short runs from
Bangor to Barre or Boston to Burlington. It wanted it known,
however, that it most assuredly would be interested in taking on
the Boston-New York-Philadelphia-Washington-Miami route. In fact,
Pan Am had been trying unsuccessfully for 15 years to get per-

mission for a New York to Florida route. It had even tried to swap stock with National Airlines which did fly that run. However, CAB refused to sanction that maneuver.

A non-passenger carrier now evinced interest also. Riddle Airlines transported cargo over the same New York to Miami routing. Acquisition of Northeast Airlines would permit it to carry passengers along with its cargo. Riddle submitted a plan which offered a low fare air-bus service along the East Coast. However, it seemed highly doubtful that CAB would approve the idea of this cargo carrier entering the stiff competition for business on the coastal run.

Early in 1961 Hughes concluded a deal for Toolco to purchase the 56% of Northeast Airline's stock which Atlas owned. This transaction had to be approved by CAB and for a while it appeared that the Board would reject it out of hand. Meanwhile financial conditions at NE were going from bad to worse and Hughes was the only person in sight offering succor. With great reluctance on May 4, 1962, a CAB examiner made a halfhearted recommendation for approval of Toolco's plan to buy control from Atlas.

That summer CAB finally approved the plan but included some severe restrictions. There was to be no transaction between Northeast Airlines and Hughes Tool Company in excess of $100,000 in any single year without prior approval of the CAB. The major purpose of this ruling was to prevent implementation of Hughes' normal operation: Having Toolco buy planes and equipment and then either reselling them, or renting them, to Northeast at a profit for Toolco. This had been done with TWA and the CAB regarded the practice with sour disapproval.

Time, reporting on the CAB action, called it a "Pyrrhic Victory" for Hughes, who was paying $5 million for Northeast Airlines which in 1961 had lost almost $10 million and was running at a current balance sheet net worth deficiency of over $23 million.

Things did not work as well as they might have done. In February of 1963, one of Northeast's new jetliners crashed in the Everglades killing 43 people. The news made nation-wide headlines, and caused a particular stir in Florida. For the remainder of the season travelers requested, "Please book me on National or Eastern—I don't want to fly with NE."

In April, 1963, a CAB examiner who had been investigating the problem of whether the New York-Florida Certificate should be made permanent recommended not only that it not be made permanent but that the route be taken away from NE entirely.

In July CAB dealt what appeared to be the critical blow when it ordered NE to give up its New York to Florida route and on a Petition for Rehearing on August 16, 1963, reaffirmed its original decision that Northeast would lose all routings south of New York. This decision was greeted with wailing and gnashing of teeth in many places, particularly in New England. Even the conservative *Wall Street Journal* printed an article condemning the decision, under the title, *Expertise-Gone-Awry.* The United States Department of Justice, then under Attorney General Robert Kennedy (a New Englander), attacked the CAB decision and made application to intervene in the dispute. The CAB turned the Attorney General down cold. The Board's attitude was simple: "It's none of your business."

At : RFK

In September the announcement was made that nine Viscounts purchased by Northeast Airlines in 1958 from Vickers of England would be foreclosed and sold at public auction to pay off some of the debt owed by NE to Vickers. This was the death rattle.

Hughes did not take these developments quietly. With the order to cease the Florida run taking effect in October, time was running out for Northeast. At the last possible moment, attorneys for the troubled airline got a court order from the Circuit Court of Appeals superseding the CAB order and holding everything in status quo until further hearings could be arranged.

To bring greater pressure to bear on the Board Hughes caused TWA to resume merger negotiations, which put CAB on notice that any possible merger of TWA with NE would be contingent upon the grant of permanent certification for the New York-Florida run. At the November annual meeting of Northeast Airlines the number of Directors was increased from 9 to 16 and seven representatives of the Hughes Tool Company were elected to the Board.

In April of 1964 the Federal Court of Appeals in Boston handed down a decision ordering the Civil Aeronautics Board to reconsider its edict taking the Florida run away from Northeast Airlines. CAB began immediate hearings to examine the additional evidence which the Boston Court said should be investigated.

Believing that a good offense is also the best defense, while CAB was considering whether to permit NE to continue the southern run, the airline itself applied for routing certificates into the Caribbean to serve the Bahamas and also to extend its service in the north throughout Canada.

While these requests were pending the CAB launched another low blow at Hughes when, in response to his application to regain control of TWA, the Board ruled that it would not even examine the issue unless Toolco first gave up control of Northeast Airlines.

Hughes acted promptly. Within days after the order he named Louis J. Hector as trustee of all the NE stock owned by Hughes Tool Company. Hector was a Miami attorney who had been a member of the Civil Aeronautics Board and who had resigned with a blast at the Board. He and maverick Hughes were kindred spirits on the subject of CAB.

In October of 1964, NE Airlines and Toolco filed a proposed Trust Agreement with the CAB. As part of the plan for Hector's trusteeship a number of directors would resign from the Board of Northeast Airlines, including Chester C. Davis, who might be regarded as Hughes' General Counsel; Raymond A. Cook, a lawyer and partner in an Eastern law firm which had long served Hughes; Robert S. Montgomery, an official of Hughes Aircraft; Maynard Montrose, President of the Oil Division of Toolco; and Raymond M. Holliday, one of Hughes' General Managers.

The Trust Indenture filed with the CAB implied that the major purpose of the trusteeship was to liquidate Hughes' interest in Northeast Airlines. Thus, the trustee was granted unlimited powers to sell, initiate and complete mergers or consolidations, transfer property, and take any and all action necessary to liquidate the interest of Hughes and Toolco in Northeast Airlines. At the time Hughes' spokesmen made it clear that the filing of the indenture didn't mean they were giving up the fight to continue the Boston-Florida run.

The CAB maintained its unbroken record of ruling against Hughes when it announced in December that after reconsideration, as ordered by the court, the Board had again voted to confine Northeast Airlines to a role as a local New England carrier and therefore NE had to relinquish all its routes south of New York.

Through President James Austin of Northeast Airlines, Hughes immediately announced "We'll fight!" and all parties returned to the Federal Court of Appeals in Boston, which had been much more sympathetic to the cause of Northeast and Howard Hughes.

Immediately following the CAB decision with respect to Northeast Airlines, a Bill was introduced into Congress which would, in effect, overrule the decision. The legislation provided that any trunk line operating with temporary authority under any scheduled line since 1957 should become permanent. Although it sounded like legislation of broad scope, it was cleverly worded to affect only Northeast Airlines.

This would not be the first time that Congress had in effect overruled the CAB. It had last done so in 1955 when legislation gave a local service carrier permanent authorization despite the CAB.

As was to be expected the CAB protested angrily against the proposed legislation. Board Chairman Alan S. Boyd was particularly vehement about the Bill and continually stressed that Congress had set up the entire regulatory system under the jurisdiction of the Civil Aeronautics Board and if Congress didn't like the way the system operated it could change it but not by legislating against the Board's rulings.

Hastings Keith, a Massachusetts Republican, sponsored the new law. He said bluntly at one point, "If there are no Florida routes for Northeast Airlines there may well be no Northeast Airlines."

In another speech Keith announced, "I cannot believe that it was the intention of Congress to have an airline which has efficiently served New England and the East Coast . . . for more than seven years, denied this operation [the Miami run] by a Board it [Congress] created to promote the best possible air-passenger service."

Massachusetts Senator Edward M. Kennedy also supported Northeast and denounced the refusal of the Civil Aeronautics Board to extend the Florida-New York run of Northeast Airlines. He announced to the press that he believed the CAB action was a "shocking misjudgment on both regional and national transportation needs." He further stated that in his opinion the CAB acted "without hearing a word of evidence of the encouraging record made by Northeast during the past year-and-a-half."

Now a new problem arose—Eastern Airlines and National Airlines jointly went to the trustee, Attorney Hector, and offered him $15 million to give up the appeal relating to the Florida run and to commit Northeast Airlines to becoming a subsidized New England regional air carrier.

Before the offer could be considered, an airline pilot named Mudge filed suit in a Massachusetts County Court to get an injunction to restrain the directors from even acting on the offer.

Many observers thought they detected the fine hand of Howard Hughes in this suit. Cleverly it argued a basic theory of law: that any time a corporation changes its basic nature it must obtain the approval of stockholders. For example, if a publicly held department store wanted to go out of that business and become a movie theater it would have to obtain approval of the shareholders. Mudge's theory was that giving up the fight for the Florida route was the equivalent of a complete change in the basic nature of the corporation and required approval of the shareholders.

The County Court granted a Preliminary Injunction restraining all action on the offer and appointed a Master to take testimony on the merits to decide whether the Injunction should be granted. The case dragged on and neither the offer nor the case ever got anywhere.

In June, 1965, Hughes received an offer to sell his stock in Northeast Airlines to the Storer Broadcasting Company. He would get about $5 per share for his stock and the Company would repay much of the debt owed by Northeast to Toolco. Since the stock on the American Stock Exchange had been ranging between $2 and $4 a share, and the chances of getting the debts repaid were small, the offer was attractive. On June 3, 1965, Storer obtained an option to purchase Toolco's majority interest in the airline.

On July 30, 1965, the trustee conveyed all of the interest of Hughes Tool Company, consisting of 973,226 shares of common stock in Northeast Airlines. Thus ended Howard Hughes' effort to amalgamate a north-south airline with an east-west airline.

Shortly after the sale Northeast Airlines common stock, which had been hovering around $4 a share, skyrocketed to $39 per share! There was little logic to this rise and, in fact, it was so absurd that at the annual meeting, George Storer, Sr., Chairman of the Board, stated that he felt that Storer stock was a rather good investment but he was extremely skeptical about the high price of the common stock of NE Airlines.

"We paid about $5 per share and last night I read it was selling at $37 per share," he said. "This is a mystery to me. I don't think it's worth that much."

That day Northeast stock closed down $4. In spite of this drop, it did manage to maintain its inexplicably high price and went into 1967 selling in the 30's. This marks one time when Hughes failed to sell at the top. If he could have sold the stock at the $30 mark rather than the $5 mark he would have realized $25 million more on the transaction. One must conclude, however, that this is a comparatively small matter to a billionaire!

Howard Hughes and His Secret Headquarters

THE YEAR 1926

PLANS WERE announced for the construction of a bridge across the Hudson River from Fort Lee, N.J., to Fort Washington in Manhattan. Later the bridge was named the George Washington.

Congress created the Army Air Corps.

Airmail service between New York and Boston was inaugurated.

Gertrude Ederle, age nineteen, swam across the English Channel—the first woman to accomplish the feat. It took fourteen hours and thirty-one minutes.

Sinclair Lewis declined the Pulitzer Prize award for *Arrowsmith,* saying that prizes tended to make authors "safe, obedient and sterile."

Popular songs of the year: *I Found a Million Dollar Baby in a Five and Ten Cent Store, Bye Bye Blackbird, Desert Song,* and *Play Gypsy.*

The Warner Theater in New York introduced the first "talking movie" in the film *Don Juan* starring John Barrymore. The sound was produced by a compatible phonograph record.

Gene Tunney became Heavyweight Champion of the World when he defeated Jack Dempsey in a ten round fight at the Sesquicentennial Stadium in Philadelphia. A record crowd attended—118,736.

Brazil and Spain left the League of Nations. Germany joined the League. Russia and Germany signed a treaty of "reassurance." Hirohito became the Emperor of Japan as Yoshohito died.

Howard Hughes was twenty years old.

21

SHORTLY AFTER arriving in California in 1926, Howard Hughes purchased 51 percent of the stock of Multi-Color, Inc. This corporation purportedly owned the patents and had the knowhow to make color movies. The far-seeing twenty-year-old believed that some day most, if not all, movies would be filmed in color.

Hughes was ahead of the times with Multi-Color. The idea was excellent in theory, but in practice it failed to work. He poured money into research, but the experimenters could not evolve a practical process for the development of motion picture color film. Ultimately, Multi-Color turned out to be one of Hughes' few financial flops.

Although the project itself failed, out of it Hughes acquired the building at 7000 Romaine Street in Los Angeles, which was used as his headquarters until 1953. At that time he sold the building to Eastman Kodak but apparently later regretted his action. In 1957 he repurchased it, and today it remains his major headquarters, message center, and general command post.

The structure is a two-story beige stucco building with no mark to identify it as a business property. Most of the time the doors are locked and no one gets in who is not expected.

The building is staffed primarily with Mormons. Hughes long ago learned that Mormons make excellent employees. They do not drink, smoke, or carouse, and they are noted for unswerving loyalty and integrity.

It is to this headquarters that Hughes generally relays his requests and commands, and it is through this same headquarters that his employees throughout the world communicate with him. As a message center, the Romaine Street headquarters operates with speed and efficiency.

An asphalt parking lot on one side of the building belongs to the headquarters. It is staffed with crew-cut young Mormon men who drive nondescript, usually older-model, battered Chevrolets. Any suspicious act in the general vicinity will cause one or more of the cars to emerge to investigate. Also, it is from this point that Hughes can dispatch a car to pick up and deliver someone to his home or other meeting place.

For many years Hughes made his home from time to time about ten minutes away from 7000 Romaine Street in either a house in Hollywood Hills or a bungalow on the grounds of the Beverly Hills Hotel. Despite his proximity he rarely went to the headquarters but preferred to communicate by telephone.

On those occasions when Hughes actually visited his Romaine Street office his primary purpose would be to dictate some specific business contract or letter that he wanted to do personally. This act was accompanied by an elaborate ritual. First, he insisted on having two different typists prepare the identical letter. Second he dictated directly to the typists, not trusting to the transcription skills of stenographers. When the typists were ready to start, he personally adjusted the typewriters so the margins of the letters would come out where he wanted them to be.

Hughes is a perfectionist who will not tolerate an erasure or even a smudge. He might dictate half a letter, then change his mind about a word and require the typist to start over on fresh stationery.

The selection of the secretaries who would work in the beige building perhaps involved more screening and more investigation than the CIA uses for its agents. The amount of intelligence material compiled on a secretary was unlimited, primarily because Hughes wanted to be absolutely certain there would be no leaks from his headquarters.

After they were selected, secretaries received unusual instructions. They were not permitted to wear nail polish or perfume. Make-up had to be kept to a minimum and, although lipstick was not prohibited, all other cosmetics were strongly discouraged.

Each girl worked alone in her private office so that no one could know what anyone else was doing. Great emphasis was placed on the following instructions to each employee: No one is permitted to receive personal phone calls at work. Away from the job it is strictly forbidden to talk to anyone about the work or about the employer or supervisor.

Hughes' personal typists led a fairly easy life. Primarily they were required to remain on call at any hour of the day or night. Other secretaries were available as substitutes if needed, but typists had to record in advance the fact that they were going to be out on any particular night. These special typists had few additional duties, but when they were actually called upon to work it was usually between midnight and morning. At those times they worked very hard. All night they typed—boring, tedious work because usually it was repetitious.

In addition to restrictions on the use of cosmetics, all typists were required to wear rubber gloves while typing or handling the paper. (This was probably because of Hughes' bacteriophobia.) When a page was scrapped a special attendant came with a container in which the paper was placed. The contents of this container were then taken to be burned. It is difficult to say whether this procedure was to maintain security for Hughes' confidential work or for the sake of sanitation—or both.

So much emphasis was placed on cleanliness to the point of antiseptic sterility that its occupants frequently called the building "the maternity ward."

Amid these sterile surroundings Howard Hughes paced up and down between the two desks where two secretaries typed as he dictated slowly and methodically an important letter or a paragraph of a contract. The girls who performed this job had to be prepared for long hours without eating. Even when there were breaks for food, no one left the premises. All food was brought in. Hughes would not trust any typist to leave the office to go out to a drugstore for food, where she might be tempted to gossip with others about the important work she was doing. Apparently he tried to ignore the awful fact that inevitably these same girls had to return to their respective homes.

The Romaine Street headquarters is a treasure house of the finest and most sophisticated forms of electronic gadgetry usable in the counter-espionage field. Various warning devices can be triggered by almost anything trespassing in the area under surveillance. There is a device which will sound an alarm if anyone tries to get information about documents inside the headquarters by use of X-ray outside the headquarters! There are lead-lined safes and burglar-proof vaults. There is electronic equipment to repel radio waves and to neutralize electronic snooping devices.

Such a mass of complex equipment carries with it the seeds of its own problems. This came to light when, during the litigation involving TWA, one of Hughes' attorneys astonished eminent opposing counsel, representing the leading banks and insurance companies of America, by accusing their forces of attempting to take illegal X-ray photographs of documents inside Hughes' Romaine Street office. It later developed that Hughes' battery-operated anti-X-ray warning system had sounded a false alarm when its battery ran down!

Publicity about the location of Hughes' secret headquarters and his inaccessibility has led to several attempts to enter the Romaine Street building illegally. No known attempt has ever succeeded.

In the 1960's some changes were made in the procedure at headquarters. Before this time, anyone who called OL 2-4500 would hear the operator reply simply by giving the phone number. Anyone asking for Hughes would be instructed to state his name, telephone number, and the nature of his business and would be informed that Mr. Hughes would be advised. A series of people then evaluated the message and made the decision about whether Hughes would be called.

In the early 1960's Hughes served notice that he was not to be called under any circumstances. His attitude, very simply, was, "Don't call me—I'll call you." Now from time to time Hughes or someone close to him does call the headquarters to check on messages. This is presently his sole contact with his empire on any formal basis.

Howard Hughes and His Photography Plane

NOVEMBER, 1937

THE JAPANESE Imperial Army was advancing on Shanghai. Troops forced their way across the Soochow River following an intense artillery bombardment. The Chinese resisted but fell back.

There were rumors that Italy would join the Japanese-German pact to create a strong three-power anti-Communist entente.

Jackman's in New York had a sensational sale of full-length fine dark mink coats at $875. Bloomingdale's offered men's suits (Burtons) with two pairs of pants (all wool) for $25.

The best sellers of the day included: *The Citadel* by A. J. Cronin, *Northwest Passage* by Kenneth Roberts, *To Have and Have Not* by Ernest Hemingway, *The Rains Came* by Louis Bromfield, *Life with Mother* by Clarence Day, and *How to Win Friends and Influence People* by Dale Carnegie.

On the stage Tallulah Bankhead starred in *Antony and Cleopatra*. There was also a hit comedy called *The Women*, by Clare Boothe.

In the movies Greta Garbo and Charles Boyer played in *Conquest*. Deanna Durbin and Leopold Stokowski appeared in *A Hundred Men and a Girl*. Paul Muni and Louise Rainer gave fine performances in the cinematic adaptation of Pearl Buck's *The Good Earth*.

Next month Howard Hughes would be thirty-two years old.

5

D-2 plane.

In 1937, after losing the Army competition for an experimental
twin-engine pursuit aircraft to Lockheed, Hughes became exceed-
ingly wroth. He had not the slightest doubt in his own mind that
his design was superior to that of Lockheed and he firmly believed
that the company had gained the contract not on merit but on social
relationships with the people responsible for making the recom-
mendations.

Hughes determined to turn his back on the Army and build a
plane so far superior to anything then existing or contemplated that
the Army would come hat in hand to plead with him to build it for
them. Suspecting that some of his best ideas had been stolen by
Lockheed spies, he redoubled his security measures.

Security became so tight at the Hughes Aircraft plant that even a
general could not breach it. Indeed, one tried but without success.
The United States Air Corps decided that it might award Hughes
a contract just to keep him doing business with it. General
Henry H. (Hap) Arnold himself was commissioned to visit the
Hughes Aircraft Company plant and inspect its facilities.

When General Arnold arrived at the plant the guards refused him
admission. Presentation of his credentials had no noticeable effect
in opening the way before him. All efforts to gain admission were
frustrated by one simple rule. "No one was to be admitted without
approval of Hughes." Later Hughes conceded that this was probably the only time the head of the United States Army Air Corps
had been denied admission to an airplane factory.

As Hughes explained, "Naturally, this incident was not intended.
I simply left instructions that no one was to be admitted and I was
unaware that General Arnold was going to pay us a visit."

Hughes put his men to work on a new design which he called the
D-2. It would be a two-engine medium-sized plane, probably a
bomber, built primarily out of wood and capable of long range and
high speed.

At this time the Hughes Aircraft plant was located in Burbank, California, but the installation was too small for the new undertaking. The D-2 would require a large area for development. Hughes also had his idea for a flexible ammunition chute to replace the archaic system of loading guns currently in use in the large planes. Therefore, Hughes instructed Odekirk to find another location. Odekirk immediately sent his engineers out to inspect California from the air until at last they found two large pieces of land they believed would be satisfactory. Many weeks later Odekirk succeeded in locating Hughes and flew him over the two sites. Hughes took one look at the Culver City property and laconically ordered, "Buy it."

Although absent from the Culver City building for some time Hughes kept himself informed about every step in its growth. He was conversant with every detail of location and construction. Odekirk, to his constant surprise, would suddenly receive a call from Hughes, who might say, "I think you are making a mistake making that stockroom in the East Wing so small. It will have to be larger in order to accommodate all of the hardware we are going to need." And Hughes was usually right.

In order to keep himself informed of progress, Hughes would frequently come into the plant in the middle of the night, walk around, make some notes, and disappear again. If someone was working at a task that intrigued Hughes, he might join the worker, remaining all through the night. He usually carried with him a brown paper bag containing a sandwich and a carton of milk. Hughes liked to eat when he was hungry and sleep when he was sleepy, without regard for the position assumed by the hands of a clock. Occasionally in the middle of the work his eyelids would grow heavy and he would be overwhelmed by a need to sleep. As suddenly as he had appeared he would disappear, much to the mystification of those with whom he worked, who might not even know his name. Rarely did anyone argue with him or question him. His air of authority and his knowledge of the subject earned him instant acceptance.

Hughes did not depend solely on these clandestine forays. He also maintained a small special force whose assignments were to keep him informed. The members of this force earned the title "Hughes spies," and the quantity of information they transmitted is an undisclosed secret.

Shortly after Pearl Harbor the Army Air Corps sent official delegations to visit all aircraft factories throughout the country in order to obtain an inventory of production facilities. Odekirk was advised that such a delegation was about to descend on Culver City, and he at once notified Hughes, who appeared in person to act as guide for the inspecting group. Everyone was surprised at his detailed knowledge of the inner workings of the plant.

He welcomed this opportunity to let the Air Corps see his D-2, which was finally taking shape. The Army showed little interest in the plane but they were greatly intrigued by the bullet feed-chute which would permit the continuous firing of 600 rounds of ammunition by the aerial gun, a significant improvement over the 50-round belt that the Air Corps was then using. Hughes received an immediate order for all the chutes he could produce, but try as he might he could raise not the slightest interest in the D-2. In spite of his considerable powers of persuasion, the Army personnel would not be swayed from their position that they had enough developmental and experimental planes on their drawing boards. What they desperately needed, as quickly as possible, was large numbers of planes in the air. Experimental aircraft would have to await a more propitious time.

By June of 1942, unable to find any method of selling the D-2 to the federal government, Hughes decided to use other resources. He therefore contacted his good friend, Jesse Jones, and laid the problem before him. Jones, Secretary of Commerce and one of the top aides to the President of the United States, with his own hand wrote a note to Franklin D. Roosevelt.

[Handwritten]
"For the President:
"June 27, 1942
"Howard Hughes, airplane designer, builder and holder of most of the world's speed records, will send into the sky at an early date his twin-motored classic bomber which will fly faster than any pursuit ship in the world. (485 miles an hour)
[Typed] "Mr. Hughes has put 6 million dollars of his private funds and several years of intensive work and study into the development of this plane, the Hughes Design No. 2. Hughes Design No. 1, which inspired his fast bomber, was a plane in which seven years ago he flew non-stop from Los Angeles to New York in 7

hours, 29 minutes. This record still stands and is by far the fastest long cross-country flight ever made. Nowhere in the world has anyone yet approached Hughes' record of 2500 miles at a sustained speed of 333 miles per hour."

The President attached to Jones' memorandum a little forwarding slip "Memorandum for General Arnold—What is there in this?"

The next day back came a memorandum from Arnold stating:

"The United States Army Air Force has been in close touch with Howard Hughes in the development of his twin-motored bomber. It will be made of plastic, and is of the light bomber type with a gross weight of somewhere from 20,000 to 25,000 pounds.

"Mr. Hughes volunteered to build this at his own expense, because he felt that he could build a vastly superior bomber and he received an outline of our desires and went ahead with his own ideas.

"He claims that our engineers do not challenge the figures, that his airplane will make about 430 miles an hour fully loaded.

"At present he is trying to sell it to the United States Army Air Forces and we are negotiating to see if we can arrive at a price agreeable to both parties."

This communication was followed by a final memorandum of July 17, 1942, in which General Arnold advised the Commander-in-Chief as follows:

"Mr. Hughes suggested the following procedure, which we have agreed to. That when the airplane is completed and ready to be submitted to the government, which is now estimated to be August or September, we will inspect and test the airplane; and if the government is sufficiently interested to give him an order for additional airplanes, that we undertake to absorb his development costs. He estimates that he has invested in this airplane, which as yet contains many unproved features from the viewpoint of construction, about three million dollars. If the airplane is of no interest to the government, he states that he, Mr. Hughes, will expect to take the loss."

As the D-2 approached completion there still was no interest by the Armed Forces in the plane other than the cryptic arrangement of General Arnold's memos. Finally Hughes sent his No. 1 man, Noah Dietrich, General Supervisor of the Hughes empire, to see General Oliver P. Echols, Chief Officer in Charge of Aircraft Procurement at the major Army Air Force Procurement Center at Wright Field. Dietrich's mission was to fasten the attention of the Army on the D-2.

General Echols told Dietrich bluntly that under no circumstances would he deal with Hughes, for whom he had an intense and abiding dislike. Dietrich argued that the D-2 was a plane which should not be ignored because of personalities. He explained that it would far outperform and outspeed any plane in existence or on any design board. He even offered to give the Army written guarantees. Patiently he probed to elicit the reasons for Echols' antipathy to Hughes. Finally the story began to take form.

Following Howard Hughes' establishment of the transcontinental record Echols had reached Hughes by telephone and asked him to fly the ship to Wright Field so that the Army staff could inspect it. Hughes simply ignored the request.

Echols was also irritated by his treatment a short time before his meeting with Dietrich. The Air Corps had decided to examine the D-2. Echols called Hughes Aircraft and obtained permission to inspect the plane. He sent a staff of engineers under the leadership of Major Ervin. On their arrival at the plant their entrance was delayed while Plant Security contacted Howard Hughes. Hughes, obsessed with fear of espionage by other manufacturers, declared that because of the secret nature of the project he would not permit a group of people to inspect the plane. He was willing to permit Major Ervin or one other expert to look at it but a group inspection was out of the question.

As Echols related to Dietrich, "That was very embarrassing to me. I had sent a mission out there to inspect the plane and they were refused permission."

General Echols recalled his group and Hughes continued work on the D-2 without official Army authorization. The Army did cooperate with Hughes to some extent when he ran into difficulties in procuring engines, propellers, turbines and similar necessary equipment. Without a government contract, he was unable to requisition official matériel but the Air Corps permitted him to request that the needed supplies be made available for its convenience. The Army provided Hughes with a special contract arranging for Hughes Aircraft Company to furnish it with a report on the D-2 for a nominal payment. Thus it became legally possible for Hughes to obtain certain critical equipment which was in short supply.

The D-2 made its first test-flight June 20, 1943, but it was not overly successful. Virtually abandoning the D-2 design, Hughes and his aeronautical engineers created a new plane which they designated the D-5.

On August 13, 1943, the Air Corps issued a special report to the Chief of Air Staff stating that the D-2 was not successful. Recognizing that the D-5 represented a modification of the D-2, the Army reported to the Chief of Air, "This office recommends against any further action tending to encourage the development of, diverting facilities to, a project which has not progressed favorably to date and which shows so little promise in the future." This conclusion was approved by the Chief of Air Staff.

In the interim Colonel Elliott Roosevelt, one of the sons of President Franklin D. Roosevelt, had become an authority on photoreconnaissance in the European theater of operations. Even before joining the Army he had had considerable experience with aviation. He was a licensed pilot, became Aviation Editor of a Los Angeles newspaper, and subsequently acted as Aviation Editor for all the Hearst newspapers. He also wrote a daily nationally syndicated column. Later he was appointed Vice President of the Aeronautical Chamber of Commerce. At one time the President's son had even served as General Manager of an airline that operated between Los Angeles, San Diego, Caliente and Encinada, Mexico.

Roosevelt was commissioned a Captain in the Army in 1940 and very shortly thereafter was assigned to the 21st Reconnaissance Squadron which was in charge of obtaining information about submarines operating in the North Atlantic. One of the tasks he was charged with was to make a photographic reconnaissance survey of North Atlantic bases. It was then that he first discovered that all the Army Air Corps photographic reconnaissance aircraft were obsolete. In fact, no one in the Army at the time had any concept of the utility of photographic reconnaissance as an intelligence weapon. The beginning of active combat pin-pointed the necessity for good aerial reconnaissance to support ground and air combat and simultaneously revealed the total lack of planes fitted to do the job.

Young Roosevelt worked on the adaptation of fighters and bombers for photographic missions. In August, 1942, Roosevelt received a promotion to Lieutenant-Colonel and was placed in charge of photo reconnaissance for the invasion of North Africa and Sicily.

He began with about 92 planes, including B-17 bombers, P-38

fighters and some British Mosquitoes borrowed for experimental purposes. They all proved completely unsatisfactory for reconnaissance work. The famed P-38's operated at a ceiling of 17,000 feet but good photo reconnaissance required a higher altitude because the German ME-109 and even the comparatively poor quality Italian planes could fly higher and so could shoot down the P-38's. Even though they made the planes as light as possible, stripping them of all armor and guns, they still were unable to evade the enemy.

General Carl Spaatz was in charge of all air combat in this particular area and he bombarded Washington with complaints about the difficulties involved in getting photo reconnaissance work done with the inadequate planes provided for the job. The argument was simple: "Give us planes and we'll fly faster, climb higher, and have less mechanical difficulties."

To add salt to the smarting wounds of the Army Air Corps, Intelligence reported that the enemy was far ahead in reconnaissance-type aircraft. For example, they had installed water-injection systems which permitted short bursts of high speed to remove a threatened plane rapidly from a dangerous situation. With greater speed and more maneuverability, the enemy consequently suffered fewer losses of aircraft.

Shortly after the invasion of Sicily, Robert Lovett, Assistant Secretary of War for Air, while touring the Western Theater of Operations, visited Elliott Roosevelt. The photo-reconnaissance chief took this opportunity to tell the Assistant Secretary of the problems of accomplishing rewarding reconnaissance flights without extraordinary loss of life.

Mr. Lovett replied, "Both our office and General Arnold have been getting a great many complaints from all theaters of operations. In fact, the ground forces are so disgusted with the lack of intelligence from reconnaissance aviation that they started agitating to take over and establish their own reconnaissance independent of the Air Force. I don't like this development."

Roosevelt agreed with Lovett and was completely taken aback when Lovett added, "I know that you perform a terrific job out here in the photo-reconnaissance field and you probably know more about it than anyone else and I want you to come back to Washington to take charge of the reconnaissance branch on a central basis."

Roosevelt cautioned, "You can't do that, sir, because of the fact of who I am. While I have had considerable overseas experience, I am the son of the President of the United States, and it will open him to great criticism if you bring me back and have me sit out the war in the Pentagon building. You will give the members of Congress who don't like Franklin Roosevelt a wonderful opportunity to smear him."

The idea gave Lovett pause but he recognized the truth of what young Roosevelt said. "I am going to talk it over with Hap Arnold."

In July, on Lovett's instructions, the War Department sent a message to the Commanding General of the 12th Air Force stating, "The advice of Colonel Elliott Roosevelt is urgently required in this Headquarters in connection with the contemplated reorganization of the reconnaissance aviation program. It is therefore requested that temporary duty orders be issued returning Colonel Roosevelt for duty in Washington at the earliest possible time that will not seriously interfere with his duties. It is desired that he bring all pertinent information in connection with the reconnaissance program in the European theater."

Colonel Roosevelt arrived in Washington on the last day of June in 1943 and received immediate orders to report to General Arnold. The General of the Air Force told Roosevelt, "This whole reconnaissance picture is very, very bad. The ground forces and General McNair are raising a tremendous amount of fuss. They are bitter about the lack of support given the ground troops in all theaters by the Air Force in the way of reconnaissance."

Roosevelt replied, "Sir, I agree that the situation is not right."

General Arnold continued, "That is not the only headache. We are even getting it from our Air Force Commanders. Now I want you to look into the whole problem of the Reconnaissance Program of the United States Army Air Forces and to figure out a way whereby we can overcome the objections and not be forced to turn over reconnaissance units to the control of the ground forces: at the same time rectify it so that both the Air Force and the ground forces in all theatres will get the proper service."

General Arnold had some further instructions. He indicated that under no circumstances was there to be any interference with the fighter or bomber programs. Once Elliott suggested the possibility of getting some of the best fighter planes, removing the guns and putting in cameras, but the General commanded imperiously, "Don't you dare do that!"

Secretary Lovett, General Arnold and Colonel Roosevelt discussed the formation of an inspection team to travel around the nation searching for a suitable plane for use in the future for reconnaissance work. They finally decided on four people in addition to themselves:

Squadron Leader D. W. Stevenson, a British reconnaissance flyer, had served under Roosevelt. He had seen action in the Malta campaign and in the air battle of Britain. As a flying officer, his record was outstanding.

Lieutenant Colonel Karl Polifka had commanded the first reconnaissance squadron in the Southwest Pacific.

Lieutenant Colonel Harry T. Edison had served as aide to Roosevelt in the African theater. He was one of the first officers to survive five photo-reconnaissance missions.

The final member of the party was Major W. R. Boyd III who worked in the reconnaissance section of Headquarters.

The group first visited Wright Field, but could find no aircraft there which could serve their purpose.

The next stop was the Lockheed plant at Burbank, California, where they looked into the XP-58. That plane, although it was designed for the possibility of use as a photo-reconnaissance aircraft, had fallen victim to a series of conflicting directives and the company could not possibly turn out anything on schedule.

Roosevelt later reported, "To this day the Lockheed factory does not know what a standard aircraft should contain in the way of camera mountings, camera openings, and other technical specifications which could very well have been standardized many, many months ago."

The inspection team concluded that the projected performance figures on the XP-58 did not promise a sufficient improvement over existing planes to warrant a procurement program. Furthermore, since Lockheed estimated 18 months to produce a prototype and at least two years to get into production there was no time to depend upon this craft.

Lockheed did possess, at about the same stage of development, the T-38, which was found to be an excellent aircraft for photo reconnaissance if it could be obtained quickly. Unfortunately the basic design engineering had not yet been completed, and a prototype could not be ready for at least eighteen months. No estimate could be given as to the date of production and therefore this aircraft too was ruled out.

Next the inspection team proceeded to the Hughes Aircraft Company at Culver City where they met with company executives, including Howard Hughes. Elliott Roosevelt and the others in the official group were shown the drawings and tests on the D-2 and then taken to Harper's Lake to observe a flight. As it stood, the plane was not satisfactory but Hughes proposed certain modifications which could overcome the objections to its use in a photo-reconnaissance program.

Hughes had already committed some changes to paper, and evolved what he designated the D-5. At this time Elliott Roosevelt held Howard Hughes in high esteem and he believed Hughes would be an ideal choice as a designer. Roosevelt was influenced by Hughes' experience with racing and long-range aircraft design over a prolonged period of time.

Hughes informed the inspecting group that he would be completely amenable to the acceptance of a contract for any number of photographic reconnaissance aircraft of the D-5 type and that the government would not have to accept any aircraft that failed to live up to minimum performance figures and required delivery dates.

Typically, Hughes agreed that if the aircraft did not conform to the specifications he personally would bear all the costs in connection therewith so that the government would pay nothing. Furthermore, despite the potential high cost Hughes pledged that if delivery dates were not met he would be willing to include contract penalty clauses.

Hughes and his staff undertook to produce the first complete photo-reconnaissance aircraft, which would be ready for flight testing within five months. To complete the factory and the Army tests, he undertook to begin manufacturing production models within twelve months from the date of the contract. He further promised completion for delivery at the rate of two a day within eighteen months.

Satisfied with the results of the trip Roosevelt, on behalf of the inspection party, strongly urged that an order for photo-reconnaissance planes be placed with the Hughes Aircraft Company.

The Army opposed this recommendation. Major General Oliver P. Echols, in charge of Air Force Plane Procurement, issued a strongly worded memorandum to General Arnold requesting that the "previous recommendation made by this office and approved by the Chief of Air Staff" with regard to the Hughes plane be disregarded. Echols based his decision on the calculation that Hughes would have to hire between 4,000 and 5,000 new people in a Los Angeles area labor market where excess labor simply did not exist. In addition, the chief procurement officer objected that the plane was made of wood and the Army had had its fill of this structural material.

He said, "As a result of our experience, it is our considered opinion that wooden airplanes are a very poor investment and there was no indication that the Hughes airplane would be any different structurewise and maintenancewise than any others."

Despite Roosevelt's affirmative recommendation the Army discouraged the project. A special conference of Army officers knowledgeable about the aircraft recommended instead that Republic Aviation's special photo-plane known then as the XL-12 should be used in preference to the Hughes Aircraft D-5 (about to be redesignated F-11). However, by no means was there unanimity of opinion. Some of those present at the meeting thought the proposed F-11 would be far superior to any photo-reconnaissance airplane then in existence. Unfortunately for Hughes' hopes, everyone substantially agreed that the FX-11 would not be ready to fly as soon as the Republic plane, as the reports stated "because of the reputation of Republic as opposed to the Hughes organization."

The Army wrapped the Hughes photo-reconnaissance plane in red tape and it was not until late 1943, almost a year after Roosevelt's recommendation, that a contract was at last prepared for 100 photo-reconnaissance planes to be built by Hughes Aircraft. Hughes was pleased. Notwithstanding all of the delays and all of the changes he now had a contract not only to build a plane for the Army but also to go into production on that plane.

The contract called for constructing three experimental planes and one static test plane. The static test plane would, of course, be disassembled and tested part by part in wind tunnels and with other testing equipment. The government agreed to pay Hughes $500,000 per plane for the four test models and thereafter he would receive an additional contract for 97 planes on a regular production basis.

Hughes and his people spent a considerable amount of time trying to devise a provision in the contract which would permit recovery for all of the research, design and engineering expense incurred in developing the D-2. However, the Army was reluctant to include any of this because of the widespread belief among Army personnel that the plane they were ordering—the FX-11—was completely unrelated to the D-2 and the D-5. A major change had been made by Hughes' agreement to fabricate the plane from metal rather than wood.

Naturally a compromise was reached which provided that eventually the Army would send out a commission to compare the new plane with the old drawings and designs. These experts would try to determine how much of the many million dollars Hughes had spent in developing the D-2 could logically be counted as design and development costs for the FX-11.

In the year 1944, with the war drawing to a close, Hughes at last obtained his contract. Shortly after, in May, 1944, twenty-one engineers including the project engineer resigned from the Hughes Aircraft Company. Of course, the Army immediately became alarmed, anticipating increased production delays, inferior aircraft, or at the very least, increased costs. In spite of this blow, Hughes weathered the storm and continued his work on the FX-11. However, time had run out. The war ended with the FX-11 still unfinished.

The Army canceled the contract for 100 planes and substituted instead a contract for three planes with the implication that in the final payment for the three planes and in covering the cancellation, Hughes would be reimbursed for the millions of dollars he had spent in development research. In spite of this, the dispute grew between the Army and Hughes over whether he would be reimbursed for the development of the D-2 and/or the D-5. Hughes and his staff insisted they should be; the Army insisted equally vehemently that the D-2 and the D-5 had nothing whatsoever to do with the FX-11.

Notwithstanding the continued disagreement Hughes finally completed the FX-11 and on July 7, 1946, a half year after the war had ended, the flying test model stood waiting on the runway. Hughes' staff tried their utmost to dissuade Hughes from testing it himself, but to no avail. Again he insisted, "I do my own flying."

Early Sunday morning Hughes began to ground test the plane preparatory to the ultimate flight test. He performed two hours of high-speed taxi maneuvers on the Hughes Aircraft Company's runway at Culver City. After each run he returned the plane to the hangar for further checking and testing. He was meticulous in his attention to each minute detail. Finally, at 5:20 P.M. he pronounced the aircraft ready for air tests.

Following a routine take off, Hughes made his first mistake. Although the flight test plan did not call for retracting the landing gear, Hughes tested it anyway. When he saw that the landing gear warning light was still red, indicating a complete retraction had not been accomplished, he climbed to a higher altitude and continued to try unsuccessfully to cause the gear to retract completely.

As he continued to experiment with the controls, he discovered that by pushing sharply forward on the control wheel as the gear retracted, the warning light could be made to go off, theoretically indicating that the gear was up and locked in place. He was still not completely satisfied with this assumption so he essayed two more trials, each completed by exerting sharp forward pressure on the control wheel.

Now, cautious as always, he decided it would be advisable before landing to have a visual check to determine that the nose gear had rotated to its proper position. He planned to fly low across the field with the gear extended, then come back across the field and observe if the spectators indicated any trouble with the position of the wheels. He began his descent and at 2,000 feet observed a company-owned A-20 climbing after take-off from the plant runway.

Wishing the A-20 to observe his landing gear, he started to climb to 5,000 feet, approaching the other plane closely on the way up. The pilot of the A-20 (unknown to Hughes it was Odekirk) not understanding the reason for the odd behavior of the FX-11, maneuvered to place maximum air space between the two planes. Hughes now tried to establish radio contact.

Army headquarters, through the authority of the Federal Communications Commission, had assigned a C-channel frequency of 150 megacycles to the Hughes Company for use during the flight test program. Ground control at the Hughes Field had been set up to operate on the assigned frequency and had made a satisfactory check test with the FX-11 a few hours before take off. No further check was made by Hughes immediately prior to the test. Now, for some reason, Hughes failed to use the C-channel frequency but instead used B-channel "any tower" call.

The Los Angeles Municipal Airport tower responded and Hughes asked the operator to contact the A-20. While waiting for the Los Angeles tower operator to reach the A-20 Hughes became aware for the first time of a strong pull on the right side of the aircraft. Not wanting to be busy with the radio during what might be some incipient emergency he acknowledged a tower reply and then apparently broke radio contact.

Hughes was now two or three miles east of his home field heading north at approximately 5,000 feet. The force became stronger, causing the plane to turn to the right. He eased the craft along, letting it turn until it was headed almost due east, then gently he stopped the turn and began to coax a 180-degree turn to the left. Removing his safety belt, Hughes moved through the cabin, meanwhile keeping his left hand on the controls. He searched out every possible place that might be the source of the trouble, but found nothing.

At last he returned to his seat but was too busy handling the plane to find time to refasten his safety belt. After seating himself, he turned on more power, revving both engines up to 2800 r.p.m., but the additional surge produced no effect. The plane was definitely losing altitude, flying erratically and giving every evidence of uncontrolled drag.

At 2,500 feet he considered bailing out, but decided he still had a chance to find out what had gone wrong. The drag had now become so strong that it was necessary to hold full left rudder and full left aileron just to keep the plane level. Although he could still control the direction of flight he had completely lost control of altitude. He was now down to 800 feet and it was apparent that his time was running out. If he was going to locate the source of trouble it would have to be at once. Thinking possibly a landing-gear door or some other underside surface might have torn loose and turned broadside to the wind he decided to drop the landing gear. If his supposition were correct the force of the wheels dropping into position might jar the obstruction loose, thus removing the source of the drag and allowing the plane to gain altitude. With the wheels down, he realized he had incorrectly diagnosed the problem and that it was also too late to avoid a crash.

He propped his feet firmly high on the instrument panel and attempted to flare the plane into the roof of a house directly ahead of him—the crash was inevitable but he hoped to exert some control over the result.

The right landing-gear and engine penetrated the second story wall and roof and the left landing gear struck the peak of the roof.

Initial impact caused the aircraft to yaw severely to the right. The right wingtip struck the neighboring house at 802 North Linden Drive in Beverly Hills and the aircraft continued to travel sideways. The next jarring contact was made by the left side of the cockpit forcibly colliding with a power-line pole. The canopy broke and the plane careened on, striking the ground across the alley from 802 North Linden Drive, then bouncing and skidding into the rear of 808 Whittier Drive, and finally coming to rest there. The plane immediately burst into flames, destroying both itself and the house at 808 North Whittier Drive.

Luckily for Hughes he hit the ground still in the fuselage with the plastic cockpit canopy gone. With his last remaining strength he forced himself out of the burning plane and collapsed. Two men saw him: Marine Sergeant William Lloyd Durkan and Captain James Guston quickly reached his side to pull him to safety. Hughes was still conscious and Sergeant Durkan asked him, "Is there anyone else in the plane?"

Instead of replying to that question Hughes asked, "Did anyone get hurt in the crash?" When they indicated that they did not believe that any person had been hurt he seemed to sigh and sag with relief.

An ambulance from the Beverly Hills Emergency Hospital arrived and took him on a stretcher to that institution. Half an hour after his arrival he was moved, still on the same stretcher, to the Good Samaritan Hospital, where he was examined by Dr. Verne R. Mason who then issued the first bulletin on Hughes' condition:

> Fracture of the left clavicle.
> Fracture of the posterior portion of the upper nine ribs on the left side.
> Fracture of the first two ribs on the right side.
> Possible fracture of the nose.
> A large laceration of the scalp on the left side.
> Extensive second and third degree burns of the left hand.
> A large second degree burn of the lower part of the left chest extending from the nipple line to the medial scapular line.
> A large second degree burn of the left buttock.
> Numerous cuts, bruises and abrasions of both arms and both legs, numerous small cuts about the face.

A later report said:

"In the early morning of July 8, 1946, hemorrhage occurred into the left pleural space, and this was followed by an effusion into the chest. This pleural space was tapped and 3400 cc. of bloody liquid was removed at three tappings. The hemoglobin content of this fluid was 18% and it is probable that 650 cc. of hemorrhage took place into the chest."

Hughes' friends and associates held no hope for his recovery. Odekirk, who had been flying the A-20 in order to better observe the test flight, took the room next to Hughes in the hospital and spent the long, sleepless night peering anxiously into the injured man's room. Reporters and movie actresses, top executives and military officials flocked to the hospital to wait for news. The first medical bulletin gave him only an outside chance to live.

At dawn Hughes regained consciousness and demanded a pencil and paper so that he could write out what he believed to be the cause of the crash.

By the second day he had reported that he thought the crash was caused by some malfunction of the right propeller.

On the third day, annoyed by his inability to move or be moved without suffering excruciating pain, he sent for Odekirk and ordered construction of a special bed he had designed, made of separate rubber squares, each square operating with an individual motor. The completed design resembled today's full-power automobile seat —each square could go up or down and turn in either direction— tilt or rake. This enabled Hughes, by operating the controlling push-buttons, to rearrange his position with a minimum of pain.

The hospital was deluged with flowers, telegrams, baskets of fruit and numerous visitors, who descended upon it in full cry. The casual observer might well have concluded that the institution harbored a world leader or at least a princely member of a major royal house. The President of the United States, Harry S Truman, wired, "I am watching eagerly all the reports concerning you. I feel sure you will win the fight. With every good wish."

On the fourth day Hughes asked for his good luck charm—a battered felt hat that he wore on all test flights, races, and other potentially dangerous occasions. Policeman E. R. Davis found it in the wrecked cockpit, dirty and water-soaked but miraculously unburned, and Hughes welcomed it as an auspicious omen.

Many Hollywood stars came to the hospital or called regularly: Lana Turner, Katherine Hepburn, Ginger Rogers, Ava Gardner,

Linda Darnell, Cary Grant and Errol Flynn were among those who figuratively haunted his bedside, although none could pass the guarded hospital door.

After a week of continued improvement Hughes suddenly suffered a relapse. He had just dictated his belief as to the cause of the accident. Then he rallied and recovered.

Despite the crash, the government accepted delivery of the FX-11 on January 14, 1947. From the viewpoint of Hughes and his staff the major remaining concern was to get paid, so the company renewed its efforts to include the engineering cost of the D-2 in the payment for FX-11.

One Army report on this matter read: "The Hughes Aircraft Company's contention that the D-2 was a prototype for the F-11 airplane is ridiculous. We might just as well say that the B-17 is a prototype of the B-29. These airplanes have the same general configuration, use similar identical rudder pedals, and, in general, contain a lot of individual parts which are used in all airplanes fabricated by the Boeing or Republic companies. Such parts are normally associated with various manufacturers and are used in order that new parts will not have to be designed. They are peculiar to the company which fabricates them. The fact that they are used does not indicate that any subsequent airplanes built are prototypes.

"The only thing that the D-2 has contributed to the F-11 is Hughes' aircraft knowhow. . . . In addition to not being a prototype, the D-2 is not an experimental version of the F-11. Aside from the general geometric shape and a few details such as the throttle handle, mixture control, flap control, etc. they are two separate and distinct flying machines. The contention that the flying characteristics will be identical or even similar is too far fetched for further comment. The F-11 is not a scaled-up version of the D-2 in that the weights are different, the air foil sections are different, the percentage of controlled area is different and many other differences exist too numerous to mention."

In spite of all opposition, somehow the costs of the D-2 were included in the F-11. A memorandum which approved this inclusion contained in longhand the comment, "I'll be damned!" It was written by Ralph R. Graichen, Civilian Deputy Director of Research and Development for the Air Force.

The crash which almost cost him his life, didn't diminish Hughes'

confidence in the FX-11. He was convinced that the difficulty had
been caused solely by the faulty propeller and that the plane was
basically sound. An Army examining board found that the crash
was due in great part to "pilot error." Hughes never accepted their
finding. He ordered another plane completed and by January of
1947 the second FX-11 was ready for testing. But Wright Field had
taken control of the second plane in the name of the Army and this
time, therefore, Hughes could not test fly it without its permission.
Routinely the company filed its request for Hughes to be the test
pilot on the first flight. Just as automatically Wright Field refused.

Hughes would not accept the turndown. Satisfied that the "Hate
Hughes Club" was still in control at Wright Field, he went immediately to Washington to see Lieutenant-General Ira C. Eaker in
an effort to get the Wright Field decision reversed. Hughes had met
Eaker briefly at a luncheon at the Press Club in Washington after
his around-the-world flight in 1938.

It was a determined Hughes who appeared one Sunday early in
February at the Fort Myers home of General Eakers. He marshaled
persuasive arguments to advance his cause. He pointed out calmly
and logically that he had flown the first craft and was the only pilot
alive who had had experience with the plane. He had designed it,
he argued, and knew its weaknesses and its strengths. It was only
natural that he should fly it.

He spoke cogently and winningly, advancing his reasons why he
should be permitted to make this test flight too. General Eaker was
swayed but did not believe it was his place to make the final decision. This right and responsibility, Eaker explained, lay with General Carl Spaatz, the Commanding General of the Army Air Forces.
However, General Eaker added, he was ready to call General
Spaatz on the telephone and ask him to join them at once, if possible, to listen to Hughes' arguments.

After Spaatz arrived, Hughes once again trotted out his boyish
but persuasive argument as to why he should be the first pilot to
test fly the FX-11.

Hughes next delivered himself of what he regarded as the ultimate and irresistible offer. "I'll have the Hughes Tool Company
execute a contract whereby it will pay the government for any
damage whatsoever occurring to the plane while I fly it."

General Spaatz could hardly believe his ears. Incredulously he inquired, "Do you mean you'll pay the government the full value of that plane if it crashes?"

Hughes reiterated, "I mean exactly that. I recognize that the plane is worth $5 million and the Hughes Tool Company will agree to reimburse the Army for the full $5 million if it's cracked up."

General Spaatz could no longer divine any logical reason to withhold his agreement, and he told Hughes so. "For on those terms I see no objection to your flying it and I will issue the necessary orders to Wright Field."

The second test was smooth and successful. The plane offered Hughes no difficulties and, following the flight test plan laid down by the Army, he was able to execute every maneuver flawlessly. The Army accepted the plane and Hughes received his payment.

When Hughes met General Eaker he was impressed by the obvious ability, sincerity and candor of the man. Shortly after General Eaker's intervention on Hughes' behalf, the General's request for retirement after thirty years of service was granted. In early May, 1947, while he was addressing the Alumni Association of Southern California, he received a phone call inviting him to dine with Mr. Hughes. He accepted and at dinner received an offer for his services, which he accepted.

Howard Hughes and His Public Relations Man

DECEMBER 1, 1941

THE RED ARMY was battling for its life on the southern front from Rostov to Taganrog.

Marshal Henri Philippe Pétain, French Chief of State, was scheduled to meet with Adolf Hitler in Occupied France for "final discussions" of Franco-German relations.

President Franklin Delano Roosevelt rushed back from his holiday at Warm Springs, Georgia, to prepare to deal with the Japanese war threat personally.

For the first time in history a war was broadcast over the radio. The British Broadcasting Corporation sent out live over its microphones the sounds of the Battle of Moscow. The Russian announcer declared, "Never will the enemy succeed in getting even a glimpse of Moscow."

The books on the best-seller list included John Gunther's *Inside Latin America;* Dr. A. J. Cronin's *The Keys of the Kingdom,* and Edna Ferber's *Saratoga Trunk.*

The stage featured Helen Hayes in *Candle in the Wind;* Howard Lindsay in *Life with Father;* and Maurice Evans and Judith Anderson in *Macbeth.* Ethel Barrymore received rave reviews in *The Corn Is Green.*

The movies of the day were Abbott and Costello in *Keep Them Flying,* Charles Boyer and Margaret Sullavan in *Appointment for Love,* Clark Gable and Lana Turner in *Honky Tonk,* Fred Astaire and Rita Hayworth in *You'll Never Get Rich,* and a star-studded cast in *Dr. Jekyll and Mr. Hyde,* including Spencer Tracy, Ingrid Bergman, and Lana Turner.

This month Howard Hughes would be thirty-six years old.

6

JOHN W. MEYER, erstwhile public relations man at Warner Brothers Studios, ex-owner-operator of the La Conga Night Club in Hollywood, former public relations man for the Caliente Race Track in Mexico and man of multiple experiences and varied occupations, went to work for Howard Hughes on December 1, 1941.

In theory Johnny Meyer worked on public relations for Hughes personally but actually Hughes assigned him to whatever spot currently had need of his specialized talents. Meyer entertained visiting VIP's, paid the bills for Army officers who wanted hotel suites, provided women, supplied alcoholic beverages and otherwise discharged the multiple duties inherent in the anomalous position labeled "Public Relations."

The possible revelations of Johnny Meyer comprised the greatest threat to Hughes during the Senate investigation of the National Defense program. Meyer was brash and uninhibited and no one could predict what he might say. For example, the following colloquy took place during one phase of Meyer's testimony.

Senator Ferguson: "You did not pad your bills, then knock down the difference?"

Meyer: "No."

Ferguson: "You are sure about that?"

Meyer: "No, I didn't. I should have, but I didn't."

Ferguson: "Will you answer me? Why do you say you should have padded them and did not?"

Meyer: "Because I get such a low salary for all the work I do, which is 24 hours a day."

Ferguson: "What is your salary?"

Meyer: "My salary is $10,000 a year."

Ferguson: "$10,000? It is a little more than that, is it not?"

Meyer: "Whatever figures out, 52 weeks."

Ferguson: "Fifty-two weeks at $200 a week."

Meyer: "Ten-four."

Ferguson: "And did you get a salary from any other company?"

Meyer: "Well, I have drawn expense checks from TWA for doing work for them."

Ferguson: "You were an expense item to TWA?"

Meyer: "That is right."

Ferguson: "How much was that expense item?"

Meyer: "Well, it would run different, whatever I would put in. We finally worked it out to try to average it at $500 a month."

When Colonel Elliott Roosevelt came to the United States to make his tour of the airplane plants in his search for the photo-reconnaissance plane, it was Johnny Meyer who was assigned to meet and entertain him. Meyer was accompanied by the beautiful movie actress Faye Emerson. Although in testifying later Meyer denied that he was going to see Roosevelt in connection with the sale of the D-2 plane, his testimony was refuted by official records. In order to secure the priority needed for airplane space Howard Hughes had personally stated that it was needed "to meet Colonel Roosevelt at New York in connection with the D-2."

Meyer testified that he subsequently dined and wined Roosevelt and his party at leading nightclubs in New York including the 21 Club, the Stork Club and El Morocco.

It was Johnny Meyer who introduced Faye Emerson to Colonel Elliott Roosevelt. When Faye Emerson and Elliott Roosevelt were married December 3, 1944, John Meyer gave the bride away and Howard Hughes paid for the Beverly Hills Hotel honeymoon bungalow as a wedding present.

As Elliott explained later, while he was at the hotel desk, writing out his check to settle his account before leaving, Meyer rushed up to him and said firmly: "You can't pay this bill!"

Roosevelt replied, "I sure can pay the bill. I've already written the check."

"Tear it up!" Meyer directed. "Howard phoned me to tell me that he desired to give you a wedding present of your stay here in California."

Perhaps Johnny Meyer's greatest problem arose in trying to answer all the questions about his gifts to females. The following is a typical extract from the official record:

Ferguson: "Now, the item?"

Meyer: "It says, 'Presents for girls, $75.00.' "

Ferguson: "How many girls?"

Meyer: "Two."

Ferguson: "And I assume you have some doubt as to what the presents were?"

Meyer: "I do."

At another point in the record, this exchange is reported:

Ferguson: "Now, what is your next item?"

Meyer: "The next item is Saturday night. It says, 'Some girls at hotel late.' They obviously didn't have dinner."

Ferguson: "How much did you pay?"

Meyer: "$50.00."

Ferguson: "What do you mean 'They didn't have dinner' when you paid $50.00?"

Meyer: "I mean they probably joined us late at the Statler."

Ferguson: "How do you account for the $50.00? What is the $50.00?"

Meyer: "Probably some presents."

Ferguson: "Well, what does it have to do with the production of aircraft?"

Meyer: "I felt this was a Hughes Aircraft item, so I charged it that way."

Ferguson: "Now, was this entertainment for Colonel Roosevelt and the party you had? Is that why you charged it in?"

Meyer: "Yes."

The mere fact that Johnny Meyer referred to Elliott Roosevelt, the Roosevelt party, or anything else connected with Roosevelt or any other person did not guarantee that it was so. Colonel Elliott Roosevelt's forthright denial at a later date of any misdeeds is entirely credible. In fact, at a later point in his testimony Johnny Meyer reported charging a hotel bill to the "Roosevelt party" at a time when it was obviously impossible for the Roosevelt party to have stayed there.

Asked why he listed this expense in such a way, he replied, "That is what I cannot understand myself."

On another account Meyer listed an item specifically to Colonel Roosevelt, and when Senator Ferguson asked him, "Why did you write that at the bottom of the bill?" Meyer answered, "I have no idea."

Finally, Senator Ferguson, after harassing questioning, demanded, "What did your reply have to do with writing the name 'Roosevelt' on it?"

Meyer replied, "I just wrote it. I just liked the name."

Senator Ferguson wanted to know why Meyer paid a bill for an officer named Colonel Brooks and Johnny replied, "It must have been 'nice to soldiers' week, I don't know."

The examination continued:

Ferguson: "This is the next one. Lorraine Wallace, for which you transferred a bill of $22.77 which was room and restaurant to your account. Now, if that was 'good to soldiers week' what did this have to do with it? Was she in the army?"

Meyer: "I do not think so. I had no idea. I do not remember. I hardly remember the young lady."

Meyer had a disarming candor which made it possible for him to respond to questions on the most minute details without the committee obtaining usable information. At one time the following interchange took place:

Ferguson: "The next item."

Meyer: "That is Miss Emerson. Lunch at the Madison Restaurant."

Ferguson: "How much?"

Meyer: "$7.50."

Ferguson: "Next item?"

Meyer: "That afternoon, some nylon hose that I bought Miss Emerson as a present. $132.00."

Ferguson: "And the next item?"

Meyer: "Cash to travel home, $20.00."

Ferguson: "Now can you tell me why you were charging up to Hughes Aircraft Company $132.00 for nylon hose for Miss Emerson and $20.00 to go home?"

Meyer: "Because she had been very charming."

Ferguson: "Very charming!"

Meyer: "Girls are very pleasant."

Ferguson: "What has that to do with aircraft production?"

Meyer: "They just went along. Every company in the business did it. We were no different."

Ferguson: "You say because she was very charming you charged up this item of $132.00 to the production of airplanes?"

Meyer: "That is right."

Ferguson: "Now would you tell us why you gave her $20.00 to go home and charged that up to the company, if she was very charming?"

Meyer: "Well, you topped me, that is very good. I will concede that."

Ferguson: "You do not have an answer to the last question?"

Meyer: "I do not. I must admit you topped me."

The whole panorama of the expense accounts involving Johnny Meyer resembled an Arabian Nights dream. From April, 1942, to December, 1946, he spent $169,661.17 in direct expenses. In addition, there were thousands of dollars in indirect expenses that the committee could neither locate nor isolate.

However Hughes disapproved of entertainment for Army officers, his own entertainment needs were served by Meyer. Johnny-on-the-spot had a way with women. Aided and abetted by a virtually unlimited expense account, he was able to persuade some of the most beautiful women in Hollywood that it would be quite profitable to perform sexual services in a certain bedroom at a certain hour for a certain Hollywood producer and industrialist.

Hughes is reported to have built a series of houses in various parts of California that were identical in every detail. This, so he could know the location of every room and every light switch. He was equally at home in each of the built-alike love nests.

Meyer caught the girls and Hughes had of them. This was one thing that money could buy and Hughes bought.

The set-up solved a variety of problems. Hughes was shy. His hearing difficulty may have contributed to his lack of confidence with young beautiful girls. He feared rejection. He was suspicious. He knew that he was fair prey for fortune-hunting damsels.

With Meyer making the deals, there were no problems. There would be no rejections. The girls agreed in advance to share their favors. There would be no money complications. Meyer had made the deal.

This, of course, wasn't the procedure with the "big name" stars. Here there was challenge and Hughes enjoyed the contest. He was inhumanly patient. His patience was the characteristic Meyer remembers and admires Hughes for most of all. Hughes made no passes on the first few dates. There were no propositions. With infinite patience, he waited. On date after date he was the perfect gentleman. So much so that the lady in question often began to doubt her own sex appeal and was much relieved when the perfectly-timed seduction finally took place.

It is difficult to determine how the Johnny Meyer testimony affected Hughes, who had a high concern for the impression made on the American public. Hughes testified that he personally disapproved of the program of entertainment for Army officers but that the policy followed by other aircraft manufacturers forced him to conform. He added he would wholeheartedly support an official end to this unofficial procedure.

Howard Hughes vs. Major-General Bennett E. Meyers

AUGUST, 1943

BENITO MUSSOLINI was on the run and was reported seen in Berlin, Tokyo, and all points between. Britain, the Soviet Union, and the United States officially notified the world that any country granting asylum to Mussolini or any other war criminal would be taken to task. This was primarily intended as a message to Argentina.

The French Committee on National Liberation in Algiers, recently liberated, announced that it had appointed General Charles deGaulle as permanent chairman of the Committee on National Defense. This ended an eight-month dispute among the French.

The Soviet Union announced that it was prepared to give Finland new peace terms and include all land up to the 1939 borders except for the area surrounding Leningrad. That land, said the Russians, would be required for the security of the city.

In the movies—Irving Berlin's *This Is the Army;* Charles Boyer, Joan Fontaine, and Alexis Smith in *The Constant Nymph;* Betty Grable in *Coney Island;* and Humphrey Bogart in *Action in the North Atlantic.*

The best sellers on the book lists included *The Robe* by Lloyd C. Douglas, *Hungry Hill* by Daphne duMaurier, *The Valley of Decision* by Marcia Davenport, *Citizen Tom Paine* by Howard Fast, and *One World* by Wendell Willkie.

In the theatre Miriam Hopkins and Conrad Nagel starred in *The Skin of Our Teeth;* Ralph Bellamy and Shirley Booth appeared together in *Tomorrow the World.*

Howard Hughes was thirty-seven years old.

7

BENNY MEYERS was a self-made general. He enlisted in the Army on September 1, 1917 and although he remained in the United States he received his wished-for assignment to the fledgling aviation section of the Army Signal Corps. Private Meyers successfully applied for pilot training and after the end of the war received his commission as a second lieutenant. In 1920, on the strength of an examination, he became an officer in the Regular Army.

By the time the Japanese struck at Pearl Harbor, Bennett Meyers held the rank of Major in the Regular Army Air Force. Gradually he achieved a position of importance in the procurement activities of the Air Force, and acquired numerous titles and positions.

The self-made General Meyers was a very industrious and able man. He conceived and wrote a two volume book on production control and had his system adopted by the Air Force. He also developed a manufacturing control system which was installed in the aircraft factories.

When asked, "What did you do in your spare time?" he answered with a straight face, "I usually had a cot in my office, and every once in a while I got to lie down in it."

By 1943 General Meyers had become Assistant Chief of the Air Staff, Matériel, Maintenance and Distribution. In this capacity he was accorded a decisive position on the staff with respect to the procurement of aircraft. On August 13, 1943 General Meyers sent a memorandum to the Chief of the Air Staff which reviewed in detail the Hughes DX-2 airplane and its transformation into the D-5.

The memo concluded, "This office recommends against any further action tending to encourage the development of, and diverting facilities to, a project which has not progressed favorably to date and which shows so little promise in the future."

Some time thereafter General Arnold, Commander of the Army Air Force, issued a verbal directive to order 100 of the Hughes photographic airplanes. Meyers sent a memorandum dated October

9, 1943, to the Commanding General, in which he outlined all the reasons why he was opposed to the contract for the Hughes Aircraft Company reconnaissance planes. He concluded his memorandum with a statement:

"It is concluded . . . by this office that we would be derelict in our duty were we to fail to call to your personal attention the many uncertainties connected with this project, as well as the amount of money involved. This might, at a later date, draw Congressional attention and public criticism upon the Army Air Forces. . . ."

In spite of his opposition, however, General Meyers was also very human. He learned that Jesse Jones was in favor of the Hughes photo-recon plane. So was President Franklin D. Roosevelt. So was General Henry H. Arnold. And very soon so was General Bennett E. Meyers. He complained about "outside pressures" but he began to push the contract. By April of 1944 General Meyers was, in his own words, raising hell about the fact that the contract was not completed. He called the Contract Officer and demanded, "Why in hell isn't this contract in here?"

Sometime in the interim General Meyers and his wife traveled to California where, according to company records, the Hughes Aircraft Company paid a bill of $524.02 for the Meyers' stay at the Town House in Los Angeles. Further, the aircraft company paid train fare in the sum of $149.68 from Washington to Los Angeles for Mrs. Meyers. Hughes Aircraft also picked up the tab for Colonel Howe and his wife who accompanied the Meyers. The total bill paid by Hughes' company for this trip was about $1500.

General Meyers collected his portion from Colonel Howe and claimed that Mrs. Meyers reimbursed Johnny Meyer, the Hughes public relations man, for the bill the company had paid.

For his part, Johnny Meyer testified, "I swear, under oath, that I received no money from anyone for any bill I ever paid."

When recalled to the witness stand in order to deny specifically the testimony of General Meyers, Johnny said, "That testimony still stands."

To buttress his story General Meyers had his wife take the stand and testify that she had put all the money in an envelope and then had tried to give it to Johnny Meyer. She continued, "He did not wish to accept it, but General Meyers had ordered me to give it to him, so I insisted that he take it. He still refused to take it, so I put it in his pocket and called his attention to it and we went from there on to the station."

The General Accounting Office audit showed that $3,314.07 of expenses were paid by the Hughes Aircraft Company for the benefit of General Bennett E. Meyers. In spite of the General's numerous explanations, the Committee, in view of all the circumstances, did not believe him.

The General came into an eyeball-to-eyeball collision with Howard Hughes. Meyers testified that he had had a plan for buying U.S. bonds on margin but needed to borrow money to make the initial purchase. Hughes and his men offered to help him but he "naturally refused" to accept. Meyers further averred that he checked the possibility of purchase with Secretary of the Treasury Morgenthau, and with Marriner Eccles of the Federal Reserve System, and concluded that it was a very good idea. According to General Meyers, Neil McCarthy, one of Hughes' attorneys, who discussed the matter with the General, called Meyers when he was at Wright Field and offered to lend him $250,000 so that he could conclude the margin bond purchase.

General Meyers found it a difficult problem to explain to the Committee why, since he taped so many phone calls, he failed to tape the McCarthy-to-Meyers call during which the bond loan was offered.

Howard Hughes' memory and testimony differed. According to Hughes, Meyers first propositioned Attorney Neil McCarthy with the suggestion that Hughes himself or the Hughes Tool Company should lend the General $200,000 with which he would be able to purchase ten million dollars worth of government bonds on margin.

The General would put up the $200,000 borrowed from Hughes plus the bonds themselves as full security for the $10 million. Of course, if the bonds dipped in price it would be up to Hughes to put up additional money to protect his $200,000 investment. On the other hand, if the bonds went up then General Meyers could make a fortune. Under this system every time the bonds went up one point General Meyers would make $100,000 and every time they went down a point Hughes would have to put up an additional $100,000. This was not the kind of financial proposition that appealed to Howard Hughes and he turned it down flatly.

Speaking of it later he was quite kind to General Meyers. "I am still convinced that there was nothing crooked in the mind of Benny Meyers and I think that is proven by the fact that he did not do anything to interfere with the contract after I refused the loan."

General Meyers was less charitable than Hughes. As the evidence piled up against him, becoming more and more damaging, he began frantically to unburden himself. He spoke about the time Howard Hughes had come to Washington in a desperate attempt to save the Flying Boat contract. Hughes, Meyers said, invited him to dinner at the Statler Hotel. During dinner Hughes revealed considerable agitation over the imminent cancellation of the Flying Boat contract, and asked Meyers, "Is there some way you can help me out?"

After lengthy discussion of this point (according to Meyers) Hughes remarked, "I sure wish you had a twin brother so I would have a guy like you to come out and run my aircraft plant for me."

Meyers replied, "I am very sorry I don't have a twin brother. I could use a lot of help myself if I had one."

Hughes: "Well, no fooling, is there any way you could get out of the Army and come to work for me? You know how badly I need someone to run my plant."

Meyers: "Howard, there would not be a Chinaman's chance in hell of me getting out of the Army, even if I wanted to. All I'm interested in now is winning the war."

A few days later Hughes was in General Meyers' home in Washington discussing the Flying Boat and he asked the General, "Is there any way you can find out from Charley Wilson or Donald Nelson if there's anything we can do to keep the Boat contract from being cancelled?"

Later, Hughes reportedly said, "Don't forget right after the war I want you to come to work for me and if you agree to do it you can write your own ticket."

On January 22, 1944, the General was in Los Angeles. He and Hughes were on their way to dinner when Hughes said, "I want you to stop by my house for a minute or two."

The General acquiesced and they sat in the den discussing company affairs, while Howard waxed enthusiastic about the potentialities of his company. He spoke glowingly of TWA operations.

"After the war or even earlier," Hughes told Meyers, "Jack Frye, the boss of the airline, is going to retire and go out to his ranch in Arizona and that job also is going to be open. You can have that one if you want it."

The General, however, was only interested in winning the war.

From Howard Hughes' viewpoint the story is different.

Hughes: "In early 1944 it was well known to the industry that I was looking for a general manager for Hughes Aircraft Company. I investigated and interviewed, I am sure, 20 prospects for that job. Manpower was very difficult to obtain during the war. Industry had expanded tremendously and every available man with ability was either in the service or had a job. It was almost impossible to get anyone with any degree of ability.

"However, I had been making a strenuous effort to find a general manager. I always felt that my design work and technical work was second to none in this country, and I believe that my results have proven that. But I did feel that I needed a good business manager out there. I had considerable trouble with my personnel; factions had grown up within my company. Some of the boys did not like some of the others, and, as you know, had no success in dealing with the Army.

"So the business phase of my aircraft company in Culver City I felt needed improvement.

"Bennett Meyers had offered me the hand of friendship and when he heard that I was looking for a general manager, he recommended several to me, one of whom was Charles Perelle. As a matter of fact, Bennett Meyers went out of his way, at least so he told me, to try to persuade Perelle to come with my company.

"He also talked to several other people on my behalf in an attempt to obtain for me a general manager.

"During the course of one of my conversations with General Meyers, pertaining to various applicants or possibilities for this job, Benny Meyers looked at me with that little smile of his and took the cigar out of his mouth and said, 'You know, I might like to have that job myself.' This was in his apartment in Washington. It was before the contract for the F-11 was signed.

"I passed over Meyers' statement and took no notice of it either then or subsequently when he made the same suggestion. He could have only meant immediately and that was impossible and if he meant after the war I had enough sense to know that general managers would be a dime-a-dozen then.

"I never considered General Meyers resigning and coming out of the service to go to work for me.

"Any statement of General Meyers that I tried to press him to come to work for me is not true."

Howard Hughes vs. Ralph Owen Brewster

(AS BREWSTER SAW IT)

FEBRUARY 12, 1947

WARREN AUSTIN, United Nations delegate, told the Security Council that the United States was fundamentally opposed to the disarmament resolution proposed by the Soviet Union to establish a commission to seek information about atomic weapons. The United States would give out no information about such weapons.

Bomb-hurling Zionist extremists fought anti-terrorists in the heart of Tel Aviv. It was the first major clash since British troops began enforcing extraordinary security measures to stamp out underground violence.

The Senate War Investigating Committee, in its first session under Republican leadership, announced that it would continue the investigation of the Howard Hughes contract to build *Hercules,* also known as the Flying Boat, the largest cargo plane in the world. Senator Owen Brewster, Republican of Maine, the committee chairman, indicated that high officials of both the Truman and Roosevelt Administrations would be called before the group.

The current movies were Tyrone Power, Gene Tierney, Clifton Webb, and Herbert Marshall in *The Razor's Edge;* Pat O'Brien and Claire Trevor in *Crackup;* Larry Parks in *The Jolson Story;* Bing Crosby and Fred Astaire in *Blue Skies;* and Claudette Colbert, Walter Pidgeon, and June Allyson in *The Secret Heart.*

The best-selling books were John P. Marquand's *B.F.'s Daughter*, Pearl Buck's *Pavilion of Women;* and Frances Perkins' reminiscenses about *The Roosevelt I Knew.*

Howard Hughes was forty-one years old.

8

IT WAS HOT. It was unprecedented. It was almost ridiculous. Was it possible, thought Brewster, that anyone could seriously contemplate that one who had been in public life as long as he had—a member of the State Assembly, State Senator, Governor of the sovereign State of Maine, former member of the Lower House of the United States Congress and now a Senator of the United States serving his second term in that august body, could possibly make such a ridiculous and bald proposition. It sounded more like Hollywood than Washington.

Why, he was chairman of this very committee, one of the most illustrious and important committees ever to be developed by the United States Congress. The Special Committee to Investigate the National Defense Program had been established at the beginning of the war and the first chairman, Senator Harry Truman, was now President of the United States.

When Harry Truman became the Vice-Presidential running mate for Franklin D. Roosevelt he resigned his chairmanship of the committee and Senator James M. Meade of New York succeeded him. Meade was subsequently followed by Senator Harley M. Kilgore and on January 1, 1947, the eminent Ralph Owen Brewster himself (generally known only as Owen Brewster) became the chairman of this most important committee.

How could he possibly find himself in the degrading position of being summoned before HIS committee to testify in an adversary relationship with that upstart Howard R. Hughes. Nevertheless, here he was, one of the subjects under investigation [and how he got that way he would never know] and his second in command, Senator Homer Ferguson of Michigan, would handle the questioning.

The whole arrangement was ridiculous! First Hughes would testify, then Brewster, then each could question the other, with the committee members acting as intermediaries. It was surely the most unprecedented state of affairs ever to involve a Senatorial committee.

Think of Hughes testifying that he, Brewster, would drop the investigation if Hughes would let TWA merge into Pan Am! Absurd!

Hughes insisted repeatedly and the Committee equally repetitiously insinuated, that there would have been no investigation of Hughes, his Flying Boat, his FX-11, and/or his personal affairs if he had agreed not to try to block Pan Am as the American flag-carrier throughout the world—which it assuredly should be. Nevertheless the idea that this investigation of Hughes and his affairs was related to the achievement of that purpose was ridiculous.

In spite of this absurd concept he would have to face the questions, which were now beginning to be directed to him. Where had it all started, and when? The Senator was prepared:

"Now, the first time this came to the attention of the Committee was in July of 1942, and I find not only the record of the hearing in the matter on July 30th, but I find also a most interesting report of a subcommittee on this Flying Boat, Cargo-boat, Project, which has apparently disappeared from the files of the Committee in some fashion, and it was only by telephoning Justice Burton in Switzerland, the first of this week, that I was able to locate a copy in his files."

No one expected this surprise report. And it was an excellent bona fide report addressed to Harry S Truman, Chairman, and issued by the eminent Senators Wallgrenn, Hatch and Burton and by Charles Clark, then counsel to the Committee. The report emphasized the necessity of not diverting from the war effort the raw materials, critical equipment, trained personnel, plant facilities and engineering skill which the Flying Cargo Ship would require in the course of its development.

In addition were all the memoranda from various responsible parties suggesting that the Hughes project be cancelled. Still it was not cancelled. The many complaints forthcoming were routed to the Committee, which was obviously the reason why the Committee had to investigate Howard Hughes.

The Senator mused over how it had really started. He had accepted invitations to deliver Lincoln Day addresses—as a good Republican Senator always did. He was scheduled for an appearance in Kansas City on Saturday evening, February 8, and thereafter he would travel to Morgantown, West Virginia; Columbus, Ohio and Baltimore, Maryland.

He arrived in Kansas City on Saturday afternoon by train, made his speech and remained overnight. A few minutes after nine he received a phone call from Mr. Hughes, calling from Washington. It was the first time the Senator had heard from Mr. Hughes since a Constellation flight he had made as Hughes' guest, together with Senators Ferguson, Vandenberg, Barkley and Truman, and Hughes himself. On that trip he had been afforded the opportunity for a very brief acquaintanceship with the rich man.

On the phone Hughes had said that he was in Washington and wanted an opportunity to confer with the Senator about the investigation. He added that if the Senator would return to Washington they could have a talk.

Brewster replied, "I can't possibly go back now because I might not be able to get to Morgantown for my speech on Monday evening and then Columbus, Ohio, on Tuesday evening. I will probably be back Wednesday."

Hughes insisted, "I cannot wait until Wednesday."

"I'll see what I can do for you," the Senator promised.

"If you will get back here on Monday," Hughes urged, "I will see that you get to Morgantown and to Columbus. I will see that you are flown up there."

Brewster agreed and met Hughes in the Senatorial office on Capitol Hill. Hughes evinced great interest in the details of the forthcoming investigation of national defense contracts.

"If you're going to have any hearings I want a hearing right now," Hughes demanded.

The Senator, learning that Hughes had no records with him and had made no arrangements for legal counsel, remarked, "I am certain that you are not ready for a public hearing in the matter and I am quite sure that the Committee is not ready. We have to go into considerable detail before we could conduct hearings of this character. The investigation has only started."

Hughes began to tell his side of the story, only to be stopped by the Senator. "Well, I am sure that the Committee will be glad to hear your story in Executive Session. That will not involve any unfortunate publicity for anyone concerned and I will call the Committee together."

The Senator immediately checked his Committee personnel. They

were not ready for an immediate hearing but agreed to schedule
one for the next morning, February 11, 1947, at 11 A.M. Hughes
duly apeared and testified for about an hour. George Meader, the
Committee Counsel, conducted the routine proceedings, following
a planned agenda and list of questions.

After the hearing ended, Hughes picked up Senator Brewster
and Senator Bricker of Ohio, in his car, and personally flew them
both to Columbus, Ohio. The Senator remembered the flight clearly.
The aircraft was a B-23 with one additional crew member who
helped with communications. The noise of the plane and Howard's
difficulty in hearing precluded all conversation.

The Senator delivered his address and after dinner returned to
the airport. To his great surprise he found that Hughes had not
waited but had flown back to Washington. In his place Jack Frye's
plane, the TWA VIP craft, had been flown up to Columbus to pick
up the two Senators and return them to Washington. Senator Brewster thought it odd that the expense of an extra round-trip flight
had been wasted.

On the return flight the two Senators engaged in some casual
discussion about proposed legislation in the airline field. Senator
Brewster was very interested in that branch of law. He was Chairman of the Subcommittee on Aviation which currently had before
it the McCarran Bill, the one Brewster referred to as the Community Airline Company Bill. He remarked that many people called
it the Chosen Instrument Airline Bill. But it wasn't that at all.

Brewster indicated his feeling that the bill was a patriotic measure—it would give the United States a flag carrier airline throughout the world. There were, of course, those carping critics who said
the bill was simply designed to grant Pan Am an exclusive to fly
outside of the United States. But this was only an accidental and
coincidental result, not the real purpose of the proposed law.

Although everyone blamed Senator Brewster for the bill, it really
was not the exclusive property of either Brewster or McCarran.
Senator McCarran was the author and originator of the proposition
while Brewster was only one of the promoters. Oddly the bill remained in Committee because of a rare instance of a 10-to-10 vote
in the Subcommittee on reporting it out. There it remained until
subsequently, after some changes, another bill was introduced.

On Wednesday, February 12, 1947, Brewster invited Hughes to
his apartment for lunch. Brewster considered this a minimum cour-

tesy to the airline magnate in return for Hughes' kindness in flying him around the country.

Hughes strolled around the apartment, admiring its furnishings, and making particular note of a painting of a llama from Lima which Mrs. Brewster and the Senator had picked up on a South American trip the previous November.

The friendly conversation ranged over a wide variety of subjects. Hughes entertained with tales of the movie world and narrated some of his own adventures. In passing, they touched on the virtues of the Community Airline Bill. It was then that Hughes mentioned for the first time the possible merger of TWA with Pan American. The Senator had never before heard mention of the possibility.

After Hughes left that day nothing more was heard from him by the Senator until his call from California some time in March. At that time Hughes said, "I have tried to get hold of you because I thought I ought to speak with you before talking with the press."

Senator Brewster thanked him politely. "It is very nice of you to call. A fellow called me from the *Journal of Commerce* and asked me whether you are going to merge and did you believe in the Community Company and I told him the answer to both questions was 'no.'"

"Well," replied Hughes, "I had to deny the merger because that put the whole TWA organization into a spin, as you can well imagine."

"Yes, it looks to me as though somebody was inspiring these stories in order to either embarrass you or me or both of us." The Senator continued, "Certainly nothing which I have said at any time could be construed that way. They may have thought they could put you or me in a hole but you can depend on it that I have said nothing at any time that could be in any way construed as significant."

Hughes: "Well, anyway, it's all over."

Senator: "Yes."

Hughes: "I didn't mention the Community Line at all. I just denied the Pan American story."

Next, Brewster encountered a great deal of difficulty in obtaining Hughes' records. At first Hughes purported to be very cooperative and was perfectly willing to show his records. But when the chips were down he backed off. The Committee had to send Francis D. Flanagan, Chief Assistant Counsel, out to California and then

Hughes offered a variety of excuses for not submitting any information. First he insisted he didn't see how his records would help the
investigation any. He alleged executive reasons why he was afraid
of any information becoming known publicly. His patents had a
long time to run and he didn't want anybody to know anything
about them. He had never made the balance sheets of Hughes Tool
Company public, since he owned all the stock. He was most reluctant to furnish any information about the entertainment expenses.

Hughes offered to furnish information concerning the Flying
Boat and the Photo Reconnaissance Plane but he couldn't allow the
investigators to look at his records. Of course, the Committee could
not accede to such a procedure because only the Committee itself
could determine that it had all relevant information, and that meant
seeing all the records.

On March 26, 1947 the Committee issued, as properly it should
have, a subpoena to Howard Hughes to produce all the files and
records at a hearing in Washington. The press was informed of the
issuance of the subpoena and also told that Howard "Wily" Hughes
had immediately notified the Committee that there was no need to
serve the subpoena because he would gladly make all the books
and records available.

Then Hughes did a switch. He offered to hire Hugh Fulton,
former Chief Counsel of the National Defense Investigating Committee, the very Committee now conducting the investigation.
Because of this action by Hughes, Fulton called Senator Brewster.

"I come to you as a friend of both Mr. Hughes and of yourself,"
he told the Senator, "and I am very much concerned about the
situation developing since it looks like this investigation is being
carried on as a persecution stimulated by Pan American Airways.
I think it is very unfortunate and might lead to unfortunate repercussions."

The Senator from Maine talked steadily to the former Chief
Counsel for almost an hour. The conversation ended with the suggestion of the attorney that no public hearing should be held.
Throughout the conversation Hugh Fulton had emphasized he was
speaking not as counsel for Mr. Hughes but as a friend of both
sides.

Fulton finally offered the possibility of a "nominal hearing" and a brief report which would permit the entire matter to pass over. The Senator grew incensed at these words.

"I don't like your attitude in regard to the Committee report," Brewster threw angrily at Fulton. "You say there could be a report without a hearing. Now I want it distinctly understood that hearings will be held and reports will be gotten out in accordance with those hearings. I cannot say that one person will not be called. It may be that Snyder [John W. Snyder, Federal Loan Administrator] and Hughes and Jones [Jesse Jones, Secretary of Commerce] or the whole list may be called and I do not like your repeated statement to the effect that you assume such and such will be done in the Committee."

Fulton walked the Senator from his office to the Senate Chamber. He appeared considerably disturbed over the manner in which the Senator had spoken but could do nothing. Brewster remained adamant.

That same evening Senator Brewster had to leave for Cairo to attend the International Parliamentary Conference. In order to safeguard the situation he sent a memorandum to the Chief Counsel of the Committee, George Meader, in which he pointed out, "I am quite indifferent to Hugh Fulton's interest and I think probably the files and material in the matter should be treated as confidential."

When the Senator returned after a two weeks' trip around the Mediterranean area, he found that Hugh Fulton had not been idle. He had held a further meeting with George Meader during which he made it known that Hughes had a lot of suspicions about Brewster's connection with Pan American Airways and about the interest of Pan American in the Committee's investigation. Fulton added that Senator Brewster would be in the thick of things if the investigation were not headed off.

But Senator Brewster had retained his courage in the face of these threats. He viewed the situation as a fundamental issue. If a member of the Senate or the Chairman of a Committee could be intimidated by actions of this character then Senatorial investigations might well cease. Obviously there was always someone who wanted to stop an investigation. The Senator had to face the decision and face it he did! He promptly appointed a subcommittee headed by Senator Ferguson who could handle the matter from then on and let the chips fall where they may.

He remembered when he later asked counsel and Senator Ferguson for a report and was told, "We think the Hughes case is getting ready."

The next episode occurred when Major General Arthur Wilson and Otis Bryan, both vice presidents of TWA, came to visit with the Senator to discuss the Community Company Bill. After he finished explaining all about the bill, Otis Bryan said, "Well, we wanted it to be clear that we were opposed to this."

Now the hearings were beginning.

The Senator looked around the caucus room at the assembled citizens, smug in his assurance that he had been a good Senator, even a courageous one, and certainly an exemplary public servant.

9

Howard Hughes vs. Ralph Owen Brewster

(AS HUGHES SAW IT)

THE SHOWDOWN was coming. He was Howard Hughes and he wasn't going to flinch from telling the Committee, the public, and the world that this hearing was nothing more than a concerted effort to compel him, under duress, to merge his potential world airline, TWA, with the first American overseas airline—Pan American Airways.

Hughes looked around the Committee Room. The podium was now being shared by Subcommittee Chairman Senator Ferguson, Senator Pepper of Florida, Senator Cain of Washington and Senator O'Connor of Maryland. Although these men were probably not a part of the general conspiracy, Senator Brewster was undoubtedly manipulating them like puppets, Hughes told himself bitterly. Right after the executive session with the Committee up on the Hill, Senator Brewster, as friendly as one could desire, had invited Hughes to drop by for a chat. The two men lunched together and the Senator made it crystal clear that the hearings would end if Hughes agreed to merge TWA with Pan American.

Hughes remembered the incident vividly. Having been warned that if he had any conversation with the tricky Brewster he should be sure to have a witness with him, he had made inquiries about a reliable person to accompany him to the luncheon. A Mr. Hefron had been sent with him. He had never seen Hefron before then, has never seen him since. He thought Hefron was probably a lawyer but his function had been that of a dependable witness.

It had all started in Kansas City when Senator Brewster invited Hughes to drop by his apartment. Hughes did not trust so private an arrangement but agreed instead to meet in Brewster's office. When he arrived there the following day Brewster launched immediately into a lecture on his Community Air Line Bill. He was a voluble conversationalist, and he included his opinions on air supremacy, jet propulsion, and fare differentials. He bewailed the difficulty of success for competitive American systems when foreign airlines could supply similar services at a lower global rate. This problem of meeting international competition was Brewster's major argument for the Community Air Line Bill which, if enacted, would have unquestionably made Pan American the American flag-carrier throughout the world and relegated TWA to the restricted position of a wholly domestic airline.

Hughes told Brewster, "I don't agree at all. I specifically disagree on your thought that England has a technical supremacy in the air over us. The United States in my opinion has always led in commercial aviation and probably always will. Some foreign countries have exceeded us in flash performance of various military types but when it comes to safe, sound commercial aviation, our country has always led and I feel sure it always will. In fact, I believe that people would be willing to pay a little premium to ride in a United States airline because they will believe that it's safer and better."

"I wish you were right," Brewster replied. "However, our own study had indicated that that's not so. I believe unless the government does something with the thought I have in the Community Air Line Bill we will fall behind in aviation."

Following this meeting Hughes had been invited to Brewster's suite at the Mayflower Hotel in Washington. Diffidently, Hughes tried to keep the conversation on general topics. As he strolled around the room he stopped to admire Brewster's "Llama from Lima" when abruptly the conversation turned to the Community Air Line Bill with Brewster trying to sell the idea. Then the Senator made the bold proposition—agree to merge TWA into Pan American and the hearings would end.

Later Hughes flew Brewster from Washington to Columbus, Ohio, where Brewster had to make a speech. Again Brewster urged acceptance of the Community Air Line Bill and the merger. He talked about Juan Trippe and mentioned other elements of the possible merger.

Hughes brought himself back to the present and listened incredulously as Brewster told lie after lie. He could hardly believe that a former Governor, a United States Senator, the Chairman of one of Congress's most important committees, could mouth such unadulterated fabrications.

Hughes yearned for the opportunity to cross-examine Brewster but this the Committee would not allow. It had already agreed to one unprecedented exception—Hughes would be permitted to ask questions of Brewster provided they were submitted in writing. In a small corner of Hughes' mind was the awareness that this was a most gracious and unique exception to Committee procedure and Senatorial protocol.

Under normal circumstances when any private citizen differed with a Senator, the Senator could use the forum as a weapon but the private citizen was relegated to what benefit he could obtain from telling his side of the story to the press. However the Hughes power and influence had been too great to disregard so the Ferguson Subcommittee had agreed, unanimously, to permit this exception to the accepted procedure for conducting a hearing.

Hughes would still have preferred the satisfaction of a real cross-examination so before acceding to the undramatic, cold, dry procedure of reading written questions he made a final attempt to obtain permission to do his own blood-letting. He argued the difficulty of submitting all the questions because of the way one answer led to another question. Everyone knew how cross-examination was built up step by previous step.

He said plaintively to Senator Ferguson, "How can anyone cross-examine a witness if he is not allowed to ask questions predicated upon the answers given?"

Finally, the Committee began to read Hughes' questions to Senator Brewster. Brewster was most agile in dodging the first question which related to the Community Air Line Bill. Next came a more difficult one: "Is it not true that you are a personal friend of Juan Trippe, President of Pan American Airways?"

Senator Brewster replied, "That is right. I have known Mr. Trippe for the past four or five years perhaps, since I have been here. I would not exactly say that it represents any great degree of intimacy."

Then the wily Brewster began to make full use of his ability to use words for his own ends. He admitted having legislative differences with Mr. Trippe and that he not only opposed him but also licked him in the Senate. He described his association with Trippe as limited to a few dinners as a guest in Mr. Trippe's home in Connecticut.

Now the interrogation began to get a little rougher. Hughes' written questions asked about Sam Pryor—a Vice President of Pan Am and a Republican National Committeeman—and about Bill McEvoy, also a Vice President of Pan Am and a good friend.

Next came the query, "Are you familiar with the address 2017 F Street, Washington, D.C.?"

Brewster was smart. He knew it was common knowledge that the address referred to Pan American's Washington entertainment facility for VIP's. "You refer to the place maintained by Pan American for the occupancy of their executives or others who may be here. I think it would be proper to add that it is a rather modest establishment, as compared with the house maintained by TWA, located at 2301 Uhle Street, Arlington, Virginia, which was a mansion of twenty rooms, with eight baths, that has been handled by the TWA for some time. I think it is now for sale for $150,000, and has a swimming pool. When you contrast that with the place maintained by Pan American, it is a comparatively modest establishment. I think I have had in the last six months, three breakfasts at the Pan Am place, consisting of eggs and bacon. That comprises the extent of my entertainment at this establishment."

Brewster cleverly had even submitted pictures of the TWA facilities at Arlington as exhibits. With its four stately columns and the wide expanse of lawn the house certainly looked the epitome of southern aristocratic mansions.

Hughes' next question was asked about Sam Pryor's winter place at Hobe Sound in Florida.

Senator Pepper, a left-wing Democrat, interjected, "That is not where I get my votes, in Florida, generally."

Brewster explained, "Twice, I think in the last two years, Mrs. Brewster and I have occupied for one week Sam Pryor's small place which has five rooms. Mr. and Mrs. Pryor were not there. We had the exclusive occupancy and I hired a cook, whom I paid $5.00 a day, and I went over to the grocery store and bought the groceries, and a Thanksgiving turkey and I left the place pretty well stocked up, when I got through, with canned goods, as a sort of expression of my appreciation of what had gone on."

Now the questions began to hit the mark. "Have you ever accepted free airplane trips from Pan American Airways in their special private airplane?"

Brewster: "I have."

Question: "How many free trips did you make to Raleigh, North Carolina?"

Brewster: "I went there once to confer with Senator Bailey on the Community Air Line Bill."

Question: "Have you accepted free airplane trips from Pan American to Hobe Sound, Florida?"

Brewster: "Well, I may have."

Then a question typical of a layman turned lawyer, "Is it not true, Senator, that by virtue of this position as Chairman of this Committee you held a whip handle in one hand which you could easily use to the embarrassment of Howard Hughes, while with the other hand you wanted from him the support of the Community Air Line Bill, or the removal of his opposition to it?"

Senator Brewster parried the question handily with the argument that he could not control the Committee since he was only the Chairman.

Next a test question: "You formed the subcommittee in order to eliminate the charge that you were using this Committee to further your own ends and after forming it why did you not disqualify yourself and step aside?"

The Senator debated the meaning of the word "disqualify" and his reply was noncommittal.

Hughes had anticipated this attitude. "Is it not correct that you remained active in this matter and that you issued all of the first announcements on the matter concerning this hearing?"

The question was framed clumsily but everyone understood that Hughes was in effect asking: "How come you, Senator Brewster, continued to control the Committee and made all of its announcements?"

The Senator denied it. Once again Hughes had anticipated the denial. "Is it not true, Senator, that you, yourself actually made the decision to start this hearing on July 28, the date it was begun?"

Again the Senator denied the point. "That is certainly not true."

And again Hughes had correctly anticipated the Senator and had prepared an appropriate follow-up question. "Then, Senator, if you yourself did not make the decision to hold this hearing, and if you left the decision up to Senator Ferguson, how do you explain the fact that Senator Ferguson was totally unaware that the decision to hold this hearing had actually been made until the day following the time that you announced the hearing to the press, on July 24?"

This was a telling blow. Brewster evidenced confusion and a quick answer was not forthcoming. Lamely, he finally remarked, "Well, I didn't know."

Having laid all the groundwork Hughes had then begun the infighting. The question: "While occupying the unique position of Chairman of a Committee with a whip over Howard Hughes did you or did you not lobby with Howard Hughes or attempt to sell him your Community Air Lines Bill?"

The Senator, no longer as belligerent, answered unsatisfactorily.

Hughes was still ahead of the Senator as a forecaster of Brewster's reactions. The question followed: "Did you or did you not admit to Hugh Fulton that you had lobbied with Howard Hughes for this bill and that you tried to sell it to him?"

Searching for a way to evade the question, Brewster said haltingly, "I told Mr. Fulton certainly that I had discussed it with Howard Hughes, but I do not recall any suggestion that there had been any intimations of impropriety."

The next question asked painfully, "Is it not true that last Thursday you telephoned Hugh Fulton and asked him if he would come down here and testify on your behalf in connection with these charges I have made against you, and is it not true that Hugh Fulton replied that he was willing to testify but that he was afraid that his testimony would hurt you because he would have to say that you admitted to him that you lobbied with me for the Community Air Line Bill and had attempted to sell it to me?"

Senator Brewster was appalled. This was a telling blow. He started out by labeling the accusation "absolutely false," then admitted that he did call Fulton. He offered as his excuse for calling, the fact that "I felt in justice to him, he ought to know that his name was liable to be involved."

Question: "Senator Brewster, is it not true that you have been referred to as the spokesman for Pan American Airways in the Senate?"

Brewster (lamely): "That is, I think, what I have been called by friends and enemies and, as all of the members of the Committee know, I hardly think that would be considered a matter which would be relevant in evidence. What I have been called at various times in my career would fill a book."

Having exhausted the written questions Senator Ferguson asked whether Hughes had any additional questions. Howard Hughes

quickly answered, "I can answer that 'yes.' I have many other questions, but I do not see any point in submitting them in this manner.
I think that Senator Brewster's statements were evasive, and in
many cases it is not possible to get a direct answer, and I think that
submitting the questions that are asked this way and having them
asked and never having his reply challenged by the Chair in any
way, just accepting the answers on every occasion, is unsatisfactory,
so I shan't submit any further in this way."

Howard Hughes was recalled to the stand. As he took his seat,
he had a strong feeling that he no longer had anything to lose. In a
way his reputation had already been ruined so he might as well
call a spade a spade.

Hughes began to tell his side of the story by following the pattern
laid down by his predecessor on the stand. "I too have been before
the public eye to a certain degree in this country. I have been doing
business in the United States for 23 years, I am a citizen of this
country, and I was born in this country. I have become fairly well
known. Nobody kicks around for 23 years in this country without
acquiring a reputation, either good or bad. Now, since Senator Brewster has brought this past-record tangle into the situation, I think
that he should have gone a step further and compared his reputation with mine."

Hughes continued, "Now, I may be a little unkind in what I am
going to say, but I shall also be unkind in the appraisal of my own
reputation. I understand that Senator Brewster has a reputation of
being a clever, resourceful, and a terrific public speaker, a man
who can hold an audience in the palm of his hand and that he has
a reputation of being one of the greatest trick-shot artists in Washington, one of the most high powers behind the scenes."

This slur on the Senator was immediately picked up by a stalwart
member of the Senators' Club. Senator Ferguson queried, "Will
you give us the source of your information?"

Hughes obliged, "Yes, I believe that I can. One man who made
that statement was Jack Frye [long-time president of TWA]. I
asked him what sort of man Brewster was and upon his recommendation I took along a witness with me when I first met Senator
Brewster. However, I have heard that general reputation voiced by
others."

Hughes drew a deep breath, preparatory to launching into a
rarity—Hughes expounding on Hughes: "Now let us examine my

reputation. I am supposed to be many things which are not complimentary. I am supposed to be capricious. I am called a playboy. I have been called eccentric, but I do not believe that I have the reputation of being a liar. As far as I know in 23 years, up to yesterday, no one has ever questioned my word. In fact, I believe I have the reputation in that respect which most Texans consider important. That is to say, if I may use a corny phrase, I believe most people consider my word to be my bond."

The room was still. It was apparent that Howard Hughes spoke as sincerely and directly from the heart as a man could do. Hughes took a sip of water from a paper cup and then continued, "For example, the motion picture business where distrust is the rule, nevertheless, Louis B. Mayer, the head of the largest motion picture company in the world, and a man who is my competitor and who does not waste any particular amount of love on me, nevertheless on numerous occasions has said to many different people that he would rather have my gentlemen's agreement than a written contract with most people."

Hughes paused, wondering whether to go on in this vein. Everyone in the room seemed interested. There was scarcely a rustle as the ever-expanding audience waited for him to continue.

"Now, the statements I made on the stand here yesterday were true. I tried not to say anything which was a half-truth. I tried not to make any statements of which I was uncertain. I think that should be taken into consideration. A man who carefully and diligently tries to tell only what he is certain of, that man should be believed before a man who makes certain obvious misstatements."

Most people who dealt with Hughes said that he often talked and acted like a trial attorney. Now he behaved like one. He continued, "Since the beginning of this affair, Senator Brewster has made a number of statements which are obviously untrue. One of these was the statement that he has no direct or indirect connection with Pan American Airways. Most people in the aviation industry know that statement is untrue; and in Senator Brewster's testimony here this morning, he admitted a close relation with Sam Pryor, the Vice-President of Pan American. Now, I ask you what is the difference between Sam Pryor and Pan American Airways? I maintain that if Senator Brewster makes one statement which is known to be untrue, there certainly should be some considerable doubt attached to the other statements he has made." [In law this is called the doctrine of *falsus in uno, falsus in omnibus*—false in one thing, false in all.]

Brewster had had enough and he cried out, "Mr. Chairman . . ."

Quickly Senator Pepper came to Hughes' rescue. He could not let such unfairness go unnoticed. Loudly and distinctly he uttered, "I think Mr. Hughes ought to be permitted to finish his statement."

However Senator Brewster was well-versed in Parliamentary procedure. He called loudly for a point of order which was granted by his club-mate, Senator Ferguson. Brewster interpolated, "In what Mr. Hughes is now stating, I think it may be important to determine whether or not those are the words of Mr. Hughes or whether they are the words of Mr. Carl Byoir, formerly publicity manager of German interests in this country, now acting as the publicity representative of Mr. Hughes. I would very much rather prefer to hear Mr. Hughes' testimony here rather than the voice of Mr. Byoir."

Senator Pepper again protested that Senator Brewster had no more right to interrupt Hughes' statement than any private citizen would have.

Over the noisy debate Hughes cut in. "I will gladly state under oath that the statement is mine." And in a fashion typical of Hughes added, "I will clarify the issue and say that in the questions given you this morning they were edited by me but to some degree were collaborated in by Mr. Slack [Tom Slack, his attorney at the hearing] and Mr. Byoir, but the evidence I am now giving is entirely my own and I am glad to swear to it."

Ferguson was still not satisfied. He cross-examined Hughes on his recognition of the fact that he was under oath and then asked about Byoir. Hughes repeated similar answers to similar questions.

Now Hughes related an interesting story. Senator Brewster had previously testified before the Committee and had also told the reporters at a press conference that the free airplane trips given by Hughes were entirely at Hughes' suggestion. The Senator had stated that he was in Kansas City and intended to return to Washington via Morgantown, West Virginia, and Columbus, Ohio. He further alleged that after Hughes had contacted him in Kansas City he arranged to fly directly back to Washington. Later, he claimed, Hughes had promised to provide TWA transportation to take him back to Morgantown and Columbus.

Unfortunately for Brewster, he had purchased a round-trip ticket *before* leaving Washington and this ticket made no provisions for stopovers en route in either direction. Furthermore, because of inclement weather Brewster had cancelled his outgoing flight and used the train to Kansas City instead, but he did not at the same time cancel his return flight to Washington. In fact, Hughes could say with complete honesty that Senator Brewster never even mentioned going to Morgantown or Columbus. It was only after he returned to Washington and conferred with Hughes that he made the request to be flown to Morgantown and then to Columbus.

Both Hughes' evidence and his explanation clearly made Brewster out to be a liar. Unfortunately for Brewster he had elected to fly from Washington to Kansas City and back via Hughes' own airline (TWA) and Hughes most assuredly had access to the records of TWA. These showed clearly that at all times Brewster had a ticket for an immediate return to Washington after his speech in Kansas City.

Brewster stated that he returned to Washington earlier than anticipated, at Hughes' request, and he further told the press the whole story, including this colloquy: Hughes had offered, "I will fly you if you come back to Washington."

Brewster stated flatly, "So I bought a ticket on TWA, Hughes' airline, and came back to Washington."

According to Hughes the innuendo, implication and the direct words were all lies. Brewster didn't have to go out and buy a ticket on TWA—he had one all along and Hughes could prove it to the Committee.

Ferguson was very annoyed at this turn in the proceedings. He interjected, "This means, Mr. Hughes, that the integrity of the United States Senate is at stake. I therefore speak for the Senate. If you have had legal advice as to what your comment should be prior to the time you came here, or what it should be during these hearings, I would advise you that it is bad legal advice. It is obvious that you are trying to take control of the Senate hearings."

The Senator pushed a paper forward so that it was obvious to all that he was reading from a poorly prepared statement. He continued, "If you believe that because you have great wealth and access to certain publicity channels, and therefore you can intimidate any member of the subcommittee, I want to advise you, Mr. Hughes, that you are mistaken and that is final. It appears that while one of your motives may be to discredit one member of the

Committee, it is apparent that your prime motive is to discredit the Committee so that your activities in the procuring and carrying out of these two government contracts will not be investigated, and brought to the public's attention. This extraneous matter, and your contempt for this Committee, will not affect or cloud the real issue. This Committee intends to carry out its functions. Now, is it clear?"

The Democratic member of the Committee, Senator Claude Pepper, refused to overlook this attack. He hastened to Hughes' defense by announcing that he did not agree with Senator Ferguson and that he believed Hughes was acting most properly.

Hughes was now ready to deliver the coup de grace. It was a trivial matter but, petty or no, it was the kind of incident that could impress the American public. Hughes was known as a ladies' man. Just the previous week the society columnist, Igor Cassini, who used the pseudonym Cholly Knickerbocker, had written that the Hughes probe was loaded with girls.

The current issue of *Time* commented on the columnist's statement. "That was enough for the summer-becalmed tabloids. They sailed into the story with shrieks of joy and thankful indignation. They were sure they saw squads of scantily clad models, actresses and whatnots, running in and out of New York and Hollywood bars, house parties, night clubs, swimming pools, hotels—hotly pursued by grinning Generals and Government administrators. Was this any way for a General to behave?"

And *Time* also ran pictures of bikini-clad damsels who certainly looked like bait for government contracts.

Senator Brewster, an old hand at recognizing the right ammunition to feed the press, had poured a little naphtha on the fire of public indignation when at a press conference he remarked that the airline hostess had refused to go along with Hughes and Brewster on the flight from Washington to Columbus, Ohio, because she was afraid to be alone with Hughes on the return flight.

Hughes now produced an affidavit from Harriet Applewick, the hostess.

Under oath she swore that she had "read Senator Brewster's statement that I refused to make the trip to Columbus with Senator Brewster in Mr. Hughes' airplane because I didn't want to return to Washington alone with Mr. Hughes in his airplane. This is the most ridiculous statement I have ever heard. There was never any thought on the part of Mr. Hughes or anyone else that I would

return in his airplane with him. It was naturally intended that I
should remain in Columbus and return with the Senator in the other
airplane to look after his needs on the return flight. Even if I had
returned in the airplane of Mr. Hughes, I would not have been alone
with him, because there was a flight engineer in the other plane
also. This accusation of Senator Brewster's is absolutely untrue."

Next, Hughes produced an affidavit from Flight Captain M. E.
Bell who piloted the TWA plane from Washington to Columbus
to pick up Senators Brewster and Bricker. Pilot Bell's statement
read:

"I was the Captain on the airplane which was sent to Columbus
to pick up Senator Brewster and another Senator on the night of
February 11, 1947. I was present when Mr. Hughes left Washington for Columbus with two Senators in his airplane. I was present
at all conversations with Miss Harriet Applewick, the hostess.

"There never was any thought of her returning with Mr. Hughes
in his airplane. I am very familiar with the operation of Mr. Hughes'
airplane. I can say to my knowledge he has never carried a hostess
in his airplane at any time. The only reason for the hostess being
present on this occasion at all was for the purpose of serving food
to the Senators and looking after their requirements."

In a sense it was a small thing but the kind of thing which
tips the balance. This clear and unmistakable contradiction of an
unsavory accusation effectively turned the tables and the accuser
suddenly became the accused. The incident foreshadowed the end
for Senator Brewster. He soon became a forgotten man in American politics, and on his next try for re-election to the Senate, he was
defeated.

Howard Hughes and His First Twenty Years

DECEMBER 24, 1905

THERE WERE internal and insurrectionary disturbances in Russia, including armed rebellion in Moscow. The Czar's manifesto of October granting civil liberties had not altered the drive for freedom.

American society was agog at the prospects of the forthcoming White House wedding. Alice Roosevelt, daughter of the President, was marrying Nicholas Longworth, a member of the House of Representatives. The coming week she would be in New York purchasing her trousseau.

The National Metal Trades Association had organized a strong group to fight the closed shop. A large sum of money had been raised to accomplish the purpose.

A new train service was inaugurated from St. Louis to Mexico City. It would take only 55 hours to make this trip.

In New York, apartments were advertised at $32.50 per month. One location, at 151 West 140th Street, offered six-room modern apartments with all the latest improvements including, "marble bath, steam heat, hot water, elevator day and night, and hall attendants."

Plays receiving national attention included Ethel Barrymore in *Alice-Sit-By-The-Fire* at the Criterion and Henrietta Cossman in *Mary, Mary, Quite Contrary* at the Garrett. Helen Bertram in *The Ginger Bread Man* at the Liberty received pleasant notices.

The New York Telephone Company was seeking young ladies between the ages of seventeen and twenty-three to learn to be switchboard operators. A refined female could receive as much as $5.00 per week salary while learning. Stenographers with "three years' experience, accurate, neat, conscientious and having references" could earn as much as $10 per week.

Howard Hughes was one hour old.

10

DECEMBER 24, 1905, Houston, Texas. At high noon the weak, watery sun filtering down succeeded in forcing the temperature to climb to a peak of 57 degrees, but it soon dropped into the 30's. Although pre-Christmas Houston frequently enjoyed a balmy temperature in the 70's, this was no such day.

Howard Robard Hughes seethed with excitement. This was a crowning day in his life. He would become a father at any moment. He thought proudly and fondly of his wife, born Allene Gano, a 20th century descendant of a French Huguenot family which traced its roots almost back to Charlemagne himself. The Gano family, well-known in Dallas, had produced several distinguished jurists. In fact, Hughes' father-in-law was a well-known Texas district judge, direct descendant of Reverend John Gano, the famous chaplain of the Revolutionary War. The chaplain is supposed to have secretly converted George Washington to the Baptist faith, and Rupert Hughes maintained that affidavits existed to prove it.

Hughes himself came from a family learned in the law. As he shuttled back and forth that day between his office (it was Sunday but he had to go some place) and his home on Crawford Street, next door to the fire station, to look in on his beautiful wife, his mind kept returning to his own family.

Hughes had been born thirty-six years earlier, in the month of September, 1869, in Lancaster, Missouri. His parents were Felix Turner Hughes and Jean Amelia Hughes, née Summerlin. The first Hughes of that line in America had been an English land grant colonist who settled in Virginia. The first Summerlin had arrived at the Isle of Wight (also in Virginia) in 1717. Hughes' father was a well-known Missouri lawyer who had become, first, President of a railroad, and later a judge. Because of his father's influence Hughes also gravitated toward the law.

After preparing at the military academies of Morgan Park, Illinois, and St. Charles, Missouri, he entered Harvard College in 1893. He graduated from Harvard and then studied law at the State University of Iowa. [Most biographies erroneously state that he studied law at Harvard Law School.] He grew so anxious to enter active practice that, without waiting to graduate, he managed to obtain admission to the bar after only two years of law school. In those days this was not an unusual procedure. He hung out his shingle alongside his dad's in Keokuk, Iowa—then a booming city at the juncture of the Mississippi and Des Moines Rivers.

The eager young attorney did not find enough excitement in the practice of law. Busy with the comparatively dull job of preparing wills and deeds, he heard the clarion call of mining and mineral exploration. Hughes gave up his practice and traveled to nearby Missouri to try his hand in the newly discovered field of lead and zinc mining. Then it was impossible for him to resist the lure of the oil strikes in Texas. For several years, in partnership with Walter Sharp, he drilled oil wells, both for the partnership and as contractor for others. It was a boom or bust business. One year he had money to burn and the next year he burned for its lack. Brother Rupert Hughes, the novelist, once remarked, "Howard would have $50,000 in the bank one year and be $50,000 in debt to the bank the next."

Sometimes the change of fortune came so rapidly that Hughes could scarcely realize he was no longer wealthy. When he had money he spent it with complete openhandedness. In fact, he had just finished a spending spree: to celebrate his marriage the year before he had taken his new bride to Europe along with the proverbial $50,000. The honeymoon lasted several months, then the couple returned—she pregnant and he broke.

The lawyer-without-brief and prospector-without-oil was remembering this as he entered the house once more on his marathon between home and office. This time there was good news. To his intense pleasure he learned he was the father of a boy. The proud parents named the new arrival Howard Robard Hughes, Jr.

There was little change in the lives of the new parents until 1907. In that year Hughes started digging a well at Pierce Junction, Texas, but was forced to abandon it because his drill could not penetrate the hard rock. He was vastly disappointed because he was sure he had oil beneath him—he could almost smell it. Then the irritation turned to frustration when the experience repeated itself at Goose Creek, Texas. Here he could not only smell the oil, he believed he could taste it in the earth which he had drilled! But when the standard fishtail drilling bit with its two cutting edges hit hard rock, it quickly blunted to uselessness.

Hughes, baffled and thwarted, complained to Sharp, "I'm damned sure there's a way to get through this rock but these fishtail bits won't do it."

Sharp had long ago recognized that Hughes was ingenious and inventive. He had frequently jury-rigged a contrivance or improvised a missing part when operations threatened to be held up for any length of time. Therefore Sharp suggested, "Howard, I think you ought to work on the idea. You've been working too hard as is. Why don't you take a vacation and try to think out a new bit?"

Hughes, impressed by the seriousness in his partner's voice, decided to do exactly that. He returned to his parents' home in Keokuk resolutely determined to work out a new drilling method that would not balk at hard rock. A few ideas were already percolating in his head. He worked for two weeks, using the kitchen bread board for a drafting table, and finally had it! He had drawn a conical bit with 166 cutting edges—the maximum he could place on a single bit. His theory was that even if each edge made only the smallest impression the cumulative effect should nevertheless be able to pierce the most impermeable matter short of a diamond.

Seething with excitement he hurried to Houston to show his idea to his partner. Sharp was delighted and impressed. They decided to keep the project as secret as possible and therefore could not have a model made locally. Hughes journeyed all the way to Springfield, Massachusetts, to find a model maker who could make a prototype for testing.

Sharp and Hughes took the new bit back to the Goose Creek location and, enforcing strict secrecy and security on the crew, fastened the tool to the drilling rig. It worked! Within eleven hours it went through fourteen feet of hard rock and shortly thereafter it brought in the first Goose Creek gusher. This well was the first in what became one of the great oil fields in the Gulf Coast area. Using the new bit Hughes and Sharp also discovered the Pierce Junction field in the area which had originally thwarted Hughes' fishtail bit.

In November, 1908, Big Howard (his new name to distinguish him from the baby) filed for a patent and within a year received United States Patent Numbers 930,758 and 930,759 for rock drills.

These two patents became the foundation of the Hughes family fortune which Little Howard would one day carry forward from a modest, by Texas standards, estate to the rarified stratosphere of the billion-dollar-plus elite.

Hughes and Sharp, protected by their patents, founded the Sharp-Hughes Tool Company, in Houston, to manufacture the drills. Those first years were far from smooth sailing. Making production models of the drill proved to be a totally different operation from the handcrafting of individual pieces. The partners encountered both personnel and production problems which they had to learn to deal with, but they persevered and in a few years had established a flourishing business.

One early commercial decision proved to be very advantageous to the young company. Instead of selling the cone-type drills outright, they rented them out to the oil prospectors, requiring that they be returned to the Sharp-Hughes factory for sharpening. This gave them complete control over their product. Until a few years ago the Hughes bit was in use in approximately 75% of the drillings throughout the world.

Anyone who wants to satisfy his curiosity about the appearance of this jewel of the Hughes empire can see the bit enshrined in the corner of the entrance waiting room at the Hughes headquarters, 7000 Romaine Street, Hollywood, California. If the seeker cannot gain entrance (frequently the case) he can peer sharply to the left, through the glass entrance doors, and see the bit clearly, resting on its pedestal.

The Sharp-Hughes Tool Company had a world-wide monopoly on this very important drilling tool. Half-a-century later a reporter asked Howard R. Hughes, Jr., "Is it true that the Hughes Tool Company is a monopoly?"

"Of course not," denied Hughes. "People who want to drill for oil and not use the Hughes bit can always use a pick and shovel."

In 1917 Walter Sharp died and Hughes, Sr., bought the deceased's interest from his widow. The Hughes Tool Company became a family affair, and a family affair it remained, although in later years it became a family of one.

Howard, Jr., entered his teens having been raised in a fashion befitting the scion of a Texas fortune. Although it was not basically an oil fortune at least indirectly it stemmed from oil, and in addition it rested on a possibly more stable foundation.

"Sonny" early showed precociousness, inventiveness and tremendous persistence. He taught himself to play first the ukelele and then a saxophone. Those who remember the child still talk about the torture of hearing Howard practice day and night until he mastered each instrument. He was hardly out of diapers when he showed his interest in things mechanical by learning to take pictures with a box camera.

He had a bicycle but he wanted a motorcycle. His mother refused permission. Undaunted he built a motor out of the newly developed automobile self-starter, attached it to his bicycle, and achieved a homemade motorized bike.

As a teen-ager he and his friend Dudley Sharp, son of Hughes, Sr.'s, former partner, built a ham radio set. Hughes became one of the first government licensed radio ham operators, with the call letters 5CY.

His formal education was erratic. He started at a private school and then moved to a Houston Public Junior High School. Although he was clever and a good student he had little interest in education. His family tried to remedy this lack by sending him to the Fessenden School at West Newton, Massachusetts, for a year.

Big Howard's letter covering little Howard's entry to the school is revealing: "Please let Howard purchase anything which he may require and which is not against the school regulations. I wish him to uphold the subscriptions for anything which would serve to increase the prestige of The Fessenden School. So you may feel free to charge my account liberally for such and should some one or two boys not be in funds or need any assistance I would be more than pleased to help them through the year."

This was not an unusual attitude for Howard, Sr. A generous man, he directed his philanthropic efforts towards poor but deserving students, cloaking his assistance in anonymity.

Howard entered Fessenden in the fall of 1920—his fourteenth year. He elected to take ninth grade work (called the "Seventh Form" at Fessenden) which was really too advanced for his academic background. In a short time he was moved back a grade into a class of thirty boys. He did well in every subject, except spelling (which he flunked) and he excelled in algebra. He achieved a winter term final examination mark of 100 in that subject!

Although he could not spell he could write fluently and made the Board of the school magazine—the *Albemarle*.

His algebra teacher offered, "Howard started out pretty easy going and at first just about passed. Then Howard decided to buckle down and see what he could really do. This got him his 100."

His geography teacher described him as "bright, intelligent and alert."

At the end of the first month the headmaster, Mr. Fessenden, wrote to Hughes, Sr.:

"Howard's conduct and work have been quite satisfactory. It is not easy for a boy who has never attended boarding school and has been indulged at home to get adjusted to so many new conditions. I think he has done well—and I believe he is going to show general improvement. He has ability but he finds it somewhat hard to keep down to business from day to day."

In another letter the Headmaster noted young Howard's complaint that Mr. Giles, the algebra teacher, gave out too much homework. But Mr. Fessenden assured the father that this was a common complaint by the students at first. Eventually all the youngsters managed to complete fifteen problems. Howard, Jr., was disgruntled because he had been enjoined from going outdoors one afternoon when he failed to complete his algebra assignment on time. Obviously the young student had adjusted to the requirements in order to have attained a perfect mark.

Howard took an active part in all school activities. He played the saxophone in the school jazz band and got the reputation of a player with a lot of style. He played on the senior football team, and although he was a substitute, even that was a noteworthy attainment for a first year performance. He played golf in the school tournament and was runner-up in the finals.

One tradition at Fessenden was for each student to recite something before the entire school. The English teacher, Mr. Fife, had the chore of preparing the youngsters for the ordeal. Howard suffered agonies over this task. He selected the shortest eligible poem he could find, "Old Ironsides" by Oliver Wendell Holmes (the great physician-poet-man of letters, not the Justice).

During rehearsals in the gym Mr. Fife could scarcely hear the whispering lad. Suddenly the teacher bellowed, "I can't hear you." His loud voice reverberated through the empty gym.

Howard, startled, hitched up his clean, drooping, baggy-kneed gray trousers, took a deep breath, and shouted out the line, "Ay, tear her tattered ensign down!" with resolute vim and vigor.

His fellow students and teachers remember Howard as a quiet boy, shy and retiring but intelligent and witty when the stimulus was great enough. He was well-liked and regarded as a "good citizen." Although later in life he sometimes was eccentric in dress —wearing dirty sneakers to a nightclub and a court hearing—at this stage of his life he was marked as a neat and well-dressed boy. His room was kept so immaculately as to impress even the teachers.

He ended his year at Fessenden in the first third of his class and on the list of boys commended for faithfulness and industry. The class prophet predicted that Howard would become a member of the English Secret Service!

About this time the center of oil drilling had moved from Texas to California. Big Howard opened a branch of his tool company in Los Angeles and began to spend a lot of time in California. He decided to bring his son from Massachusetts to California and enrolled him at the Thacher School in Ojai. This was a residential and resort city about twenty-five miles from Santa Barbara, cosily nestled in the Santa Ynez Mountains.

The school had been founded by Sherman A. Thacher, a Yale graduate and the son of a Yale professor, who came to Southern California to homestead 160 acres of land as a rancher. In 1889 young Thacher made the mistake of accepting an East Coast student for tutoring. He performed his duties so satisfactorily that soon there followed a second and then a third student.

By the turn of the century Mr. Thacher had given up ranching and become the headmaster of a new school which became one of the outstanding preparatory schools in the United States. In addition to preparation for college the school also offered a full program of outdoor activity including horse back riding and camping.

Young Howard did very well at Thacher School and was apparently happy there. Then suddenly during the spring term, when he was sixteen years old, his father broke the news to him that his mother had died in the operating room of a Houston hospital.

Big Howard had been deeply in love with his wife and he mourned her passing. Nevertheless, he was an outgoing, gregarious man and after a respectable period of mourning, he began to be seen in public escorting models and actresses. He soon became known as one of the big Texas spenders.

This was the period designated later as the "Roaring Twenties" when America had just finished its first great war and had ushered in prohibition as a national experiment in futility. Among the upper class elite lavish living was the order of the day. Aged and mellow whiskies and vintage wines were replaced with bathtub gin and bootleg champagne. The way of life gave rise to a philosophy which held that the major object of living was the enjoyment of sensual pleasure.

Young Howard could hardly fail to be impressed. However, he recognized the need for continuing his education and he did have a lively curiosity, especially about mechanical science. He completed the year at Thacher and while his admission to Rice Institute in Houston was pending he was admitted to a course at the California Institute of Technology.

Young Hughes later entered Rice, where he made good grades, excelling in mathematics. At the end of his first term, just as he turned 18, his father died. Big Howard had been talking business in his office when he was suddenly struck down by a severe heart attack. He fell to the floor, never to rise again.

After the funeral the elder Hughes' will was read to the assembled mourners. Although he had recently prepared a new will, he never got around to signing it. The old will that remained in force was in fact more than a decade old. It still left half the estate to the deceased Allene, twenty-five percent to young Howard and the residue to other relatives. Under Texas law Howard inherited his deceased mother's share but he still had the family as partners in the tool company.

The tax returns placed the total of the estate in the neighborhood of one million dollars. The debt deductions claimed by the executors in order to reduce taxes were indicative of the kind of man Howard, Sr., had been and revelatory of the life he had led. There were Brooks Brothers' bills for over $2,000 covering suits, shirts, haberdashery. Jewelers' accounts exceeded $5,000, including items not of a type used by a man.

As soon as Howard fully understood the situation and realized that he had his grandparents and uncle as business partners he began to negotiate to buy out their share. When he first approached them they laughed at him, saying he was too young. He was an "infant" in the eyes of the law and could not enter into contracts until he was 21.

He marked time for a while, taking a trip to Europe with Mrs. Walter Sharp, widow of his father's old partner, and her son Dudley, his boyhood friend. He visited London, made his first commercial air flight from London to Paris, gambled at the casinos and came back determined to gain control of his inheritance without partners.

A statutory provision of the Texas Civil Code stated that if a minor could convince the court that he had the ability to handle his own affairs he could be declared competent and thereafter enter into binding contracts. Young Hughes started his long career with law and lawyers with this event. He went into the Probate Court and obtained the declaration that he was competent.

Shortly thereafter he negotiated the purchase of his grandparents' and uncle's interest in the Hughes Tool Company. The price has never been made public but the net result of his purchase was that as a mere stripling of 19 he totally owned one of the most prosperous business enterprises in Texas.

Immediately after completing his purchase he moved into the Tool Company's building, took over Big Howard's office and began to learn all aspects of the business. Despite his youth he acted out his executive role with the aplomb of an experienced entrepreneur. He hired a number of talented men, one of them an accountant named Noah Dietrich. Dietrich eventually became Hughes' chief lieutenant and the relationship was to last for more than thirty years.

Hughes played the adult man in another way: he took a wife. He had known Ella Rice, daughter of the founding family of Rice Institute, for several years. She was his senior by a few months and during their late adolescence and early maturity Howard could hardly compete with the older beaux who flocked around the dark-haired beauty. However, when he came into his inheritance, became the sole owner of the Hughes Tool Company, and began to assert himself as a man, he was able to win the girl he had longed for for so many years.

On a hot summer day in the year 1925, he and Ella were married in one of Houston's high society events of that year. The tool company was running smoothly and now that he had Noah Dietrich to depend on, he believed Toolco (the familiar name for Hughes Tool Company) could run by itself. He was becoming restive in Houston and decided to investigate new fields of endeavor.

He was not yet twenty years old.

Howard Hughes and
His Motion Picture Camera

THE YEAR 1925

IT WAS a good year. The chief events consisted of the signing of the Locarno Treaties, the growth in power and prestige of the League of Nations, and progress toward the settlement of Europe's debts to the United States. It looked as if the world had finally ended war.

There were almost one hundred shows playing in New York. These ranged all the way from *Earl Carroll's Vanities* and the Paris edition of *Artists and Models* to *Abie's Irish Rose, No, No Nanette,* and George Bernard Shaw's *Androcles and the Lion.* A number of Shakespeare plays were on the stage including *Hamlet* (in modern dress), *The Merchant of Venice,* and *The Taming of the Shrew.*

Some new motion pictures worth noting included *Stella Dallas;* Lon Chaney in *The Phantom of the Opera;* Eleanor Glyn's *Soul Mates* with Edmund Lowe; and Eric von Stroheim's *The Merry Widow,* starring Mae Murray and John Gilbert.

The Paige Company ran a large advertisement of the new Jewett Six for $995 f.o.b. Detroit.

Howard Hughes, already a married man, celebrated his twentieth birthday.

11

By 1925 the words "Hollywood" and "movies" were synonymous. The demand for American movies was worldwide and insatiable. Hollywood became the movie capital not just of the United States but of the world. As for the pictures themselves—each strove to out-do all the others.

In a city of great producers, Sam Goldwyn was one of the greatest. His entrance into the film industry in 1913 was a major factor in the changeover from Wild West thrillers and white slave shockers to the beginning of the Hollywood feature picture as it is seen today.

As Mr. Goldwyn studied the medium he concluded that the key to the good movie lay in the ability of its author. Enthusiastically Sam Goldwyn determined to make stars of his writers and envisioned the theater marquee advertising not so much the actors as the author. His first step was to organize a company known as Eminent Authors, Inc. He signed contracts with Rex Beach, Mary Roberts Rinehart, Gertrude Atherton, Basil King, Gouverneur Morris, Leroy Scott and Rupert Hughes. Thus it was that in the early 20's Rupert Hughes came to Hollywood and began to write for films. Although Sam Goldwyn's idea was not successful he did get publicity for the money spent plus one script by Rupert Hughes entitled *The Old West* which brought in box office returns of more than a million dollars.

Also in 1925 Howard Hughes and his wife came to Hollywood and for a while they lived with Uncle Rupert. Howard, always curious about something new, followed him around, watching movies being made. And Howard was bitten by the movie bug.

One day an actor named Ralph Graves approached him with an idea for a picture. Graves needed funds to promote it and told Hughes his story of a Bowery bum with a heart of gold who adopted a child. The tattered Good Samaritan kept bumping into all sorts of unusual and dire predicaments. Howard liked the plot (one biographer relates the unlikely story that he burst into tears, he was so moved) and he agreed to put up the money.

Typically, when Howard Hughes first ventured into the business of making movies he refused to start a new corporation because, he said, he had enough corporations around so why waste money on another one. He found a corporation called Caddo Rock Drill Co. —a wholly-owned subsidiary of Hughes Tool Company. He ordered his lawyers to amend the charter and change the name to Caddo Productions. This became Hughes' first corporate vehicle for the making of motion pictures.

In the making of his first picture Howard acted as both financier and producer and Hollywood set out to take the greenhorn. It did! The Hollywood of that day (as today) did not like anyone who began at the top. There was an unwritten rule that in order to make a movie one had first to learn all about acting, directing, lights, camera operation, and all the other techniques of the motion picture medium. However, for Howard Hughes certainly no such apprenticeship would be necessary. After all, Howard had seen many movies, knew something about cameras, and had a pretty good idea of what he wanted. Enthroned in a director's chair he caused the picture *Swell Hogan* to be committed to film and after it was finished he looked at it and knew that it was no good. He never released it.

During the filming of *Swell Hogan* Howard was the butt of many jokes. Everyone knew that the greenhorn from Texas was being taken. Although the film budgeted at under $50,000 it actually ran over $80,000. Howard could afford it and he signed the checks.

Quick-witted and alert, Howard Hughes learned his lesson and profited from this first venture into the world of moviedom. He came to understand the importance of competent actors, fine directors, and above all a good story. He disappointed the Hollywood elite, so ready to give him the razzberry, by refusing to turn tail and run. Instead he selected another script called *Everybody's Acting* and with the instinct of the true gambler, sank twice as much money into it. This time, however, he hired an experienced director, Marshall Nielan, and obtained a good story.

Although Hughes haunted the set, peering into every nook and cranny of the operation, he refrained from his customary interference. He was prepared to acknowledge that the professionals knew what they were doing and he lacked sufficient knowledge to improve upon their performance.

Exercising great restraint he permitted his employees to shoot the picture, prepare the silent film titles, cut and edit the film and put it together, all without interference. Nevertheless he was learning all the time. Nothing went on that he did not scrutinize, appraise, and feed into his memory bank. He had no intention of adopting a "hands-off" policy forever. To him, this was a period of apprenticeship.

The film starred Betty Bronson, Ford Sterling, Louise Dresser, Henry B. Walthal, Raymond Hitchcock and Lawrence Gray. Despite a hackneyed plot the reviewers said of the picture, "Cleverly directed episodes, and a tried and trusted formula not calculated to weigh heavily on one's mind, at least serves its purpose by providing sane and agreeable entertainment."

Hughes, flushed with the heady wine of his first success, now began to comb both Hollywood and the hinterlands looking for unknown actors and actresses whom he could turn into stars. He read scripts by the dozen and dreamed of those colossal successes which Hollywood so loved to predict and so rarely achieved. And on his third try Hughes accomplished what to many in the industry is the zenith of a movie career—his picture won an Oscar.

The award winning film—"Two Arabian Knights"—was a comedy starring two unknowns who later became famous—Lewis Wolheim and William Boyd. Also in the cast were Mary Astor, who provided the love interest; Ian Keith, DeWitt Jannings and Boris Karloff. Donald McGibney wrote the screen play and Lewis Milestone directed it. The picture featured unusual, magnificent and expensive photographic effects. Hughes also employed an imposing array of well-costumed extras.

The picture opened at the Paramount on Broadway and was so well received that a most unusual happening occurred—after its engagement at the Paramount ended it moved to the Rivoli for a long run. Only once before had a movie enjoyed such a reception: that film was *Underworld.*

M. Hall, the reviewer for the *New York Times*, commented, "If common sense direction, intelligent acting with general humor have succeeded in this instance, then it should inspire other producers to abandon the old bag of tricks and make fun without using the china closet, the kitchen or the chimney."

Other reviewers commended to their readers the "genuinely clever comedy" and the "intelligent direction and acting."

Hughes let two years go by during which he contented himself with being a successful producer while letting others actually make the movies. Then he got a big idea and readied himself to produce the super-colossal epic of them all.

Hughes' vision, which later became the subject of one of a multiplicity of lawsuits, was to make an aerial epic about the heroic American flyers of World War I. In the past aerial photography usually had consisted of photographing model planes against a backdrop of sky. No producer or director had as yet successfully brought to the screen an authentic realistic movie about aviation.

This theme was a natural for Howard: aviation enthusiast, pilot, and knowledgeable participant in all elements of flying. Partially in preparation for just such a picture and partially because he simply wanted to learn all there was to know about flying, he had haunted the airfields in the environs of Hollywood, taking instruction in flying as a novice. He told each aviation school he knew nothing about flying and let them teach him. At each place he learned something new. Now he was prepared to turn this experience to financial advantage in his forthcoming epic of the skies.

He bought up more than eighty old planes and hired over a hundred stunt pilots. He called his opus *Hell's Angels.*

Louella Parsons in her story about Hughes entitled, *The Man Nobody "No's"* said, "I remember watching this picture being made. Even I was appalled at the way Howard was spending money. At one time he had twenty-four cameramen shooting battle scenes. Howard was creating his own war and it was almost as expensive as the real one."

The production was made with the elan of an Indian potentate building a new Taj Mahal. Although Hughes had the famous director Lewis Milestone under contract he did not use him because Milestone was not an aviation enthusiast. Instead he hired Luther Reed of Paramount who had been an aviation writer before becoming a Hollywood director. For the starring role of the British pilot competing for the hand of an English society girl, he signed one of the top stars of the time—Ben Lyon.

Hughes borrowed Lyon from Warner Brothers where he was under contract at that time. For the part of the British high society girl he signed Greta Nissen, a blond Scandinavian who was then *de rigeur* in the movies. She was one of the most beautiful actresses of the period and, although she spoke little English, in the silent era it made no difference. Finally, Hughes hired Harry Behn, the author of *The Big Parade,* to write the script.

As soon as everything was set to begin shooting the film, Hughes' own private war began too. He and Director Luther Reed argued bitterly over how to shoot the aerial dogfights. Hughes kept rewriting the script, thereby earning everyone's consummate displeasure. Even the actors tried to avoid him because he kept insisting that they take certain risks in the air.

Occasionally the stunt pilots would refuse to take one of the rickety old planes off the ground. Hughes, infuriated at what he considered their deliberate thwarting of his wishes, would order the reluctant pilot out of the cockpit and take over the controls himself to demonstrate the feasibility of the maneuver and the airworthiness of the plane in question.

His tactics sometimes backfired. On one occasion the pilots were having difficulty getting a squadron of the old relics off the ground in formation. After several attempts, all but one of the planes completed the maneuver. Hughes turned his ire on the pilot who failed to keep in formation, removed him from the plane, and took over himself. The squadron prepared to take off once more. Hughes attained an altitude of 100 feet before the antiquated craft went out of control and plunged to the ground. The plane was completely demolished and Hughes wound up in the hospital in serious condition. This was the first of a series of airplane crashes that he somehow always managed to survive.

Hughes, young, resilient, and eager to get back to work, recovered quickly and, still bandaged, returned to the fray.

Always the perfectionist, he spared neither people nor expense. Each day as he examined the rushes he rearranged schedules and rediagrammed dogfights. In his first views of the aerial sequences he sensed something lacking. He sat in the projection room, running the film over and over again, calling in anyone who passed to watch with him.

Again and again he questioned his captive audience in an effort to pinpoint the trouble. No one could give him the answer. To most people the realistic experience of seeing balloons burning and real planes flying in the air and plunging to the ground was so novel and exciting that they could only lavish praise on the bits of action.

Hughes, not satisfied, morosely stared at the scenes flashing on the screen.

Suddenly he recognized what was wrong. They were shooting in the last months of 1928 and, as if to spite him, the Los Angeles sky remained blue and cloudless. And without clouds the viewer had no sense of the movement of the aircraft. The shots were static, motionless.

Hughes scrapped the footage already shot and organized a search through the valleys for cloud formations to use as background to supply the fighting planes with the appearance of action they needed. However, this one time Howard could not command what he wanted. No one could possibly reproduce moving clouds. He could use painted backdrops but he scorned such subterfuge.

He wanted cloud formations so brilliant and so grandiose that they could not possibly be mistaken for anything but the real thing. Howard began to rise very early. Before dawn he would arrive at his private air field in the San Fernando Valley to check flying conditions. Once airborne he roamed the skyways seeking clouds. If he found none within reasonable shooting distance he would return, muttering that there would be no shooting today because of the clear sky. This resulted in the posting of a sign: "War postponed today—no clouds."

Hughes was one of the youngest men on the set. He had reached his twenty-third birthday during the shooting. Many of the men were considerably older than their boss. Most of the pilots were World War I-trained aviators, now in or near their thirties. To the majority of the hundreds of fliers, actors, prop-men, electricians, and others who composed the cast and crew of *Hell's Angels*, Hughes was a rich kid playing at motion pictures. He was tall, gangly, sometimes awkward, usually negligently attired, but always intense, busy and persistent.

He irritated people in many ways. When a scene called for shooting in a London rain, he insisted on shooting it in an actual rain. This was not then the custom. In the real rain actors got wet and their clothes became soggy and their tempers short. They even caught colds. Most Hollywood productions were shot in a simulated rain with jury-rigged sprinklers that gave the audience the illusion of rain but kept the actors comparatively dry. Hughes wanted realism with a capital R.

Although there are claims that the cast and technicians held Hughes in contempt and called him "junior," "sonny," "the kid," "boy" and other appellations less dignified, Ben Lyon, star of the film, denies this. Lyon recently recalled that though everyone recognized Hughes as young and inexperienced, nevertheless "everyone had the highest respect for him."

Some brave soul might occasionally risk a practical joke such as turning on the propeller of a plane against an outhouse Hughes occasionally used, but Hughes disregarded all horseplay. His eye was fastened on his single target—to produce the best aerial war story ever to emerge from Filmland.

Hollywood was still in its lusty youth and moviemaking was relatively unsophisticated. Movie stuntmen suffered a high rate of injury and even an occasional death, but *Hell's Angels* produced a new record for casualties. In one sequence a plane struck a high tension wire and the pilot was burned to a crisp.

In another flying sequence the pilot encountered a storm too strong for him to cope with and the plane crashed, scattering bits and pieces of man and machine over the landscape. A scene required both pilot and crew to bail out but one member of the crew either could not or would not jump and he perished in the crash. There were mid-air collisions, engine failures, and other more bizarre and unpredictable accidents. By the time shooting was finished, the cost of *Hell's Angels* could be measured in millions of dollars, gallons of blood, and many lives.

Hughes struggled constantly for verisimilitude. He refused to use backdrops, miniatures, newsreel footage or the similar tricks which other producers used. When a scene required infantry battalions locked in combat, Hughes actually hired almost 2,000 extras to fight the battle and scattered a score of cameramen to photograph it. When the script called for a balloon to be shot down in flames he paid thousands of dollars for a real Zeppelin and then burned it.

The shooting of *Hell's Angels* took Hughes from 1927 until early 1930. During this time a revolution was brewing in Hollywood. In 1926 the Bell Laboratories had perfected a synchronizing process in which sound and film were so interlocked that as the camera showed the speaker's mouth moving the sound track reproduced the utterance. As soon as the process, called Vitaphone, was ready,

the executives at the Laboratories tried to interest the top Hollywood moviemakers in using it. However the sages of the American
film world looked, pondered, discussed, and concluded that the
invention was of no interest to them.

During one of these demonstrations in Hollywood Sam Warner's
attention was caught. At this time Warner Brothers was in financial
difficulties and was on the verge of going out of business. Sam induced his brothers to take a final desperate gamble. They started
with sound recordings of short subjects but these were roundly
condemned by both newspapers and magazines. Sam Warner, over-
worked and unhappy, died during these months of experimentation.

Radio was becoming more widely used as entertainment and the
people gradually adjusted to its continuous noisy assault. William
Fox introduced a process similar to Vitaphone, called Movietone,
and he induced many theatre owners to wire their theatres for
sound.

In 1927 the surviving Warner brothers conceived the sensational
idea of having an actor sing during a feature film and allowing the
audience actually to hear the song instead of merely watching an
unheard singer. They decided on a script entitled *The Jazz Singer*
and selected Al Jolson to star in it. Except for a few words and
some singing by Jolson, the picture was in the main a silent film.
Nevertheless, *The Jazz Singer* enjoyed immediate success with its
awed and excited audience. Warner Brothers quickly became one
of the major film producers in Hollyood. Warners, flushed with
success, next filmed a musical complete with sound, called *The
Lights of New York* and followed this with a talkie to end all talkies
—even the credits were spoken! This film was called *The Terror*.

In 1929 *Variety* summed up the development of sound pictures
by saying, "It didn't do any more to the Industry than turn it up-
side down, shake the entire bag of tricks from its pocket and advance Warner Brothers from the last place to the first place in the
league."

Howard Hughes was not one to ignore such developments. Although he already knew the answer he held a routine sneak preview
of *Hell's Angels* in a neighborhood theater and watched in pain as
the restive audience rustled, squirmed, talked, and ignored the
brilliant aerial scenes, the exciting dog fights, and the spectacular
combat scenes he had so painstakingly filmed. Hughes suffered
wordlessly as he watched Greta Nissen's mouth open and close in

her mouthing of the nonsense syllables which were interpreted by English titles to give semantic meaning to the action.

When he left the theater the young producer announced, "We will do it over."

Several million dollars had been spent in making the silent picture. Not a single Hughes associate or adviser agreed with Howard's decision to remake the epic. A multi-million-dollar movie was a rarity in those days; only a few films had ever cost as much. Hughes' associates were devastated at the prospect of spending more millions to add sound.

In spite of all the more or less cogent arguments advanced by his associates, Hughes remained adamant. He would not permit his name to be attached to a silent film at a time when sound was the new sensation.

The addition of a sound track to *Hell's Angels* was complicated by the fact that its star, Greta Nissen spoke with a thick Norwegian accent which disqualified her from the role of an English girl. No one yet knew anything about dubbing in another voice. Miss Nissen had to be replaced and all the scenes in which she appeared had to be reshot. Hughes began a desperate search for a replacement. He looked at existing screen tests. He arranged tests for dozens of actresses, including Ann Harding, June Collyer, and Carole Lombard but none satisfied him.

After months of waiting around, Ben Lyon and James Hall, the stars of *Hell's Angels*, happened to be visiting the set where a comedy was in the process of being made. In one dance scene using approximately 100 extras, Ben Lyon noticed a beautiful blonde. When the scene was finished he introduced himself to her and asked, "How would you like to play the lead in *Hell's Angels?*"

The attractive young actress replied, "All right. What do I do?"

Lyon said, "You don't have to do a thing. Meet me when you break for lunch at 12:30 and I will take you to Mr. Hughes."

Harleen Carpenter, the blonde extra, had arrived in Beverly Hills as the 16-year-old bride of a youthful playboy, scion of a wealthy family. The role of housewife had not been challenging enough to satisfy her so she adopted the stage name Jean Harlow and, despite her husband's objections, went to work as an extra in the movies.

At lunch time Lyon took Harlow to Hughes' headquarters. She wore a most striking and revealing black satin evening gown which set off to advantage her shapely figure and glowing platinum blonde hair. While she waited in the outer office Lyon entered the inner sanctum.

"Howard," he said, "I have found the girl for the lead in *Hell's Angels.*"

Hughes, having already tested almost everyone possible without any success, thought Lyon was joking. However, when Lyon insisted he was serious, Hughes came out, looked at the girl and told Lyon, "If you really think she can do it, shoot a test tonight at 7:30."

The following day Hughes saw the test, approved it, and signed Harlow to a long-term contract at $125 per week.

With his female lead selected at last, Hughes went back to the set. Again the cameras began to grind. Again the picture became his life.

The making and remaking of *Hell's Angels* was such a challenge to Hughes that he concentrated on it to the exclusion of all other activities including that of being a husband. While Hughes' neglect and absence from their home were nothing new to Ella Rice Hughes, in the past he had at least reappeared after 24 to 48 hours and reassured her that she still had a husband. Now, however he remained away from home for days on end.

The young wife led a lonely existence. She had little in common with the movie colony, took only a slight interest in the making of motion pictures, and was primarily interested in the friends and family she had left behind in Houston. Hughes' concentration on *Hell's Angels* became the final straw to break up the marriage. While Hughes was immersed in the problem of taping the sound and fitting Jean Harlow into Gretta Nissen's part, Ella quietly packed her bags and left for Houston and a divorce. Hughes offered no opposition. He made a property settlement in excess of one million dollars, payable in installments.

The divorce was but one of a series of annoying events that plagued the young film maker during the shooting. *Hell's Angels* also involved him in numerous law suits for which he would develop an affinity.

One portion of the *Hell's Angels* story was taken from a one-act play entitled *Somewhere in Mexico* written by Robert Mears MacKay. MacKay had sold the play to Director Marshall Neilan, who in turn sold it to Hughes.

The suit against Hughes was brought by Richard Barry, an old-time professional writer who had gotten his start covering the Japanese army invasion of Manchuria in 1905. Barry's first story, which appeared in a 1911 issue of *Argosy*, was entitled *Breaking of an Insurgent*.

Robert Mears MacKay's story entitled *Somewhere in Mexico* paralleled the Barry yarn except that the scene was Mexico rather than the Philippines.

The major defense at the trial was that both stories were based on the experience of a famous Cuban hero of the Spanish-American War, José d'Estrampes. Hughes also showed that the story had appeared in the *New Orleans Times* on May 13, 1906.

Hughes won the case in every court from the lowest (Federal District Court of New York) up to the United States Supreme Court. One of the most interesting aspects of this case was that the plaintiff's action against Hughes was based upon the parallel similarity of the words and scenes found in the Barry story and the MacKay play. The attorney defined the similarities between the two stories by showing two columns side by side in his brief—the left column containing the paragraphs in question from one version and the right column the related alleged infringing paragraph.

This was exactly the same technique used by the Howard Hughes forces thirty-five years later in order to convince the same court that a biography of Howard Hughes was plagiarism of other articles which the Hughes forces had purchased. In the later case the Second Circuit Court of Appeals also rejected the argument of parallels and Hughes lost.

Hell's Angels set many new Hollywood records. Its total cost was greater than any other film up to that date: well over $4 million. Production, too, set a new record for length of time: it began October 31, 1927 and did not end until May 1, 1930. The cameramen shot 2,254,750 feet of film. Even in those days the cost was approximately $250,000 for raw film stock and development.

Some idea of the significance of this total footage can be obtained from this comparison: Normally, a typical feature film lasting 90 minutes will have 8,000 feet of film. The average producer will shoot ten times as much film as he is going to need and make a selection from it. The director of *Dr. Zhivago* used 20 times as much as he needed. Hughes shot almost 300 times as much as was required.

Some of the other accounting figures relating to the film show

$2,113,000 cost of flying sequences, exclusive of film cost. Out of this $562,000 was spent to purchase and recondition airplanes and $754,000 was salary for flyers and players. Over $1 million went into interior sequences and $540,000 for sets and costumes.

One sequence involving the shooting down of a Zeppelin cost almost a half million dollars. Hughes used 87 airplanes, 137 aviators, and 2,000 extras for the infantry battle sequence, 1,000 extras for the London Charity Ball scene, 35 cameramen and 12 cutters.

He maintained eight separate locations for the filming of the aerial sequences. The main flying base was at the field named after his movie production company, Caddo Field at Van Nuys. A training school camp was maintained at Inglewood. The German field was at Chatsworth. There were other fields at Santa Cruz, Encino, Ryan Field in San Diego and March Field at Riverside, California. And the Oakland Airport was also pressed into service.

The opening of *Hell's Angels* showed Hughes' flair for publicity. The picture opened at Grauman's Chinese Theater in Hollywood in June, 1930. Hughes had Hollywood Boulevard lined every few yards for a mile with special arc lights. He also had fan-shaped clusters of colored searchlights placed in the overlooking Hollywood Hills to play on the theater. Beginning in the early evening of the opening night, planes zoomed overhead, dropping flares and small parachutes carrying flags and banners.

Huge representations of the planes in action hung above the streets in long sequences. There were large cutouts of Grummans and Fokkers, British DeHavilands and Snipes, a Gotha bomber and even a Zeppelin. An endless parade of shiny limousines passed in review before the huge crowds lining the streets to watch the largest aggregation of Hollywood stars ever assembled enter the theater.

Tickets for the opening were $11.00 apiece—a new high even for a Hollywood first night—even though less than a year before, the United States and the entire world had plunged into a deep depression.

Sid Grauman, owner of the theater, was on hand to welcome personally the hundreds of dignitaries who came to see the show. Through the flagstoned entrance containing the footprints of the famous passed Charles Chaplin, Dolores Del Rio, John Gilbert, Gloria Swanson, Bebe Daniels, Louise Fazenda, Lionel Barrymore, Jesse Lasky, Maurice Chevalier, Cecil B. DeMille, Leslie Howard,

Irving Berlin, Lawrence Tibbett, Ina Claire, Florenz Ziegfeld, Billie Burke, Jerome Kern, Jo Davidson and many others. Assembled in the audience to watch the World Premiere of *Hell's Angels* was probably the greatest aggregation of talent of all varieties ever gathered under one roof.

Preliminaries started at 10:00 P.M. with Frank Fay as Master of Ceremonies for a one hour vaudeville show. Appearing on the stage were Captain Roscoe Turner and his then-famous pet lion cub Gilmore, both of whom had just landed at the Los Angeles Airport after breaking the record for the East-West flight from New York to Los Angeles. It was 11:00 P.M. before the first frames of *Hell's Angels* finally flashed on the screen.

M. Hall in his *New York Times* review expressed the sentiments of audience and press alike, that the picture involved a strange combination of brillance and banality. The war and aerial scenes were regarded as "marvelous," "thrilling," and worthy of raves. In fact, most reviewers agreed that these scenes were the finest ever seen in any Hollywood motion picture. The remainder of the film, including the love scenes, was regarded as dull.

In spite of sporadic protests lodged by German officialdom at the unflattering image of their military, the film was an international success. In Hollywood, it ran for 19 weeks at Grauman's Chinese Theater, drawing capacity crowds. It was also the first picture to open simultaneously at more than one major New York theater.

Robert Emmet Sherwood, the famed American playwright and Pulitzer Prize winner, wrote: "One shouldn't jump to a natural conclusion that it is an extra-ordinarily fine picture because it isn't. If the lamentable truth must be known, it is pretty much of a mess. It is one of the most exciting news stories that the cinema has ever evolved, and therein lies the secret of its terrific appeal."

The perceptive Mr. Sherwood also pointed out that although Americans continually economized and praised thrift, there nevertheless existed an incurable fondness for rank extravagance. He commented, "The high, wide and handsome spenders, such as Death Valley Scottie or Diamond Jim Brady, are bound to become, in their immodest ways, national heroes. So is the young Howard Hughes. His shrewd and understanding press agents have broadcast the news that he took a fortune out of oil wells and spent it on *Hell's Angels*. As a result of this, countless numbers of solid citizens want to see the picture just to find out what he got with all that money."

What Hughes received for his money, Sherwood says, was "about five cents worth of plot, approximately thirty-eight cents worth of acting, and a huge amount of dialogue, the total value of which may be estimated by the following specimen. Boy: 'What do you think of my new uniform?' Girl: 'Oh, it's ripping!' Boy: (nervously) 'Where?'"

Mr. Sherwood crowned his review with the remarkable prediction: "The leading players include an obstreperously alluring young lady named Jean Harlow, of whom not much is likely to be heard."

Hell's Angels became both a financial and a popular success. England loved it. The *London Times* said it had "no equal on the screen." The *Daily Express* called it "the greatest masterpiece the screen has ever known." The *Sketch* remarked, "London was thrilled as never before."

As was customary in Hollywood, Hughes attempted to cash in on the success of *Hell's Angels* with two quickly made imitations. The first, *Cock of the Air*, used a screen story by Robert E. Sherwood and Charles Lederer and starred a blue-ribbon cast including Chester Morris, Billie Dove, Mat Moore, Walter Catlett, Louis Alberne, and Katya Sergeiva. It was described by the *New York Times* as "a mad war romance with many strange interludes."

The story concerned an American flying lieutenant and an actress known to him as "Whatever." It was more a collection of incidents than a story and included a checker game in a night club using champagne cocktails for checkers. The slapstick comedy encompassed seltzer squirting, face slapping with pancakes and disappearing clothing. The Hays Office censored portions and a reviewer lamented that it was not cut more because it was not the kind of picture "that could be any the worse or any less coherent for a generous pruning."

The major importance of this film in the life of Hughes was its promotion to stardom of his then current female companion—Billie Dove. Miss Dove was a Broadway show girl, unusual because she was small and fragile in a period when the ideal of female pulchritude was tall and lissome. Hughes met her at a cocktail party and was instantly smitten. Billie Dove, however, was unimpressed and ignored him. Told by a friend that the attentive man was "the" Howard Hughes her attitude was "so what"?

The next day the bachelor millionaire began to inundate Miss Dove with gifts. He sent carpets of flowers and cases of jewels. He let it be known to his sensitive and acute army of spies throughout Hollywood that he wanted to know Miss Dove's whereabouts at all times. If he received word she was out riding he would buzz her in a plane. No matter where she went he was not far behind.

Like most young women, Billie Dove could not long ignore such attention from the wealthy young movie producer whose most recent picture, *Hell's Angels,* had made him a hero to the movie industry. Soon wherever Dove was, there was Hughes. And naturally he wanted to star her in a picture. Unfortunately, the first vehicle—*Cock of the Air*—was unsuccessful.

Almost simultaneously Hughes produced another air war picture called *Sky Devils.* This too was a mediocre imitation and was received coolly. Despite the fact that it included Spencer Tracy, William Boyd, Anne Dvorak, Yola d'Avril, and Forester Harvey, it did not quite come off. A reviewer called it: "Farcial rivalry . . . and clever flying feats. . . . *What Price Glory* of the air produced by a Mack Sennett." It was rowdy, boisterous and full of fights, bottles broken over someone's head, auto and plane crashes and slapstick comedy. The action was vague, unmotivated and confused.

Meantime Hughes had been reading numerous scripts in his search for one suitable for Billie Dove—whom most of Hollywood believed he would marry any day. He finally found one called *Age for Love,* from a novel by Ernest Pascal. He hired Frank Lloyd to direct it and assembled a star-studded cast to complement Miss Dove—Edward Everett Horton, Mary Duncan, Charles Starrett, Betty Ross Clark, Adrian Morris and Lois Wilson. He had the novelist himself write the screen adaptation and Robert E. Sherwood did the dialogue. Unfortunately it turned out to be an unfunny comedy.

He had now made three bad pictures in a row.

His three failures convinced Hughes that the formula for *Hell's Angels* could not successfully be imitated. He observed the warm reception accorded a few recently released gangster pictures.

Hughes decided this could well be the new success formula. Deciding at the same time to give up personal direction of his films he selected a man whom he regarded as the best director in Hollywood—Howard Hawks—in spite of the fact that his past relationship with Hawks had not been friendly.

While Hughes was filming *Hell's Angels,* Hawks had been making a rival air epic, *Dawn Patrol,* and the two men found themselves in direct competition for the stunt pilots available in the Hollywood area. At another time Hughes began a legal action against Hawks for infringement of copyright in connection with a British play which Hughes had purchased and which he believed Hawks had copied.

Hughes nevertheless admired the competence of Howard Hawks. Unfamiliar with the workings of the Hughes mind, Hawks was shocked and surprised one Sunday morning to receive a call from Hughes inviting him to play golf at the Wilshire Country Club and to discuss a business matter.

Hawks replied, "You have an unjustified lawsuit against me and I wouldn't play golf with you if you were the last man on earth."

Hughes, prepared for this reaction, replied, "I'm ready to drop the action. Let's talk."

Hawks insisted on proof first and golf later. Within minutes Hughes' attorney called Hawks to corroborate the news that he had already received instructions to terminate the litigation.

The golf game proceeded in accordance with Hughes' plan. Although at the first hole Hawks had no intention of directing Hughes' pictures by the 18th hole they had made a deal.

The noble experiment with prohibition was almost at an end. Most people had had enough of the Volstead legislation (the law prohibiting the sale of liquor). The huge profit in the import and illegal manufacture of booze had swelled the coffers of the underworld. The stakes were huge and the battles bitter as the gangsters fought to control the trade in alcoholic beverages.

More citizens knew the name of Al Capone than that of the Vice-President of the United States or of members of the Cabinet. Even today, many decades later, Capone is remembered by almost everyone, but few can name Herbert Hoover's Vice-President, Attorney-General or Secretary of State.

The callous cruelty of the Czars of the illicit liquor trade intrigued the law-abiding citizenry. Actors like James Cagney and Edward G. Robinson achieved stardom portraying film gangsters. To the experienced observer of the new wave in movies it became obvious that the drawingroom comedy was passé and the violence of the street mob portraying American gangsterism was *de rigueur.*

Hawks and Hughes set out to make the best of the gangster

movies. They assembled a talented group of people, including Ben Hecht, one of the best-known Hollywood script writers, to do the play. Though he really wanted only the title, Hughes bought the rights to a book called *Scarface* by Maurice Koons (penname Armitage Trail). It was about the Capone gang in Chicago.

Ben Hecht, in his autobiography *A Child of the Century*, tells of this time when his agent, Myron Selznick, signed him to write the movie *Scarface* for Howard Hughes. Hecht says, "I told Myron I didn't trust Mr. Hughes as an employer. I would work for him only if he paid me a thousand dollars every day at six o'clock. In that way I stood to waste only a day's labor if Mr. Hughes turned out to be insolvent." The deal was made that way and every day a messenger from the Hughes menage delivered to Ben Hecht one thousand dollars.

Hughes publicized the fact that he was doing a biography of Al Capone. One night Capone's henchmen came to Hecht's hotel after midnight. They entered the room with scowling faces and guns bulging from their pockets. Somewhere they had obtained a copy of the script which they showed Hecht, asking, "Are you the guy that wrote this?"

Hecht admitted he was.

Next, they asked, "Is this stuff about Al Capone?"

"God, no," Hecht said feelingly, "I don't even know him."

Next they discussed the gangsters whom Hecht did know. Finally satisfied, the emissaries left, agreeing they would tell Al that the story was about some other guys.

As they reached the door one of them turned to Hecht and said, "If the stuff ain't about Al Capone, why are you calling it *Scarface?* Everybody will think it's him."

Hecht, thinking fast, explained that because Al was so famous and fascinating the title *Scarface* would make everybody want to see it, figuring it was about Capone even though it really wasn't. "That's part of the racket we call showmanship," he said.

After pondering they agreed, "All right we'll tell Al." Then one added, "Who's this fellow Howard Hughes?"

"He's got nothing to do with anything," Hecht assured them, speaking truthfully at last. "He's the sucker with the money."

"Okay. The hell with him!" The visitors left.

As usual, Hughes could not find a male lead who satisfied him so he started his customary search for new talent. Howard Hawks

discovered a young actor playing the lead in a Jewish theater in
New York City. Director Hawks and Producer Hughes watched his
performance and agreed that he would do nicely. His name was
Paul Muni. For the second lead they selected another young un-
known named George Raft. Ann Dvorak, Boris Karloff, Karen
Morley, Osgood Perkins and Vince Barnett rounded out the cast.

Hughes' contest with the movie censors is an excellent vignette
of the mores of the times. First he had to obtain a seal from the
Association of Motion Picture Producers known then as the Hays
Office. On first viewing of *Scarface*, the horrified Hays Office
suggested wholesale cuts and changes. Secure in the control
they exercised over the content of films, they even told Hughes
that at the end Scarface should be hanged instead of being shot
by the police. The censors believed that execution by gun shot was
too benign a punishment for such a depraved gangster. Therefore,
reasoned these brilliant guardians of public morals, to permit the
fatal shooting was tantamount to giving official approval to heinous
anti-social conduct.

Hughes unexpectedly agreed to compromise. He reshot some of
the more violent scenes, deleted a few of the gorier episodes, and
changed the name from *Scarface* to *Scarface, the Shame of a Nation*.
However on the ending he remained adamant. Scarface remained
unhanged, dead instead by bullet wounds.

The picture was completed and ready for release in 1932. Now
Hughes faced the inept and capricious local censorships which
prevailed in many cities and states. The New York censors refused
their approval—too much violence. The blue-nosed Pennsylvania
censors and their Ohio counterparts found the picture too strong
for the delicate sensibilities of the citizens of their state.

When the New York Censorship Board banned *Scarface* in spite
of the Hays Office Seal of Approval Hughes issued the following
statement to the press:

"It has become a serious threat to the freedom of honest expression in America when self-styled guardians of the public welfare,
as personified by our film censor boards, lend their aid and their
influence to the abortive efforts of selfish and vicious interests to
suppress a motion picture simply because it depicts the truth about
conditions in the United States which have been front-page news
since the advent of Prohibition.

"I am convinced that the determined opposition to *Scarface* is actuated by political motives. The picture, as originally filmed eight months ago, has been enthusiastically praised by foremost authorities on crime and law enforcement and by leading screen reviewers. It seems to be the unanimous opinion of those authorities that *Scarface* is an honest and powerful indictment of gang rule in America and, as such, will be a tremendous factor in compelling our state and federal governments to take more drastic action to rid the country of gangsterism."

Hughes followed through by bringing a legal action to compel the New York Board to abandon its censorship of the film. The anti-censorship forces rallied to his support and the *New York Herald Tribune* commented editorially, "Hughes is the only Hollywood producer who has the courage to come out and fight this censorship menace in the open. We wish him a smashing victory."

Hughes' action was successful. The combination of an unprecedentedly violent movie combined with the publicity engendered by censorship caused *Scarface* to become one of the most successful of the gangster pictures. In addition, both Paul Muni and George Raft enjoyed a meteoric rise to stardom as a result of their roles in the film.

Opposition to the film developed, too, among Italian groups who requested both officially and unofficially that the film be banned. The strongest effort was made by the Sons of Italy in Massachusetts who specifically asked the Governor and the Attorney-General to prohibit the showing of the film because it portrayed Italians in a bad light and implied that the majority of gangsters were Italian.

A number of states exercised no censorship and in those places Hughes permitted the picture to be released. He contrived to obtain the endorsement of several crime commissions and, aided by good reviews, he forced the censors in New York, Pennsylvania, Ohio and other places to pass the picture uncut. Everywhere it was well reviewed and well patronized.

Following the artistic and financial success of *Scarface* Hughes went on to make what many students of the film industry regard as his finest movie—*The Front Page.*

Choosing another Hecht play, the young producer proved he could make a good picture without recourse to spectacular aerial scenes or bloody violence on the ground. *The Front Page* was a newspaper story directed by Lewis Milestone. Once again Hughes starred a newcomer who went on to make screen history—Pat

O'Brien. Adolphe Menjou, Mary Brian, Edward Everett Horton, Walter Catlett, Slim Summerville, and Clarence H. Wilson were also in the cast.

The film told the story of a prisoner who escaped from jail by borrowing the Sheriff's pistol during a re-enactment of the crime. Its major themes involved Chicago politics and newspaper activity. The reviewers described it as a "witty and virile talking picture." The *New York Times* called it "a distinct tribute to the talking film."

Ernest Marshall wrote from London about its opening on Piccadilly Circus: "It is a long time since London critics have found an American film so much to their taste as Howard Hughes' production of *The Front Page* now on for an indefinite run at the Rivoli in the Strand." He added that it was through films of this nature that America would counteract the Soviet propaganda that the United States was inhabited almost entirely by bloated capitalists.

Approval of the film was not universal; one critic called it a "travesty and foul libel upon journalism."

The Front Page marked a new phase of Hughesian ingenuity. Instead of attacking problems of extramarital sex, nudity and other prohibited topics broadside and thus becoming embroiled with the censors he used clever devices to convey the ideas to the audience without depicting them in such fashion that the censors could take exception.

The subtlety of *The Front Page* made it a prototype for what later became a regular Hollywood style. Both box office returns and the critical reviews attested to the success of the film. At last Howard Hughes was ready to rest on his movie-making laurels. Almost a decade would pass before Hughes returned to movie-making.

Howard Hughes and
His Trip Around the World

SUNDAY, JULY 10, 1938

JUSTICE BENJAMIN CARDOZO of the United States Supreme Court died last night.

Britain dispatched more Cairo troops (the 11th Hussars) to Palestine to put down the violence, shootings, and the stabbings of the rebellious Jews. The casualties in Palestine that week rose to 12 killed and 24 wounded.

Generalissimo Francisco Franco's insurgents hammered from the sea, the land, and the air against the government defenders in Spain.

The U.S. Public Works Administration announced a grant of $8,325,000 to construct the long projected Criminal Courts Building in New York City.

An editorial in *Pravda* indicated that there is a melancholy picture in Soviet retail trade. Although workers have plenty of money there is nothing to buy. It is said the shelves are either empty or piled with unseasonable goods. The salesmen are rude and careless and many villages do not have a single store.

Berlin announced further measures restricting the commercial activities of Jews. After August 6, Jews will no longer be allowed to act as tourist guides or marriage brokers. The licenses of all Jewish peddlers will expire September 30. On October 6, Jews will be prohibited from acting as private detectives or doing any investigating. On January 1, 1939 Jews

159

will not be allowed to be active in any business or profession.

The books being read were Mary Roberts Rinehart, *The Wall;* *China Fights Back* by Agnes Smedley, *The Age of Consent* by Norman Lindsay; *The Yearling* by Marjorie Kinnan Rawlings and *Lisa Vale* by Oliver Higgins Prouty, the author of *Stella Dallas.*

The theaters were playing *Our Town, Pins and Needles, Room Service,* and *You Can't Take It With You.* On the screen were Margaret Sullavan in *The Shopworn Angel;* Gracie Fields and Victor McLaglen in *We're Going to Be Rich;* Ginger Rogers in *Having a Wonderful Time,* with Charles Boyer; Melvyn Douglas in *Fast Company,* and Kay Francis in *My Bill.*

Howard Hughes was thirty-three years old.

12

In January of 1937 Hughes was awarded the Harmon Trophy for having made the most outstanding contribution to aviation in 1936. In the latter year Hughes had established many speed distance records. He flew from Burbank, California, to New York City to receive the trophy, in the process breaking his own West-East cross-country record by completing the coast-to-coast flight in 7 hours, 28 minutes, 25 seconds. His first major award afforded him great pride and pleasure at having established himself not as a playboy-stunt-pilot but as a serious flyer who had contributed materially to the advancement of aviation.

The role of pioneer flyer he had assigned himself required him to make ever greater contributions to aviation performance and safety. Aviators were planning a number of onslaughts on Lindbergh's record flight from New York to Paris. Some prophesied a non-stop flight from New York to Berlin. Hughes had larger plans.

He would prove to the world the safety of flying by circling the globe. He had day-dreamed about such a trip since 1933 when that one-eyed adventurer, Wiley Post, had become the first man to make a solo flight around the world.

Post's flight had captured the attention of the world partly because of his style: he was a seat-of-the-pants, spur-of-the-moment, catch-as-catch-can flyer. Hughes would mournfully shake his head and say, "That's not the way to do it." When Hughes engaged in such an operation, he was a long-time planner, a meticulous and painstaking programmer who wanted every jot and tittle of the trip worked out in advance.

In August of 1936 Hughes filed a request with the United States Bureau of Air Commerce for permission to make a foreign flight. This agency supervised aviation at that time and Hughes' general application with them asserted that both the destination and the purpose of the flight were to be kept secret. It also provided that any additional information would come directly from him and from no other person. Shortly before this he had obtained a license for the operation of an aircraft radio station. Required to give a purpose, he specified a "round-the-world flight." It is indicative of the character of the man that he began in 1936 methodically to plan for a flight that would take place two years later.

He experimented with a number of planes for the projected flight but rejected them all until he tested a Lockheed monoplane with the speed and capacity he wanted. He spent most of 1937 and the beginning of 1938 modifying the plane and testing supplies and equipment to be included on the flight.

Hughes was a close friend of New York City's glad-hander, Grover Whalen. For months Whalen had been trying to convince Hughes to become the advisor on aeronautics to the forthcoming 1939 World's Fair which would be held in New York. He also knew about Hughes' planned flight and asked him to name the plane *New York World's Fair 1939*. The projected flight would thus serve to focus world-wide attention of aviation enthusiasts on the Fair, which they could visit to see the progress in aeronautics since the Wright Brothers had made the first flight of 59 seconds 36 years earlier at Kitty Hawk.

Hughes devoted his whole-hearted attention to the meticulous selection of his crew. He finally decided on four outstanding experts to go with him and a number of men to back up the operation from flight headquarters on the Fair Grounds at Flushing, Long Island. The crew members included Richard Stoddard, a 38-year-old radio engineer, as chief of communications. Stoddard had been a radio operator on steamships; later he earned his airplane pilot's license and joined the National Broadcasting Company as an engineer working in the field of technical radio communications. He succeeded in getting a leave of absence so he could go with Hughes.

The navigator was Thomas Thurlow, a 33-year-old Army flyer who had graduated from all of the Army navigation schools and then had become an expert in the development of special navigation instruments for the United States Air Force.

Edward Lund, the engineer mechanic, was a Montanan who had devoted his life to working on engines in an effort to obtain maximum speed from them. For many years he had worked for the Dodge Motor Company and later for the Douglas Airplane Company. He was probably one of the foremost experts in the United States on airplane engines.

The fourth man was Harry P. McLean Connor, also an expert navigator. Connor had been the navigator for Roger Q. Williams on the first nonstop New York-to-Bermuda flight in 1929. In 1930 he served as navigator and co-pilot for Captain Errol Boyd on a record-breaking flight from Montreal to London via Newfoundland. Connor would be Hughes' co-pilot and alternate navigator to Thurlow.

Although the flight was made long in advance of modern knowledge of correct nourishment for space pilots, Hughes showed his instinctive grasp of the exigencies of a new situation. Instead of merely ordering a selection of food for the trip, he carefully tested the potential nutritive value of more than 20 kinds of breads before selecting the variety to be used for the sandwiches which would constitute the major portion of the provisions for the flight.

He equipped the plane with the most elaborate piloting and navigational facilities of any private plane in the world. His equipment was exceeded in sophistication only by that used in the aircraft flying the trans-Pacific run and in the South American clippers used by Pan American Airways. He installed a newly-perfected "Sperry Gyro pilot" which would act as both an automatic pilot and a steering device for special use on overwater flights.

Hughes' radio communications equipment was different from anything previously used. The Federal Government approved special call letters which used the customary "K" and added the initials the press generally used when referring to him, "HRH." The plane would carry a powerful small set which could reach not only the major sending and receiving stations in the United States and in the rest of the world but also could maintain contact with a special station to be set up at his headquarters on the World's Fair grounds in Flushing Meadows, Long Island.

Finally all the plans were completed and a flight date was set—July 9, 1938. The small commissary on board was stocked with 15 gallons of drinking water, 10 pounds of ham and cheese sandwiches made with the special bread that Hughes had tested, three quarts of coffee and several quarts of milk. The *New York Times* commented that if Hughes followed his normal eating habits on long-distance flights, the crew would consume the food and Hughes would drink the milk.

The plane took on 1750 gallons of gasoline and 150 gallons of oil, sufficient to fly almost 5,000 miles. The longest flight planned was less than 4,000 miles, and this fuel load represented a safety factor in excess of 1,000 miles.

The flight plan provided for flying at 15,000 feet to 16,000 feet altitudes, especially over the mountains of Siberia. Consequently Hughes placed aboard the aircraft the most modern oxygen equipment available.

On Saturday, July 9, Hughes flew the big silver monoplane to Floyd Bennett Field where he began final inspection, paying special attention to the plane's two 1100 horsepower engines. Weather reports were being received from the United States Weather Bureau, the Coast Guard Stations and a number of ships at sea. William C. Rockefeller, long-time Hughes employee and head of the meteorological staff, took charge of correlating and analyzing these reports. Weather conditions were excellent for the take-off when suddenly Hughes discovered that the nine cylinders on each of the two engines had become slightly pitted from the new high-octane gasoline used on the California to New York flight. Without a moment's hesitation, Hughes ordered, "Put in new ones."

At once the scheduled take-off was postponed and a squad of mechanics went to work installing new cylinders. While the work was being completed, satisfactory weather reports continued to come in so Hughes ordered the workmen to continue around the clock. Assured at last that the replacement was proceeding properly, Hughes took off for the city purportedly to visit his current female companion, Miss Katherine Hepburn.

Hughes returned to the field accompanied by Sherman Fairchild, an avid aviation pioneer himself, and by Captain Charles Stoffer, one of the pilots from *Hell's Angels*. In a plane piloted by Stoffer, Hughes circled the field several times studying both the wind sock and the ground in order to prepare his take-off plan.

After he landed, Hughes told his friends, "If I had known what the situation is I probably wouldn't have used this field. But, since there is wonderful weather I think I am going to use it and take off tonight anyway."

Hughes had selected the runway which had the smoothest and hardest ground at its end. However, during the check flight he had noticed a fence at the end of the runway and he requested the airport officials to remove it in order to give him a few hundred additional feet for take-off. Take-off time was drawing near so Hughes went to the hangar office to check the latest weather report. Then he announced that they would leave shortly.

It was late Sunday afternoon and Hughes was warming up the motors when a new difficulty arose. The motor on the right side seemed to have a faulty magneto. An emergency call went out to the Wright Company which cooperated on that beautiful Sunday by sending its manager to the storeroom for a new magneto. Once that was installed all was well.

Hughes commanded, "Let's get off before something else happens."

As the plane made ready to take-off, Grover Whalen rushed up to tell Hughes that he had to participate in a leavetaking ceremony. Reluctantly Hughes approached the platform in front of the Administration Building where hundreds of assembled onlookers waited before the news-reel cameras and microphones.

Grover Whalen praised Hughes and his companions lavishly. "In a few moments you and your companions will be taking off on a flight to Paris. You have with you all the factors that make for success—skill and daring, courage, and mechanically perfect equipment. This flight will remind the world of the good will and understanding that has long existed between great democratic nations."

Hughes replied: "We hope that our flight may prove a contribution to the cause of friendship between nations and that through their outstanding flyers, for whom the common bond of aviation transcends national boundaries, this cause may be furthered. We are glad to bear invitations from the New York World's Fair, 1939, to these flyers, for we feel that they understand that with the development of air transportation, increased communication will further international cooperation and friendship."

Hughes then turned to the reporters and photographers who had been trying in vain to reach him for two days. "I want to apologize to the newspaper men and photographers if I seemed rude and impolite last night and this morning. I had received favorable weather reports and I had only the thought of hopping on my mind. I did not mean to be rude or impolite, and I want to apologize right now."

For this impromptu explanation he received a small cheer from the assembled representatives of the press who were especially

pleased when he consented to pose for them. Previously their requests for pictures had met with brusque refusal.

Hughes shook hands with some of the dignitaries who had come
to see him off. Included in the group were the noted flyer, Viola
Gentry, and Roger Q. Williams, who had made the first non-stop
round-trip flight between New York and Bermuda. The amenities
completed, Howard and his crew moved toward their plane.

Hughes, described by the *New York Times* as "the despair of
American Tailors" wore a wrinkled pair of gray trousers, scuffed
tan shoes, a white shirt open at the throat and a tan hat. Wives of
the married crewmen rushed forward to kiss their husbands good-
bye. Tommy Thurlow jumped on his father's back for a parting
hug. The unmarried Hughes and Lund had no feminine relatives or
friends to bid them farewell.

Just before they boarded the plane a small, unanticipated additional weight was added. At the very last moment Mrs. Connor,
wife of co-pilot Harry Connor, slipped through the police cordon
and firmly attached to the tail a wad of chewing-gum. She announced, "That's for good luck."

Once they were all aboard Hughes wasted very little fuel in
warming up the engines. The weather was hot and the plane had
been standing in the sun for a long time. Hughes felt that the
motors were ready for flight without the customary warmup.

At 13 seconds after 7:19 P.M., Sunday, July 10, with the throt-
tles wide open and a cloud of dust trailing the wings (65 feet from
wing-tip to wing-tip), the ship, shimmering like quicksilver in the
setting sun, went roaring down the 3500 foot runway.

The huge tires sagged under their burden of 2500 pounds and
the plane seemed slow and earthbound, but by the time the halfway
mark was reached on the runway the wind screamed loudly as it
passed the sleek sides of the forward-darting craft.

Electronic timing instruments did not yet exist, and consequently
Mr. John P. V. Heinmuler, Chief Timer for the National Aeronautic
Association, had to drive down the runway with a stop-watch to
obtain the exact split-second when the silver monoplane would rise
off the earth on its skyward journey.

Heinmuler tells his experience in timing this flight in his book,
Man's Fight to Fly. He reports that the plane used up its 3500 feet
of paved runway and went on into the rough that extended beyond.
As the wheels began to stir up the dust of the dry July ground he

was horrified to see one of them begin to bend inward. Sure that he was witnessing the beginning of a disastrous crash, he glanced at his stop-watch. However, within 30 seconds the plane emerged from the cloud of dust, seemed momentarily to settle back to the ground, and then, brushing the tops of the red clover that carpeted the south end of Floyd Bennett Field it turned slowly and rose into the darkening sky.

Hughes had 15 to 20 feet of altitude as he reached Jamaica Bay where he began a steady ascent. Well above the tops of the houses he turned north over the Rockaways to follow the Great Circle Route which would take him over the east coast of the United States to Newfoundland. From there it was a short hop over-water to Ireland and then on to Paris, and touchdown at Le Bourget Field. The first leg of the trip would cover a distance of 3641 miles.

The weather was good and initially communications were fine. At 8:26 P.M. the craft reported passing over Boston. At 9:30 P.M. Rockland, Maine, was beneath them, and at 9:55 P.M., Nova Scotia slid by.

At 10:30 P.M. the plane was hooked into the Columbia Broadcasting System for a national broadcast. Richard Stoddard, the radio technician, started off by reporting that the weather was clear and the trip was proceeding smoothly. Their major problem was a high internal cabin temperature—90 degrees. Then he introduced Howard Hughes who, after a casual word or two, reported that Tommy Thurlow was too busy plotting their position and Lund, the flight engineer, was too busy with his own duties to do any talking.

At 1:36 A.M. the plane reached the tip of Newfoundland. Flying at 7450 feet, with an average speed of 192 miles per hour, they were ready to leave land behind and start across the ocean when the automatic trailing antenna broke. They were forced to suspend all communications until, by using an emergency hand-rigged device, they could put out a new antenna. Unexpectedly adverse winds and weather cut down their speed and increased gas consumption enough to make questionable whether the fuel supply would be sufficient for the remainder of the trip.

At 2:30 A.M., with the plane 230 miles out into the Atlantic from the tip of Newfoundland, and 1400 miles from New York, Hughes reported back that he had had to increase the output of the engines in order to maintain their altitude and therefore his fuel consumption was much greater than he had anticipated. Use of a direct route to Paris as originally planned had now become uncertain.

Hughes himself spoke. "I hope we get to Paris before we run out of gas, but I am not so sure. All we can do is hope we will get there. I hope we will have enough gas to reach land. I am throttling back the engine as fast as the reducing load permits."

At the Fairground headquarters Odekirk, Rockefeller and the others waited with heavy hearts for further bulletins. After a while things began to look a little more cheerful because as the gasoline was used up, the plane got lighter and the speed increased. Over Newfoundland Hughes had averaged about 162 miles per hour but out over the ocean they picked up to as high as 192 miles per hour. The original flight plan had called for an average cruising speed of between 145 and 155 miles per hour with the prevailing winds counted on to lift the actual speed to 175 miles per hour. The goal was Paris in less than 24 hours.

The route was almost exactly the same as that pioneered by Charles A. Lindbergh eleven years before on May 20, 1927 in 33 hours and 30 minutes. Using a better plane and superior engines Hughes calculated he could cut Lindbergh's time, which was still the record for the New York-to-Paris flight, by about one-third or 10 hours. (Wiley Post, who then held the round-the-world record, had flown from Floyd Bennett Field to Berlin in 24 hours and 45 minutes.)

At 9:30 A.M. (New York time), well ahead of schedule, the plane was sighted over Kenmare, County Kerry, Ireland, just 600 miles from Paris. At 11:00 A.M. it was again sighted nearing Paris and at 11:55 A.M. Hughes landed at LeBourget Field. In an elapsed time of 16 hours and 35 minutes he had covered 3,641 miles at an average speed of 219.6 miles per hour. This was almost exactly half the time it had taken Lindbergh to make the same flight a decade before.

The plane traveled so fast that officials, newspapermen, photographers and others, accustomed to lengthy waits at LeBourget Airfield, were taken completely by surprise when the plane landed at 11:55 A.M. (New York time). They had taken their time arriving, anticipating that Hughes would require a minimum of twenty hours to complete the trip. As a matter of fact, as Hughes neared his destination, he was traveling fast enough to outstrip reports of his progress. Approaching the coast he had flown over the *Ile de France* which announced to the world that as soon as they com-

pleted plotting their position, it would be made public. While
the calculations were being made, Hughes landed!

American Ambassador to France, William C. Bullitt, and his staff
did arrive in time. As Hughes and his men left the plane, the Em-
bassy staff stood waiting to shake hands. Ambassador Bullitt invited
Hughes to his home for a shower, a meal, and a rest but Hughes
declined the invitation because he had to stay at the field to supervise the readying of the plane for the next leg of the journey.

Hughes did reluctantly consent to say a few words on the air.
"We certainly want to thank all these people here at LeBourget
Field for the help they have given me."

It was now early evening in Paris and everyone in the city seemed
to be streaming out to the field to get a look at the wonderful American "flying laboratory" as the French newspapers called it, and at
the eccentric and laconic millionaire who flew it. The French police
had to assign two platoons of French mobile guards, wearing shiny
black helmets and armed with rifles, to form a moving square
around the plane as it was moved from its landing place to a hangar
for servicing.

Careful inspection revealed a twisted stay in one of the wheels
of the landing gear, probably caused by the bumpy ground on take-
off. A repair job was certainly indicated. Hughes and Lund examined
the damage with sinking hearts and requested some of the French
mechanics on the field to look at the wheel. With Gallic casualness,
the mechanics shrugged and muttered, "It's done!" One explained
that it would be necessary to send to the United States for new
parts or to spend a week waiting for them *if* they could be tooled
in France.

Someone on Ambassador Bullitt's staff recommended an American sergeant who had real Yankee ingenuity. An urgent call went
out for Sergeant Cook and, in the best tradition of hairpin and tooth-
pick repair, Cook miraculously fixed the damaged part with improvised angle irons. In the meanwhile, the four members of the crew
got some rest. Hughes snatched a light meal at the airport restaurant and returned to help Sergeant Cook make the repairs.

The reporters kept badgering Hughes for an interview, but got
nothing but grunts for their efforts. Many newsmen took it upon
themselves to file stories that the round-the-world flight had ended,
but they were wrong. At eight o'clock all was in readiness for take-

off and the unlikely-looking mobile guard unit escorted the plane back to the runway.

At 8:24 P.M., eight and a half hours after arriving in Paris, the Lockheed monoplane, under questionable flying conditions, took off for Moscow. The weather was soupy and at 8:52 P.M. Hughes radioed back, "We are flying blind."

The flight plan from Paris to Moscow routed them over Belgium, Germany, Poland, Lithuania and Latvia. They could then pick up the Leningrad Highway and follow it into Moscow Central Airport. They had one routing problem in that, in obtaining governmental clearances, the Hitler government had been very coy. With all the preparations for war going on in Germany in 1938 the Nazis were not inclined to permit a strange plane, especially an American one, to fly over German terrain making notes, possibly taking pictures and no one knew what else. As a consequence when they began to cross Germany the messages started to come in, "Who are you— identify yourself—" etc., etc.

However, with all the time he had lost in Paris fixing the wheel, Hughes was not about to detour around Germany, so, hidden from sight by the weather, he gave orders to his crew to ignore all radio warnings.

The weather became so bad that they were forced to climb to 16,000 feet and go on oxygen. At that altitude ice began to form on the wings and it appeared that the combination of ice weight on the plane plus poor weather would form a truly dangerous combination which would force them down. Suddenly the weather began to clear so they could lose altitude to the level where the ice melted. At 4:15 A.M., New York time, the plane landed at Moscow Central Airport.

The Soviet Government cooperated fully in readying the plane speedily for flight. A 2500-gallon tank car filled with the type of gasoline used by the plane rolled up to Central Airport, a special crew stood by in readiness to make repairs, refuel, or do anything else necessary.

The Russians were particularly anxious to reciprocate the fine treatment recently afforded to the Russian flyers who had pioneered a long distance flight over the Polar Route from Moscow to the United States. These flyers, Yumasheff, Baidukoff and Gromoff, were present to greet Hughes.

The Soviet citizens went wild over the American ship and flyers.

Hundreds of people streamed out to the airport and the Soviet Foreign Office opened a special entrance to issue passes and admittances. The Soviet press was quite kind and applauded all the exploits of the flight, even quoting a Russian guard who noticed on the tail the trademark of Lockheed and purportedly said, "Look, they fly the Red Star." He pointed to the stabilizer and tail of the plane. "It will bring them luck. It is fine to show Fascist vultures that we democracies fly better than they do."

Through all the hustle and bustle Hughes watched the clock. He wanted to leave as fast as possible and told the official greeters, "I would appreciate it if you could refuel as quickly as possible. We would like to leave in 20 minutes." This, of course, could not be done, but everyone concerned labored earnestly to make time on the ground as short as possible.

They were making good time; they were about a day ahead of Wiley Post.

Walter Duranty, Moscow correspondent for the *New York Times*, reported that many important Soviet officials were on hand to greet Hughes. Even Alexander A. Troyanovsky, Soviet Ambassador to Washington, on leave in Moscow, was there to shake hands with Hughes. All of the American officials were also there, including Alexander C. Kirk, United States Chargé d'Affaires, and Lieutenant Colonel Philip R. Faymonville.

Hughes quickly shook off the visitors and went out for a bite to eat. The Soviet government had thoughtfully provided a typical American meal including what they imagined every American ate for breakfast: cornflakes. However, Hughes instead requested and received a typical Russian breakfast, including caviar and black bread.

Hughes was extremely anxious not to lose any time. After eating rapidly he went to the Administration Building to study the maps, weather conditions and other information which the Soviet experts had prepared for him. Of course, this was not what the Muscovites had planned and they were quite disappointed when Hughes rejected a sight-seeing tour of Moscow, a huge lunch and a hotel suite. The Russian trans-polar flyers, understanding Hughes' impatience, explained to all the officials the importance of his getting away quickly.

At 6:30 A.M., New York time, on Tuesday, July 12, the plane took off from Moscow for Omsk, its next destination. Just before they sealed the cabin the Russians brought a large jar of caviar which Hughes regretfully rejected because of his inability to carry any additional weight, but he did accept a large bottle of mineral water. As Hughes had climbed into the plane the last view the Russians had of him was the one which pleased them most—clearly visible was a patch on the seat of his pants. The Soviet press was quite taken with the millionaire who traveled in patched pants.

Omsk was about 1300 miles away from Moscow and because of the weather the projected flying time was estimated at eight hours. However, in almost exactly seven hours and thirty minutes, at an average speed of 184 miles per hour, the *World's Fair, 1939* reached the Omsk Airfield, a flat meadow with a grass landing strip.

In Omsk the flight was delayed because the available gasoline was not airplane-engine fuel and Hughes had to add ethyl. He had prepared for this eventuality by carrying a supply of ethyl but delay was inevitable because the additive required that the gasoline be strained for foreign matter. This operation took more than four hours to complete but at 6:37 P.M., New York time, they were once again airborne and bound for Yakutsk.

This leg of the flight covered over 2000 miles non-stop and it was Wednesday, July 13, 5:00 A.M. (New York time) when they arrived at Yakutsk. The elapsed time was ten and a half hours at an average speed of 207 miles per hour.

At Yakutsk the Russians who met them were puzzled by the name of the plane: *New York World's Fair, 1939.* The officials of the city were familiar with the International Date Line and knew that on one side it might be Thursday and on the other side Friday. Now, however, they had the concept that perhaps somewhere in the world there was a line on one side of which it was 1938, as, for example, at Yakutsk, while on the other side of the line it was 1939, where the New York World's Fair was. This misunderstanding was quickly cleared up with an explanation of the meaning of the aircraft's name.

The next leg of the journey carried the flyers from Yakutsk, deep in the heart of Siberia, to Fairbanks, Alaska, a flight of almost 2500 miles, which would consume more than half a day. In addition, on this leg of the flight they would have to go over a series of mountain ranges, including the Verkhoyansk range which had heights to 8000 feet. Hughes' maps of the area were inaccurate and in some places the mountains were 2500 feet higher than those shown on the maps.

Part of Hughes' plan worked well. The flight from Yakutsk to Fairbanks would be during daylight hours. Following his flight plan Hughes flew between peaks that towered far above him. He gradually increased his altitude until he was flying at 12,000 feet, where he could safely clear the range.

By this time the Hughes round-the-world flight had become front-page headline material in every newspaper and on every radio station throughout the world. The baseball games, the bullfights, and the soccer games were all forgotten and everyone wanted only to know where Hughes was at the moment. As a result, the welcoming throng at Floyd Bennett Field was building up and getting out of hand.

Police Commissioner Louis J. Valentine formulated plans as though he anticipated an insurrection or a riot! He ordered four police captains, a hundred sergeants, and over a thousand foot-patrolmen to take positions on the field and, assisted by a flying squad of 24 motorcycle police, to keep the plane constantly surrounded and safe from souvenir hunters.

While Grover Whalen, Police Commissioner Valentine and Hughes' staff were getting ready for the welcome in New York at 8:15 P.M., New York time, Hughes landed at Fairbanks, Alaska, after a flight of 12 hours and 17 minutes. For the almost 2500 miles Hughes had averaged 200 miles per hour.

One of the visitors at Fairbanks was Mrs. Wiley Post, recent widow of the round-the-world flyer whose record Hughes was now breaking. Hughes greeted Mrs. Post effusively and expressed his unsurpassed admiration for her husband's feat.

"Having just followed Wiley Post's route but doing it with a crew of five rather than alone," Hughes told her, "I can really appreciate his accomplishment!"

The weather between Fairbanks and New York was uncertain so Hughes selected several alternate landings for the next refueling stop. Both Winnipeg and St. Paul were alerted to stand by for refueling but while aloft Hughes abruptly changed course and headed for Minneapolis. St. Paul learned of the change of plan but somehow the message never reached Winnipeg, where anxious watchers were about to send out search planes when they heard on the radio that the missing plane had landed in Minneapolis. After a short refueling stop they took off immediately on the last leg of the flight to Floyd Bennett Field.

Early on the morning of July 14, 1938, more than 20,000 people were at the field to welcome Hughes and his crew. The police kept them back from the runways, but the mob crushed against the wire fences, straining to catch the first glimpse of the landing. Many people had passes to gain entrance to the field, many others contrived ways and means of achieving that objective. When the big monoplane touched down at 2:37 P.M. after a total flight of 3 days, 19 hours and 17 minutes, Hughes and his men descended from the plane into a mob of well-wishers.

One riotous interview on the field broke up all the elaborate plans for the welcome. Hughes landed on a runway other than the one where he had been expected. As the plane touched down Grover Whalen and Mayor LaGuardia raced over to the anticipated stopping place. When the door opened Whalen and LaGuardia were waiting but so were hundreds of reporters and many other people.

Never before had such an elaborate setup for radio broadcasting been devised. Millions of people throughout the world were listening to the complex radio hookups which would carry the words of the great flyer. Listeners were rewarded with the following conversation:

"Get out of here." (This was the first thing that anyone heard of the actual arrival.)

"It's taking up too much time."

"Ah! Shut up."

Then the unmistakable voice of Grover Whalen came through: "Did you have any trouble?"

This was followed by the weak, tired voice of Howard Hughes, "No, none at all."

Next were several unidentified voices:

"Grab his hat off!"

"Better get in the plane."

"Hey, Howard!"

Then followed the high-pitched, gravelly voice of Mayor La-Guardia, "Seven million New Yorkers offer their congratulations for the greatest record established in the history of aviation. Welcome home. . . ."

After an unintelligible jumble of words Hughes' tired voice was heard to say, "I am ever so much honored. Thank you very much."

Grover Whalen, realizing that the welcome at the field was getting out of hand, steered the official party into cars and took them to his home in Manhattan, a remodeled row of stables. There Whalen gave Hughes time for a shower while he sent a man out to buy him a shirt.

When the reporters assembled for their interview, Hughes said he would answer only those questions which dealt with the flight. In spite of this, many of the reporters asked when he was going to see or marry Katherine Hepburn. He refused to answer any questions of a personal nature, or pose for pictures.

When a reporter mentioned that Hughes had smashed Wiley Post's record Hughes corrected him sharply. "In my opinion, Wiley Post's trip was absolutely beyond comprehension. It is something like pulling a rabbit out of a hat or sawing a woman in half. Unbelievable."

Throughout the several days of interviews and personal appearances, whenever anyone discussed the magnificence of the Hughes flight, he took the opportunity to praise Wiley Post's achievement. It was obvious that Hughes was enormously impressed by Post's success in making the trip alone.

In a press interview Hughes disclosed for the first time that he had been planning the flight for a long time and that it had been no spur of the moment matter. In fact, planning for the trip had begun approximately two years earlier. It had, for example, been necessary to overcome the unwillingness of various governments to let him fly over their territory, carrying new and unusual American flying instruments and photographic equipment.

At last the exhaustive and exhausting press conference ended and the four crewmen got into separate cars to be taken to their quarters at the Hampshire House. Hughes slipped away to enter a waiting limousine which took him to Katherine Hepburn's New York residence. As the car approached her town house Hughes saw that a crowd had gathered, obviously anticipating his arrival.

Changing his mind, he ordered the driver to take him to the Drake Hotel where he checked in and disappeared. There is a difference of opinion about whether he slipped out to spend some time with Katherine Hepburn or whether he simply had milk and cake and went to bed. He certainly had to have some sleep because at noon the next day Hughes and his crew would ride in a triumphal ticker-tape parade down Broadway.

Sitting beside Grover Whalen in the open touring-car Hughes at first appeared stiff and unyielding. The crowds shouted; they threw ticker tape from the stock market "machine" and torn phone books shredded into confetti; the paper snow filled the sky and covered the street. The welcome was boisterous and good-natured. As always in public Hughes presented to the crowd a frozen, unbending appearance.

He could not, or would not, make a public show of emotion, joyful or otherwise. But as the crowds lining the sidewalks and thronging to the open windows of the large buildings on both sides of the route continued to cheer he was impelled to make a feeble little gesticulation of the hand which was greeted with a loud roar of approval. This apparently pleased him and moved him to greater efforts. Soon, he was beaming broadly and waving his hat over his head in cowboy style. The warm welcome and the unrestrained friendship and admiration of the huge crowd got under his skin and for once Howard Hughes came out of himself and enjoyed the limelight.

Many of the well-wishers broke through the police lines and rushed to the car to have a closer look or even possibly to touch the hero. One or two thrust out their hands and Hughes, simply to be civil, shook them and found that the act gave him pleasure. He was soon shaking hands with almost everyone who could reach the car.

For a person for whom crowds had always been anathema, Hughes' enjoyment of this particular demonstration was remarkable. He even smiled when an enthusiastic well-wisher threw out a large piece of the phone book without shredding it and it landed in his lap.

New York in the middle of July was hot and sticky. There was no air-conditioning and when finally they reached City Hall where Mayor LaGuardia was to present the Key to the City to Hughes and his crew, the room set aside for the ceremonies was an overheated oven.

Mayor LaGuardia delivered the welcoming speech which was seconded by an old Texas friend of Hughes, Jesse Jones, the Chairman of the Reconstruction Finance Corporation. Jones said that he had recognized Hughes' genius when he saw him as a child working in his father's tool shop. After many more speeches, finally Hughes was called upon.

He said, "I haven't a great deal to say about this because I am afraid I might get a little nervous and not say just what I want to." He then pulled out some papers and as he unfolded them added, "I can't say everything I want because some of the speakers took part of it away from me. I will just have to do the best I can. At least you can be sure that no one has written this for me but myself."

Hughes showed his obvious pleasure at the laughter this remark provoked.

"I'm not very good at making speeches and I agreed to make this one only because there is something about this flight that I want everybody to know. It was in no way a stunt. It was the carrying out of a careful plan and functioned because it was carefully planned."

He explained that he had used the most advanced and modern equipment possible and a good deal of thought.

"The airplane was fast because it was the product of over 200,000 engineering hours. Young men trained mostly at the California Institute of Technology, working in a factory in California, put in 200,000 hours of concentrated thought to develop that machine. Flying at all times at the altitude which was most favorable to the operation of the plane with a load aboard constantly varying as the fuel was consumed, we completed this flight without at any time using more than 590 horsepower of the 625 horsepower per engine approved by the Department of Commerce for normal cruising."

Hughes paid his respects to the purpose of the flight in the field of international cooperation and expressed his hope that this flight would stimulate the sale of American airplanes to foreign airlines. This was a time when the United States was just pulling out of the depths of the worst depression in its history and employment opportunities were a matter of great significance. He suggested the possibility that this flight would provide more jobs in the airplane factories of the United States.

With the ceremonies ended at last, Hughes was forced to use his whole bag of tricks to escape both the official party with their good wishes, and the hundreds of New York citizens who simply wanted to look at him. He executed a previously planned maneuver in which the limousine he rode in stopped at an office building. There he jumped out, dashed into the building, ran through an exit on the other side where another limousine waited, and was whisked away to pick up Katherine Hepburn for a private evening.

Hughes apparently enjoyed the adulation of the crowd for his achievement. Unlike him though it was, he accepted requests to speak at receptions across the country. The content of his speeches was basically the same. He usually paid tribute to Wiley Post, always shaking his head ruefully as he said, "That was one of the most remarkable feats of all time. I really don't know how that man could have done it all alone." Then, he would emphasize that flying had achieved the status of a science and was no longer a seat-of-the-pants affair. He continually emphasized that carried out properly and scientifically, flying was both certain and safe.

He particularly enjoyed his reception at Houston. Despite the fact that this was the center of his financial empire, the home of the Hughes Tool Company, he rarely was able to spend any time there. Now he addressed a gathering near the plant where thousands of employees of Toolco saw him in person for the first time. Whether he meant it or not, he tactfully acknowledged his indebtedness to them, saying, "I realize that were it not for you men and women and your diligent work, I would probably be pushing a plow."

Repeatedly, varying only the words, he offered the following simile: "When you use your vacuum cleaner in the home, you don't talk about how smart you are—you talk about how smart the man was who invented it." He gave credit to the engineers, the scientists, the factory workmen, the test pilots, and all those others who had made this plane possible.

Addressing a banquet in the evening like a true Texan, he told the assembled guests, "Being from Texas particularly fits a person for flying around the world. There is nothing you can see anywhere you can't see in Texas. After you have flown across Texas two or three times, the distance around the world doesn't seem so great. We didn't see any mountains on our trip that were any steeper than the mountains of West Texas. We didn't see any plains broader than the plains of Central Texas. And we didn't see any swamps that were any wetter than the swamps of Houston."

Hughes was a hero even to the left wing press. Epitomizing the feelings of the left from Moscow to New York, the *New Republic* said, "Simple in manner, careless in dress, unconscious of social distinctions, he devotes his superior capacities to the conquest of new difficulties." The weekly called him "a man of broad interests and intelligence," and completed its panegyric with the statement, "Hughes has not allowed himself to be spoiled by inherited wealth."

For a time Howard Hughes was the toast of Texas and many parents named their children after him. As Hughes traveled westward on his return to California the press turned him into a national hero, with its multitudinous reports on his life and exploits. *Time* described him as the young man who looked like Gary Cooper and flew like Lindbergh.

Howard Hughes and His Bosomy Western

THE YEAR 1940

HITLER SAID he foresaw victory in 1941.

The United States was working around the clock to become the arsenal of democracy and deliver the war materials necessary for the allies to win the war.

The Japanese indicated clearly that they did not want to fight the Western powers. A *New York Times* headline read, "Japan is not anxious to fight for the Axis" and a feature story proclaimed, "Powerful internal forces would come into play to prevent an attack on us for the benefit of Germany."

One of the difficult problems confronting British officials was combating unseen German air raiders flying at great heights, sometimes five to seven miles up, under cover of darkness and beyond the effective range of anti-aircraft fire.

In the movies: Clark Gable and Hedy Lamarr in *Comrade X;* Walt Disney's *Fantasia;* Charlie Chaplin in *The Great Dictator;* and Henry Fonda and Dorothy Lamour in *Chad Hanna.*

Hits on the stage: Ethel Waters in *Cabin in the Sky;* José Ferrer in *Charlie's Aunt;* Olsen and Johnson's *Hellzapoppin;* Al Jolson and Martha Raye in *Hold on to Your Hats;* Ethel Merman in *Panama Hattie.*

Books: Ernest Hemingway, *For Whom the Bell Tolls;* Taylor (Janet) Caldwell, *The Earth Is the Lord's;* Clare Boothe, *Europe in the Spring;* Willa Cather, *Sapphira and the Slave Girl;* Howard Spring, *Fame Is the Spur;* and Kenneth Roberts, *Oliver Wiswell.*

Howard Hughes was thirty-four years old.

181

13

In 1940, after a lapse of eight years, Howard Hughes decided to make another motion picture. For his return to Filmland he selected the story of Billy the Kid. Although involved with many other ventures, including his tool company and his aircraft company, Hughes found time to assemble the basic elements of what would become a landmark motion picture. As Murray Schumach, Hollywood reporter for the *New York Times* wrote in his book on movie censorship, *The Face on the Cutting Room Floor,* it was Howard Hughes' film which brought "mammary madness" to the movies. Schumach added it was a "Hollywood fixation that has still not abated."

The script was not extraordinary. Billy the Kid was portrayed as a typical young western lout whose major interests in life were horses and girls. In a bar Billy meets, and in a barn rapes, the heroine—Rio—with sufficient finesse to avoid tearing her dress.

Billy the Kid and Rio's steady boy friend, the well-known gambler, Doc Halliday, meet and become friends. (Doc doesn't know that Billy has raped his girl.) During one of his frequent pistol duels, Billy is wounded. Sought by the Law, Billy turns to Doc for help and Doc arranges for Rio to hide him and nurse him back to health, warning Rio that it is vital that Billy be kept warm. Rio, remembering how Billy raped her, debates silently whether to let him die, but her better nature triumphs and she cares for him diligently. When Billy has a chill and nothing seems to help, Rio gets into bed with him and warms him with her body. When Doc returns, he creates a scene. Billy, to placate his friend, offers Doc an intriguing alternative.

He says, "There is the best horse in the West. You can have that horse, or I'll get on it, ride away, and leave you Rio."

Doc had been using Billy's horse and the implication is clear that, having enjoyed both Rio and the pony, Doc would prefer the pony.

Even before shooting began Hughes launched his publicity campaign. At a cocktail party he had met Russell Birdwell, the Hollywood press agent who had handled the publicity for *Gone With the Wind*, and he had not forgotten him. Hughes hired Birdwell to ballyhoo *Billy the Kid* with a campaign that would dwarf *Gone With the Wind*. After a midnight session with Hughes at his Hollywood bungalow Birdwell happily undertook the task.

Hughes outlined frankly for Birdwell his intention to make sex a major feature of the movie. Furthermore the heroine of the picture would be a woman whose breasts could symbolize sex to America.

Birdwell started his promotion immediately and the first results were predictable. Early in December of 1940 Joseph Breen, then head of the office responsible for granting Seals of Approval to motion pictures, wrote to Hughes:

"I 'see by the papers,' as Mr. Dooley used to say, that you have begun shooting on your picture and it occurs to me that you ought to let us have a copy of your shooting script, with a view toward examining it, against the possibility that there may be some details in it, which will have to be deleted or changed in the finished picture."

Even Howard Hughes could not ignore or deny such a request, so he sent a copy of the script to the Breen office.

When *The Outlaw* was filmed a quarter of a century ago neither the sexsploitation film nor the nudie movie had yet made its appearance in the commercial cinema. The Hollywood Code was stringent and imperious. Sex had to be subdued; evil had to be punished; the body must be clothed; a woman's possession of breasts could be hinted at, but never demonstrated; all in all, subtlety was the order of the day.

The Breen Office, surrounded by rules and regulations governing the permissible and verboten in movie-making, now found itself confronted by a script which contained such *bon mots* as the following:

Doc Halliday learned that Rio had gotten into bed with Billy to keep him warm and Doc was not pleased. In defense of the humane maneuver, Billy the Kid remarks: "Well, you went off with my horse."

Doc replies, "Well, you were not in any shape to use it."

To which remark Billy retorts, "A fair exchange is no robbery."

At another point Billy offers to return Rio to Doc. Billy tells him, "If you want her back you can have her and welcome. Now what do you think about that?"

To which Doc Halliday replies, "I don't want her now. Cattle don't graze after sheep."

The rape scene included a daring line. Billy says, "Hold still, lady, or you won't have much dress left."

Later, when Rio gets into bed with the wounded Billy to keep him warm one of her first remarks is, "Be careful, your wound, you'll hurt yourself."

Mr. Breen, having read the script, dashed off a hasty note to Howard Hughes stating that the shooting script contained elements which would render the movie unacceptable to his office. He suggested that changes be made in the objectionable dialogue. In addition, suspecting that Hughes intended to pioneer in the field of partial nudity, Breen also recommended that Jane Russell be fully covered and, in scenes where she was going to wear a nightgown, she should also wear a bathrobe.

With respect to the scene where Rio gets into bed with Billy the censorship office naively suggested that "care will be needed . . . to avoid sex suggestiveness." All in all, the letter, the first shot in what would become the battles of the missives, listed twenty-three specific objections.

Hughes almost certainly perused Joseph Breen's suggestions. He then proceeded to ignore them all.

Faced with the threat of censorship, Hughes protected the picture with unusual security precautions. Even the actors were not permitted to see the rushes.

In the search for a female star for *Billy the Kid* Hughes scrutinized and rejected over five hundred applicants. One day an agent showed him a photograph of Jane Russell and he at once approved her for the lead.

Ernestine Jane Geraldine Russell was a $10-a-week receptionist in a doctor's office. She was nineteen years old and had graduated from high school one year before. She lived in a Van Nuys, California, ranch house with her widowed mother and on Friday evenings she played piano in an orchestra with which her four brothers also performed. Her mother, who had been an actress, named Jane after the famous actress, Jane Cowl. The stage-struck mother had insisted that the child take acting lessons.

Shooting of *Billy the Kid* began on location in the Arizona desert with two hundred and fifty actors and technicians. Each day's shooting was flown back to Hughes in Los Angeles by private plane.

Every day Hughes would return the plane to Director Howard Hawks, with suggestions that usually called for additional expenditures of money.

Hawks was appalled by the extravagance. He said he wanted to resign as director. Hughes could not possibly accept a simple resignation, but when he saw that Hawks was not following his suggestions and that the picture was not developing as he visualized it, he arranged to take over himself by what was probably the most unusual method in the history of American filmdom.

Hawks was on location in Arizona, surrounded by hundreds of actors and technicians, multitudinous props and equipment, and all the other paraphernalia of movie-making. Hughes arranged for his scouts (spies?) to advise him of the first day when the director left the area to search for locations for later scenes in the film. On that same day Hughes sent his chartered train to pick up the entire company, all costumes, equipment, and other accoutrements, and return them to Hollywood. When the director returned to the location he found that his entire company had vanished, bag and baggage!

Hughes was so busy during this period that he could not always be on the set as director. Consequently, he appointed the script writer, Jules Furthman, as assistant director and instructed him on what was expected of him during Hughes' absences. Unfortunately, Furthman had some ideas of his own, one of which was that he would not work after 5:00 P.M. Hughes, of course, kept in touch with Furthman with telephone calls at completely unpredictable hours of the night. The writer instructed his housemaid that he was not to be awakened at night. Hughes had a persuasive and compelling manner and could usually convince most maids to violate orders. Late one night—well after midnight—Hughes called, only to be informed by the maid that she could not call Furthman. Automatically Hughes argued that the matter was urgent and Furthman must be called.

The maid replied, "He has a gun. He told me that if I woke him up again he'd shoot me."

Hughes also had explosive difficulties with two very experienced actors, Thomas Mitchell and Walter Huston. Hughes, always the perfectionist, insisted on retakes until he achieved exactly what he had in mind. Thomas Mitchell, playing the sheriff, was short-tempered, proud, and had no great love for Hughes. The actor could frequently be heard advising the director in a scornful, booming voice that he knew absolutely nothing about directing a picture.

The entire cast was on edge but Hughes kept fighting for the performance he wanted.

In the midst of the shooting, and to Hughes' great annoyance, MGM began to make a picture about the young outlaw and even had the effrontery to call it *Billy the Kid*. The MGM vehicle starring Robert Taylor was completed long before Hughes had reached the halfway mark, so he had to change the title of his picture to *The Outlaw*.

Faithful to his original plan, Hughes focused a great deal of cinematic attention on Jane Russell's breasts. Advisers close to Hughes during the making of the film suggested that he play it with a light touch for laughs. Schumach, in *The Face on the Cutting Room Floor,* quotes one of the workers on the set, "Hughes was a great student of the obvious. He believed in putting everything on the floor. He had Jane Russell bend over Billy and had the camera peering down to her navel. He claimed this shot had never been done before. He was right. No one else in Hollywood would have dared to try it."

During the making of *The Outlaw* Hughes suffered a serious head injury in an auto accident. He tried to direct the film by telephone from the hospital, using Furthman as his amanuensis. This proved to be one of his less successful ideas and before long, his head swathed in bandages, Hughes was back on the set in person intent on completing his epic. Perfectionist that he was, no matter how much of Jane Russell's breasts the camera revealed, Hughes remained unsatisfied. He commented, "We're not getting enough production out of Jane's breasts."

In one scene Jane was tied by leather thongs between two trees. The leather was wetted down to cause it to shrink, thus stretching the hapless victim on a crude but effective rack. Although the scene was shot and reshot, Hughes still did not obtain the proper effect. Finally he concluded that the problem was caused by the brassiere Jane wore. At once he sent for a drafting board. Utilizing his knowledge of aerodynamics, cantilevering, and other engineering principles, he designed a new bra for Jane Russell which would give her breasts the proper prominence as they heaved about in her agony. In certain quarters Howard Hughes is probably better known for this brassiere design than for anything else he ever accomplished.

At long last, in the spring of 1941 the picture was ready for screening by the Production Code Office. Joseph Breen viewed the film, then wrote to Hughes:

"We had the pleasure this afternoon of witnessing a projection-room showing of your production, titled *The Outlaw* and as I have already told you, the picture is definitely and specifically in violation of our Production Code and because of this cannot be approved." After enumerating a number of defects the letter continued, "There is undoubtedly an inescapable suggestion of an illicit relationship between Doc and Rio and between Billy and Rio . . . also we object to the countless shots of Rio, in which her breasts are not fully covered."

In disputes over the granting of a Seal of Approval, the procedure up to this point had been standard. However, the letter sent by Breen to his boss, Will Hays, was out of the ordinary:

"In my more than ten years of critical examination of motion pictures I have never seen anything quite so unacceptable as the shots of the breasts of the character Rio. This is the young girl whom Mr. Hughes recently picked up and who has never before, according to my information, appeared on the motion picture screen. Throughout almost half the picture the girl's breasts, which are quite large and prominent, are shockingly uncovered." He continued in this vein and finally warned that this might launch a trend to "undrape women's breasts."

In spite of demands for changes and cuts Hughes refused to give in. A legal battle was inevitable. Hughes appealed from Breen's decision. The officials of the Motion Picture Association of America conducted a hearing on his appeals. At this time Hughes gathered stills of all of the famous female breast pictures ever shown in Hollywood movies. These he had posted around the hearing room. When the officers of the association met to solemnly deliberate on whether or not to grant a Seal of Approval to *The Outlaw*, the august censors found themselves surrounded by enormous stills of all the conspicuously endowed stars from Jean Harlow to Rita Hayworth, Ann Sheridan, Marlene Dietrich, and Betty Grable. Hughes also had a witness, a mathematician, who, using drafting instruments, showed how Jane Russell's breasts were no more public than those of many others. Finally, after considerable infighting, the association appointed special committees to make extraordinary studies. Hughes agreed to some changes, and a Seal of Approval was granted on March 23, 1941.

One amusing aspect of the controversy developed over the words "a fair exchange is no robbery." This had to do with the ethics of exchanging a lady for a horse. Hughes considered this line too highbrow and changed it to "You borrowed from me, I borrow from you."

Breen objected to the change in language, and Furthman, the script writer, asked Breen to suggest substitute wording. Breen offered, "Why don't you say, 'Tit for tat?' "

Hughes was delighted and the picture was shot that way, although Jack Buetel had difficulty keeping a straight face when he used the line. However, in the final cutting prior to the grant of the Seal the Hays Office demanded that this line be stricken and the original Hughes line restored. Hughes accepted the change.

In February, 1943, the picture was ready for its premiere at the Geary Theatre in San Francisco. Russell Birdwell, the highly paid publicist for the picture, brought in fifty columnists and their wives on a three-day junket to San Francisco for the premiere. One report indicates that the first-night audience, consisting of the fifty, their wives, and sundry invited dignitaries, sat politely embarrassed as the picture unfolded. The picture grew steadily cornier and the polite stares grew incredulous. Finally, the audience broke down completely, laughing at the serious scenes, groaning at the funny ones, and guffawing raucously at that scene of scenes when Jane Russell, intent on nursing the wounded Billy, gets undressed with the announced intention of getting into bed with him because he is supposed to be kept warm and there are not enough blankets.

Of the first night critics only one, Hughes' old friend Louella Parsons, was kind to the picture. A typical review said, "The general impression was that Red, the horse, stole all the honors."

Birdwell was an accomplished publicist. Following Hughes' instructions to make both Jane Russell and *The Outlaw* household words, he covered the American periodical scene like a blanket, and by the time *The Outlaw* appeared, Jane Russell and her treasures were familiar to most adult Americans.

Unfortunately, this kind of publicity was not enough. Using his own ingenuity and without guidance by Hughes, it is said, Birdwell schemed to get the picture censored by the authorities. Presumably there were phone calls and complaints to the police but nothing happened. Then a whispering campaign started. "You ought to see Reel 3. It's the wildest thing you've ever seen." The Geary Theatre began to get calls which asked, "When will Reel 3 start?"

By this time San Francisco had become a major port of embarkation for the Pacific War Theater and had a large transient population of soldiers and sailors. Word spread rapidly that there was something called Reel 3 in *The Outlaw* that ought to be seen by everyone.

As a result of these rumors, business increased and so did censorship. The local police heard the story of Reel 3 and finally they seized it. In a jury trial in Municipal Court the film was cleared.

Judge Twain Michaelsen said, "I cannot bring myself to the legal conclusion that the picture, *The Outlaw*, has left you ladies and gentlemen of the jury in a state of moral suspense, or of mental lewdness and licentiousness, bewitched and seduced. . . ."

The advertising grew wilder. One women's group wrote to the Hays Office, "A very disgusting portrayal of a feminine star of *The Outlaw* was displayed throughout the San Francisco Bay Section on large billboards."

Even Darryl F. Zanuck, head of the 20th Century Fox studio, wrote to Joseph Breen, "The whole advertising campaign on this picture is a disgrace to the Industry."

The supreme promotion coup occurred when, as one commentator said, "The picture's publicity man had achieved a literal new high in vulgarity. Over Pasadena, a skywriting plane traced *The Outlaw*, then drew two huge circles side by side and placed a dot in the center of each."

Suddenly with no warning, and no explanation, the film was withdrawn. Despite the high production cost, despite all the money spent on the publicity campaign, despite the censorship battles, the picture simply vanished. Howard Hughes had called his chief engineer, Glen Odekirk, and ordered him to drop everything and come to Los Angeles. Once there he was instructed to build a special room at the headquarters at 7000 Romaine Street, lined with lead walls, and make it the repository for the original negative of *The Outlaw*.

It was not that Hughes had lost interest in the picture. He was simply too busy at that moment building a plane that the Army might buy, maintaining production on Army material contracts, and designing and constructing the Flying Boat.

Three years later Hughes found time to return to *The Outlaw*. According to the film industry rules Hughes had to submit all advertising to the Advertising Code Authority in order to keep his Seal of Approval. Hughes duly submitted some of his copy to the Authority but when it began to evince some disapprovals, he authorized advertisements without regard to its endorsement. The United States was blanketed with *Outlaw* advertisements in newspapers, magazines and on billboards. Anguished screams of protest were voiced by the bluenoses.

Life magazine said, "The unmitigated vulgarity of the movie itself was outdone only by the offensiveness of its advertising. This Hughes personally prepared and directed, and he has the dubious distinction of having authored the slogan 'HOW WOULD YOU LIKE TO TUSSLE WITH RUSSELL?' "

This slogan to which *Life* objected appeared under a large photograph of Jane Russell which highlighted her breast development. The same photo was used with other lines such as:

"WHAT ARE THE TWO GREAT REASONS FOR JANE RUSSELL'S RISE TO STARDOM?"

"WHO WOULDN'T FIGHT FOR A WOMAN LIKE THIS?"

"THE GIRL WITH THE SUMMER-HOT LIPS . . . AND THE WINTER-COLD HEART."

Irritated by Hughes' disregard of their approval, the Motion Picture Association took an action which was probably unprecedented at that time—it withdrew the Seal of Approval which it had previously granted. MPA offered as its reason for such action the fact that, in direct violation of the rules of the Association, Hughes had used unapproved advertising matter.

Threatened with loss of the Seal of Approval of the Association, Hughes instituted legal action to obtain an injunction to prevent the withdrawal. Even for the litigious Hughes, this was a radical action because a victory would, in effect, result in destruction of the power of the Association to police films and their advertising, and consequently would destroy the M.P.A. itself.

The continued functioning of the Hays Office was of paramount importance to the film industry because it represented an insulating barrier against individual censorship by forty-eight states and hundreds of local communities. The Office had not been organized

to make movies cleaner or better. It functioned primarily to protect
the industry from being inundated by censorship problems. Will H.
Hays, Postmaster General of the United States under President
Warren Harding, had resigned from the Cabinet to head the or-
ganization. It was a time when the typical fare offered to the view-
ing audience consisted of such titles as *Hot Lips, Virgin Paradise,
Scrambled Wives, Her Purchase Price*, and similar works of art.
Shortly after the end of World War I almost every state in the
Union was either considering, or had already adopted, censorship
legislation.

The existence of these individual boards with their diverse and
multitudinous requirements gave a nightmare quality to the working lives of the movie-makers. To make movies differently for each
state was expensive and difficult. The establishment of the Hays
Office rendered unnecessary these individual censorship boards. To
a considerable extent the Hays Office was successful in accomplishing what it had set out to do. Although not all state censorship
disappeared, much of it became painless and harmless.

Now along came Howard Hughes to threaten all of this expensive
and valuable machinery. He threatened it in two ways. In the first
place he attacked in the courts the entire association and its Seal
of Approval system, and in the second place he began national distribution of *The Outlaw* without a Seal. Up to that time no producer of an expensive Hollywood production had ever dared such
a step.

The Hughes Tool Company, owner of *The Outlaw*, filed the legal
action in the Federal District Court in New York.

The Hughes Complaint charged that over 90% of the theatres
in the United States would not show a picture unless it had the Seal
of the Association.

Having set forth the facts in its suit, Hughes Tool Company
offered two major arguments:

First, the system of approval constituted illegal censorship and
was therefore a violation of the First Amendment of the United
States Constitution which prohibited abridgment of freedom of
speech. Toolco therefore requested the court to declare the Hollywood system of censoring movies and film advertising illegal and
further requested modest damages of $1 million.

Second, Toolco argued, the entire association, its producers, and
its methods were in violation of the federal Sherman Anti-Trust

Law. Such a system of seals was a restraint on interstate commerce in violation of the Sherman Act and for this violation the plaintiff asked for slightly larger damages of $5 million.

In addition, the court was asked to enjoin the association from continuing its operation and to prevent the withdrawal of the Seal from *The Outlaw*.

A battery of the finest attorneys in the country offered oral arguments and submitted fat briefs. Nonetheless the court refused the injunction and ruled against Hughes Tool Company on the following grounds:

It had been clearly shown that on various occasions the makers of *The Outlaw* used advertising which had not been submitted to the Advertising Code Administration and which was of "such character as to incur the condemnation of public authorities and its consequent withdrawal."

Furthermore, said Federal District Judge John Bright, the facts made it clear that Howard Hughes "has sought and still seeks to arrogate to himself the decision of what advertising should be indulged in, regardless . . . of the rules and regulations of the Association of which his production company was a member."

In commenting upon this advertising the court remarked, "The advertising now in controversy in substance consists of pictures, cuts and lithographs of a lady, Rio, featuring more her breasts, legs and positions than the saga of Billy the Kid. . . ."

In considering the seriousness of censorship and the demands made by the Advertising Code Administration the judge pointed out that a series of pen-and-ink drawings was rejected because the administration felt "slightly too much of the breasts were shown" and that the office had suggested "a slight retouching, that is, by raising of the blouse a fraction of an inch" would render it completely satisfactory and permissible. However, Hughes had adamantly refused to give that fraction!

Other objectionable shots "showed a man and woman together in the hay in a compromising horizontal position."

The court found that the entire system adopted by the Motion Picture Association was fair and to hold it invalid would be against public interest in favor of a private selfish interest. At one point in its opinion the court stated:

"Plaintiff's real complaint seems to be that because he claims to have invested two million dollars and that *The Outlaw* is the only picture which it has produced since 1941 and its entire status as a producer is at stake on this one production, the defendant's 'threat to revoke the Seal' must be gauged on the basis of financial loss that may be involved and of plaintiff's capacity to go on producing motion pictures."

Judge Bright answered by saying that this problem was one of Hughes' own making. Thus, in his legal jousting with the Seal granters Hughes came out second best.

He didn't do much better in his battles with state and city censorship. State after state, and even municipalities, where there were local censorship boards, insisted upon cuts and changes. In some places the cuts were so injurious to the picture that Hughes had to carry his fight to the courts, where he usually lost.

A Maryland judge upheld a complete ban on the picture and made a comment that has gone down in movie annals as one of the famous opinions of the film. He remarked that Jane Russell's breasts "hung over the picture like a thunderstorm spread out over a summer landscape."

In Ohio the entire conversation between Doc and Billy the Kid that took place after the young gunman had recovered from his illness and after Rio had warmed him with her body in bed, was deleted. Since it was an integral part of the action it created a jolting gap.

New York also made a number of cuts, including deletion of the line, "Cattle don't graze after sheep" used by Doc to explain why he was no longer interested in Rio.

In Massachusetts, in addition to alterations and deletions, the movie was prohibited from being shown on Sunday.

Censorship problems cropped up all over the world, wherever *The Outlaw* was screened. In Alberta, Canada, the censors even required changes in the trailer shown to advertise the picture as one of the coming attractions at a particular theatre. In Ontario, the censors cut the entire conversation between Billy the Kid and Jane Russell during the rape scene. In Australia and Great Britain the censors objected to the amount of visible flesh of Jane Russell's breasts.

All of the publicized difficulty with censorship boards, the courts, and the Motion Picture Association had its effect on the box office. When the picture opened in a Los Angeles theater in 1946 the sidewalk in front of the movie house was jammed by 10 o'clock in the morning and although it had been customary for all the theaters in the area to show double features, this theatre abandoned the practice during the showing of *The Outlaw*.

The *Los Angeles Daily News* reported, "What packed them in was . . . an opportunity for anatomical research."

The picture arrived at the Broadway Theater in New York on September 12, 1947. *The New York Times* reviewer was most uncomplimentary:

"This is strictly a second-rate Western, loud and tedious and crudely acted for the most part and a great deal more soporific than swashbuckling. Of course, a great attraction of the film was supposed to be some torrid love scenes, but there have been enough cuts to leave it hanging pretty much in the air.

"It is a long-drawn-out story which could have been told in one-tenth of the time about a friendship between two gunfighters who quarrel for two hours as to who owns a horse and in between they shoot a few people, escape from Indians and a sheriff and take a half-breed girl along for decoration."

The reviewer admitted that Jane Russell was "undeniably decorative in low-cut blouses" but added that she was "hopelessly inept as an actress."

The critics did differ on one point. *The New York Times* called the picture "unintentionally funny."

On the other hand, John McCarten, writing in the *New Yorker* (and neither the reviewer nor the organ was celebrated for kindness to second-grade movies) had a different opinion. McCarten said that having seen Hughes publicly he had been of the opinion that the man was rather solemn but after seeing *The Outlaw* he believed Hughes was a wag. He continued that "with sardonic ingenuity" Hughes combined the diametric opposites of a Western and a burlesque. Jane Russell, he pointed out, was the antithesis of the shy girl in calico and Jack Buetel was the antonym of the strapping desperado. Together they made an amusing picture. The *New Yorker* reviewer noted that many people would not agree that Hughes did so consciously, but he insisted: "I am confident that no man could have handled the history of the Kid in this manner unless he knew what he was up to."

Time said the picture was going to be "either the best or the worst picture of the year."

The *Hollywood Reporter* of September 15, 1947, stated, "Judged by *The Outlaw* which flatly states Hughes directed and produced it, and which statement Hughes has never denied, Hughes' determination is compounded of arrogance, stubbornness and contempt for all people, not only Senators."

For a few years the picture played in those relatively few theaters that would show a movie which did not possess a Seal. Then Hughes capitulated and made the necessary changes and deletions which would win back the Seal of Approval. Even the Catholic Church's Legion of Decency altered its absolute condemnation rating to a B rating which meant, "Morally objectionable in part for all people." This was a not unusual classification and the furor abated. The film was good box office. Wherever it went people poured in to see it.

Murray Schumach in *The Face on the Cutting Room Floor* says, "*The Outlaw* proved that bad publicity, if there is enough of it, can be good box office." This same author also wrote, "Regardless of Hughes' motives, he brought some refreshing honesty to Hollywood's approach to sex. He made the American public laugh a little at its own prudery about the female breasts. If ever a cinematic Rabelais emerges from Hollywood, he will be indebted to this unusual industrialist. Hughes lacked artistry. But he is not afraid to show, on a movie screen, that sex, even without a license, can be fun."

All comments on *The Outlaw* at that time tended to be prejudiced by the viewpoint of the viewer or reviewer. Many years later George N. Fenn and William K. Everson wrote *The Western,* which was the first definitively analytical book on the cowboy movie, and in their analysis they give considerable credit to Hughes and *The Outlaw.* They call the film largely responsible for a complete change in the Western movie on the erotic level. Prior to *The Outlaw,* Westerns were devoid of sex. After the Hughes contribution, the Western began to exploit or utilize sex and "the Western heroine took to provocatively tight and unbuttoned shirts and blouses, equally undersized men's trousers, silk stockings, and flimsy negligees and similar accessories."

It is still difficult to conclude whether Hughes was a panderer for a sex film, a sincere advocate of freedom from censorship for Hollywood, or a tongue-in-cheek moviemaker who was kidding his audience. Regardless of which view one takes there can be no doubt that in *The Outlaw* Hughes made a major contribution to American film art. He started his epic when it was illegal to show the inside of a woman's thigh or more than one inch of breast cleavage and succeeded in shattering the entire moral touchstone of movie-making. Today when the completely nude female breast, nipple and all, is standard fare in many movies, those who prefer the modern frankness must extend a vote of thanks to Howard Hughes.

No discussion of *The Outlaw* would be complete without a post-script referring to the unusual publicity jackpot hit by a young English press-agent, Suzanne Warner. Anything was permissible in the campaign to give the picture the utmost publicity coverage.

In London, although critics unanimously sneered at the picture, it played to record crowds all over and broke the record at the London Pavilion. Part of this success was due to the ingenuity of Miss Warner who hired a psychologist with a psycho-galvanometer to go to the Pavilion and measure the reaction and emotional response of people watching the film.

Miss Warner and her psychologist tested people against the background music alone, without the film, and the reading came to 15 centimeters. Then they tested members of the audience, and critics particularly, while watching the picture. Dick Richards, critic of the London *Sunday Pictorial,* registered 28 centimeters when he saw Jane in a loose, low-cut bodice. A lady moviegoer who asserted a complete indifference to any sex on the screen hit 29 centimeters when Jane was getting into Jack Buetel's bed. All in all, Miss Warner had a field day with one of the world's most inaccurate measuring devices. However, this was typical of the kind of publicity gimmicks used to promote the movie.

The present successor to Breen is Geoffrey M. Shurlock, who says about the picture, "The breast exposure that caused the uproar in *The Outlaw* would not create much excitement today. Still Hughes corrupted the whole world on this mammary gland business. He started the exploitation of big breasts. He started the cinematic avalanche of breasts."

Howard Hughes and
His Motion Picture Studio

MAY, 1948

JEWISH FORCES seized the southwestern part of Jerusalem after savage fighting with the Arabs.

The United States proposed that the United Nations Trusteeship Council create a temporary trusteeship arrangement for Jerusalem and offered to participate in troop forces to maintain order in the Holy Land.

Making a survey of television, Nathan M. Rudich, television editor of the *Theatre Arts Magazine*, told an Institute for Education meeting that the general saying "Television is here" might be supplanted soon with the saying, "Television was here and it is rapidly passing us by." His point was that there were very few programs that had any value aside from sports telecasts.

Before a shrieking crowd of 100,000 people the 74th running of the Kentucky Derby at Churchill Downs found the horse Citation coming in an easy first. Eddie Arcaro was the winning jockey.

The top books being read were Lockridge, *Raintree County;* Wilder, *The Ides of March,* and Williams, *House Divided.* In the non-fiction class the Kinsey Report, *Sexual Behavior in the Human Male,* was very popular.

In the movies Fred MacMurray and Frank Sinatra starred in *The Miracle of the Bells;* Burt Lancaster and Lizabeth Scott were in *Walk Alone;* Robert Young and Marguerite Chapman starred in *Relentless.*

In the theater we had *A Streetcar Named Desire, Born Yesterday, Brigadoon, Harvey, High-Button Shoes* and *Mr. Roberts*.

In business there was a paradox—while General Motors Corporation set a new peacetime high-mark for earnings, Chrysler reported its profits were sharply down.

Howard Hughes was forty-two years old.

14

In 1905 John R. Freuler of Milwaukee invested $900 with a Milwaukee ex-policeman who thought that money could be made showing movies in a public nickelodeon. They opened a store-front emporium and began to supply exhibitors with products for their own nickelodeons. Benjamin F. Keith of Boston—a master of vaudeville—soon joined them in the business.

The Milwaukee operation became the Western Film Exchange and later the Mutual Film Corporation. Soon Mutual was well known as a distributor of films for use in small movie houses or nickelodeons.

Mutual Film Corporation was a dynamic innovator. It was responsible for the system of paying astronomical salaries to stars. For example, in 1916 Charlie Chaplin received $670,000 for twelve two-reel comedies, this at a time when the average wage of a worker was between $1 and $2 per day!

In 1927 Joseph P. Kennedy, father of the late president, acquired the controlling interest in the Keith-Albee-Orpheum Corporation. Like many other American corporations, Keith-Albee was unable to withstand the depression and on January 27, 1933, it went into receivership. At this time it became known as RKO Corporation.

Floyd Odlum, the West Coast financier, first became interested in RKO in 1935 while the company was still in receivership. By the time receivership ended in 1940 Odlum owned the largest single block of stock and became chairman of the board. The company began its new operation with a sound financing plan involving $8 million in cash and no debt. *Fortune* commented on Odlum's viewpoint at the time:

"Odlum's approach to RKO was simplicity itself. He was not a boyish personality bent on amusing himself with a motion-picture studio. (From an adolescent's point of view probably the most ir-

resistible toy that man had ever devised.) He had no neurotic
appetite for power over people. Nor was he an egocentric, determined that every foot of film should bear his personal imprimatur.
He simply wanted to make RKO into a vigorous, profitable company, then sell his stock at a price reflecting that improvement."

For several years Odlum devoted himself to rearranging per-
sonnel and revising operations at RKO until he had a moneymaker.
RKO finished the year 1943 with a profit after taxes of upwards of
$7 million. For several years thereafter, in spite of many difficulties,
RKO showed a profit.

In 1946 Odlum brought in Dore Schary to take charge of production. At that time filmdom was suffering from some illnesses.
The proceeds from international distribution, long a stable source
of income for the cinema producer, were frozen in most countries.
Although the shows could be exhibited, the profits could not be removed—primarily as a result of a dollar shortage in most foreign
countries. Also, Congressman Parnell Thomas had started a Communist witch hunt, and he fixed his eye on the movie industry.

Odlum decided to sell his RKO stock. In the year 1946 the value
of a share of stock had fluctuated between $15.00 and $28.00. The
company enjoyed a prestige position in the motion picture industry. It maintained major studios in Hollywood and in Culver City,
ninety acres of land in Los Angeles, and a film-producing company
in Mexico City. Also, RKO had a wholly owned subsidiary which
controlled a chain of one hundred and twenty-four motion picture
theaters throughout the United States. Fifty-three of these were
owned in fee and the balance were leased. There were twenty-six
theaters in New York City alone. The nation-wide chain ranged
from center city theaters in major cities to two in Sioux City, Iowa,
and one in Champaign, Illinois. The company had a net worth in
excess of $100 million with an earned surplus of $23.5 million. It
had paid out dividends to shareholders averaging $3.5 million an-
nually for several years.

There were 3,924,911 ¾ shares outstanding, and Floyd Odlum
owned 929,000 of them. This gave him undisputed control. His
asking price for these shares was approximately $9 million (about
$10 per share—below market). There were not many interested
prospective buyers, and Odlum got his first serious offer in mid-
January of 1948 when Howard Hughes flew down to see him in
San Diego. They discussed the proposition for only an hour, after

which Hughes announced he was going back to his home in Beverly Hills to think about it.

Floyd Odlum issued a release to the press, "Under today's almost panicky conditions in Hollywood, no one has the combined money and nerve to meet the faith of Atlas Corporation [Odlum's own company] in the industry."

The statement was probably intended to sting Hughes into action, but it was not the movie-maker's nature to respond to gibes.

Hughes did negotiate with Odlum, but not in an ordinary way.

Always suspicious of wiretapping, of being overheard and of being spied upon, Hughes' wariness became even greater after his experiences in Washington during the Senate investigating committee hearings in 1947. He had obtained evidence, which did not become public until a few years later, that Mrs. Frances Dustin, Senator Brewster's administrative assistant, had made a payment to Lieutenant J. W. Shimon of the District of Columbia Police, who had tapped Hughes' hotel phones. Later Lieutenant Shimon claimed he had not received any pay for wiretapping. Nevertheless a policeman named John McHale testified that he saw Shimon putting a thousand-dollar bill in his pocket after talking to two unidentified men. Reasonably good evidence also indicated an attempt to plant a microphone in Hughes' hotel room.

Hughes, therefore, refused to sit down with anyone in an office to negotiate. Instead, meetings took place in parked cars on lonely streets in the middle of the night, in airplanes, anonymous hotel rooms, and railroad stations.

When Hughes wanted to confer with someone, he would arrange to have that person notified to stand by for a phone call at a specified hour. Then he would be notified to wait on a certain street corner at a particular time, where he would be picked up by a dark blue car. This might be followed by several transfers to other cars and the trip might finally end on a desert road, in a small hotel room, or in the front seat of another nondescript battered car.

Negotiations with Odlum continued in this unorthodox manner for four months. In May, 1948, Hughes bought Odlum's stock and took over control of RKO. He paid $9.50 per share, or a total of $8,825,500. The market price had been dipping rapidly so this was slightly above the market.

Fortune gives as the reason for his purchase that he was moved by "two of his abiding interests, prestige and money." Unquestionably, he was especially interested in the one hundred and twenty-four theaters of which he gained control in the transaction. He had always experienced a considerable amount of distribution difficulty, ,but he had confidence in his own productions and believed that if they were exhibited properly they would make money. The RKO deal gave him a means of distribution. Also, he had two films rapidly approaching completion—*Mad Wednesday* and *Vendetta*. The two pictures had cost him in excess of $5 million and he wanted to be sure of outlets.

When Hughes assumed control of RKO, its president was Peter Rathvon, Odlum's finance man. Hughes assured Rathvon that he wanted him to stay on as president, that he could function without interference, and that he would probably have a freer hand in management than ever before.

Hughes said he did not even intend to become a member of the board. He also said that Dore Schary, head of production, would remain under the supervision of Mr. Rathvon.

A week after Hughes assumed control, he met Schary for the first time. The two men were completely dissimilar. Hughes was a pragmatist whose major interest was in box office returns and Schary was a sensitive gifted artist concerned primarily with turning out an artistic product. The first meeting between the two men did not go well. Immediately after the introduction Hughes remarked, "I hear you don't like me."

Schary replied, "Well, I hear you don't like me either. We can either talk in terms of gossip or talk business."

"You can run the studio—I haven't got time," Hughes answered.

As always, Hughes *said* that he would abdicate responsibility and authority but in practice he continually arrogated it to himself. Within two weeks Hughes was questioning Schary on his reasons for making a picture called *Battleground*—a story about the Battle of the Bulge.

Schary explained, "I think that war films are going to be in vogue soon and I would rather lead than follow the parade."

"I don't think that war pictures are a good idea at this time," Hughes retorted. "I believe that public opinion polls have reported against them.

"And another thing," asked Hughes, "why are you making the film *Bed of Roses* and why did you star Barbara Bel Geddes in it?"

Patiently Schary explained that both he and the director, Anatole

schary; MGM
war films

dietrich

Litvak, believed that Miss Bel Geddes was an unusually talented actress and it was time for RKO to start building up its own stars. Miss Bel Geddes was one of their selections for stardom.

Hughes refrained from further comment—he wanted to think about it. Both pictures were ready for shooting; the sets were completed; all preparations were made and within a few days the cameras would begin to roll.

Two days after the initial conversation took place, Hughes called Schary and told him to halt production of the two films. Schary promptly resigned and Hughes quipped publicly, "It saved me paying him two weeks' salary."

Questioned about who would succeed Schary, Hughes told reporters, "It will be someone you least expect—a shocker." Actually, he had no one in mind as yet.

Schary went to work for MGM, the largest studio in the industry, as head of production. The following year he made sixty-four pictures, including *Battleground*, the script of which he had bought from Hughes. He filmed it for $1,780,000 and turned it into the No. 2 box office success of 1948 with a potential gross of close to $5 million. In addition he started a new fashion in war films which continued for many years.

Shortly after Schary left, Peter Rathvon followed him. Odlum, still chairman of the board, and still interested in RKO because he retained warrants to purchase 300,000 shares of stock, believed it was important to the financial well being of the corporation to retain the services of Rathvon. He tried to make peace between Rathvon and Hughes. Odlum prepared a letter outlining a division of authority between the two men and Rathvon agreed to remain if Hughes would accept the agreement in writing. Hughes read the letter, refused to sign it, and Rathvon exited.

Hughes had assured everyone that there would be no firings for sixty days. He kept his word, but as soon as the sixty days had passed the firings started. Seven hundred employees were discharged during the summer of 1948. Odlum resigned as chairman of the board and Hughes replaced him with Noah Dietrich, the general supervisor of the Hughes empire. Ned Depinet was elected president, and an executive committee was drawn from the experienced producers at RKO, including Sid Rogell. Hughes still remained away from RKO. He maintained an office at the Goldwyn Studios about a mile away and transmitted his orders by personal

messages or telephone. The story is told that on one occasion when
he wanted to see a movie set, he had it dismantled and moved
over to the Goldwyn lot for his approval. However, although he did
not visit the RKO studios, he certainly did not refrain from assuming active management. He told reporters, "My life is not exactly
going to be dull for the next two years. I am really cooking at RKO
and things are going to pop. I'll make news for you. The only
thing that could stop me would be my death—an event that would
be a story."

One of Hughes' first activities was to sell to RKO those films
personally owned by him, including *The Outlaw, Mad Wednesday,*
and *Vendetta.* He next signed a production company to make three
movies for RKO, starring Ann Sheridan. Then he purchased the
rights and the partially completed screen play of *Jet Pilot,* being
filmed by an independent producer. He wanted to make it into a
modern *Hell's Angels,* using jets instead of old relics. However the
studio was not doing well and around Christmas of 1948 suspended
all production. The final picture being shot that year was Jane
Russell, Groucho Marx, and Frank Sinatra in a comedy entitled
It's Only Money.

Fortune quipped on this point, "RKO's only money connected
with picture making was a cool loss of $5,600,000 for 1948."

The studio announced that things would be much better in 1949,
and that it planned to release forty-nine major films, thirty-one of
them to be made by RKO itself. What was not reckoned with, however, was Hughes' interference. He clearly demonstrated an ambiv-
alent attitude toward his studio. On the one hand he wanted his
executives to do a good job and to have authority, responsibility and
a lot of leeway. On the other hand, he *knew* that he had a better
grasp of the movie industry than any of *them* and he didn't want
to see them making mistakes which he knew he could prevent. As
a consequence he allowed his executives to operate the studio but
they were well aware they had to clear all significant matters with
him. This frequently resulted in a stalemate.

An executive might get wind of a good story that would probably
make a fine movie. By getting there first with the best offer he
could scoop the other studios and become the owner of the property. The operation was, however, a stroll through an economic
mine field which could at any moment detonate and wreck the job
of the unfortunate executive who guessed wrong. Therefore, it be-

came the better part of valor at RKO to obtain Hughes' approval before closing any deal, an action not easy to accomplish.

To clear something with Hughes meant calling his headquarters at 7000 Romaine Street and leaving word that it was urgently necessary to talk to him. This put into operation the invisible chain linking him with his headquarters. Messages went out that, for example, Sid Rogell wanted to talk to Mr. Hughes. However, Mr. Hughes might be in New York, Chicago, Miami, Mexico City, Paris, or any point in between and, of course, he might just as possibly be in one of his haunts at nearby Las Vegas or San Francisco or even a stone's throw away in his lavish bungalow on the grounds of the Beverly Hills Hotel.

On the other hand he might not be taking calls at the time. Or he might not be in a mood to talk to Mr. Sid Rogell. Or, he might be too busy making his own calls to Tokyo, New York, Istanbul or Great Zimbabwe, to answer any calls himself. In any case, it was always a gamble whether Hughes would be reached within minutes, hours, days, weeks, or months.

Hughes probably learned quickly that he was wanted because he employed a marvelously efficient network of espionage experts. Everyone in, or on the fringes of, the movie industry, knew that a tidbit of information furnished to Hughes was worth at least a $100 bill. Bellhops, chambermaids, grips, electricians, top stars and extras, fifth assistant cameramen and top producers, newspaper columnists and bookies, all cooperated. To some it meant extra spending money, to others it might mean the financing of a picture, the purchase of a script, or an upward boost on the ladder to stardom. *espionage network*

Whether true or apocryphal, there is a yarn illustrative of a significant Hughesian attribute. Once one of Hughes' men reached the end of his patience and his labors on behalf of one or the other of Hughes' endeavors and decided, since there was nothing on the fire at the moment, he would take a vacation.

He was, of course, aware that a vacation was scarcely worth attempting unless he could achieve escape velocity from Hughes' orbit. He left California on a plane bound for New York, with everything checked through including baggage. When he reached Chicago where the plane touched down for a brief period, he quietly and quickly left the aircraft and checked into an obscure Chicago hotel to spend a few days completely out of contact with the Hughes empire. Within ten minutes after entering his room he received a call from Howard Hughes which purportedly ran along the following lines:

"What the devil are you doing in Chicago? (no pause for reply) I'm in New York and I want to see you promptly. Take the next plane which will be leaving in fifty minutes and be at my hotel tonight at midnight." The conversation was over and so was the startled executive's brief vacation.

The obverse side of the coin of Hughesism is illustrated by the following: One of Hughes' men was called and told to stand by because Mr. Hughes wanted to talk to him. This was a customary procedure, known by the denizens of the Hughes world as "being on the hook." This man was now "on the hook." He advised the caller that he would be at a certain hotel in a certain room and was told, "Remain there and try to stay in your room as much as possible. Mr. Hughes will be calling you."

on the hook

The unfortunate employee remained in his room awaiting the call from his boss. He had meals sent in and day after day, week after week, he stayed in his room, waiting for the phone call that never came. On the day he had checked in he had noticed in a tree outside his window a small bird building a nest. He watched the bird bringing twigs and grass and filler and saw the nest completed. He observed the bird settle down in its nest and lay its eggs. He saw the bird sit on its eggs, watched as the baby birds broke the shells and emerged into the world. And when the maturing babies tested their wings and finally flew away he was still sitting by his window. It is quite probable that Mr. Hughes did indeed remember the waiting man; he just wasn't ready yet to contact him.

Under such business administration it is easy to understand why RKO did not prosper. The movie industry was highly competitive. Good scripts, good actors, and even good executives were snapped up as soon as they came into the market. RKO executives had to stand by and watch while Mr. Hughes pondered each move. In addition, the more desirable people in the industry didn't want to work for RKO where they would be subject to the whims and eccentricities of the phantom of Hollywood.

competitive

As the corporation lost money, the directors grew uneasy. Some of them became especially restive when they saw Hughes treating RKO as though were a personal corporation in his own vest pocket—which it was not. In fact, Hughes owned only 25% of the

~25% ownership
RKO.

company—it was not one of his wholly-owned subsidiaries. Nevertheless, he did treat it, at least to some extent, as though it were a private proprietorship. In 1949 he sold another personally owned picture, the Jane Russell vehicle *Montana Belle*, to RKO. Only when the transaction was completed did the RKO Board of Directors learn about it.

Although the Hughes method of operation was subjected to much criticism, it had little effect. Up to this point Hughes had remained aloof from direct management, but now he had himself elected Managing Director of Production. In this position, he added little to the inefficient operation. The picture *It's Only Money* was not yet finished and Hughes made continual changes in it. He changed the title to *Double Dynamite*. He didn't like the gowns worn by Jane Russell and ordered complete reshooting of some scenes so that his voluptuous star and her stellar attractions could be highlighted by new styles. The film, scheduled for completion by the end of 1948, was not finished until 1951.

An Ann Sheridan vehicle scheduled for 1949 never got started. Instead the production company hired to make the movie sued RKO for almost a million dollars and RKO settled the dispute by purchasing the script for a sizable amount. Then the studio became involved in a squabble with Ann Sheridan over the legality of her selection of her own leading man. This disagreement joined the long list of legal disputes involving RKO.

Jet Pilot, which was going to be a modern *Hell's Angels* and put the Hughes name back on the lips of everyone in the movie industry never even got off the ground. The millions spent in trying to get the film started appeared to be wasted. Even the uniforms used in the footage already shot became obsolete because of an official change in Air Force uniform.

The year 1949 produced a large loss for RKO—a deficit for the year of just under $5 million. As soon as the figures were announced the exodus of directors began. Most of the independent directors handed in their resignations.

Even Sid Rogell decided that it was time to go. The final straw for him was the breach of a deal in which, as Executive Producer of the studio, he had negotiated for months with Jack Skirball of Gold Seal Productions, Inc. to conclude a contract in which the latter would make some important pictures, the first of which was to be

Appointment in Samarra, a story by John O'Hara, scheduled to star Gregory Peck.

According to Rogell, Hughes participated in the negotiations every step of the way. Rogell talked to Skirball by day and Hughes took over at night. Finally, Rogell closed the deal with Skirball with an oral agreement and a handshake and the studio released its publicity—all with Hughes' approval (said Rogell). Then, nothing happened!

No contracts were forthcoming and the deal was not implemented. Rogell left RKO and Skirball began to press for his contracts, to get the actors, and to obtain the cooperation of the studio so that his project could get off the ground. Instead of cooperation, Skirball got his "walking papers." Hughes sent a message that the deal was dead and Skirball should get off the lot.

Another lawsuit joined the long list of cases against Hughes, who testified:

"I at no time told Mr. Rogell to close the deal. I at no time told him to discuss the deal in terms of $125,000 plus 20% of the profits with or without Gregory Peck. I at no time told him to make or close an oral production-distribution agreement with Mr. Skirball or anyone else."

Rogell, called to the stand, gave directly opposing testimony. In deciding the case, Judge Joseph Vickers, after issuing the dictum that there was "no comparable case in the Industry," rendered the decision that there was unquestionably a valid agreement and that therefore Skirball was entitled to $375,000 damages plus interest.

One of Hughes' major contentions in this action was that RKO just didn't make verbal agreements. Although Hughes was involved in much litigation, normally his cases were consistent and if a score was kept it would probably show that he won more cases than he lost. However, in the Skirball case, Hughes was clearly in the wrong because in a recently completed action involving the actress Jean Simmons, Hughes and RKO had taken the position that Miss Simmons was bound by an oral contract to RKO.

To succeed Executive Producer Sid Rogell, Hughes brought in Sam Bischoff, a thoroughly experienced independent producer. However, Hollywood quickly noted that Bischoff did not get Rogell's office, which remained vacant. Instead, Bischoff was assigned to a smaller office further down the line. It was obvious that Hughes was reserving the top production spot at RKO for someone else.

Soon everyone knew who that somebody was—Hughes wanted none other than the independent producing team of Jerry Wald and Norman Krasna. Thus began a weird negotiating marathon. For weeks Wald and Hughes discussed terms. Finally Hughes bought the Wald-Krasna contract from Warner Brothers and signed Wald and Krasna to a five-year contract with RKO in one of the largest financial deals Hollywood had seen in a long time.

The contract included a provision that Wald and Krasna would make $50 million worth of feature pictures for RKO release, at the rate of twelve films a year over a five-year period. The pictures were to be financed 40 percent by Howard Hughes personally and 60 percent by the Mellon Bank of Pittsburgh and the Bankers Trust Company of New York. Wald and Krasna each received a salary of $2,500 a week plus a 25 percent equity in each of the films.

A major press conference in RKO's board room commemorated the completion of the agreement. Wald and Krasna, drunk with negotiating success, could not promise enough. The studio told the assembled reporters, publicists, magazine writers, and hangers-on that teams of experts would be assigned to scour the world for new stories. Many important film properties were already lined up, including *Stars and Stripes*, a story about the USO with Al Jolson; *Size 12*, a Jerome Weidman story about a fashion model business; *Call Out the Marines*, a story of the origin of the Marine Corps; *Mother Knows Best*, which would star Mae West and Jane Russell, and *The Harder They Fall*, bringing the Bud Schulberg novel to the screen.

The Hughes-Wald-Krasna deal was unusual. Hughes, although retaining close control, agreed to make his decisions within a week. Also, he retained a veto power over any film which would cost more than $900,000. The year 1950 had four months left—scarcely enough time for the new deal to put RKO in the black. Once again, the financial loss was substantial: nearly $6 million.

Another development also hurt Hughes and RKO. For some years the government had been maintaining an anti-trust action against RKO, contending that the same unit should not make movies and also own theaters. The action was finally settled with a ruling that split off the RKO theaters from the parent company. The stockholders of the major RKO company received the individual stock of the theater corporation.

The year 1951 began hopefully, but even Wald and Krasna could not break out of the straitjacket of Hughes' decision-making. True, they did succeed in making and releasing four movies: *The Blue Veil, Behave Yourself, Clash by Night,* and *Lusty Men.* But it was a long way from the announced goal of twelve pictures.

The 1951 annual report to shareholders contained some financial legerdemain in order to show a small profit. A footnote to the annual statement revealed the wizardry that turned a deficit into a profit— RKO decided to delay amortizing the cost of films until twenty-six weeks after the release of each picture. This turned a million-dollar loss for 1951 into a $300,000 profit, but it fooled no one.

The year 1952 showed no improvement. In fact, the first nine months revealed another $5 million loss which might have been worse had not RKO scraped the bottom of the barrel. Out came a two-decade old movie called *King Kong* which was re-released with surprising success. During the last three months of 1952 Hughes completely shut down the RKO studio, blaming "the hunt for Communists." (Most people believed this shutdown was really to ease the crushing burden of overhead on a studio that was making neither pictures nor profit.)

By September of 1952 Hughes had had enough. He entered into a contract with a five-man syndicate to sell them his RKO holdings, which consisted of 1,013,420 shares of stock, at a price of about $7 per share for a total of $7,345,940. This was not a bad price for a stock that was then selling at 4-3/8. The syndicate consisted of Ralph Stolkin, Abraham Koolish, Ray Ryan, H. G. Burke, and Sherrill C. Corwin.

As part of the deal Hughes agreed to lend RKO $8 million so that the company could pay off a $5 million demand loan at the bank and still retain some working capital. The syndicate's payments were not going to be very difficult. They would give Hughes a certified check for $1,250,000 and pay the balance of approximately $6 million over two years. Hollywood puzzled over this arrangement because it was not like Hughes' normal business operations. Between the credit extended on the sale and the promise of the loan, Hughes was extending credit of close to $14 million to five people who were far from gilt-edged or blue-ribboned.

Hughes' public relations people explained that Howard Hughes had many important and substantial interests including TWA and Hughes Tool Company, and of all his enterprises RKO was unquestionably the least important. In spite of this, RKO consumed

85 percent of his time, which left him only 15 percent for more important affairs. What the release neglected to point out was that those companies which consumed the 15 percent portion of his time were prospering, while the company which claimed the bulk of his time was failing.

The syndicate installed Arnold Grant, an attorney with a motion picture practice, as chairman of the board and Arnold Picker, a United Artists distribution man, as executive vice president. The word in the industry was that RKO was losing money at its usual rate of about $5 million a year.

Grant and Picker tried to run a paying operation but the *Wall Street Journal* chose that moment to print a background story on Stolkin and Koolish. Their business history was well known, but only to the Better Business Bureau, the Federal Trade Commission, and the Fraud Section of the Post Office Department. These two men had had intermittent difficulties in the operation of mail order enterprises, insurance businesses, and the sale of punch boards. Some people accused Hughes of giving the information to the *Wall Street Journal* but there is no proof of this allegation. At any rate the news did not help the syndicate achieve a profitable operation of RKO. In fact, it became impossible for them to arrange the necessary financing to complete the deal, so they had to forfeit. Hughes got back his stock and a vacant board of directors. He also retained the $1,250,000 down payment plus a $250,000 installment payment that had been made. Now it more closely resembled a Howard Hughes deal than it did in the beginning.

Hughes reinstalled his own people on the board and began once again to operate the studio. He made James R. Grainger, president, and Grainger's son, Edward, became production manager. The company ended the year 1953 with the largest loss in its history—and with production virtually at a standstill.

In March, 1954, a story prophetically called *Second Chance* reopened the studio. Hughes planned to emphasize a new process—three-dimensional movies. He apparently believed that this new process would catch on and become a moneymaker.

After the deal with the Stolkin syndicate Howard Hughes, so frequently the plaintiff in legal actions and so free in resorting to the courts, began to feel the sting of litigation on his own back. Many shareholders instituted lawsuits against him for his handling of RKO. The stockholders' suits were brought in various places, including Nevada, Delaware, New York and California. These suits made many allegations, but a central theme could be detected: RKO stock, publicly held by 15,000 shareholders, had lost 80 percent of its value during Hughes' stewardship.

One suit alleged that Hughes had "saddled unfair commitments" on RKO, causing millions of dollars of loss. Another suit charged Hughes with operating RKO under a system of "pique, caprice and whim" to the enormous detriment of the investors.

The stockholders also charged that Hughes presently was *making* millions of dollars in profits from various maneuvers, including the sale of his own properties to the company, and the sale of his stock to outsiders, while at the same time the corporation itself was *losing* millions. It was charged that he operated the company with a total disregard for the profit-making features of the enterprise. He was accused of everything from violation of the Securities and Exchange Commission laws and regulations to common law fraud and deceit.

Among the items alleged in the various lawsuits was the fact that Hughes had kept sitting around RKO, doing absolutely nothing but drawing breath and salary, such assets as Ursula Thiess, Mona Freeman, Mara Lane (then England's Marilyn Monroe) and others of similar ilk. It was further alleged that he had bought an entire French ballet company in order to obtain the services of the French actress, Jeanmaire, and then failed to make use of her. Another allegation was that Jack Buetel, who co-starred with Jane Russell in *The Outlaw*, sat around Hollywood for five years mowing his lawn, playing golf, watching motion pictures and waiting for his weekly paycheck (from RKO), but never made another movie.

Two brave stockholders, Louis Schiff and Jacob Sacks, owners of the vast amount of 200 shares, actually dared to file a petition in New York to appoint a receiver for RKO! Supreme Court Justice S. Samuel DeFalco heard the case and reserved decision. The complaint alleged that Hughes exercised effective working control over all of RKO and although he did not have complete ownership, he operated the corporations as though they were wholly-owned Hughes subsidiaries.

The suit also pointed out that RKO lost over $38 million during the Hughes regime with $6 million of the loss in the preceding year. Many reasons for this loss were alleged including the regularly averred fact that although much talent was paid at astronomical salaries, it was never used to the advantage of the corporation.

Hughes went to work to resolve his dilemma. First he had to dispose of his 929,000 shares of the theater-owning-company stock which he had obtained as a result of the antitrust ruling which divorced the theater company from the studio. Hughes sold the 929,000 shares to a group headed by David J. Greene, New York investment counselor, and had the sale approved by the Securities and Exchange Commission. This stock had been selling at $3.87½ a share on the New York Stock Exchange but Hughes received $4.75 a share for his holdings. He had now received approximately 50 percent of the consideration he originally paid to Floyd Odlum.

He then began negotiations to sell either all or part of his production studio holdings and discovered that as a 25 percent owner of that corporation he lacked enough control to satisfy most people who might desire to run RKO.

On February 8, 1954, Hughes astonished Hollywood and astounded financial circles by making an offer which, in effect, would pay off all RKO Studio shareholders. Outstanding shares at the time were selling *under* $3.00 per share.

Hughes offered to pay $23,489,478 in cash for all of the RKO assets. This would be sufficient to pay off all shareholders (except Hughes) at a price of $6 per share! The Hughes offer provided that the RKO Board would have to accept the offer within one week and the majority of stockholders would have to approve before the end of March. He set the deadline for the transfer of all the assets to himself as April 12, 1954.

The publicity release which made this most unusual proposal stated: "There have been expressions of dissatisfaction among shareholders. I have been sued by certain of the stockholders and accused of responsibility for losses of the corporation. I would like to feel that I have given all the shareholders of RKO Pictures Corporation an opportunity to receive for their stock an amount well in excess of its market value at the time when I first became connected with the company, or at any time since."

Eliminating the legal language surrounding the offer, what Hughes was saying to all the shareholders was in effect: "You appear to be dissatisfied with the way I run things. Since I took control of this company the shares never got to $6.00 apiece and therefore most of you never had a chance to sell for this price. At the present time if you go into the market to sell your shares you would not get $3.00 a share for them. In addition, if a great number of you went in to sell, the price would probably go down much further than that. However, let no man ever say he lost money because I didn't run a company properly. Therefore, I offer you $6.00 for every share of stock you have. I am offering to double your money, and take all the risks myself."

Wild trading rapidly forced the RKO' stock up. By noon there were 15,000 separate buy orders on the floor of the Stock Exchange, with bids ranging from a few hundred shares to several thousand shares. The first trade after the noon mark was for 200,000 shares at 5 3/8. This represented the largest transaction on the New York Stock Exchange since a 500,000 block of Western Airlines stock traded five years before.

Trading became so disorganized that in a few days the stock, with a maximum value of $6.00, if everything went well, actually passed over the $6.00 mark and traded higher because speculators were forced to cover short sales.

On February 13, 1954 the RKO Board met in a closed session at the Biltmore Hotel in Atlanta, Georgia. The next day in Atlanta, Board Chairman Grainger announced that the directors had accepted the Hughes offer and called a special shareholders meeting for March 18 in Dover, Delaware.

Speculation abounded on what Hughes had in mind, but he was not talking. Despite the best efforts of hordes of reporters to reach him he remained completely inaccessible. A Los Angeles attorney, Bernard Reich, announced that Hughes would not get out from under the suits he had filed against him. Reich intended to do everything legally possible to keep those suits alive.

In a few days the two intrepid litigants, Schiff and Sacks, who owned a few shares of RKO were in action in the Chancery Court in Delaware, the place of incorporation of RKO, to enjoin the sale on the theory that unless Hughes was stopped he would obtain net assets worth almost $100 million at a cost to him of a little over $23 million. The suit was also designed to stop the shareholders' meeting of March 18. The plaintiffs had a pending action for receivership in New York and they wanted the Delaware court to halt all proceedings on the proposed sale until their New York suit could be decided.

On March 9, 1954, testimony started in Wilmington to determine whether Hughes could go ahead with the sale. Accountant C. B. Apt testified concerning his disagreement with various elements of the RKO financial statements. However, Hughes' attorneys were able to show clear explanations from the Price, Waterhouse audited statements. It was also shown that in Atlanta the directors had valued the net worth of the corporation at something under $15,000,000 despite the fact that Hughes was willing to pay close to $23,000,000 for it.

The plaintiffs continued to maintain their case. They charged that the assets did not include a proper evaluation of funds blocked in foreign countries, other assets in foreign countries, under-evaluated real estate holdings, the film library of several hundred features and four hundred short subjects carried on the books at $1.00 per film, etc., etc. However, the learned Chancellor advised the plaintiffs that none of this was enough to stop the sale and they would have to show that the board was involved in fraud in accepting the offer.

After the refusal of the court to grant an injunction against the sale, the stockholders met on March 18th in Dover and in less than an hour voted more than 2,000,000 for the sale to fewer than 100,000 against. At that meeting the only significant opposition to the acceptance of the offer came from Lewis D. Gilbert, the owner of 100 shares of stock, who was a professional antagonist of corporate shenanigans. Shortly after the meeting, the suit in Delaware was dismissed. Then, one by one, the other suits throughout the country were dismissed as either groundless or moot.

The sale was completed when Hughes wrote a personal check for $23,049,478 and became the first sole owner of a major Hollywood studio.

Hughes now owned the assets of RKO, and RKO had cash which it offered to all shareholders who wanted to tender their shares for redemption.

Many people speculated on what Howard Hughes was going to do with the studio. W. R. Wilkerson, writing in *The Hollywood Reporter* on April 1, 1954, predicted that within a year RKO would become the greatest studio in the world. Others, less charitable, predicted that within a year the studio would be disbanded. For a while the favorite cocktail topic in Hollywood was, "What will Howard Hughes do with RKO?"

The movie colony soon learned Hughes' plan for RKO. He was going to sell it. He began to negotiate with Thomas Francis O'Neil, president of General Teleradio. This company operated a radio network and four TV stations and was heavily involved in the film purchasing business.

O'Neil had just recently bought for $1.5 million, films held in the vaults of the Bank of America as a result of default by the pledger in the repayment of loans. Negotiations began with the familiar around-the-clock telephone marathon, including calls in the middle of the night, disturbing to O'Neil but routine for Hughes. Finally the two men seemed to be close enough on terms to warrant a personal meeting. O'Neil flew to California, where he met with Hughes at the Beverly Hills Hotel. As O'Neil described it, they would eat, talk, argue, watch television, take catnaps, and then return to negotiating. O'Neil opined that Hughes knew more corporate law and taxation than any attorney he had ever met. Finally, they reached an agreement which Hughes had typed up. Now Hughes pulled another one of his tactics. He refused to have the agreement signed in California because he did not want it governed by California law.

O'Neil, by this time thoroughly bewildered, consented to board a plane with Hughes, who piloted the aircraft himself to Las Vegas. At last, on Nevada ground, the contract was signed. O'Neil was immediately flown back to his home in Akron, where he went to bed to sleep around the clock.

In fact, the arrangement was beneficial to both sides. O'Neil paid Hughes $25 million. Hughes had already received close to $10 million for the theater corporation. He kept RKO Radio, which itself had a fair amount of cash and a tax loss carry-forward. Later Hughes merged this corporation with Odlum's Atlas Corporation and received a consideration worth another $10 million. Hughes now ended his eight years in RKO with a profit approaching $10 million. It was all in capital gains with a relatively light tax bite.

O'Neil acquired, in addition to the real estate, sets, cameras, and other motion-picture-making accoutrements, a library of seven hundred and forty films. Up to this time most studios had been turning down offers to sell their backlog film to television, because Hollywood had no wish to encourage what they considered dangerous competition. However, O'Neil was on the television side of the fight rather than the picture-making side, and shortly after purchasing RKO he sold his backlog to TV for more than $15 million. He was also able to sell current RKO releases for over $10 million.

This covered his payment to Hughes and the remainder of RKO was all his at no cost.

Hughes was now out of the motion picture business, but from time to time there were announcements that he would return. As late as the summer of 1966 Greg Bautzer, a Hughes trouble-shooter and one of his attorneys, announced that Hughes was considering going back into the film-making business.

Howard Hughes and the Million-Dollar Bit

THE YEAR 1925

HARLAN F. STONE was appointed a Justice of the United States Supreme Court succeeding Joseph McKenna, who resigned.

An amendment to the United States Constitution to outlaw child labor was ratified by California but was rejected by South Carolina, Oklahoma, Ohio, Kansas, Texas, North Dakota, Delaware and Washington.

Gaston B. Means and Thomas B. Felder were convicted by a Federal Jury in New York of conspiracy to bribe United States Government officials. They were fined $10,000 and Means was sentenced to two years in prison in one of the most famous American bribery trials to date.

Photographs of the inauguration of President Calvin Coolidge and Vice President Charles G. Dawes on March 4th were transmitted for the first time by telephone by A.T. & T. to New York, Chicago and Washington and were published in the evening newspapers of the same day!

Lieutenants C. H. Schildhauer and J. R. Kyle established a new record for sustained flight of 28 hours, 35 minutes and 27 seconds.

John Scopes was arrested in Dayton, Tennessee for violation of the state law prohibiting the teaching of evolution in a high-school class.

America proclaimed its sovereignty over Swain's Island in Samoa.

Howard Hughes was nineteen years old.

15

After Howard Robard Hughes (the father) obtained patent numbers 930,758 and 930,759 for a new form of cone-type bit and drill to be used in a rotary drilling system, a continual battle raged over infringement attempts. The father, and later the son, had to fight tooth and nail, claw and hammer to keep away the imitators, the copiers, and the appropriators.

Clarence E. Reed, who had been an auditor for the Hughes Tool Company in the early years and later became secretary-treasurer of the company, made one of the first serious attempts to invade the patent. In the early 1920's he left Hughes Tool Company, formed the Reed Roller Bit Company, and tried to acquire his own patents. One of these was a minor improvement over one held by Hughes.

Hughes, Sr., had improved the bit with a system for oil lubrication so that when the bit hit rock it would not overheat and lose its sharpness. While oil was the primary lubricant, water could be substituted, though it was not as satisfactory because of a tendency of the disks to clog. Reed worked out a system of closing a slot at the rear of each cutting disk which restricted the passage when the bit was flushed with water and prevented the clogging of the disk. He had begun to market his own bits when Hughes Tool Company, now under the aegis of young Hughes, brought a legal action against him. Toolco won the litigation on the theory that, though Reed had made an improvement on the Hughes bit, he had appropriated the use of the bit to do so and this was illegal. Reed fought his case through the federal courts to the United States Supreme Court but lost every round.

Other companies, such as the Chicago Pneumatic Tool Company and the Southwest Tool Company, essayed their own improvements on the Hughes bit. In every injunction action Toolco successfully stopped the illegal infringement of its patent.

Howard Hughes and his staff watched over the bits as though

they were diamonds. As soon as the nineteen-year-old Howard took charge of the company he established a system of research which in 1931 was formalized into a research department with a central laboratory in Houston, Texas. The department had two major objectives: (1) to reduce the total number of bits necessary to complete the drilling of a well, and (2) to increase the efficiency of the bits, thereby speeding up the rate of drilling.

At that time there was much rotary drilling for oil and gas in East Texas. Hughes Tool Company assigned a number of its research personnel in that area to conduct an orderly and extensive performance control of the bits in the field. To keep control of its bits, Toolco abandoned their new practice of selling them outright, and leased them instead as they had done originally. The leasing agreement required that each bit had to be returned to Toolco for tests and analysis when it lost its sharpness.

With the knowledge accumulated in the early thirties, Hughes Tool Company changed over to a complete bit service. Instead of simply selling two or three styles of bits, it began to manufacture many different types—each designed for a particular rock formation or drilling condition. The leasing contract specifically provided:

> When the original cutter teeth and/or bearings have served their useful life, the user will surrender the bits to Hughes Tool Company upon request. In accepting delivery, the user agrees not to surrender any of the tools as mentioned above to other than a duly authorized representative of Hughes Tool Company.

Every bit manufactured by Toolco was stamped "Property of Hughes Tool Co., Inc." Hughes maintained at his central research laboratory a wide variety of scientific and technical personnel to test the bits, conduct metallurgical investigations, and make chemical analyses. The field organization had grown to almost two hundred men, who delivered new bits to the site of drilling rigs and picked up the worn-out ones. Each bit had a serial number so the home office could keep a record of its performance. As each was returned to the central laboratory, it carried complete information about circumstances of use, rock formations drilled through, conditions encountered, and performance.

One court, in deciding a case in favor of Hughes, said: "Such research has enabled Hughes not only to eliminate flaws appearing in its bits, but to constantly improve the design and operating qualities of its bits, and to extend the useful life thereof."

One of the problems in handling these bits was that no one could see what was going on where the bit was actually operating. Some of the bits would drill as far down as three miles beneath the surface of the earth. In its efforts to manufacture bits suitable for specific conditions, Toolco gradually increased production to four hundred and seventy-five different sizes and types, which could accommodate all segments of the drilling industry. Some idea of the size of the business can be gained from the fact that in an average year Hughes Tool Company leased eighteen thousand *experimental* bits.

As the bits became more expensive a new form of competition appeared. Companies began to retip the worn bits. With an acetylene torch and a suitable metal they restored each worn tooth as nearly as possible to the original form, size, and position. The work was performed under water to prevent the metal from losing its temper.

As soon as the retipping process began to cause substantial inter- retipping ference with Toolco volume, Hughes took legal action. Counsel pointed out that most of the bits used in the retipping process were either stolen, retained in violation of the leasing agreement, or otherwise illegally acquired. The major argument advanced by Toolco was that, if the bits were not returned, interference with the research program resulted, and the company was unable to maintain complete records of all its bits. The courts, impressed with the cogency of the arguments advanced, enjoined the retipping procedure.

In defense the retippers attacked the Hughes leasing practice as an antitrust violation similar to that outlawed by the federal courts in connection with shoe machinery. However, Hughes and his people had prepared their cases too carefully to be caught in that trap.

Toolco argued that it merely leased bits and created no other restrictions. The United Shoe Machinery Corporation, on the other hand, had insisted on long lease terms, restrictive provisions, and other conditions which adversely affected anyone desiring to use a competitor's machinery. Toolco was cagy. The company said, in effect, that they had the best drilling bit in the world and anyone who wanted it could lease it. If that arrangement was not satisfactory, the prospective customer could lease someone else's bit instead. The court sustained Hughes' monopoly.

Howard Robard Hughes, Sr., had achieved a notable distinction when he invented the original bit with one hundred and sixty-six cutting edges. Howard Robard Hughes, Jr., insured that the original invention proliferated, improved, and acquired the stature of the world's greatest underground cutting tool.

166 edge
cutting tool

Howard Hughes and His Anti-Communist Crusade

APRIL, 1951

PRESIDENT TRUMAN issued a revised draft order which approved deferment for college students of superior scholastic standing or those achieving a high score in a national aptitude test to be given in May and June.

United States tanks and infantry succeeded in pushing across the 38th parallel at two points on the western front in Korea. Prime Minister Jawaharlal Nehru came out in favor of an immediate truce in Korea and said that India would gladly help in negotiations.

Secretary of State John Foster Dulles finally outlined the peace proposals that would be offered to Japan. It was to be a peace of "reconciliation."

In the movies: Bette Davis in *Payment on Demand;* John Wayne in *Operation Pacific;* Joan Fontaine and Joseph Cotten in *September Affair;* Judy Holliday in *Born Yesterday.*

The best seller books were Jones, *From Here To Eternity;* Schulberg, *The Disenchanted;* Wylie, *The Disappearance,* and in the non-fiction field, *Kon-Tiki* and *Washington Confidential.*

Howard Hughes was forty-five years old.

16

In 1936 Joseph R. McCarthy started his political career as a New Deal Democrat. Shortly thereafter the Democrats lost their majority in his county so he switched to the Republican Party. In 1946 he was elected to the United States Senate from Wisconsin on the Republican ticket. Very soon after being seated Senator McCarthy started a wave of witch-hunting unprecedented in the annals of the United States Senate. He perfected a form of political blackmail by Congressional Committee, immune from legal retaliation or almost any other form of attack, which became known as McCarthyism.

One of the major vehicles for advancing McCarthyism was the House of Representatives Subcommittee on Un-American Activities. This Committee roamed the nation asking a now well-known question, "Are you now, or have you ever been, a member of the Communist Party?"

In 1947 Congressman J. Parnell Thomas asked this question of the first ten of nineteen prominent Hollywood writers. Then he stopped. The ten included Dalton Trumbo, Ring Lardner, Jr., Albert Maltz, Lester Cole and Adrian Scott. These men came to be known as the Hollywood Ten. The nine who were not reached by the Committee were forgotten.

Each of the ten refused to answer on the ground that his politics was none of Thomas' business. They were all convicted of contempt of Congress and sentenced to $1,000 fine and a year imprisonment.

The United States Supreme Court by a decision of six to two (Justices Hugo L. Black and William C. Douglas dissented and Justice Tom C. Clark abstained) refused in 1950 to review the convictions. (On the very day the convictions of the Hollywood Ten were upheld by the United States Supreme Court the man who had asked the questions, erstwhile Congressman J. Parnell Thomas, was in prison for conspiracy to defraud the United States Government.)

The climate of the early fifties was one in which it was both patriotic and fashionable to hunt Communists. In April of 1951, the same House Subcommittee came to Hollywood and called to testify before it a number of other writers, one of whom was Paul Jarrico.

In 1951 Paul Jarrico was thirty-six years old and a graduate of the University of Southern California. He had tried to follow in the footsteps of his lawyer father, but, after a few weeks in law school he dropped out because he really wanted to be a writer. He was fairly successful and in January, 1951, signed a contract with RKO to prepare a screen play to be titled *The Las Vegas Story.* It was scheduled to be one of RKO's leading movies for 1951 and would star Jane Russell and Victor Mature.

Jarrico worked on his script for nine or ten weeks and was doing the final polishing when word got out that he was to be called before Representative Harold H. Velde, an Illinois Republican who headed the House Un-American Activities Committee at that time.

Jarrico issued a statement that he would under no circumstances cooperate with that committee and declared, "If I have to choose between crawling in the mud with Larry Parks, or going to jail like my courageous friends of the Hollywood Ten, I shall certainly choose the latter."

As soon as Howard Hughes learned of the committee's interest in Jarrico and Jarrico's attitude toward it, Hughes had him fired from his $2,000-a-week job. A few days later, learning that Jarrico still had access to the studio, Hughes ordered him "eliminated" (Hughes' own word) and barred from the studio. In addition, he ordered his people to rewrite the story taking out all of Jarrico's contributions, and omitting his name from the screen credits.

The screen writers were well organized and had a collective bargaining contract with all major studios. This agreement provided that screen credits for the respective writers would be decided by the Screen Writers Guild. There was no question that the studio had a right to fire Jarrico, because Jarrico's individual contract with the studio provided for his dismissal or termination at will. However, there was a real question whether they could use his script and deny him credit. Many RKO people tried to convince Hughes that leaving Jarrico's name in the credits could do no harm, but Hughes was adamant.

Acting under the collective bargaining agreement between the

Writers Guild and RKO, the Guild (as was customary in such cases) wrote to Hughes requesting a meeting to discuss the matter of screen credits.

Hughes replied personally that he had no intention of permitting credit to be given to Jarrico. He stated baldly, "I do not know whether your members want to strike or not . . . if they do . . . they would just as well get on with it."

This was really throwing down the gauntlet to the union, which requested that the matter be submitted to arbitration under the collective bargaining agreement. Hughes refused, pointing out that, whatever decision was reached in arbitration, he would not give screen credit to Jarrico or to any other person who refused to answer the questions of a Congressional Committee.

The members of the Guild sensed that Hughes was trying to provoke a strike. Business was not going well at RKO; the studio was losing a lot of money; many believed that Hughes wanted to close the studio and blame it on someone else. The leaders of the Guild warily refused to give Hughes such provocation and began a legal action instead.

Hughes filed a counter-action in the form of a Declaratory Judgment requesting the Superior Court for the County of Los Angeles of the State of California to declare that RKO had a right to deny Paul Jarrico screen credit for *The Las Vegas Story*.

Bringing a legal action was routine for the litigious Hughes who had instigated court fights for lesser reasons. However, this particular case was a bit unusual because, since Hughes had run the entire show himself and had publicly accepted personal responsibility for his actions, he would probably have to testify. Customarily he shied away from Court appearances at all costs.

The case became celebrated because it was one of those rare instances in which Hughes was subjected to direct depositions by an opposing attorney and was forced to appear for cross-examination in an open Courtroom.

Paul Jarrico was represented by the Hollywood attorney, Edward Mosk. After the pleading (the complaint filed by Hughes and answered by Jarrico, who filed a counterclaim) Mosk's next step was to try to get Hughes to appear for a deposition. (A deposition is a pre-trial maneuver used in modern legal practice to try to ascertain what the testimony will be at trial. It helps to cut down the length of trials, eliminate surprises, and enable attorneys to prepare their cases better.)

Under normal practice the attorney simply notifies his opposite number that he desires to take the deposition of someone under the control of the opposing attorney, a date is set, and all parties sit down with a court stenographer present so the attorney requesting the depositions can ask questions and have them recorded officially.

In the case of Howard Hughes this was easier said than done. Attorney Mosk, after addressing numerous requests to Arthur Groman, counsel for both Hughes and RKO, still received no cooperation. Consequently he determined to serve Hughes with a subpoena. This turned out to be an impossible task. For many years and in many cases litigants have tried unsuccessfully to serve the elusive Hughes with subpoenas, but it is doubtful that anyone has ever actually completed legal service upon him.

However, Mosk persisted, making legal feints in all directions and maintaining pressure on attorney Groman. Finally Groman telephoned to say that he would have Hughes available for a deposition but only on one condition. As Mosk said, "Ordinarily one is not confronted with conditions when exercising legal rights." But the case had been so strange from the beginning and the difficulties of serving Hughes had seemed so insurmountable that Mosk agreed to listen. He was told that he could set a date and time for the taking of the deposition. The place would have to be left entirely up to Mr. Hughes and Mosk would not be informed of its location in advance.

Mosk remarked reasonably to Groman at this point, "If I don't know where it is how am I going to get there?"

Groman replied, "The arrangement will be that you will be told to stand on a street corner at a designated spot where a car will pick you up and deliver you to the location of the deposition."

Since no better alternative suggested itself, Mosk agreed to the condition.

On the appointed day at the specified time Attorney Mosk went to the corner and waited. Shortly thereafter he was picked up by a limousine, taken to the Beverly Hills Hotel and directed to a large conference room.

While the attorneys sat around making small talk, a man came into the room carrying a sealed bottle of pure water. A few minutes later Howard Hughes entered and sat down. At this point, in his presence, the water tender opened the bottle of water. (Hughes insisted that his water bottle always be opened in his presence.)

Hughes was pleasant, even charming, and answered all questions responsively except when Mosk tried to pin him down as to where he lived. At regular intervals Hughes excused himself to go to the bathroom. He had a urinary difficulty and could not wait extended periods of time.

Unexpectedly, when the attorney was about half through his questioning, Hughes rose quietly and, leaving Mosk with his words hanging in midair, left the room. He had set up a special phone system in an adjacent room. Hughes' own attorney remonstrated; Hughes ignored him.

Hughes had been gone for more than an hour when one of his men (Mosk calls him "his man Friday") came into the room and whispered something to Groman. The attorney said apologetically that Mr. Hughes would be tied up for a while, but he would like to buy them all dinner in the hotel dining room while they waited.

The deposition had started at about 5:00 o'clock and it was now 8:00 o'clock. They enjoyed a leisurely dinner until 10:00 o'clock, at which hour Mosk returned to the conference room to finish taking the deposition. With frequent interruptions while Howard Hughes either went to the bathroom or talked on the telephone to Tokyo or some other distant place, the deposition limped to completion around midnight.

At last, on November 17, 1957, the case came to trial before Judge Orlando H. Rhodes. Hughes and RKO argued that the court should take judicial notice of the fact that in the United States at that time the American public "feels ill-will and scorn towards persons believed to be Communists or Communist sympathizers." Furthermore, Attorney Groman argued that the judge should recognize that "the American public believes that a person who, when asked by a government committee if he is or has been a Communist, declines to answer on the ground that his answer might tend to incriminate him, is a Communist or Communist sympathizer."

In view of the foregoing, said Hughes and RKO, "it would hurt both the picture and the studio to permit the name of Paul Jarrico to be associated with it."

The proof offered of the plaintiffs' contention was almost ludicrous. First, they had Psychological Services, Inc., make a public opinion survey. The pollsters selected the city of Muncie, Indiana—a "typical American community." They obtained interviewers from the Ball State Teachers College of Muncie and sent them out to question people about their opinions of those who "took the Fifth Amendment." Both the examination and the cross-examination revealed that the venture was unscientific and had little value as proof of the theory.

In addition, Hughes' attorney called a number of American Legionnaires and other superpatriots to testify how they felt about anyone who pleaded the Fifth Amendment. Typical of the RKO witnesses was William A. White, an attorney formerly associated with the District Attorney's office of Fresno County, California. White was commander of the American Legion, Department of California.

White testified: "If a person refused to answer the question as to whether he was ever a Communist, he either has been a Communist or is now a Communist, a member of the Communist Party." He asserted that this was the general belief of the members of the American Legion. This theme ran throughout the plaintiff's case.

Jarrico's defense, ably presented by Attorney Edward Mosk, was twofold. The defendant argued correctly that writers' screen credits were not the business of the studio because it had given up jurisdiction over this matter in a contract with the Screen Writers Guild. Second, claimed Mosk, Hughes had not acted in good faith because he was using the Jarrico incident and the surrounding affair as an excuse to close down an unprofitable studio.

Attorney Mosk offered some persuasive evidence to support his charges against Hughes. He showed the existence of a contract between RKO and the Screen Writers Guild which provided that disputes concerning credits for writers would be determined by the Guild. Furthermore, the Guild had stepped into this issue and had determined that Jarrico was entitled to credit. (Mosk's contention that Hughes wanted to close down RKO was borne out by the fact that not too long after the Jarrico incident Hughes actually did close down the studio.)

Unfortunately for Jarrico the Guild at the time lacked unanimity of opinion. Some well-known writers like Leslie Charteris even resigned from the Guild because the organization took a position favoring Jarrico.

After a few days of trial preliminaries the time arrived for Hughes

to appear and testify under cross-examination by Mosk. Hughes did
not wear to court the tennis shoes he had worn during the deposition but, according to Mosk, he exhibited acute discomfort in his
regular shoes. The attorney also observed that Hughes was ill at
ease when wearing a jacket and tie. The moment he left the stand
during any intermission, off would come his jacket and he would
unbutton his shirt collar.

The ubiquitous sealed bottle of water was placed on the witness
stand to be opened in Hughes' presence. Specially installed ear-
phones were available to make it easier for him to hear the proceedings clearly. The first colloquy, as was customary in all Hughes'
testimony, concerned his place of abode. The testimony ran as follows:

Mosk: "What is your name?"

Hughes: "Howard Hughes." (Hughes rarely, if ever, uses his
middle initial or name in legal matters.)

Mosk: "Where do you live, Mr. Hughes?" (No response).

The Judge: "Repeat it, I don't believe he hears it."

Mosk (louder): "Where do you live, Mr. Hughes?"

Hughes: "You mean my domicile or present location?"

Mosk: "Where do you live?"

Hughes: "Well, I still ask you, do you mean my legal domicile or
where I am living at present?"

Mosk: "Where are you living at the present time?"

Hughes: "Well, I spent last night at the Beverly Hills Hotel."

Mosk: "Do you consider that to be your home, Mr. Hughes?"

Hughes: "Not my legal domicile. No."

Mosk: "What is your legal domicile?"

Hughes: "Well, I still consider that to be Houston, Texas."

Mosk: "What is your occupation?"

Hughes: "Manufacturer."

Hughes clearly accepted full responsibility for the action taken
with respect to Jarrico. He testified. "I gave an order to discharge
Mr. Jarrico from the studio. A week later I discovered that he was
still periodically coming in to the gates of the studio, and I raised a
very serious objection about this, and I was told he was no longer
being paid, but his services were free for that week; and I immediately gave orders that he should not be permitted to enter the
studio, whether his services were free or otherwise. . . ."

Hughes testified that he said: "We are not going to use the work

[Jarrico's writing] any way, so I don't want him admitted to the studio any further. I want every piece of paper that he has laid hands on thrown in the wastebasket and burned up."

Hughes also showed the strength of his obduracy when he issued a statement to the press, and later testified about it at the trial, in which he stated that there was no point to arbitrating his dispute with Jarrico because "my conscience cannot be changed by a committee of arbitrators."

Hughes also averred that he told those asking for arbitration: "Any arbitration of this matter would be without meaning, because regardless of what the outcome of the arbitration might be, RKO will not yield to Jarrico's demands."

Howard Hughes on the witness stand gave a remarkable demonstration of keenness in grasping the import of the questions and elusiveness in being pinned down in answering. Mosk wanted to show that RKO had never received any written objections from exhibitors to pictures bearing Jarrico's name in the credits. He asked Hughes whether, from the time that Jarrico was called before the House Un-American Activities Committee to the time of the filing of the lawsuit, RKO had received any letters from exhibitors objecting to Jarrico. Although it was obvious from the record that RKO had not received any such letters, Hughes testified, "I do not know whether RKO received such letters or not."

Mosk probed, "You personally saw no such letters?"

Hughes replied, "I do not recollect seeing any. I may have but I don't remember seeing them."

Mosk continued, "You have no recollection of any executive of your organization calling any such letters to your attention?"

"Well, that, I do not want to say. There was a great deal of discussion within the industry during the period of time you mention concerning all Communists, and I don't remember any referring directly to Mr. Jarrico, but there may have been such discussions."

Mosk, reaching the apex of his case, showed that the picture in question carried the unusual introduction: "Howard Hughes Presents The Las Vegas Story." Mosk then pointed out that the entire theory of the Hughes declaratory judgment action was that the securing, developing, and maintenance of good will and the favorable regard of the movie-going audience for a studio depended in a large measure on the standing with the American public of the names that appear in the screen credits.

When no objection was forthcoming to this line of reasoning, Mosk threw his bombshell. He showed that *Time* magazine in a July, 1948, issue had quoted someone as saying with respect to Howard Hughes, "Howard will never die in an airplane. He will die at the hands of a woman with a .38."

The courtroom buzzed. Reporters dashed to phones to call in special stories. Attorney Groman jumped to his feet and vigorously objected "on the ground that the question is vague, ambiguous, uncertain and indefinite. It is hearsay, on the ground that it seems to be innuendo to refer to a certain unnamed person or persons, and on the further ground that. . . ." And on and on he went.

Nevertheless, the bomb had gone off with maximum effect. Those few people left in Howard Hughes' circle who had not yet read the *Time* article certainly knew about it now.

Mosk was trying to show that Hughes' name was not an asset to the film but nevertheless Hughes featured it prominently. He made his point in vain.

Unfortunately for Jarrico, the climate was wrong for a writer to win such a suit. McCarthyism was at high tide and the bulk of the people in the United States had no sympathy for anyone who refused to stand up and shout from the housetops that he was not a Communist. The guarantees of the Fifth Amendment were all but ignored. Judge Rhodes ruled against Jarrico and in favor of Hughes and RKO on all counts. The case went all the way up to the United States Supreme Court, where the Hughes position was sustained.

Hughes apparently enjoyed his role in this case very much. He received public applause and citations and awards from the Veterans of Foreign Wars, the American Legion, the non-union *Los Angeles Times,* and the Los Angeles City Council. Then Senator Richard Nixon praised Howard Hughes for his activities and the eulogy was entered in the Congressional Record.

Hughes made one of his rare public appearances, in a speech to the Hollywood Post of the American Legion. He told them, "I don't pretend to be an authority on Communist influence in the motion picture industry, but I feel I know as much about it as most of the laymen around here, and I think it might be worthwhile for someone in the industry to call a spade a spade."

The assembled legionnaires applauded wildly. Hughes went on to explain that there were two schools of thought in Hollywood. One segment believed that the Reds exerted considerable influence in the movie industry and another group argued that Hollywood was free from Communism. The second group, stated Hughes, believed that the House Un-American Activities Committee had no legal authority to investigate the motion picture industry.

Hughes continued, "Well, I happen to be one person who has some experience in other industries apart from the motion picture industry and, while I do not want to draw comparisons, and I do not want to say how many Reds there are in the motion picture industry because I want to be absolutely truthful, still I feel the influence is substantial."

He explained that a great number of people in Hollywood gave money to many organizations without recognizing that some of them were Communist fronts. In addition, there were other "people we don't even suspect" who were actually actively working for the Communist cause. Hughes gave no names.

Applauded by the four hundred members of the Legion Post at 2035 North Highland Avenue, Los Angeles, he said, "If there were only one Communist in Hollywood, that would be one too many."

Discussing the privilege against self-incrimination he commented, "When a person refuses to answer whether he is or ever has been a member of the Communist Party on the ground that it might incriminate him, he is not talking about politics, he is talking about crime. Did you ever hear a Democrat or Republican refusing to state his party affiliation on the grounds that it would tend to incriminate him?"

Then he went on to castigate not only the members of the party and the "fellow-travelers" but also those who defended their rights. "I am absolutely shocked at the people whom I would least expect who stand up and defend those who have not the best interest of our country at heart."

The ingenuousness of his argument runs through the address: "If anybody thinks that the Communist Party is the same as the Democratic or Republican Party, I can answer it this way; we are not fighting Democrats or Republicans in Korea!" This brought down the house. Hughes stood there, smiling benignly, while applause rang out for several minutes.

Finally Hughes concluded, "I can say one thing, in spite of all the movement to whitewash the Industry, to say that there was no Red influence in Hollywood, to sweep this matter under the carpet and hide it and pretend it does not exist, in spite of that, there is a sub-

stantial number of people in the Motion Picture Industry who follow
the Communist Party line."

Hughes obviously spoke from the heart. It was apparent to his
audience that he had a real interest in the subject. The mere fact
that a matter could bring him out of his self-imposed exile from
public life and put him on the rostrum of ordinary organizations to
make speeches was in itself revelatory of the strength of his feelings.

In the Jarrico case Hughes won on all fronts. The Screen Writers
Guild brought a mandamus to compel him to arbitrate but that was
lost and on April 28, 1953, the Guild voted 242 to 61 to drop the
legal action.

Other instances indicate that Hughes was and probably still is
fanatical on the question of Communists in America. Sheilah Graham, a widely-read Hollywood gossip columnist and author of a
number of best-selling books, related this incident. One day one of
Hughes' errand boys, a Mr. Gaye, called her while she was confined to her bed with influenza. The message ran: "Mr. Hughes will
be calling in five minutes and please be sure no one else is in the
room or able to listen on the extension."

While the wording itself was typical, the insistence of Mr. Gaye
that she should be alone and his reiteration, "Are you sure you're
alone?" went beyond the normal preliminary to a Hughes call.
Sheilah Graham recognized that it must be something "very important."

She assured Gaye that she was alone and, despite her illness,
readied herself with pencil and paper for the world-shaking news.

Precisely five minutes later the phone rang. The voice of Howard
Hughes said, "I've got a scoop for you, and I'd like to see you right
away. I'll send a car for you." She noted that his voice was filled
with excitement.

Miss Graham explained, "I have the flu. Can't you tell me on the
telephone? I'm feeling quite ill."

Hughes was very sorry but he could not talk about it on the telephone.

In her weakest voice, Miss Graham faltered, "I'm not sure I can
get up."

"This is the biggest scoop of the year," Hughes insisted.

The columnist certainly did not want to lose the "biggest scoop
of the year" so, with resignation, she replied "All right, I'll get
dressed, I'll wrap up and I'll come."

"Do that," Hughes replied, and hung up.

Ten minutes later a car arrived to pick her up. The chauffeur took her on a circuitous drive which lasted for more than thirty minutes. It had, by now, grown dark and Miss Graham could not identify her whereabouts any longer. Finally the car drew up at what appeared to be the back entrance of a one-story bungalow. From the shrubbery, the garbage cans, and the enormous Spanish building outlined against the sky, she recognized that she was at the back entrance of a Beverly Hills Hotel bungalow. Since the hotel was at most a three-minute drive from her home, she concluded that the drive must have been intended to confuse her.

Hughes opened the door. He settled her into an armchair in a small living room and paced up and down agitatedly. Miss Graham sat sniffling and sneezing, anxious to get the story as quickly as possible and to return home to bed.

She remembered other stories Hughes had given her, such as an exclusive concerning Cary Grant's elopement with Betsy Drake, with Hughes himself as the best man. This story certainly had to be more important than that. At last Hughes told the waiting Miss Graham that he had absolute proof that a certain Hollywood film official who was courting Elizabeth Taylor was a Communist. She waited patiently for him to continue, but nothing more was forthcoming.

Miss Graham demanded, "Is this a scoop? Is this what you want me to print? Of course I can't use a story like that."

Hughes persisted, "But I have proof."

The writer replied, "But I have no proof. Besides, it isn't my job to print he's a Communist. Why don't you tell the FBI?"

Hughes ignored her suggestion. Instead he tried to convince her of the truth of his statement. "This is a big story. If I give it to Louella or Hedda, they'd make it a big thing."

Miss Graham doubted that. Even those columnists would not print such a story without proof. Finally she rose. "I'm sorry, I must leave now. I'm not well."

She never saw him or talked to him again.

Hughes also supported the fight led by the American Legion against Charlie Chaplin and particularly against Chaplin's film *Limelight*. The great comedian, who was identified by rightists with the left-wing movement, had left the United States with some indication that he would never return after the Attorney General announced legal objections would be raised to Chaplin's return. The American Legion, other veterans' groups, and the right wing started a movement to bar the showing of Chaplin's new film *Limelight*, which had been booked by many film circuits, including 20th Century, Skouras, Randforce, and RKO.

When *Limelight* was shown at the RKO-Albee Theater in Brooklyn, the Legion forwarded a strong protest to Hughes and threatened to picket the theater. Under normal circumstances, if it had involved obscenity, pornography, a religious issue, or almost anything but Communism or radicalism, Hughes would probably have been in the forefront of the fight to prevent the self-appointed vigilantes from invoking their absurd censorship. But this issue involved a Hughesian pet hate—suspected Communism—and he immediately replied to John D. Home, Chairman of a Legion Post Committee on Un-American Activities:

"I have been prevented from having even the slightest connection with or voice in the management of the theater corporation." (Hughes referred here to the Justice Department antitrust action to split the moviemaking company from the theater-operating company.) "Nevertheless, starting last Friday, I have been making a most concerted effort to persuade the management of the theater corporation to take the necessary legal measures to cancel all bookings of *Limelight*. It is my strongest hope and sincere belief that this will be done."

Hughes was successful; RKO theaters did not show the film.

Howard Hughes and His Many Managers

JULY 7, 1924

THE DEMOCRATS appeared to be hopelessly deadlocked at Madison Square Garden in an endeavor to name a candidate for the Presidency of the United States. After 77 ballots William G. McAdoo of California led with 513 to Al Smith's 367.

The Ku Klux Klan reported eminently successful mass meetings in Long Branch, New Jersey; Binghamton, New York, and elsewhere throughout the country. Total attendance at all meetings was claimed to be over 50,000.

World champion heavyweight boxer Jack Dempsey announced he would be too busy making a movie to do any fighting this year.

People were reading Rupert Hughes' book *A Golden Ladder* and Edison Marshall's *Seward's Folly*.

In New York, theatre goers saw *Abie's Irish Rose, White Cargo, The Zeigfeld Follies* and *George White's Scandals*.

In the movies the top pictures were Jack Holt in *Wanderer of the Wasteland;* Harold Lloyd in *Girl Shy;* Rod La Rocque in *The Ten Commandments,* and Douglas Fairbanks in *The Thief of Baghdad.*

Howard Hughes was 18 years old.

17

Hughes was not the kind of personality to administer or operate a business. He had brilliant and inspirational ideas, he had a flair for engineering which resulted in products the world had never seen before; he could make many contributions to the success of an endeavor. Tight operational control, however, was not his forte, and he was forced to search continuously for competent supervisors and managers to implement his plans. Many of his appointments were shrewd and long-lasting.

His first choice was Noah Dietrich, who had replied to a routine newspaper advertisement. Dietrich was a certified public accountant who joined Hughes in 1924 in the bookkeeping department but soon became the company overseer. Hughes was nineteen when he selected Dietrich to run the Hughes Tool Company, and the association remained mutually satisfactory for more than three decades.

Dietrich became managing director of all of Hughes' properties. He himself admitted that he was also the Hughes "hatchet man." Many of his assignments would not come under the heading of "fun." For thirty-two years—no matter who else became associated with a Hughes enterprise—Dietrich remained second-in-command. Even corporate presidents might be appointed and told they had varying degrees of authority, only to find that aside from Hughes himself, Dietrich was the real boss.

Although the two men had differences from time to time, these were never significant nor serious until 1956, when Dietrich discovered that Hughes had ordered jet aircraft, conventional aircraft, and parts to the tune of more than a quarter-billion dollars.

Dietrich at that time had his office at the 7000 Romaine Street headquarters. One day he received a group of contracts for presentation to the board of directors of Toolco for approval. When Dietrich had finished summarizing the finances involved, he advised Hughes that he was convinced Hughes was making a colossal error. Hughes refused to listen and Dietrich, instead of continuing the argument, left for East Africa on a safari and did not return until fall. When he got back to the office he found that the orders were still there. He began a new round of talks with Hughes, trying to achieve either the cancellation of the huge orders or some form of long-term intelligent financing to meet what would inevitably become a back-breaking, bone-crushing payment schedule.

Dietrich had another problem. He was now sixty-eight years old and wanted to work out a retirement schedule. Although he had been receiving a base salary of $75,000 per year, he had not put aside any substantial sum of money. These two issues brought the relationship to a climax of irritation. All Dietrich could talk about was the danger he foresaw in the unfinanced jet orders, and his own contract. He wanted an interest in the Hughes Tool Company through warrants, rights of stock purchase, or some other method which would place him in a position to make a fair capital gain. He claimed that Hughes had promised him this many times.

The finale came one Sunday evening in May, 1957, when Hughes called Dietrich and asked him to come over to the Beverly Hills Hotel to see if they could reach a meeting of the minds. When Dietrich got to the hotel, he did not see Hughes but was called to the telephone.

It was Howard Hughes, blandly disregarding the subject of discussion. He told Dietrich, "I want you to go down to Houston immediately and do the best you can to improve Toolco's balance sheet."

Dietrich sensed that he was reaching a point of no return with Hughes. He refused to do the job unless Hughes would complete an agreement for the capital-gains arrangement he wanted.

Dietrich said, "It will only take five minutes."

Hughes replied, "You're holding a gun to my head."

Dietrich finally stated flatly that unless he received the agreement he was through.

Hughes' reply was typical—two words: "Starting when?"

Dietrich was against the wall. There could be no backing out now. He replied, "Right now."

Each sensed that there was nothing more to be said so they broke the connection. The next morning when Dietrich arrived at his Romaine Street headquarters he found the door to his office padlocked, and learned that a score of his personal staff had been notified during the night that their jobs had been eliminated and there was no need for them to return. Thus ended the relationship of thirty-two years between Howard R. Hughes and Noah Dietrich.

In April, 1959, Noah Dietrich brought a legal action against Howard Hughes for $2,111,965. The unusual suit charged fraud and deceit—a type of allegation difficult to prove and avoided by lawyers whenever possible. The suit alleged Dietrich was prepared to retire in September, 1956, but Hughes asked him to wait and he would then get $1 million in severance pay plus $833.33 a month for the rest of his life. The suit stated that Hughes would not put this offer in writing but that it was orally agreed upon. Finally, the suit alleged that Hughes owed Dietrich his salary for the last month; the sum of $6,250 was unpaid and he requested an equal amount as the legal penalty under the California State Labor Code for failure to pay salary.

The suit also added some additional damage items, such as $74,000 as his share of a promised percentage of the earnings of Hughes Enterprises. There was an allegation of $1,759 of expenses paid by Dietrich and not repaid and to this was added the round sum of $1 million as punitive damages.

The suit began to drag through the courts and then something unusual happened.

Noah Dietrich happened to start writing a book about his relationship with Howard Hughes. Carbon copies of the first three chapters just happened to fall into the hands of—of all people—a press agent in New York's Pan Am building who was once employed to keep Hughes' name out of the papers.

Witnesses to the next part of the drama won't discuss it. But a reliable source indicates that Dietrich agreed to drop his suit and not to write his book and Hughes agreed to pay Dietrich $1,000,000 over a period of twenty years at the rate of $50,000 a year.

Dietrich is again in the Hughes camp. When he is approached by a reporter for an interview, the first thing he does is to stall or say "no." The next thing he does is to notify Greg Bautzer of the approach.

Bautzer is said to be one of the only two men who can reach Hughes at any hour of the day or night. His phone call is usually returned within five minutes.

The relationship and the subsequent rupture were atypical only in the length of time involved. For example, it was Jack Frye who induced Hughes to go into the TWA operation. Frye served as Hughes' president for exactly ten years. In 1947 they quarreled and Frye quit.

Frye was succeeded by Ralph Damon, whom Hughes took from American Airlines. Damon was a very unhappy executive who lasted for seven years and then died of a heart attack. *Fortune* described him as a "frustrated and embittered man."

For a year Hughes searched for a man to replace Damon. At last he decided on Carter Burgess, at that time Assistant Secretary of Defense. Burgess remained for less than a year during which time he never saw Howard Hughes! When he quit he made his reasons quite clear. He objected to Hughes' system of interfering in company operations without consulting the company's president and he took exception to Hughes' procrastination on policy questions.

Burgess was followed by Charles S. Thomas. He, too, was not given any real authority.

Books could be filled with the tales of Hughes' relationships with his executive officers. In many cases, after taking office the unbelieving executive never again saw Howard Hughes, who could be contacted only through an intricate system. It was necessary to call headquarters at 7000 Romaine Street, leave a message, and remain available. The caller might have to remain available for days, weeks, or even years and still never hear from Hughes. Hughes might be in the building, next door, or on the other side of the world. No one knew. This type of liaison was too frustrating when added to the normal problems of any Hughes enterprise, and many of his managers simply walked out.

Typical of his relationship with managerial talent is the story of Hughes and Charles W. Perelle. A famous American industrialist, Perelle was born in Juneau, Alaska, of a Finnish mother and an Italian father. He spent his youth on the bleak area north of Sitka where his father was the superintendent of a gold mine. He studied at the University of Washington and at Boston University and after the crash of 1929 drifted into Seattle and went to work for Boeing as a part-time painter's helper. He rose to be manager of a major division of Boeing and in 1940 switched to Vultee. There he became general manager and received one of the highest commendations from General William S. Knudsen of the War Production Board for introducing assembly-line techniques into aircraft manufacturing.

Unquestionably brilliant and capable, he developed a reputation as one of the best production men in the aircraft industry. When Vultee merged with Consolidated Aircraft in 1943 he became senior vice president in charge of manufacturing. It was at this time that Hughes, looking around for someone to manage his volatile and unorganized aircraft company, approached Charles W. Perelle with an offer. (Perelle, it will be remembered, had been recommended to Howard Hughes by General Benny Meyers.)

Perelle listened attentively because he was having his own problems with Harry Woodhead, president of Consolidated-Vultee; and the management of Hughes Aircraft Company looked like a challenging and interesting job. However, Perelle was much too knowledgable to accept any job without some reasonable assurances.

The most important condition for Perelle was that he be the boss of operations. He knew that he faced serious problems in trying to manage the Hughes properties. In the first place there was Hughes himself: a chronic interferer who would not keep a hands-off policy and who had a tendency to flit in and out, making a decision here and ordering a change there, and then disappearing for indefinite lengths of time. In addition, there was always the chance that a long-term employee of Hughes would suddenly show and say, "I am authorized by Mr. Hughes to make all decisions in this field and I have decided that what you are doing is wrong."

Perelle told Hughes that he would not come to work unless his position of absolute authority was rendered unequivocally clear.

The longer Perelle delayed the more anxious Hughes became to have him. It was typical of Hughes to insist on having what was hard to get. As Perelle remained adamant Hughes grew more accommodating until finally they reached an agreement. Hughes would arrange a banquet at the Ambassador Hotel in Los Angeles and would invite every major official of the Hughes operations. On that occasion Hughes would announce that Perelle was going to be the boss, the absolute boss, and the only boss.

The banquet was finally held, and true to his word and probably with the best of intentions, Howard Hughes arose to inform his assembled employees, officials, and managers that he was appointing Charles W. Perelle as general manager of all properties. Perelle would give special attention to the Hughes Aircraft Company, which was then without any manager, but he would also take an interest in the tool company, the airline, and in all other Hughes ventures.

He made it clear that Perelle would become the over-all boss and that Noah Dietrich would stick to accounting and finance.

But the Hughes Empire just wasn't geared to operate in such a fashion. Immediately upon taking office, Perelle discovered that he was involved in an operation unlike anything he had ever seen or imagined. There were numerous and varied restrictions and difficulties which required an okay from Mr. Hughes himself before they could be changed—and Mr. Hughes generally could not be reached. If he could be contacted at all, it meant a call in the middle of the night or a visit some time after midnight. Perelle could learn to live with this, but there was more, much more.

In analyzing his accounts one day Perelle discovered that he had on the payroll a man named John Meyer who maintained an office and a secretary at Hughes Aircraft but apparently rendered no service to the company. Perelle made inquiries as to what Meyer did and received sly generalities in reply. Finally, he sent word out that unless Mr. Meyer could justify his existence on the payroll he was to be removed. Johnny Meyer's response was to proclaim that he would be there a long time after Perelle had gone and that as a matter of fact Perelle had done so badly that Hughes was considering closing down the aircraft operation altogether. Hughes' brash public relations man proclaimed publicly and privately that Perelle could never fire *him!*

At the end of October, 1945, Perelle wrote a letter to Hughes, which is a glimpse into the Hughes empire.

HUGHES AIRCRAFT COMPANY

29 October 1945

Personal and confidential

MR. HOWARD R. HUGHES,
7000 Romaine Street,
Hollywood 38, California.

Dear Howard:

I have from time to time verbally called to your attention some of the many problems confronting the operations of the Hughes Tool Company and the Hughes Aircraft Company.

There is some doubt in my mind as to whether or not my comments have impressed you sufficiently enough for you to recognize their importance. I am, therefore, as a matter of record, reviewing the situation for you in order to clarify some of the misinformation and misquotes, of which you undoubtedly are aware.

You will recall that prior to my actually assuming duties for you a banquet was held at the Ambassador Hotel, at which time you publicly announced that I was to have complete and unrestricted control of your operations. This is a matter of record. That this policy has not been carried out is also a matter of record, as I will subsequently point out to you.

I would like to call your attention to the fact that your original invitation to me to join your organization as executive in charge of the Culver City operations only was rejected as not being a position of sufficient magnitude to be attractive to me. Unable to accomplish this objective, you later included under the terms of my contract other more attractive fields of endeavor. That I have been precluded from functioning to your benefit or the benefit of the company in any of these organizations is evident.

Prior to my coming with you, you made the statement that you had absolutely no organization upon which you could depend. I am now in a position to concur with you in that statement. In spite of all the opposition and restrictions encountered, I now feel that we have been able to put together something in the way of an organization which has possibilities of functioning. That nothing short of a miracle has been achieved at the Culver City plant during the past year is a matter of factual record, some of which is set forth in subsequent paragraphs of this letter.

Contractual relationships with the Government were at absolutely the lowest level that I have ever encountered. The attempted short-circuiting of Wright Field has had serious repercussions. I know from personal experience that it was impossible to discuss this program with any one individual without the presence of other Government officials. The F-11 contract apparently had a very bad "tinge," which added to the difficulty we were encountering. . . . The many restrictions placed upon our operations by the War Manpower Commission and the Salary Stabilization Unit are well known to you.

We were frozen with a salary scale far below that which we should have had because of bad past practices. The lack of a priority of any kind for the Cargo Ship made progress tedious, and as I have stated before, the lack of an overall comprehensive program enthusiastically supported by all members of management of Hughes Tool Company further complicated our problem.

The three departments—Aircraft, Radio, and Armament—were combined into a single operating unit, thereby effecting great economies. The three purchasing departments were merged into one, the two plant engineering departments were combined, the two tooling departments were integrated, and the two industrial relations departments were merged. In payroll reductions alone these administrative changes effected a saving to the company of more than $25,000 monthly. Charges for rents have been reduced through the consolidation of operations, excess personnel have been eliminated, and some of the payroll parasites without assigned duties have been dispensed with. Reductions in executive personnel have likewise been accomplished.

Apparently this company had made no effort to maintain good relations or to cooperate with the Treasury Department. There was no Treasury-approved salary plan. Numerous inexcusable Treasury Department violations were on file. These were subsequently corrected; a salary plan in accordance with accepted Government practices was installed and Government approval obtained.

That we have been completely in the dark from an operating point of view with respect to accounting information is a fact well known to everyone connected with this operation. This has been discussed on many occasions and at great length with all concerned. The present practice of absorbing large amounts of expense which in no way contributes to the operation is, of course, very detrimental. The practice of carrying on our payroll persons who in no way contribute to the operation serves only to add to our overhead.

The apparent hidden expense accounts from the Hollywood operation still further aggravate the condition. A continuation of these practices, which serve only to cause abnormally high overheads, will preclude us from any competitive field of operation from a standpoint of pricing. This practice must be stopped and true operating figures available, or we will price ourselves out of business.

ARMAMENT DIVISION

Armament sales, as you know, to the Government were prac-

tically nil. Government approval had not been obtained for any
of the division's products. Immediate steps were taken to have
tests conducted at both Wright Field and Patuxent, with the
result that both Army and Navy approval were obtained. Thus
new and heretofore unobtainable business was opened up to
us, and contracts in the amount of $7,622,973 were entered
into as a result of this program. These contracts, of course, were
subsequently terminated with the cessation of hostilities.

F-11 PROJECT

As you know, there has been considerable delay in the F-11
Project. This can be accounted for, not excused, by some of the
following facts: At the time we discussed a March delivery date
which you had set, you advised me that engineering was 90%
complete. And, certainly if engineering had been 90% complete
it was reasonable to expect that an airplane could be produced
during the ensuing six months. However, subsequent investigation revealed that the engineering was less than 40 percent
complete and that all of the engineering done at the La Brea
Division prior to its transfer to Culver City had to be thrown
out. As of today the engineering still is not complete. No doubt
the figures were given to you optimistically in order that contracts with the Government could be retained. As I recall, you
advised me that serious consideration was being given by the
Army Air Forces to cancellation of the F-11 Project, and that a
change in management was imperative if the contract was to be
retained.

The poor quality of engineering as accomplished by the engineering department is no doubt well known to you. The complete lack of experience in the design and construction of airplanes in general, as well as the fact that they were lacking in
experience in the design of metal aircraft, was in itself a tremendous handicap. The ability of a group of engineers to function
as a unit in the design of aircraft can only be achieved by long
experience working collectively on basic types of airplanes and
airplane construction. This fact is well-known in all industry.
Even the experience of the engineering department at Houston
is publicized as such in the oil tool field. Further, the lack of
desire to profit from the experience of other qualified people
has led to constructional difficulties of serious proportions.

These faults have not been solved, partially because of the
various fixes which have precluded action in the matter. The

internal bickering in the Engineering Department caused by various conditions existent prior to my coming here, including the fact that too many people previously had an opportunity to approach you directly, has not been completely eliminated as yet. Time is the only cure for some of these ills.

The type of contract which we have covering the F-11 has also contributed materially to the conditions which are very unsatisfactory from a performance point of view. The tieing in of an experimental plane with a production order has long been recognized as a fallacy in the aircraft industry. That considerable improvement in the performance from a manufacturing point of view has been achieved is evidenced by the fact that the costs are now far below that anticipated by you and the Government at the time the contract was negotiated.

The various attempts by the Government to cancel this project as a whole have contributed materially to retarding progress. Wright Field had been shortcircuited and antagonized to the extent that it was necessary for me to devote considerable time to overcome a rather volatile situation.

Pressurization of the F-11, as such, was a complete failure because of irresponsible engineering and inspection. Less than one-half pound of air could be pumped into the fuselage. This has not been entirely corrected yet, due to a lack of proper engineering from the beginning. The continued failure of the induction system on actual test is a further contributing factor. The failure of the hydraulic system—faulty valves bursting due to poor design and inferior quality of vendors' workmanship accepted by our inspection results in our having to redesign and remanufacture with considerable delay. Many, many other reasons for delay could be cited; these are but a few of the most obvious examples.

The termination of the 98 airplanes, the cessation of hostilities in the Jap War, the mandatory reduction to a 40-hour work-week on Government contracts . . . all contributed to a further delay in the program. These are statements of fact for your information. Whether or not a more expeditious program could have been achieved is a matter for conjecture. I know of no one in this organization, other than myself, who, from either an experience point of view or knowledge of the problem, is qualified to comment one way or the other.

CARGO SHIP

Progress on the Cargo Ship is somewhat analogous to that on the F-11. There have been some delays, partly occasioned by the Government's classification of the project as nonessential and the red tape resulting from the cumbersome Kaiser-Hughes set-up at the inception. The confused contractual arrangement and the divided responsibility now set up, which you had promised to clear up and which you have not cleared up, leaves this program completely suspended, and no completion dates can ever be ascertained under the present conditions. This has been called to your attention numerous times and despite your comments to the effect that you didn't mean exactly what you said when you advised me I was to have complete responsibility for this program and make my own decisions, I do not now and never will concur in any program which has a divided responsibility.

Shortly after I came here and when all of the surfaces were practically complete, a 4,000 pound tail-heavy condition developed which necessitated redesigning and rebuilding the tail surfaces. This can be attributed only to inferior engineering. [In view of Howard Hughes' assertion that, "I designed every nut and bolt that went into this airplane. I carried out the design to a greater degree than . . . anyone has ever designed any of the recent large airplanes," Perelle was something less than tactful.]

Nevertheless, the project as a whole, in my opinion, considering the various problems, has moved satisfactorily. The numerous day-to-day errors which are attributable to inadequate engineering, poor inspection, etc., have gradually been overcome. You cannot build quality into individuals overnight; it must be achieved slowly. The poor administration of the Engineering Department, and on occasions our inability to obtain qualified personnel, is a situation with which I am sure you are familiar. The many restrictions placed upon us by the low wage scale with which Hughes Aircraft Company found itself saddled did not attract adequately trained personnel. The lack of a comprehensive program was a further contributing factor.

As you know, I originated the program for the launching of the Cargo Ship at Government expense, and this program resulted in the successful negotiation of a contract now awaiting your approval, which awards us an additional $1,500,000.

RADIO DIVISION

In the short period that the Radio Division had been in existence prior to my taking it over it had incurred a deficit of several hundred thousands of dollars. Certain changes were made by me in personnel who were unwilling to acknowledge my authority or cooperate with us in the basic program. Through subsequent negotiation with the Government we acquired some very lucrative contracts, totaling $719,841.30, which bid well to improve activity in the department and should result in further increment to the company providing we can have a continued workable policy. . . .

ACCOUNTING DEPARTMENT

While it is a long recognized and accepted business practice to have a controller to perform the necessary checking of the accounting program of a company—and again I wish to call your attention to the fact that this was discussed with you prior to my coming into the organization and accepted by me—at no time did I ever accept or ever consent to the accounting department reporting to anyone other than the general manager.

Far more drastic action would have been taken by me months ago had it not been for the fact that this point was not clarified by you with the other parties involved, and also had it not been for the fact that Mr. McDonnell continued to tell me he was resigning. Because of his pending resignation I saw no point in attempting to change his point of view. There can be no compromise in a situation of this kind. I refer you again to your public pronouncement at the Ambassador Hotel, which is a matter of public record.

That the various top officials of the Hughes Tool Company in Houston from time to time have openly discussed, and with Army officials, the thought of closing or relegating the aircraft division to a plaything for your personal use is also a matter of record. This results in the lowering of employee morale within the plant and in the discouragement of qualified people outside the plant from becoming associated with us.

The various commitments, promises, and public comments made by your Mr. Meyer, as your spokesman, to the effect that he was closing down the Culver City Division, that he was making personnel changes, and that you were so dissatisfied with my performance that you had given me an ultimatum of

90 days in which to perform or be thrown out, have all greatly added to the confusion, not to mention my personal embarrassment. These conditions have all been called to your attention before. I merely wish to make them a matter of record at this time. The public apologies of Mr. Meyer only serve to authenticate his original misstatements.

At the time I came to Culver City Mr. Meyer was on the payroll, but was not on the job, although he maintained an office and secretary. He refused to acknowledge the authority of management and contributed absolutely nothing to the regular operations of the plant, despite the fact that he secured Selective Service deferment from the armed forces as a member of the working organization.

My duties and responsibilities as vice-president in charge of manufacturing of the Hughes Tool Company have been completely ignored by the Houston organization. They have refused to cooperate even to the extent of sending me comprehensive reports of operations. No attempt was made to provide me with office space, temporary or otherwise. Plants were shut down completely, personnel changed in others, etc. and public announcements appeared in the newspapers, without even the courtesy of advice to me. I have not at any time been properly posted on activities of the Hughes Tool Company.

You advised me that you anticipated certain difficulties in setting me up in the Houston organization, not because of me as an individual, but because of an inherent resistance to anyone coming into the company whose abilities along certain lines had national recognition. That you have not been prepared to face the difficulties encountered is very evident to me. And, again, I must call your attention to the responsibilities which you incurred when inviting me into the organization under these conditions. As I have previously explained to you, I would be quite capable of taking care of myself within the Houston organization, without your support, although my efforts might for some time be ineffectual and at considerable expense to you due to the great resistance inherent in that organization.

The activities of my directorship on the Board of Transcontinental and Western Air, Inc., have been discussed with you. As I recall your comments on a particular night in the Town House, you stated that I would have complete voice in representing you on the Board of TWA. I subsequently found that this is not the case at all.

Likewise, you advised that the president of TWA was to report to me for whatever actions and/or decisions would be required on behalf of TWA and/or the Hughes Tool Company. This, too, as you know, has not been accomplished in any sense of the word. Various restrictive measures imposed by Hughes Tool Company have precluded my functioning to any extent whatsover. As I previously told you, I am not interested in wasting my time with ineffective or dummy directorship or management titles. The recent financing program wherein you, Mr. Dietrich, and Mr. Frye completely short-circuited me in its development is evidence of bad faith on your part in the execution of the spirit and intent of my contractual arrangements with you.

From the foregoing you can readily see that I must necessarily have considerable doubt in my mind as to whether or not you were acting in good faith at the time you gave me your word in the foregoing matter.

This record is prepared for your perusal, and I am herewith asking you what action you propose to take regarding these all-inclusive problems, pertaining particularly to the over-all benefits which should accrue to the Hughes Tool Company by a more comprehensive program as we discussed prior to my joining the organization.

The letter was signed:

Sincerely,
C. W. Perelle

Explicit though it was, the letter seemed to have little effect on Perelle's relationship to the various Hughes projects. Although there was some effort by Hughes and his people to be more politic and circumspect in invading Perelle's authority, in actual fact, there was no real change.

Within two months after receipt of Perelle's letter, Hughes personally took some of Perelle's Engineering Department personnel to do art work on the movie, *The Outlaw*.

Shortly thereafter Perelle and Hughes were deeply embroiled in a sharp contest. On the surface the problem was that the government contract for the construction of the Flying Boat was practically at an end as far as money was concerned. Perelle instituted discussions with the Reconstruction Finance Corporation to obtain new allotments. The RFC agreed to make available additional funds in order to complete the giant ship but when the new contract form arrived Hughes refused to sign it because it contained, among other provisions, the stipulation that RFC had a right to choose the test pilot who would first fly the boat. Hughes wanted to fly it himself.

Perelle argued with Hughes for three months in an effort to induce him to change his mind. As the arguments became more acrimonious Perelle realized that there was no future for him in the Hughes organization.

Shortly thereafter Hughes and Perelle were negotiating on the best way to end their business relationship. One major problem was that Perelle had originally refused to become associated with Hughes without obtaining substantial stock options. These Hughes had given him and now they had to be bought back. A payment of $250,000 freed another Hughes manager for other things. Perelle became the President of the Gar Wood Corporation, manufacturer of speed boats, and later moved on to become president of ACF Brill, Philadelphia bus manufacturer.

Howard Hughes and His Around-the-World Airline

THE YEAR 1938

HITLER MOVED into Austria. Douglas Corrigan made his famous "wrong-way" flight from Brooklyn to Dublin. The fifteen day international crisis ended on September 30 when the British and French yielded the Sudetenland to the German Nazis. Japan occupied the Canton and Hankow districts in China. Mussolini and Hitler inaugurated the Rome-Berlin axis. The war in Spain became quite bloody. Chile, Italy, Salvador, Venezuela and Germany all withdrew from the League of Nations.

Howard Hughes was thirty-two years old. He began to assemble an airline.

18

In 1928 a combined air and rail passenger service was organized to get someone in a hurry from New York to Los Angeles. The organization was known as Transcontinental Air Transport. Not long after its formation, TAT merged with Western Air Express to form Transcontinental and Western Air, Inc. In 1930 T & W instituted the first coast-to-coast passenger service entirely by airplane. The company's aircraft made many stops and the trip took almost as long by air as it did by train; nonetheless it was possible to purchase a ticket and board a plane in New York and fly all the way to California.

In the early thirties the famed New York-to-Paris pioneer flyer, Charles Lindbergh, became technical adviser to the firm and it began to be known as "The Lindbergh Line." It then became part of the North American Aviation holding company complex. Subsequently it shifted to the control of General Motors, where it was placed under the wing of their young vice president, Ernie Breech. Shortly after this, the airline industry was considerably shaken by an investigation conducted by then Senator Hugo L. Black (later Supreme Court justice), and legislation was enacted which divorced airline control from combination with other industry. General Motors was compelled to give up control of T & W.

General Motors sold the airline to Lehman Brothers, and a young pioneering pilot saw his opportunity.

Jack Frye started in aviation during World War I. After the Armistice he moved to California and set up a flying school and also performed as a stunt pilot. Shortly thereafter he operated a sort of scheduled passenger and taxi service with one converted Fokker plane in which he ferried movie stars from Hollywood out to their hideaways in the Arizona desert. Frye's company was eventually absorbed by Transcontinental and Western Air, Inc. In 1936 Frye became the president of the airline and continued to maintain his air transport license by flying regular routes over the line. He was the only top airline executive who ever did so on a regular basis.

Jack Frye had wonderful dreams and plans for the airline, but the shareholders refused to put up the necessary capital.

In one of his efforts to raise capital, Frye called Howard Hughes —they knew each other as expert fellow aviators. Frye explained to Hughes that his airline needed money to purchase planes, equipment, and facilities. He said he had some great ideas but he couldn't convince the shareholders.

Cautiously Hughes asked, "How much money?"

"Fifteen million dollars," and, knowing something of Hughes, Frye added, "in cash."

Hughes replied, "Great God, Jack, don't you realize that's a small fortune?"

Frye telling the story, adds the fillip, "And I was certainly relieved to hear him call it a 'small fortune'—to me it was a gigantic one!"

Hughes thought about the situation and concluded he liked the idea of being the major owner of a transcontinental airline. He set about purchasing majority control of the line from the existing shareholders, paying somewhere between $1 million and $7 million. (Mystery still shrouds the exact price.) He next obtained bank loans for the airline, and placed orders for equipment.

Hughes found a kindred spirit in Jack Frye and they whiled away many a night planning gigantic futuristic passenger liners that could cross the country faster than the speed of sound. Palatial quarters would be provided for the passengers who would be entertained with gourmet meals and the latest movies. People who heard these stories shook their heads sadly, muttering, "They sure are a crazy pair!"

The more Hughes worked on the airline the more interested he grew. In 1939, for a price of $1,500,000 he acquired another 20 percent of the common stock and finally, by the early forties he owned 5,200,000 shares, or 78.2 percent, of the company, having paid an average of $12 per share or approximately $80 million for more than three-fourths of the outstanding stock of what would become shortly one of the major airlines of the world.

In his proprietary supervision of the airline Hughes spent most of his time poring over the specifications for planes, engines, and parts. He studied manuals and engaged in interminable bull sessions with engineers about the technical side of flying and flight equipment. He frequently ignored problems of financial policy in order to worry about the layout of a plane or the make-up of an engine. *Fortune* commented that Hughes' "deepest satisfaction came from serving TWA as a super-conscientious test pilot and mechanic."

He and Jack Frye are credited with contributing tremendously to the development of the famed Lockheed Constellation, which became a standard commercial airline plane. Hughes was one of the first to obtain a Constellation and one of the first to fly it. In fact, Hughes and Jack Frye flew their first Connie on a scheduled TWA coast-to-coast flight carrying seventeen passengers and setting a new world record for the flight of 6 hours and 58 minutes at an average speed of 353 miles per hour.

In those early days Hughes planted the seeds which would one day flower into a giant world airline. Even before World War II he laid plans for airline routes around the world, and he ordered planes that could fly both the Atlantic and the Pacific Oceans. Unfortunately for these plans, World War II took away much of his equipment and the airline had to mark time until the war ended.

In 1945, with the world once more at peace, Hughes began to try to expand the company into a true around-the-world airline. His first step was to add Europe, Africa, and Asia to the routing. In addition to obtaining these coveted routes, he contributed some important technical assistance to other countries which earned him a most favored status. Actually Hughes never did manage to make TWA a literally "around-the-world" airline—he never got a trans-Pacific route. In 1967 TWA advertised itself as "the only major U.S. domestic trunk airline whose routes span the U.S.A. and extend three-quarters of the way around the globe servicing major markets in Europe, Africa and Asia."

A typical instance of international technical assistance was the arrangement TWA made with Ethiopia in 1945. TWA entered into a contract with the Ethiopian government to provide all needed administrative and technical assistance to establish the Ethiopian Airlines. President Truman gave his approval and blessing and saw to it that the United States Government donated three Army Air Force C-47's that had been left at a Cairo airfield when the war ended.

This fledgling carrier's original airfields were bumpy landing strips built by the Italian Air Force when Italy occupied Ethiopia between 1936 and 1941. TWA spent a long time building new strips. Hughes solved some of the Ethiopian flying problems in his own inimitable fashion. For example, the airfield at Mendi, a city not far from the Sudan, was on a steep slope ending in a gorge. Hughes' solution required the pilots always to land uphill, regardless of the direction of the wind, and to depart by going downhill and taking off at the end of the strip over the gorge. Ray Vicker writing in the *Wall Street Journal* called it "a skier leaving a ski-jump."

In some places there was no telephone service between the airfield and the nearest town. It became the duty of the incoming plane to buzz the village to inform waiting passengers that they should hurry to the air strip if they intended to catch the next flight.

The plan did not call for TWA to run Ethiopian Airlines. On the contrary, Truman, the State Department and Hughes intended to teach the Ethiopians how to run their own airline. At first, Ethiopians were able to hold only menial jobs on the line, while TWA personnel held all key positions. Meanwhile, TWA set up a training program and gradually the Ethiopians could replace TWA personnel in all capacities.

Hughes planned the operation so that after approximately a quarter of a century Ethiopia would be running its own airline. This schedule appears to be holding up, and by 1970 it is probable that TWA will have worked itself out of a job. Unquestionably Hughes and TWA personnel did a fine piece of work. Ethiopian Airlines is one of the safest in the world and has never had a fatal accident.

This kind of activity by Hughes made TWA welcome in many lands and enabled him gradually to build up routes to compete with Pan American—the only American airline then going overseas. Once Hughes had his routes in Europe, Asia, and Africa he had to expand with large quantities of equipment and new, modern, expensive aircraft. Thus began the financial problems which would end in a crisis of massive proportion: a struggle between one of the richest American individuals—Howard Hughes—and the wealthiest corporations in America—the insurance companies and the banks.

It all began innocently in 1945 when Hughes persuaded the Equitable Life Assurance Society of America to lend Transcontinental & Western $30 million, an amount which was increased to $40 million in 1946. Equitable, like all lenders in the United States, insisted on certain restrictions. The major ones, which would be felt in the future, were that Transcontinental & Western could not borrow additional money elsewhere without the consent of Equitable.

In 1946 Hughes' airline encountered serious difficulties. First, there were several crashes, which were financially expensive and caused people to travel on rival carriers. Next, the Constellations that Hughes had worked on so assiduously were grounded by the federal government for safety reasons pending certain modifications. Finally, the newly unionized pilots went out on strike, with the net result that Transcontinental & Western began to slide into the red with frightening rapidity.

Without an immediate financial transfusion the airline could not meet its payroll; and there could be no additional borrowing without the consent of Equitable. After considerable negotiation, Hughes agreed that Hughes Tool Company would lend $10 million cash to the airline; in return, Toolco would receive notes payable (convertible into common stock) and the power to name a majority of the directors of the airline. Equitable's consent to this new arrangement included an agreement that, if the airline ever defaulted on its payments to Equitable, the Hughes Tool Company airline stock would go into an Equitable voting trust which would give the insurance company management control of the airline.

Little mention of the arrangement was made in the financial journals, but this marked the first time that Howard Hughes had agreed that, under certain conditions, an important company under his complete control could be run by an outsider. Hughes never committed himself to a course of action that he didn't understand thoroughly, so he must have been sorely pressed to permit this arrangement.

In the midst of the financial negotiations Hughes in 1947 quarreled with Jack Frye, who left. For a time Hughes acted as his own president without portfolio, but in 1949 he persuaded Ralph Damon, formerly of American Airlines, to become the head of the company that, on May 17, 1950, changed its name to Trans World Airlines, Inc.

During this period TWA continued to lose money and Hughes did little to correct the situation. Some people accused Hughes of permitting these conditions because he benefited from them. The legal situation was as follows:

Hughes Tool Company enjoyed large earnings. It did not pay much money out in dividends because Howard Hughes, as sole owner, would also be sole recipient. This, in effect, created legal double taxation. Hughes Tool Company paid taxes on total earnings. If, for example, it earned $1 million, it had to pay out approximately $500,000 in federal taxes. This left the company with $500,000 net income. If Hughes now received $500,000 in dividends he would have to pay personal income tax on that amount, which could range up to 90 percent of the total sum, or $450,000. On the other hand, *"UPT"* if Toolco paid no dividends at all, it might become subject to the Undistributed Profits Tax, which was a special tax on profits retained by corporations beyond the needs of the company.

It was here that the financially troubled airline took on a special value. Since Hughes Tool Company was the major owner of TWA and TWA was losing money and needed financial support, Hughes could say to the federal government, "Look here, we at Hughes Tool Company can't pay out our earnings because we need that cash to bolster up the position of one of our major subsidiaries, TWA." It was an effective argument and, in fact, Toolco never did have to pay the Undistributed Profits Tax. It has never been ascertained whether this situation was planned, accidental, or a combination of the two.

In the middle 1950's the commercial airlines entered the jet age. Howard Hughes began to study jets with the same intensity he had once devoted to the gasoline combustion engine. One famous technician, Welwood Beall, who was credited with being the major force behind the 707 jet while he was chief engineer at Boeing, states that unquestionably Hughes was one of the most knowledgable men in the United States about jets. At that time the airlines could choose between five jets—all in the planning stage and not yet tested. There were the Boeing 707, General Dynamics Convair 880, Douglas DC-8, and the British Britannia and Comet. Insiders said that Hughes knew more about those five planes than any other person in the world.

In studying the General Dynamics plane, Hughes worked directly with Jack Zevely, sales manager for Convair, and with many of Convair's engineers. This was a new and impressive experience for the Convair people. Hughes' knowledge of aircraft design and aeronautical engineering came as a great surprise to them. He frequently made suggestions that their most talented engineers had not thought of.

Hughes took an active interest in every part of the plane. Ex-

perienced sales and engineering personnel were accustomed to the
fact that some aircraft purchasers worried about flight characteristics, others were concerned with speed and range, and still others
were worried about fuel economy. Only Hughes seemed interested
in everything, even to the extent of preparing his own blueprint for
toilet installations in the aircraft!

Hughta

The General Dynamics men were completely awed by Hughes'
conferences—which might go twice around the clock before Hughes
disappeared to get some sleep. Whole teams of Convair personnel
were reduced to exhaustion before Hughes required rest.

When the plane was finally completed and named the 880, Jack
Zevely said that, although some people believed it was named for
the eighty-eight seats in the plane, this theory was erroneous.
Actually, he explained, the name came from the number of sessions
the Convair people held with Howard Hughes to discuss everything
from where to put the coffee maker to the prices and delivery
schedules.

"To give the devil his due," said Zevely, "he was driven by the
unshakable idea that Howard Hughes is the world's greatest airplane engineer. He drove like hell, and his only desire was to have
the world's greatest airplane."

Characteristically, while engrossed in his comparison shopping,
Hughes procrastinated while other airlines placed orders. In
October, 1955, Pan American became the first airline to order jets,
placing its major orders with Boeing. American Airlines, the leading
domestic carrier, followed suit in November, and shortly thereafter
the remaining airlines began to place orders with one of the five
sources.

It was not until February of 1956 that Hughes finally ordered
some jets for TWA. Typically, when he did, it was on a grander
scale than anyone else's. He wound up ordering 133 Boeing 707's
for a total $166 million, 30 Convair 880's from General Dynamics
for $120 million, and some needed piston planes for $89 million.
Therefore, what with a few other commitments, Hughes had obligated the airline and to some extent Toolco and himself personally
for a total of $375 million. (This was the financial plunging that
had caused Noah Dietrich to blow his stack and led to the parting
of the ways of Hughes and Dietrich in May, 1957.)

In spite of Hughes' vast expenditure, his procrastination had
placed him far behind other airlines in delivery priority.

At this point Hughes came up with an idea he hoped would improve his position in line. He decided to corner the jet engine market, so he ordered three hundred and fifty jet engines from General Electric and from United Aircraft. These two companies were the major sources of jet engines, and he believed that if he controlled the engines no one could get delivery on planes without coming to him for help. He would then be able to schedule deliveries for everyone, including himself.

These obligations he had contracted involved a heavy burden of cash down payments, progress payments as the planes were completed, and equally large sums to be paid on deliveries. Between 1956 and 1960 Hughes had obligated his companies and himself personally for very close to a half-billion dollars. During all this ordering of equipment his only discussion was held with the chief engineer of TWA, Robert Rummel, and with no one else!

In mid-August, 1957, Hughes suffered another misfortune. Ralph Damon, who had been president of TWA for seven years, died and Hughes encountered the executive personnel problem noted earlier. For a year this giant airline had to be operated by a committee. Hughes at last selected Carter Burgess, who remained as president for eleven months. Once again, the airline ran without a president until July, 1958, when Hughes convinced Charles S. Thomas (formerly head of Foreman & Clark, a chain of men's clothing stores on the West Coast; an erstwhile Lockheed director, and Secretary of the Navy from 1954 through 1957) to come in and take over the job of running TWA.

In the interim, running like a ship without a rudder, TWA was losing large amounts of money. This was not Hughes' only problem in the year 1957. Toolco, which had been a highly profitable enterprise from the beginning, suddenly experienced a drop in earnings from $60 million to $20 million. The drilling tool field was becoming competitive and the "million-dollar bit" was no longer the gold mine that it had been. At the same time Toolco had to find money to support the orders for jets which Hughes had placed.

TWA owed the tool company a substantial sum of money and, in addition, in 1957 Hughes had been forced to commit TWA to a common stock offering to its shareholders which would permit each shareholder to buy one additional share of stock for each share owned. This procedure helped TWA because it increased its equity capital by $43 million, of which Hughes Tool Company provided

$35 million. Of course, this also increased the equity of Toolco in TWA.

By 1958 practically every major airline in the United States, including American, Pan American, Eastern, and United, had made satisfactory long-term arrangements for jet acquisition. TWA, however, was still without a plan. Instead of long-range planning, Hughes still engaged in short-term maneuvers. For example, one day Hughes called the Boeing executives in Seattle. "I believe that TWA is being discriminated against in your delivery schedule," he argued. Boeing executives angrily denied this, but the discussion resulted in a postponement of payment—and that may have been the real purpose of the call.

Under ordinary circumstances information on precarious corporate finances is highly confidential. No major company wants it known that one of its big customers is not paying on time and, of course, the company unable to meet its scheduled obligations does not boast of it. Unfortunately for Hughes, Boeing was putting out a new issue of securities and had to file a prospectus with the Securities and Exchange Commission. The law requires that the prospectus include all information concerning the financial status of the business. This information had to disclose that Hughes Tool Company had failed to make its required progress payments for the jets and that extensions had been granted. The financial community quivered over the revelation.

Hughes was now desperately in need of an adviser to assess fairly the involved world of high finance and come up with a plan.

No one could dispute Hughes' contributions to TWA, notwithstanding its poor financial condition and lack of permanent financing. Insofar as the company could be viewed as an operating unit, it was on the threshold of becoming a profitable enterprise.

Hughes had an excellent plan for a gradual increase of his jet fleet and the phasing out of piston planes so that by the middle of the 1960's TWA would no longer be using any nonjets. Actually this happened on April 7, 1967. He also had either completed, or on the drawing board, new and modern terminal facilities in Los Angeles, San Francisco, Tucson, Phoenix, Dayton, Washington, Boston, New York, and many overseas points including Paris, Rome, and Milan.

It was Hughes' idea to have the TWA flight center at Kennedy International Airport designed by the late Eero Saarinen, and this structure has since become an architectural showplace. The aircraft industry regarded the TWA maintenance facilities at Kansas City as the finest in the world. In addition, Hughes created a flight crew training center which was so good that the other airlines sent their personnel to TWA for training.

In view of all these factors he had much to point to with pride when he went out to obtain long-term financing. Asking for money, though, was not something Hughes could do alone. Normally Noah Dietrich would have taken care of it for him, but Dietrich had been gone for a year. Instead Hughes induced Robert E. Gross, chairman of Lockheed, to take on the job.

Gross had his own personal interest in the Hughes empire. He wanted to sell Hughes the Electras Lockheed was manufacturing and he also wanted to buy Hughes Aircraft Company, which was gradually developing into a fine electronics concern. (Gross had made a lucrative offer for Hughes Aircraft as early as 1953.)

While Gross tried to make concrete plans with various members of the American financial community, Hughes pursued his own methods. He stalled for time. He conducted interminable telephone conferences with his own executives, his creditors, bankers, friends, and other interested parties. Reports indicate that at one moment he would be full of confidence, threatening those he accused of trying to profit from his troubles; a moment later a note of desperation would creep into his voice and the listener would hear what *Fortune* described as "intonations of a disaster in the making—a disaster being contrived by unnamed forces that were unscrupulously bent on undoing all that he had created."

Robert Gross, as Hughes' first emissary to Wall Street, spent considerable time with George Woods, head of First Boston Corporation, attempting to work out a plan for financing TWA. Gross suggested both the acquisition of funds from the public sale of certain assets owned by Hughes, and borrowing money by offering liens on Toolco assets.

George Woods instructed his organization to study the situation and to develop certain proposals. He then sent word to Hughes that he was prepared to meet with him either in California or in the East. One evening Hughes phoned Woods in New York and suggested, "Why don't you put your ideas on paper and send them to me and let me study them?"

By this time Woods had had his fill of working with a ghost.

Sharply, he replied, "That is not the way I do business, Mr. Hughes. I am accustomed to dealing with a face, not a voice."

Unable to work out anything productive, Gross at last suggested to Hughes the possibility of selling TWA. Hughes was adamant. "Come what may I will never sell the airline."

At about the same time Hughes told his friend Floyd Odlum, "I'll live in a garret before I surrender TWA."

Gross tried again to resolve the dilemma. He went to see Winthrop Smith, senior partner of Merrill, Lynch, Pierce, Fenner & Smith—the largest investment banking house in the world. Smith assigned brokerage personnel, including William Forrester, one of his top men, to work out a deal for the public sale of the stock of Hughes Aircraft Company.

The theory was that this asset was of little personal benefit to Howard Hughes, but the stock sale could raise enough money to relieve Hughes' entire financial problem. Actually, the Howard Hughes Medical Institute owned all the stock but, as will be seen in another chapter, by a series of financial maneuvers the money could be used for the benefit of Howard Hughes and Toolco.

At the beginning of the study Forrester was optimistic because he had the impression that Hughes would agree to a selling price for Hughes Aircraft stock based on the fifteen-times-earnings yardstick. This was a customary estimate in corporate circles and would give Hughes $225 million—a substantial contribution toward solving his financial problems. Just when the Hughes Aircraft deal was ready to be written up for signature, the stock of Litton Industries (another company heavily involved in electronics) rose abruptly to a selling price of twenty-times-earnings.

Without ever being granted a personal meeting, Forrester got word from Hughes that he too wanted a twenty-times-earnings ratio. Forrester now either had to come up with some method of closing the gap or give up. Hughes' formula was too rich for those interested in the transaction, so Forrester went back to New York. At this point Robert Gross gave up too.

Now the situation was bleak indeed. In the first quarter of 1959 TWA lost almost $4 million, but at least Hughes, TWA president Charles Thomas, and the airline personnel had done one thing right. Their pilots, crews, and technicians had been thoroughly trained to handle the incoming jets.

In the spring of 1959 TWA received delivery of its first jet, and

Thomas immediately scheduled a regular flight between New York and San Francisco. When the second jet arrived it too was added to the schedule. The coast-to-coast nonstop jet flights were an instantaneous success. They began to operate at 96 percent capacity with a utilization rate of almost nine hours a day. The planners began to revise their theory that each jet would replace two piston planes when it became apparent that each would replace at least three, and possibly four piston planes. Other advanced planning at TWA also paid off handsomely. TWA had inaugurated a replacement parts, overhauling, and checking system for jets throughout the world. TWA could operate its new jets immediately wherever it had routes.

With the jets operating successfully, the TWA financial picture turned around from a loss in excess of $1 million a month to a profit of close to $1 million a month. Now a ray of sunshine appeared. Instead of the possibility that it might take a long time for the public to accept the jets it quickly had become apparent that they were instead instantaneous money-makers. It was obvious that the airlines were not going to need as many jets as they had at first anticipated. Hughes proceeded to cancel some of his orders, thus cutting down substantially on future indebtedness. Now he could present a far more interesting financial picture to the potential investors.

Not without optimism, Hughes turned his efforts to a new source: Fred Brandi of Dillon, Reed and Company, another giant American investment banking house. In the middle of March, 1960, Brandi came up with an idea that looked good because it left Hughes Tool Company in complete control of TWA and provided $340 million in cash to meet the commitments coming due in the next several years. The money would come from the major American banks plus Equitable and certain other life insurance companies, including Metropolitan Life. Of all the participants in the plan, only Metropolitan Life was new as a Howard Hughes creditor.

The first step in firming up such financing is a letter which specifies the intentions of all the parties and is called a "Letter of Intent." Brandi prepared the Letter of Intent and also a Purchase Agreement which set forth all the details of the financing. It was a good package but it contained one point which might become a tender spot. This was the provision that if at any time there was "an adverse development" the lenders could give Hughes Tool Company and TWA notice and if the adverse development was not corrected within ninety days, the TWA stock held by Hughes Tool Company had to be deposited with trustees. They thereafter would run TWA. This voting trust could effectively remove the control of TWA from Howard Hughes and give it to the creditors.

Meanwhile the insurance companies and the banks would provide $160 million in new senior money. Toolco would provide $100 million which would be subordinated to the senior money, and the banks would provide an additional $50 million in the form of a revolving account for TWA directly. In order to meet immediate commitments, the banks would make available a credit of $40 million to assure an uninterrupted flow of jets.

It appeared that this transaction would solve TWA's problems. With satisfactory long-term financing, Hughes' airline could now join the ranks of other American airlines which had comfortably adjusted to the jet age.

Then the little firecracker in the financing plan called "adverse development" became a time bomb.

Charles Thomas, just a few days before the signing of the financing contracts on July 21, 1960, announced his resignation. When Thomas had joined TWA as president, Hughes had made his customary offer of a handsome salary and pie-in-the-sky as far as power, management prerogative, and stock interests were concerned. Thomas was no novice, so he left himself an "out" by telling Hughes that when he got the chance he wanted to work in California, where his wife and family lived.

Fortuitously, according to Thomas, and deliberately according to Hughes, in June, 1960, Thomas happened to be vacationing at Pueblo Beach, California, where he was approached by an old friend who asked whether he would be interested in becoming associated with the Irvine Ranch, a 193,000 acre tract of undeveloped real estate just outside Los Angeles. The offer was attractive and put Thomas in a position to make his final demands of Hughes. He asked for a clear definition of powers, provisions for deferred payments, and stock options.

Hughes turned Thomas down flatly, declaring he would not bargain at the "point of a gun." He added that as soon as the contemplated financing was completed, he was confident that he and Thomas could reach a satisfactory agreement. Thomas interpreted the conversation as another of Hughes' procrastinations so he made his resignation public.

This effectively postponed the settlement. Because of failure to make proper payment on the existing loan, Equitable Life Assurance Society of the United States now had the power to throw TWA into bankruptcy. However, Equitable declined to exercise its rights.

The creditors offered a plan for extending the amount then due, approximately $27 million for one month. The offer was predicated on Hughes' acceptance of the revised financial plan which had just been aborted. In addition, under the new plan Hughes would have to find an acceptable president for TWA or agree to have his stock placed in the hands of a trustee.

At this point the Civil Aeronautics Board announced that they were investigating a proposal by Hughes for the merger of TWA and Northeast Airlines. This had been an important program worked out by Hughes, and he had gradually acquired control of Northeast. This control was exercised through Atlas Corporation and the CAB said that it might well be illegal.

The over-all outlook was bleak. TWA, Hughes Tool Company, and to some extent Hughes himself, were behind in payments to banks, insurance companies, and the aircraft manufacturers. American lending agencies refused to advance Hughes any funds unless he was willing to give up control of TWA. To make matters worse, CAB indicated a renewed interest in investigating the affairs of Hughes, TWA, and his whole airline program.

Most men faced with these ominous problems might have run for cover, ready to accept almost any way out. Hughes didn't. Instead he stalled for time. The deadline of September 1 set by the insurance companies for the extension passed and Hughes did nothing except argue that he deserved more time because he was negotiating in good faith. With respect to the now overdue payments, Hughes pointed out that it would be bad for the nation's economy if the insurance companies pushed a major airline like TWA into bankruptcy. Sensing the validity of his argument the potential lenders hesitated.

One necessary member of the financial syndicate was Metropolitan Life Insurance Company, with whom Hughes had never before been involved. Its chief financial officer was Harry Hagerty, a man with a reputation as a hard-headed bargainer. Metropolitan presented a very real problem for Hughes at this stage. Not only had it never done business with Hughes or any of his corporations, but it was not anxious to become involved with him—except on its own terms.

In mid-September, sensing that he was getting nowhere with the insurance companies, Hughes tried to pull off a new coup. He approached General Dynamics Corporation and several banks with a proposition. At this time Hughes already owed General Dynamics nearly $5 million each for a score of Convairs; $50 million worth of these jets were waiting at the San Diego plant to be delivered and General Dynamics insisted that Hughes had to pay for insurance and maintenance for the interval between completion and acceptance of delivery. (Hughes, of course, would have been happy to accept immediate delivery but he was unable to raise enough money to pay for the planes.)

Under Hughes' new plan, financing would cover a term of seven years with the banks handling about 60 percent of it and General Dynamics itself handling the other 40 percent. General Dynamics was interested, because it wanted desperately to find a solution to what looked like a severe problem, but it could not get the consent of either its own creditors or the banking interests.

Hughes made a few feints in various directions, searching for at least a temporary solution. Nothing worked.

By November Hughes was forced to admit privately that the situation was precarious. His personal intelligence sources informed him that some of the banks were preparing to go into court and had instructed their counsel to ready the necessary papers. In addition certain of the banks were even taking over the TWA cash accounts, and shortly the airline would lack money for continued operations. The Civil Aeronautics Board, observing the operation closely and recognizing the possibility of an imminent crisis, warned Raymond Cook, who had been handling TWA's financial matters for four years, that—unless some financing arrangement was concluded promptly—the CAB was going to conduct an open hearing into the possible effect on the public interest of depriving Hughes of control of the airline.

By December the situation looked hopeless even to Hughes, who told Cook to go back to the syndicate and tell them he was ready now to accept the original deal. The lending group, by now chary of Hughes' dancing maneuvers, asked TWA and Hughes Tool Company specifically to request the loan in writing. This application would have to specify all of the terms and conditions as previously outlined. It contained proposals to Hughes such as the agreement to trustee his stock and give up control of the airline, to provide for a 22 percent premium if he tried to refinance the deal within two years, and certain other provisions that were anathemas to him. However, both TWA and Toolco signed the letters, which were forwarded to Dillon, Reed. At last it looked like the deal was back on the track when, without warning, Raymond Cook was fired and replaced by Greg Bautzer.

Bautzer was tall, dark, and handsome, and married to actress Dana Wynter. As an attorney he represented many movie stars and handled Hollywood legal problems. He also was adept in dealing with Howard Hughes.

Bautzer flew to New York and through his actions made it apparent that he was not ready to cooperate in a deal which he believed would emasculate Howard Hughes as far as his future relationship with TWA was concerned. Instead, he presented numerous plans for substitute deals, none of which could be carried out. At last, the conclusion of the main Dillon-Reed deal became inevitable and on December 3, the boards of directors of TWA and Hughes Tool Company met and approved the arrangements. On December 7, Attorney Bautzer announced that Howard Hughes himself had signed the letters of agreement and it now seemed certain that the deal would be completed. On December 8 the bankers released some of the details to the public. The plan called for the banks and insurance companies to lend TWA $165 million; stockholders of TWA would receive an offering of $100 million in the form of subordinated debentures with warrants to purchase stock attached. Hughes Tool Company would buy $78 million worth of these debentures and pick up any more that were not subscribed by the stockholders.

Most importantly, the control of TWA would leave Howard Hughes and the Hughes Tool Company and be assigned to a three-man board to be known as the voting trustees. This voting trust would last for ten years. Toolco would name one trustee, and the insurance companies would select the other two. If Hughes accepted these terms, he unquestionably gave up control of TWA—the step he had often sworn he would never take.

At the beginning of December everything pointed to the likelihood that Hughes was going to do exactly what he said he would do in the agreement. He even named his trustee: Raymond M.

Holliday, financial vice president of the Hughes Tool Company. The lawyers and the bankers were very busy that December preparing loan documents, debentures, and all of the paper work required by complex financing of such scope.

First, all of the TWA stock owned by Hughes Tool Company had to be transferred from Toolco to the three trustees. This would make them the legal owners and would enable them to vote the stock without hindrance by anyone. The transfer was scheduled to be made by the Farmers Bank of Delaware as the local agent in Wilmington, Delaware, on December 28, 1960. On the following day the lenders would turn over the funds to TWA in New York. The turnover of funds had to be coordinated with the registering of the mortgages on the airplanes at the headquarters of the Federal Aviation Agency which maintained an office in Oklahoma City for this purpose.

The selection of the two trustees to represent the lenders was a difficult task. They had to be men of impeccable character, high caliber, and extensive knowledge of business operations. Although such men existed in sufficient numbers, they were always busy and in positions of importance and trust. Such men could not be manipulated by the whims of those requiring or desiring their services.

Ernest Breech was in Detroit that December of 1960, winding up his affairs at Ford Motor Company, where he had just retired as chairman of the board of directors. He was doing some serious thinking about what would occupy his time after he left Ford when he received a call from Grant Keen, vice president of Equitable, inviting him to become one of the voting trustees for TWA. The idea did not appeal to him and he tried to avoid committing himself, but Keen convinced him that it was his duty to accept. (Breech, it will be remembered, had been a pioneering executive of the airline when it was T & W and he was the youthful vice president of General Motors.) The second trustee selected by the lenders was Irving S. Olds, who had some time before resigned as chairman of the United States Steel Corporation and was now a partner in the New York law firm of White & Kase. Holliday, as Hughes representative, was the third trustee.

After the appointment of the three trustees, the next job was to transfer the stock from Hughes Tool Company into the names of the trustees. This was scheduled and would be handled by Holliday. Although it was not necessarily a big job, the officers and clerks of the bank in Wilmington were well prepared and ready on December 28th to handle all details of the operation when they received a call from Mr. Holliday advising that he could not go to Wilmington until he heard from Greg Bautzer, the only person in direct contact with Howard Hughes. The information was at once relayed to the representatives of the lenders, who immediately warned Bautzer that, if Hughes tried to snarl up this deal, foreclosure proceedings would be started without further delay.

Greg Bautzer, as always, was suave and ready with excuses. It appeared that Breech and Olds wanted to make some changes in the document which governed their conduct and Bautzer had to be sure that these changes were not in any way injurious to Howard Hughes or the Hughes Tool Company. In fact, the changes related primarily to liabilities of the trustees and other provisions having nothing to do with Howard Hughes. Little wonder that many of the officers of the lending agencies became skeptical, especially when the day passed without further word from Hughes.

On December 29 some of the lenders began to get angry and indicated that they had lost patience with Howard Hughes. If this deal was not consummated on schedule there would be no deal at all. Apparently the word got back to Hughes and it became known that Mr. Holliday was on his way to Wilmington. However, Bautzer explained that although Holliday was going to Wilmington he still had no authority to execute the forms which would transfer the stock from Toolco to the trustees. It was already Thursday and those who wanted to see the deal consummated were growing nervous. The next day was Friday, the 30th, and no business would be transacted on Saturday, December 31.

By Thursday night Bautzer had reached Hughes, who gave his consent, and Holliday signed the transfer papers and returned to New York. The closing was scheduled to be signed at the Chemical Bank in New York at 3:00 P.M. It was assumed that both Bautzer and Holliday were on their way when one of the bankers got a call from Dana Wynter, Bautzer's wife, that Bautzer was exhausted from overwork and had been ordered by his physicians to go to bed and rest. He could in no circumstances be disturbed.

Holliday arrived at the Chemical Bank on schedule but when he saw the documents he said, "I don't see how you can expect me to sign all these, especially with the main lawyer sick. I won't sign anything until we either get Bautzer here or a new lawyer."

Someone suggested that perhaps Holliday could reach Bautzer, so he put a call through to Bautzer's room at the Hampshire House. He was informed that Bautzer had gone to Roosevelt Hospital. It looked more and more like a typical Hughes maneuver to gain time, but the lenders said flatly it was today or never. Everyone was watching the clock because it took two steps to complete the deal. Holliday had to sign the documents, and the mortgages had to be registered with the Federal Aviation Agency in Oklahoma City, whose offices closed at 5:30 P.M. New York time.

The last moment drew near and Holliday, in a private room, tried frantically to reach either Bautzer or Hughes by telephone. Someone thought of getting the Federal Aviation Agency in Oklahoma City to extend its working time, and that office agreed, giving the bankers until 7:30 New York time to complete the deal. The mortgages were already in Oklahoma City ready to be handed across for recording as soon as Holliday signed. Seven o'clock came and went and the bankers sat stolidly staring at the second hand on the clock. Finally, about ten minutes before the deadline, Holliday reported that he had reached Bautzer and received permission to sign. The telephone line had been held open to Oklahoma City and the FAA people were told that it was all right now for the mortgages to be stamped and registered.

For the first time Hughes had lost an important fight.

Those who had been watching the contest made many predictions as to Hughes' next step. Some said he would find a new interest to occupy him: Return to making movies or become involved with electronics at Hughes Aircraft. A few speculated that Hughes could never accept defeat but would slug it out with the bankers who had forced him to abdicate.

The first important meeting of the board of directors of TWA was scheduled for January 26, 1961. At that time the new directors and the trustees could institute a program of needed reforms.

On the day before the scheduled meeting Ernest Breech told Raymond Holliday and Maynard Montrose, another board member controlled by Hughes, "You can tell Howard not to worry as long as I am here. I'm working for all the stockholders and I believe that his interest is our interest. I want all of his suggestions to come to me through you." However, Hughes aborted this meeting by instructing his directors not to attend. Without a quorum the board meeting had to be canceled.

The new trustees, secure in their power, would not be put off by the lack of a quorum. They took immediate legal action to call a stockholders' meeting for February, at which time they voted the stock which had been transferred to them at Wilmington at the end of the previous year. They elected a completely new board of directors, although it did include the six Hughes men.

The new board selected Charles C. Tillinghast, Jr., as president and chief executive officer of TWA. Tillinghast, an attorney, was originally active in the management of Bendix Aviation Corporation. The board gave him an unusual employment contract to induce him to move from Bendix to TWA. His was a peculiar position, for he knew that Hughes could regain control of TWA simply by paying off the lenders.

While this would require several hundred million dollars, a man like Hughes was always unpredictable. If Hughes could somehow acquire the funds, in spite of the additional liability of a $16-million penalty, he could pay off the debt, reacquire his stock, call a new meeting, elect a new board, and fire Tillinghast. Consequently, the board had to give Tillinghast a provision in the contract which guaranteed that if he was dismissed he would be retired with full pay. Hughes vociferously and vehemently expressed his objection to this provision.

The new board had the bit in its teeth and it was out to run TWA notwithstanding Howard Hughes. The members showed their complete autonomy by employing an independent law firm (Cahill, Gordon, Reindel & Ohl) to determine if the corporation had any legal claims arising from past activities. This could be interpreted as aimed directly at Howard Hughes and the Hughes Tool Company, but Breech explained that the board wanted to find out if anyone had done anything injurious to the corporation which would require legal redress. He said they wanted to find out "if, for the protection of the Board, we should sue anyone at all, not just Hughes. As a director you are just as guilty for not suing as if you had contributed to the damage."

In taking over the management of TWA, Tillinghast as president and Breech as chairman of the board adopted a forward-looking expansion policy. They placed an order for twenty-six Boeing jets which would cost close to $200 million and they began negotiating for new loans with the insurance companies. In granting the new loans the lenders insisted on a contract clause providing that if the voting trust was ever terminated for any reason the new loans would be payable in full immediately. Hughes could easily read this as a new weapon against him, and he did not take kindly to it. Through his chief counsel, New York attorney Chester Davis, he advised the board that he was opposed to contracting new indebtedness and also opposed to the order for the Boeing jets.

While these points were being debated, John S. Sonnett, one of America's top corporation experts, developed an idea for a case against Hughes Tool Company. His theory was simple. It stated that, since Hughes Tool Company had supplied airplanes and financing to TWA, it had prevented outsiders from coming in to supply those commodities. This action violated both statutory antitrust laws and the common law duty between the parent and a subsidiary where the subsidiary has minority interest.

Sonnett and his law firm specifically recommended that TWA bring an action against Howard Hughes and Hughes Tool Company. Unquestionably Hughes had inside information as to what was going on and he knew about this possible suit. He sent an offer to Tillinghast to provide TWA with another $100 million of new money for common stock. Incidental to the offer Hughes wanted the voting trust terminated.

The new Hughes offer seemed to have an effect contrary to what Hughes had anticipated. The board rejected the offer and instructed counsel to bring suit. Legal action was brought in the Southern District of New York on a multimillion-dollar claim. Plaintiffs requested complete divestiture of any stock interest by Hughes or Hughes Tool Company in TWA.

The Hughes forces at once brought a countersuit in which they claimed substantial damages and they brought in all of the lenders including the insurance companies as additional defendants. TWA now encountered the same problem people always had in suing Hughes. It would be almost impossible to get any kind of judgment against Howard Hughes personally without some form of service upon him. Still, in a suit involving hundreds of millions of dollars, there were enough funds to employ numerous process servers.

Writer James R. Phelan described this period when the detectives, marshals, process servers, and hundreds of others were searching for Hughes, as follows:

"So many people were looking for Howard Hughes that at times Southern California resembled the chase ballet in *High Button*

Shoes. The pursuit had its origin in a massive legal battle between Eastern financial interests and the billionaire Western owner over control of Trans-World Airlines.

"The Easterners engaged a posse of private investigators to serve Hughes with various court orders and writs, and Hughes promptly deployed a counter-intelligence force to frustrate them. The drama of this war, enhanced by the intriguing fact that Hughes had not been seen in public for years, attracted a group of writers and photographers for national magazines. As the safari progressed, it was joined by a crowd of spear-carriers, including a Los Angeles lawyer who specialized in suing Hughes, the way some lawyers confine their practice to maritime law."

The anti-Hughes forces, armed with a practically unlimited war chest, hired several agencies to try to locate him. These entered into active competition, creating a great many false alarms, feints, and cul-de-sacs that kept the hunters flying futilely hither and yon. Many people, eager to participate, added to the general confusion by offering false clues. One story involved an Oriental mystery woman who purportedly possessed a recent photograph of Hughes taken by her brother. She tried to sell the photograph for $1,500, meeting in dimly lit bars with a number of the ferrets and persuading them that she had the only photograph in existence of Hughes taken since 1952. (The photograph turned out to be a fake.) How many of the eager sleuths paid anywhere from $100 to $1,000 for a print is not a matter of record.

An ironic aspect of this search was that Hughes was really paying the bill for both sides. From the standpoint of his own defense, he was obviously defraying all costs. As owner of 78 percent of TWA he was also paying more than three-fourths of the cost of the search to find him. Many anecdotes arose from this duality. Leadership of the operations of both hiders and seekers was in the capable hands of former FBI agents. One day the Hughes leader found the anti-Hughes leader resting, and the Hughes man told the anti-Hughes man, "You know, practically all of your expenses and salary are coming out of Mr. Hughes' pocket and he does not expect you to rest on his time. Mr. Hughes expects everyone whom he is paying to give him an honest day's work."

One day word got around that Hughes was going to be at his headquarters at 7000 Romaine Street in Los Angeles. A lawyer representing the anti-Hughes forces arrived with a subpoena which

commanded that Hughes lay aside all of his business and appear
in the Federal District Court in New York, bringing with him what
amounted to a few carloads of records. As usual the front door to
the Romaine Street building was locked and the lawyer hammered
on it in vain. (Most of the more experienced Hughes-seekers had
been to Romaine Street weeks before, and knew what to expect.)

Convinced at last that the door would remain locked, the lawyer
actually stepped back and read the entire subpoena to the closed
door! He was blissfully unaware that concealed in trucks, cars,
behind hedges, and in nearby buildings, scores of eyes were watching him. And many a Hughes hunter had to restrain himself from
bursting into a raucous guffaw.

The army of hunters never did find their quarry, and Hughes
successfully evaded service. The majesty of the law, however, could
not be thwarted; nor could the inexorable turning of the wheels of
justice be stopped by one man, skilled as he was in the art of disappearing.

The lawyers for TWA at last devised two tricky legal methods
for reaching Hughes. They started another action in the Chancery
Court of Delaware, because the real owner of the bulk of TWA
stock was Hughes Tool Company, a Delaware corporation. Then,
in order to acquire jurisdiction over Hughes they requested an
order of that court to sequester Hughes' stock so that he could not
collect dividends, vote the stock, or otherwise handle it as his own
unless he appeared in court. Hughes' lawyers tried to parry this
blow with a number of legal gimmicks, the major one utilizing the
common practice of a "special appearance" in court. Under this
legal doctrine, lawyers could appear and argue, but this did not
confer on the court jurisdiction over the parties because the appearance was "special" and not "general." However, the Delaware court
ruled against Hughes, stating that what Hughes was trying to do
was to defend the case without subjecting himself to the jurisdiction of the court. Now all decisions were against Hughes.

In the federal case, TWA managed to schedule depositions for
September 24, 1962, with all counsel being advised, registered
letters mailed, advertising appearing in appropriate places, and
every other possible means taken to notify Hughes that he had to
appear to testify. When September 24 came and went and Hughes
did not appear, the court adjourned the depositions to October 29,

1962, and when he again failed to appear more adjournments were granted.

Hughes steadfastly refused to come into court and finally, reluctantly, the federal court ruled that Hughes had forfeited his case for failure to appear. Now it only remained to determine the amount of damages Hughes and Hughes Tool Company would have to pay TWA. The federal court, in a decision by Judge Metzner, appointed J. Lee Rankin as a special master to hold hearings and fix the amount.

Counsel for Hughes appealed this to the Second Circuit Court of Appeals. There the major issue turned out to be whether Hughes and Toolco actions had been approved by the Civil Aeronautics Board. Hughes and his lawyers argued that the federal court had no jurisdiction over these issues; in any case, it was good defensive tactics to argue that they were only following CAB orders.

In spite of this argument, the Second Circuit affirmed Judge Metzner's ruling that the existence of the Civil Aeronautics Board did not eliminate the jurisdiction of the federal court, and that approval by the CAB did not eliminate possible legal violations of other kinds by Hughes and Hughes Tool Company.

One of the biggest blows to the Howard Hughes case was that, as a result of his failure to appear in court, his counterclaims were dismissed—not just dropped involuntarily by the court, but "with prejudice," which meant that he could neither renew them nor use them as the basis of a new suit.

Hughes now took the case to the United States Supreme Court, where he was momentarily heartened because the High Court issued a Writ of Certiorari. This meant that the court ordered the records to be sent to it for examination, after which it would hear arguments on the appeal. Following this, however, the Supreme Court dismissed the appeal as having been "improvidently granted." This has a number of interpretations. It probably meant that the court decided it should not have heard the appeal in the first place but had made a mistake. On the other hand, it could be interpreted as a decision by the High Court that it should not hear an appeal of this nature until the case was completed.

Obviously, the matter would not be complete until the special master decided the amount of damages. Theoretically, the special master could find that there were no damages, in that Hughes and Hughes Tool Company never did injure TWA and consequently there was nothing to grant damages about. If such were the case there would be nothing for the United States Supreme Court to hear. This theory has given rise to the belief that the United States Supreme Court will one day hear the case again. That there will be another appeal to the High Court is reasonably certain.

The proceedings on damages before the special master are still pending. The official position of Howard Hughes and the Hughes Tool Company is that "no damages will be awarded and that any judgment which might so award damages would be reversed on appeal."

This was the status of Howard Hughes and his airline as of April, 1966. With Hughes either directly or through his spokesmen still reiterating, "I'll never give up TWA," on Monday morning, April 11, 1966, Hughes surrendered and the major financial news of the day was that Hughes was selling out his entire 6,584,937-share holding in TWA. On that day his holding consisted of 75.18 percent of the outstanding stock of TWA, and a national underwriting syndicate headed by Merrill Lynch, Pierce, Fenner and Smith, Inc., would handle the sale.

The news came as a complete surprise to the financial world and became the conversation piece of the day. It was headline news in practically every newspaper that carried business news of any kind. The headline in the *National Observer* was typical: THE SECRETIVE MR. HUGHES TOSSES IN THE TOWEL.

At the time of the announcement the stock was selling at about $80 a share. Taking into account the total number of shares involved, this would be the second largest underwritten offer of already issued stock in the history of the world financial community. The only larger offering of its kind was the sale of the Ford Motor shares in 1956, which involved approximately $650 million.

The considerable amount of legal work involved was completed with great rapidity and the sale was consummated within one hour on May 3, 1966. The final price was $86.00 a share with an underwriting discount of $3.00 to the syndicate and with net proceeds going to Hughes Tool Company in the sum of $546,549,771. Analysis revealed that Hughes had paid an average of $12 a share for the stock, or a total outlay of about $80 million. Since he received in return approximately $550 million he had achieved a profit on his holdings of some $470 million. The taxes which had to be paid on the profit were sizable, and there were close to $1 million of legal and accounting expenses. Nevertheless it appeared very likely that Hughes, through the Hughes Tool Company, would be at least $350 million *in cash* richer as a result of the sale.

This was a typical ending to a Howard Hughes saga.

During his management of TWA it had limped along and, although it grew larger and stronger until it became one of the major airlines in the world—it didn't make money. However, when, on April 17, 1961, Hughes was forced out and replaced by Charles C. Tillinghast, Jr., that man, as president, assisted by a team of specialists to run the company, achieved these results: the $15 million loss of 1961 was reduced to $5 million in 1962 and converted to a $20 million profit in 1963. This rose to $37 million in 1964, and exceeded $50 million in 1965.

At the time Hughes was forced out, the stock was selling at less than $10 per share and it dipped to a low of $7.50 per share shortly thereafter. Then it rose steadily, reaching a high of almost one hundred. So it was that Howard R. Hughes became one of the wealthiest men in the world in spite of himself!

Although the sale of his TWA stock ended Hughes' legal interest in the airlines, it did not end TWA's legal interest in Hughes. The law suits by TWA against Hughes Tool Company and Howard Hughes remained alive. In fact, on May 26, 1966, Trans-World Airlines announced that it had increased its claim against Hughes and Toolco by some $145 million to $300 million, an amount exclusive of the tripling of the damages under the anti-trust law. In the meantime, Herbert Brownell was appointed as the new master to hear the action with respect to damages. Hearings have begun but are not yet completed.

A TWA spokesman, commenting on the increasing amount of damages, said that a re-examination of the grounds for the lawsuit had revealed that TWA's profit during Hughes' stewardship had been adversely affected, and other airlines had cut into TWA's share of the market because of mismanagement by Toolco and Hughes. TWA cited a series of supporting reports from such authorities as R. Dixon Speas Associates, aviation consultants; Price, Waterhouse & Company, one of the nation's largest accounting firms; Drexel, Harriman, Ripley, Inc., eminent Wall Street investment bankers, and Coverdale Colpitts, well-respected consulting engineers.

In the past the litigation had contained an element of humor because anything that TWA got from Hughes Tool Company or Hughes himself went back into TWA, of which Hughes directly or indirectly owned approximately 75 percent. Thus it appeared that only the lawyers would profit.

The litigation is obviously a deadly serious matter to Howard Hughes because Hughes and Toolco no longer have any financial interest in TWA. Any award of damages would be viewed by Hughes as being cut directly from his own hide.

Howard Hughes and His Electronics Company

MAY 2, 1947

PRESIDENT MIGUEL ALEMAN of Mexico, after addressing a joint session of Congress in Washington—the first Mexican official so to do—received a ticker tape parade down Broadway.

The United States joined Britain to defeat a proposal that the United Nations General Assembly permit the Jewish Agency for Palestine to state its views before the Assembly. The Soviet Union, Czechoslovakia and Poland voted for the proposal. Against were the United States, Great Britain, China, France, Canada, Egypt, India and Sweden.

Secretary of State Marshall accepted the proposal of Soviet Foreign Minister Molotov for the resumption of joint negotiations in Seoul on the future of Korea.

Japan put into effect a new Constitution renouncing war forever and subjecting the sacred Emperor to the will of the people.

Broadway was showing Arthur Miller's *All My Sons,* Ethel Merman in *Annie Get Your Gun,* Fredric March in *Years Ago,* Ralph Bellamy in *State of the Union.*

In the movies Loretta Young appeared in the *Farmer's Daughter;* John Garfield and Joan Crawford were in *Humoresque;* Rex Harrison in *Notorious Gentleman* and Claudette Colbert and Fred McMurray were in *The Egg and I.*

Howard Hughes was forty-one years old.

19

In 1934, shortly after Pilot-Mechanic Glen Odekirk jokingly suggested that Hughes build his own plane, Hughes ordered Odekirk to find a structure suitable for designing and constructing a racing-plane. Odekirk leased some space up at the Glendale, California airfield, and began to put in a stock of parts and tools.

When Hughes arrived fresh from a vacation in Florida he hired additional help, including a number of men from the California Institute of Technology. Within a few months twenty men were hard at work cloaked, as was usual for Hughes, in secrecy. For a while the enterprise went without a name, but at last, in order to identify this operation from others in which he was involved, Hughes had a sign painted proclaiming it the "Hughes Aircraft Company." It was not a separate corporation but merely a division of Hughes Tool Company of Texas, organized to manufacture racing planes but never really serving that purpose.

Hughes Aircraft functioned primarily to modify the planes Hughes used to break world speed records, including the aircraft used in his flight around the world. The actual manufacturing of airplanes, however, required repetitive and detailed operations not in the Hughes' spectrum. In addition, since Hughes had become the major owner of an airline, theoretically government authorities would not approve of his also building the airplanes which the airline would fly.

Hughes continually conceived of projects for his aircraft company, including planes he intended to sell to the Army. These ideas, implemented by Odekirk, soon made the available space at Glendale inadequate and finally Hughes authorized a search for a suitable piece of land on which to build a new factory.

Odekirk and others flew all over California looking for a good site for an aircraft factory. Hughes had laid down certain minimum requirements. There had to be enough land to accommodate an airstrip. The site must be near enough to metropolitan areas to

ensure an adequate flow of employees. This tended to impose narrow limits on the available choices. After searching for several
months Odekirk located two choice spots. He described these to
Hughes, who wanted to see them from the air.

On the particular day selected for the survey, the weather over
the site on the outskirts of Culver City, a section of southwest Los
Angeles, was calm, while that over the other site, in the San Fernando Valley, was turbulent, so Hughes made a quick decision—
the Culver City plot. On this spot they built a huge sprawling factory and an excellent level airstrip. It was here, too, that Hughes
built his Flying Boat and his photo-reconnaissance plane.

When World War II ended, many of Hughes' key personnel
drifted away. They believed that Hughes would give up his aircraft
plant because it had never really accomplished very much. These
people grossly underestimated him. After considerable thought
Hughes decided that the next world-wide business growth would
occur in the field of electronics and he would therefore build the
finest electronics corporation in the world.

His first problem was to find someone capable of running it, and
he set about trying to interest General Harold L. George who had
run the military Air Transport Command during World War II and
who, now retired, was in Peru operating a local airline. Hughes
wrote to General George and asked him to head the Hughes Aircraft Company in its change-over to an electronics operation. George
turned him down.

Startled and piqued, Hughes at once put through a call to Peru.
After lengthy discussion Hughes prevailed upon George to consent
to come to Los Angeles with his wife and children at Hughes'
expense.

General George, accompanied by his family, checked into the
Beverly Wilshire Hotel and left word at the Romaine Street headquarters that he was waiting. He waited and he waited. Days later,
he received word that Hughes would meet him on the street. At
the appointed time and place a battered car with Hughes inside
pulled up. The two men drove aimlessly around while Hughes
talked, trying to sell George on the electronics idea, but the general was not buying.

By this time George was briefed on Hughes' reputation for interfering in operations, the impossibility of reaching him for decisions, his long absences, and all the other legends, and he kept

mentioning them. Hughes never took offense—he probably recognized most of the problems. However, he talked persuasively to General George about his revolutionary idea. He wanted to build an electronics company that would employ the best brains in the world; they would bring in scientists and engineers capable of creating miracles. He talked about landing space ships on the moon and performing other electronic miracles, and to the practical-minded, cigar-smoking general it all sounded like science-fiction.

But Hughes could be most persuasive when he wanted to. General George, tempted with an offer of $50,000 a year and an exciting new venture, could resist no longer and agreed to go to work for Hughes Aircraft. Hughes added Charles B. Thornton of the Ford Motor Company, and his old friend, Lieutenant-General Ira Eaker, to the Management Section. To handle the technical side of the operation he hired two brilliant scientists—Dr. Simon Ramo of the California Institute of Technology and Dr. Dean Wooldridge of Bell Telephone's Research Department. These two gifted men were given the broadest latitude in hiring the people they needed and in deciding on projects to be developed.

With his team of experts assembled, Hughes set about obtaining government contracts in the electronics field. His earliest efforts involved a missile-guidance system and an airplane radar system. The radar project was an effort to combine airborne radar, a Sperry gunsight, and an electronic computer in such fashion that, without visual contact, an air-gunner could shoot at an enemy plane. The missile-guidance system was intended to permit an aircraft to launch an air-to-air missile at another aircraft and then to guide it after launching.

The government did not at first take the electronics venture seriously. Ramo and Wooldridge, however, began to develop a really promising electronic fire-control device. One test after another was successful and it looked like the diligent scientists were about to solve the problem. Simultaneously the Air Force became concerned because it lacked an interceptor device for the air defense of the United States—one which would function reliably in bad weather.

The desires of the Air Force and the work of Ramo and Wooldridge coincided, and late in 1948 Hughes Aircraft signed a contract to develop an all-weather fire-control unit for installation in the Lockheed F-94. This contract, involving $8 million, was comparatively small but, as General George said, it turned out to be

Hughes Aircraft's "dress rehearsal for mobilization." Not long after, the Korean fighting broke out, and orders for military equipment flooded the industry. Hughes Aircraft became the sole source of supply for the fire-control systems of all interceptors—North American Aviation's F-86, Northrop's F-89 and F-94, and even the Navy's McDonnell Aircraft F-2H4.

Up to the Korean conflict most of the industrial giants of America had left this type of electronics manufacturing to small outfits like Hughes Aircraft. However, in 1950 the Air Force sponsored a design competition for an electronic fire-and-navigational control system to be used in the F-102 Supersonic Interceptor. This newly developed fighter plane would become a mainstay of the American defensive and offensive systems, and production of its electronic firing and navigational systems would involve millions of dollars.

More than twenty companies competed for the design award, including General Electric, Westinghouse, and organizations new to the field who were seeking to diversify. Hughes Aircraft exhibited remarkable ingenuity in winning this competition and shutting out the major American corporations. The company acquired a near-monopoly on the Air Force's sophisticated electronics requirements, especially in the fire and navigational control fields.

Delivery figures indicate the rapid rise of the company. In 1949 Hughes Aircraft delivered $8,600,000 in equipment. This rose the following year to $151 million and approached $200 million by 1953.

Hughes was delighted with the turn of events. He gave his people at Hughes Aircraft carte blanche in ordering equipment and personnel, with the result that the Culver City establishment in the mid-1950's had one of the finest electronics laboratory facilities in the world and employed some of the best brains in the industry.

Over a thousand physicists, electronics engineers, mathematicians, and other high-grade professional technicians worked for Hughes Aircraft. An incomplete roster would include the names of Dr. Ralph P. Johnson, formerly Deputy Director of Research of the Atomic Energy Commission; Dr. Harper Q. North, who had been one of the outstanding research men at General Electric; Dr. Andrew V. Haess, one of the nation's most talented scientists; Dr. Lester C. VanAtta, previously the foremost expert on antennae for the United States Navy; Dr. Allen E. Puckett, an expert in aerodynamics, and Dr. Burton F. Miller, who had headed the Electrical Engineering Division of the Manhattan Project at the University of California.

Although theoretically the scientists at Hughes Aircraft could have anything they wanted, in practice it did not work so smoothly. Hughes Aircraft was still a division of Hughes Tool Company which meant that major requests had to be approved by Toolco. Unfortunately, Noah Dietrich, who ran Toolco, was not personally enthusiastic about the aircraft company. Dietrich seemed at times to believe that the aircraft company was nothing more than a hobby for Howard Hughes, and as supervising manager, he was not disposed to waste too much money on a hobby. For a while General George managed to get along by calling Hughes in the middle of the night or by leaving word at the Romaine Street headquarters that he wanted Hughes. Usually within a reasonable time he had his answer.

This picture changed abruptly in 1951 when Hughes moved his base of operations from California to Las Vegas, Nevada. Here he rented four suites in four different hotels along the Strip and maintained communication only with certain selected personnel at Romaine Street. This created long delays in the exchange of messages and sometimes weeks went by while George waited for Hughes to return a call.

In the meantime Hughes Aircraft was getting large orders and it needed working capital. In fact, the actual amount of business done by Hughes Aircraft at that time was even larger than that turned out by Hughes Tool Company. Nevertheless Toolco ran the aircraft company, lock, stock and barrel and no one from the aircraft company was ever elected to the Board of Directors of the tool company. The result was that when the Toolco Board met to consider a decision about aircraft company affairs nobody there really understood the problem or had any empathy with the people running the aircraft company.

One of the first serious complaints arose when, in order to meet the Air Force schedule, Wooldridge and Ramo felt it necessary to double the laboratory staff, which would necessitate considerably more space. They sent a request through George to Hughes for additional facilities requiring an expenditure of close to $4 million.

Weeks passed before the answer came back that any additional facilities would have to be built at Las Vegas. Hughes at this time had acquired much land on the outskirts of Las Vegas, but he never told General George or anyone else in the aircraft company about his plan to divide the company facilities in this fashion.

George, Wooldridge, and Ramo rejected Hughes' idea to move a major portion of Hughes Aircraft to Las Vegas. They believed that such a separation would injure the operation and they feared their scientists and engineers would refuse to live either in the desert or in the turmoil of Las Vegas.

Without resolving the matter satisfactorily General George began construction of additional facilities at the Culver City plant. Hughes became churlish. Up to this point his major interest had been in the solution of unusual engineering or electronics problems. Suddenly he became interested in all problems in and about the plant, including construction plans for the new facilities. He issued an order that all blueprints had to be submitted to him for approval.

The architect's drawings would be sent to him and would come back, sometimes within a day or two and sometimes within a week or two, with unlikely alterations such as a change in the position of the windows or some rearrangement of corridors and with detailed instructions on the most minor points. At one time he insisted they change the color of paint, commenting, "I favor light colors."

Once while the Hughes Aircraft management breathlessly awaited Hughes' decision on expenditures involving millions of dollars for new laboratory facilities, they received an imperious demand for a detailed breakdown of the disposition of four years' proceeds from the sale of candy bars, milk, and other refreshments, sold in the plant vending machines. In another ukase, Hughes insisted that they change all the procedures for purchasing and cleaning seat covers for company cars!

Hughes and General George became involved in a dispute over the grass runway which was part of the original plant. While this had been satisfactory for light use, it became totally inadequate to handle the hundreds of military planes landing and taking off in tests of the control systems installed at the plant.

The runway was a muddy morass during the rainy season and rough during the dry season. At one point conditions deteriorated so much it became necessary to stop the testing, and George insisted on authorization to pave the runway. It took an unbelievable two and a half years and an official Air Force protest that the runway was damaging its equipment before Hughes agreed to have it paved.

Some of Hughes' decisions infuriated his executives. He owned 1,200 acres at the aircraft company site, but the plant itself used only something under one-tenth of the acreage. Facilities at the plant were highly congested, and excellent use could have been made of the additional land. For example, Dr. Wooldridge required broad areas in which to test his experimental radar antenna. The land was available and it would only be necessary to build antenna towers. The real estate in question was zoned for agricultural use and carried a very low tax rate. Hughes insisted that no change be made because industrial zoning would bring about an increase in taxes. In spite of the fact that the government would have borne the additional expense, Hughes refused to consider any change.

It is possible that the managerial staff of Hughes Aircraft might have survived all of these frustrations and irritations if it had not been for Noah Dietrich. When Hughes Aircraft first began to do business, Dietrich had been amused and treated it as a Hughes plaything. However, when the company thrived, Dietrich launched a campaign to become general manager. In the past, Dietrich had been successful in defeating every aspirant to a major position in the Hughes empire. He originally rid Toolco of Colonel Rudolph C. Kuldell, a retired Army engineer who ran the company until replaced by Dietrich. He superseded Jack Frye, head of TWA until 1947. Now Dietrich wanted to run Hughes Aircraft.

At the beginning of 1950 Dietrich set out to undermine the authority of General George and his assistants. General George and Charles D. Thornton, the assistant general manager, requested bank lines of $35 million for the year 1952 in order to meet an estimated $150 million of anticipated delivery. Dietrich refused their request, cutting the amount to $25 million, which he negotiated with the Delaware National Bank in Pittsburgh.

The reduction in credit forced the management to attempt to induce the Army to make partial payments, to postpone paying bills, and to take other action to try to make $25 million do the work of $35 million. Dietrich finally was forced to raise the amount to that originally requested.

A showdown came when the accountant's 1951 inventory audit showed a shortage of $500,000 in the finished parts inventory. General George immediately instituted an investigation which revealed that four men on the assembly line, trying desperately to meet delivery schedules, had bypassed inventory procedures to take finished parts directly to the assembly line.

This meant that a finished part might have been installed in the final product for delivery to the Army without being accounted for on the way. Although the practice was irregular, it apparently was necessary and there was no evidence of fraud.

General George explained all this to Noah Dietrich, who refused to accept it and insinuated that the missing parts had gone to the black market.

General George said furiously, "What you have just stated is in fact an accusation of fraud, lack of integrity, and deceit on the part of certain principal executives."

The charge was withdrawn but the bitterness remained. As Dietrich took over more and more control of the affairs of Hughes Aircraft, word drifted down that he was beginning to run the show. The people at Hughes Aircraft were unhappy about this. A fundamental philosophical difference existed between General George and Noah Dietrich. George had established a system where management and staff acted as a team. The "thinking boys," as the general called them, and management personnel worked together on the same problem. This system might or might not work elsewhere but it demonstrably worked at Hughes Aircraft, which seemed to solve its problems more satisfactorily than almost any other electronics group in the country.

Dietrich, on the other hand, felt that these people should have nothing to do with management. At a meeting of the upper echelon of the Culver City operation, the subject turned to sales, expenses, budgets, and other financial matters and Dietrich directed that the scientists and technical personnel leave the room during the discussion. They had nothing to do with that problem, he said. General George refused to accede to Dietrich's request.

By June, 1952, the Culver City management group had had enough of Dietrich's interference, so they prepared a letter headed IMPORTANT COMMUNICATION which they forwarded to Hughes. George, Thornton, Wooldridge, and Ramo signed the statement which accused Dietrich of trying "to seize personal power without regard to the consequences." They made it clear that Dietrich's actions were hurting the company and would interfere with meeting the Air Force schedules. They asked for an immediate audience with Hughes.

Hughes treated this request as a move in a war of nerves. He neither acknowledged receipt of the communication nor scheduled the requested meeting. Shortly thereafter Hughes was seen showing the plant to a group of strangers whom he did not bother to introduce to anyone, but who were identified as Westinghouse executives. It was rumored that Hughes planned to sell the aircraft company and that Westinghouse wanted to buy it. The rumor did not disturb the aircraft company personnel, who were confident they would be welcomed by Westinghouse or any other established American corporation. Their greatest problems arose from working for Hughes.

The Hughes Aircraft executives met to discuss the matter. These people had developed some of the most sophisticated electronics systems in use by the United States Armed Forces. They had revolutionary ideas on the drawing board. They knew they were capable of generating hundreds of millions of dollars in business both with the government and commercially. They were especially eager to become involved in methods of airport flight control. They decided that if the company were to be sold they should help locate a buyer. They learned that Dan Pepper, then head of Penrose Corporation, was interested and had formed a syndicate, which included some of the major Wall Street financial houses, to buy Hughes Aircraft.

Significantly, Pepper's syndicate was prepared to offer the principal executive of Hughes Aircraft the opportunity to become an owner of a part of the equity—a possibility Hughes had never suggested.

Pepper had a number of meetings with Hughes in Los Angeles, but he got nowhere. Hughes would never set an asking price nor would he show any of the company's figures. It soon became apparent that Hughes was not going to sell, so Pepper returned to New York.

Now the company executives realized that Hughes had no intention of selling Hughes Aircraft—apparently he only wanted to know how much buyers would pay for the property. (He had gone through almost the same act a few years before, with Wall Street asking him to name a price for Hughes Tool Company. When he finally received a firm bid of $230 million, he turned it down.)

Company management then took a different tack. They wrote Hughes that they could no longer accept responsibility for meeting the schedules set by the Air Force in their contracts, and that they were prepared to so notify the Air Force.

This ultimatum elicited a response from Hughes. On September 20, 1952, George, Thornton, Wooldridge, and Ramo were directed to present themselves at the Beverly Hills Hotel, where Hughes maintained his hundred-dollar-a-day bungalow.

An affable Howard Hughes greeted them. He wore slacks, and a coat with leather elbow patches over a new white shirt. Hospitably, he provided food and liquor and freely he praised the work the men had been doing. He was very sorry that he could not get down to the aircraft company plant more often, he assured them, but they must understand how busy he was running RKO, refinancing TWA, and handling the purchase of property near Las Vegas. He even joked with them that RKO was "a bad nuisance—it represents about 15 percent of my business and takes 85 percent of my time."

Then he told them that they were allowing their emotions to cloud their judgment—after all, they all had the same goals—there were no real differences between them. In spite of Hughes' attentions to them and his persuasive and confidential manner, General George and his companions remained unconvinced. They made it clear that they required—indeed demanded—complete authority to carry out their responsibilities to the aircraft company.

Hughes retained his equanimity. He remarked that internal quarrels over the control of a company were not unusual in large corporations. They must consider the problem he faced because he relied so completely on Dietrich to take care of his "whole picture." Their insistence on having their own way and their unswerving solidarity and collective action he seriously considered a "Communistic practice."

A few days later Ramo, Wooldridge, and Thornton, with the approval of General George, flew to Washington to tell the Defense Department what was happening and to prepare them for the imminent blowup. The die was cast; all possibility of rapprochement with Hughes was ended. Washington decided that it could do nothing.

At this moment the appearance of a new buyer brought about a temporary truce. Although Hughes had no real interest in selling, Robert Gross of Lockheed made a serious offer to lease the aircraft company's facilities for ten years. Lockheed was prepared to buy the entire inventory, including the work in progress, and to make an additional payment for good will.

Negotiations between Hughes and Gross fell into the accustomed pattern. In battered Chevrolets in the middle of the night they rode around arguing and bargaining. Many of these meetings were held near Las Vegas. Hughes would pick up Gross and they would go for a drive in the fresh desert air. Hughes continually increased his price. He asked $34 million, and after Gross agreed, he wanted $36 million.

When Hughes raised the price to $50 million, Gross gave up and went back to California. The $36 million offer had been generous. Hughes would have ended up with the cash from Hughes Aircraft —about $10 million, the nonelectronics part of the business with a net worth of about $9 million, and the liquidated value of other assets in the amount of $15 million. This made a grand total of close to $35 million, the sum Hughes had invested originally in the Culver City plant. Hughes would have had his investment liquidated plus the $36 million profit paid by Gross. He would have continued to own the physical plant, which would have returned to him at the end of the ten-year lease.

Meanwhile, on the Dietrich front the war continued. Dietrich held up agreed-upon executive bonuses for 1952. He ordered General George to cease negotiating with the Air Force on prices. Ramo and Wooldridge decided to make one more attempt to arrive at a solution with Hughes. In July, 1953, they met with him and spoke directly and sincerely about how much was at stake. They reminded him of the vast potential of Hughes Aircraft and how much they could do with it if he would let them.

Hughes listened politely. He assured them he would never sell the plant, that everything would be all right, that he would straighten out all of their problems.

"You are full of promises," they told him.

Hughes replied, "Be patient, I may have a little trouble making up my mind, but once I do, I move fast."

The two men waited for twenty days and then submitted their resignations. As soon as this news became public the Pentagon called General George to find out what his future plans were.

"I intend to stay so long as I am able to do any good," he replied.

George's good intentions went down the drain when Dietrich fired George's comptroller without consulting George and announced he was moving his own office to the Culver City plant. George immediately notified Hughes that unless the comptroller was reinstated and Dietrich restrained from further interference he would resign.

There was no reply. On September 11, 1953, their month's notice up, Ramo and Wooldridge left the plant. On September 14 George sent in his resignation. A wholesale exodus followed. Dr. Johnson, head of research and development, resigned. Dean Smith, sales manager, resigned. Sixteen senior members of the technical staff handed in resignations.

At last Hughes left Las Vegas for Los Angeles, where he met with George. He made an emotional appeal to the general to stay on, reminding him of all that he had done for him, how important it was to the company, and bringing up any other factors that might influence George.

The general was adamant. He was not going to stay if he was going to be kicked around by Dietrich while he struggled to break through the wall with which Hughes surrounded himself. George had thought a lot about the problem. He wanted a board of directors to run Hughes Aircraft, made up of two directors from Hughes Tool Company, two directors from Hughes Aircraft itself, and one outsider—some nationally known figure who would be satisfactory to him and who would in effect take the role of arbitrator.

Hughes complained, "You are proposing to take from me the rights to manage my own property. I'll burn the plant down first."

"You are accomplishing the same result without matches," George retorted.

The Air Force was by now thoroughly disturbed by developments in the plant which was its sole source for important electronics equipment. They notified Hughes that he must make every effort to hold the staff together.

One night Hughes called a meeting of the scientists at the plant. They probed and questioned him until at last he agreed to offer them a full statement on revised policies for future plant operation. Later they learned that Hughes had told the Air Force that they were going to stay, although they had not yet made such an agreement. They insisted on another meeting, this time with General George and Charles Thornton present.

Charles J. V. Murphy, writing about *The Blowup at Hughes Aircraft* in *Fortune* said, "There ensued another extraordinary gathering, with Hughes listening sternly while the scientists told him that he had all but wrecked a successful management and, even worse, had imperiled a national defense program. Hughes asked for three months to work things out."

By now everyone recognized that Hughes would say anything to keep them but would do nothing afterward. At this crucial point the Secretary for the Air Force and the assistant secretary of matériel arrived from the Pentagon. Secretary Talbott told Hughes, "You have made a hell of a mess of a great property and, by God, as long as I am Secretary of the Air Force you're not going to get another dollar to do business."

Hughes offered a typical reply, "If you mean to tell me that the government is prepared to destroy a business merely on the unfounded charges of a few disgruntled employees, then you are introducing Socialism, if not Communism."

The Air Force asked several key employees to stay on and make sure the contracts were carried out. In addition, they made it known to the rest of the electronics industry that the Air Force would be unhappy if anyone began to steal talent from Hughes Aircraft. In this makeshift manner the company limped along.

Wooldridge and Ramo, after leaving Hughes, started a small electronics company called the Ramo-Wooldridge Corporation, which was spectacularly successful. Hughes brought in a new manager, William C. Jordan, formerly president of Curtiss-Wright; and production schedules continued somehow to be met. The Air Force meanwhile developed a plan by which it awarded a contract to a company and then forced Hughes to sell it his equipment and plans for the fire-control systems.

In the midst of all this turmoil Howard Hughes came up with one of his brainstorms. On January 10, 1954, he announced the formation of a nonprofit institution for medical research. He called it the Howard Hughes Medical Foundation and his first gift to the foundation was the assets of the Hughes Aircraft Company. Dr. Verne Mason, the physician who had attended Hughes when he crashed in 1946, became the first director of the foundation.

The events of 1953 had shocked Howard Hughes out of his customary complacency. He was deeply hurt and disappointed over what he regarded as the defection of General George and scientists Ramo and Wooldridge. He persuaded some of the lower-echelon people to remain under a new system in which a three-man administrative board would make all decisions and operate Hughes Aircraft. The board consisted of William C. Jordan, general manager of

Hughes Aircraft; Howard Hall, one of the Hughes' attorneys; and a third man. Any two of the three could make a policy decision without prior consultation with Hughes. Initially the jurisdictional authority of Dietrich was left unsettled.

Jordan did a good job of placating the men and warding off Dietrich but at the end of six months he left, pleading ill health. His public statements contained nothing but praise for Hughes and the company.

Hughes found himself in the position of the boy who cried "Wolf" too often. This time he did not let matters drift. He quickly put together a new management committee and brought in Laurence Hyland from Bendix Corporation, to act as general manager. Hyland was almost exactly what Hughes needed—a determined, competent individual who would brook no nonsense.

At last Hughes Aircraft Company could soar ahead. All the basic elements of Hughes' original plan for the world's most sophisticated electronics company were there. The organization employed thousands of people familiar with every branch of modern scientific knowledge. The plant contained some of the best electronics laboratory equipment available anywhere. The company had the basic patents and the know-how to make the finest electronic fire-control systems. Already on the drawing board were plans for a missile system, known as the Falcon Missile, which would become part of the American Defense System. The entire enterprise was now too well organized, too well founded, too well stocked with wisdom, ability, and competence to be destroyed by an internecine fight.

During those two years two important events took place. In 1956 Noah Dietrich went on safari during his differences with Hughes and ended the pressure of his drive to control Hughes Aircraft. In 1957 Howard Hughes got married and at least for a time lost his desire to be the active head of the world's finest electronics company. Instead, he permitted those who knew how to do so to run the company.

All of the preparatory work, the skilled complements of personnel, the excellent equipment, the fine reputation, began to pay off in 1958. Beginning in January of that year Hughes Aircraft Company negotiated millions of dollars of contracts for the development of a variety of electronics systems. They acquired a $20 million contract to complete two advanced versions of the Falcon Missile, a $40 million contract for a new aircraft fire-control system, and other multimillion-dollar contracts for various electronics systems. On March 13, 1958, the company announced its plans to hire 2,000 additional scientists and engineers and 1,500 more technical employees.

From this point on there was a steady flow of millions of dollars worth of contracts. Hughes Aircraft Company became the leading contractor in the field of electronics control of weapons firing. It was also the only company manufacturing, and improving, the Falcon Missile. The volume of work made it mandatory to obtain more space. Before the end of 1958 the company had rented another plant with 156,000 square feet of space in Newport Beach, California.

None of the work at Hughes Aircraft consisted of the simple manufacturing of electronic hardware but, in spite of the highly sophisticated and advanced nature of the varied operations, there was always time to accept new challenges. In 1959 the firm accepted a contract without a specified dollar recompense to develop "unorthodox approaches" to deflect and confuse enemy missiles. In July of 1959 the company announced that it was experimenting with a small but highly accurate atomic clock to be fitted into a satellite while a twin clock would be retained on Earth. The purpose was to learn if a clock placed in orbit around the Earth would operate at a different rate from its twin on the ground. This project would explore one aspect of Einstein's theory on relativity.

The seventh decade of the twentieth century saw still more expansion at Hughes Aircraft. A new plant was built at El Segundo, California; a missile plant at Tucson, Arizona; and another plant at Fullerton, California.

In 1960 Hughes Aircraft Company received its first contract with the National Aeronautics and Space Administration (NASA)— a beginning from which would later rise contracts in the multimillion-dollar range for the construction of some of the most unusual space vehicles yet known. The initial contract amounted to less than $1 million for building an experimental engine to power a space ship. The company produced an ingenious and inspired plan which astounded and delighted NASA. (Competitors say it is unlikely that the engine could possibly have been built for the allotted $500,000. However, Hughes Aircraft Company was working under so many contracts that the extra costs could probably have been balanced. It required the talents of a highly skilled government auditor to pass through the labyrinth of accounting involved in these contracts.)

One contract was for $3 million to manufacture high frequency radio receivers for the Air Force. Another was a $10 million Army contract to build a mobile truck-mounted missile-control system. A contract with industry called for development of a narrow light beam—a laser. A $5 million contract with the Army was to build a radar system for the Monitor Missile. This would be followed by a $70 million Army contract to construct defense command posts for the Monitor Missile. An Air Force contract for $65 million called for building Falcon air-to-air guided missiles.

And the really big one was a contract to develop a small satellite capable of receiving telephone and television signals and relaying them back to Earth. This satellite would be placed in a stationary orbit over the equator and would act as a relay point. Hung at a height of 20,300 miles, three such stationary satellites evenly spaced in orbit could provide a complete communications system for all of Earth. This satellite, later called Syncom I, occupied a substantial segment of the Hughes plant when NASA let the first contract.

Concentration on the space program did not keep the company out of other fields. In 1961 Hughes Aircraft accepted a $20 million contract to develop a control system for the Nike-Hercules anti-aircraft missile. A $10 million contract for the Polaris submarine missile control, a contract to develop Project Artemis (the Navy's long-range submarine detection system), and opening talks with NASA for construction of a spacecraft to make a soft landing on the moon—these too became part of Hughes Aircraft Company's participation in the space age.

Before the end of 1961 the Hughes people had demonstrated to NASA a degree of competence on the communications satellite project that earned them a specific contract to build the first Syncom. In addition, they continued to work on the Falcon air-to-air missile and on another $50 million of miscellaneous electronics contracts.

In 1962 business remained in the multimillion-dollar class with work from all branches of the United States Government, foreign governments, and private business. The Swiss government ordered a fire-control system for an amount of money not specified. Boeing gave Hughes a $27 million contract to produce an electronic data analysis system for the Minute Man solid fuel missile. Work was going ahead also on the Falcon Missile and on Syncom I.

As 1962 drew to a close Syncom I neared completion. After a number of dry-run tests, launch was scheduled for February 14, 1963, at Cape Canaveral, Florida. The satellite measured 28 inches long, weighed 150 pounds, and was designed to receive radio signals from specific points on earth and relay them to other points. Tension was high at Hughes as the satellite lifted off and moved toward its orbit. Then something went wrong with radio communications and for ten days the scientists struggled to find out what had happened. Finally on February 24, 1963, the telescopes in a South African observatory located Syncom I. Satellite control found it could turn Syncom's batteries on and off and make it respond to signals. While this first effort at a synchronous orbit was not a complete success, it was far from a failure. One valuable lesson learned from Syncom I was that the plan to have perfect equatorial alignment was too difficult to maintain and was not necessary.

The Hughes scientific staff went back to the drawing board and worked feverishly around the clock. By July 6, 1963, they were back at Cape Canaveral with Syncom II. This time the orbit pattern would be a figure eight in which the satellite would travel slightly north and then swing slightly south of the equator.

Syncom II was shaped like a drum, weighed 86 pounds, and measured 28 inches in diameter and 15½ inches in height. It had 3,840 silicon solar cells to power its battery and was equipped to handle telephone signals, teletype, and even facsimile. It was not yet ready for TV. Shortly after launching it achieved a perfect orbit, then began to drift slightly. NASA scientists used radio signals to start the hydrogen peroxide jets which would move it back into orbit. Everything worked perfectly. It became immediately possible to make telephone calls between the United States and Europe via satellite without using the Atlantic Cable.

Hughes Aircraft now received a contract to build another synchronous orbit satellite. This one, named Olympic Star, would include the capability of relaying television signals. (It received its name because it would be used as the TV relay station for worldwide transmission of the Olympic games.) On August 19, 1964, from the same point, now called Cape Kennedy, the Olympic Star was launched and it, too, worked perfectly. People all over the world watched telecasts of the Olympic games from Tokyo—a new high in television coverage, and a new gem in Hughes Aircraft's crown of accomplishments.

Meanwhile, the government of Japan announced that it was going to adopt what was now known as the Hughes Air Defense System—a complete electronics system which could alert a central command post to approaching aircraft. This would mean uncountable millions of dollars in contracts for the company. Hughes Aircraft was also one of the first firms to get a contract from the new Communication Satellite Corporation, known popularly as Comsat.

The United States Army requested development of an anti-tank missile to be mounted on a truck or tank. The Air Force authorized a $61 million contract to increase the radar sensitivity of its supersonic fighters. There were standard contracts from NASA to build satellites, and unusual contracts such as one to develop a system of launching missiles from helicopters.

In 1964 Hughes negotiated a contract with NASA to develop a moon exploration unit called the Surveyor. On December 11, 1964, a dummy model of Surveyor was orbited but had to be abandoned as unstable and redesigned. Less than a year later, on September 22, 1965, a 2,000-pound model of the new Surveyor was successfully launched from Cape Kennedy. Now all signals were "go" to make the actual landing of the Surveyor on the moon. The unmanned lunar probe was launched on May 30, 1966. Object: soft landing on the moon.

To do so it would travel 231,483 miles in 63 hours and 36 minutes. The complexity of this launch may be glimpsed when it is realized that Surveyor had to be aimed at a point in space where the moon *would be* at a given time in the future and that it had to land in a predetermined area.

Surveyor weighed 620 pounds and was designed to travel at a speed of 6,000 miles per hour. It had to be capable of control throughout the flight, reducing speed while still in space and maneuvering into position to touch down on the moon's surface at a speed of less than eight miles per hour. It arrived exactly five seconds late and landed precisely ten miles from the selected point of impact. At touchdown its three landing legs opened as planned and absorbed the shock of first lunar contact. Immediately after landing, Surveyor began to radio pictures of the moon's surface to the eagerly waiting Earthmen. Both the launching and the accomplishments of Surveyor after the moon landing rank as one of man's most advanced scientific achievements.

Surveyor's pioneering triumphs were appropriately topped by Surveyor III on April 22, 1967, when its tubular arm dug a trench on the moon's surface.

Hughes Aircraft Company was also actively engaged in the construction of communications satellites for Comsat. These "Early Bird" satellites serve as a link for commercial TV, telephone, and telegraph between North America and Europe. On August 14, 1965, Comsat launched the first of the "Early Bird" satellites manufactured by Hughes Aircraft. Pleased with the perfect orbit and successful operation, Comsat went ahead with plans for a complete global communication system to be completed by 1967 and invited all the nations of the world to sign up to use it. Forty-six countries accepted the invitation. Obviously, Hughes Aircraft would make the system.

There is no doubt that by 1967 Hughes Aircraft Company either had completed, or was well on its way to meeting, the visionary goals set for it by Howard Hughes when he first revamped the company to create "the world's finest electronics company."

Howard Hughes and
His North-South Airline

THE YEAR 1956

NASSER SEIZED the Suez Canal. The world's tiniest kingdom once described by W. Somerset Maugham as a "sunny spot for shady people" became one of the top spots in the news when its handsome young ruler, His Serene Highness, Prince Rainier III, married Grace Kelly, a Hollywood movie actress.

Communist Party boss Nikita Khrushchev delivered a long denunciation of Stalin, starting an uproar in the Communist world.

John Gunther's *Inside Africa* stayed on the bestseller list an amazingly long time for a specialized type of book. Also making the bestseller list for an unusual length of time was John Schindler's *How to Live 365 Days a Year*. The national book award went to John O'Hara's *Ten North Frederick*. Senator John Kennedy published *Profiles in Courage*. MacKinlay Kantor's *Andersonville* won a Pulitzer Prize.

In the theatre: *The Diary of Anne Frank;* Shelley Winters in *A Hat For Lorraine;* Bert Lahr in *Waiting for Godot*. The Comédie Française after 275 years of existence made its first appearance in the United States with the production of Molière's *Bourgeois Gentilhomme*. In the field of musicals the smash hit was *My Fair Lady* with Rex Harrison and Julie Andrews.

Howard Hughes was fifty.

20

DURING WORLD WAR II a large percentage of Howard Hughes' time was devoted to the development of the "Spruce Goose" and his photo-reconnaissance plane, and to the manufacture of war material. What time that was left he used to build up the technical strength of TWA.

With the end of the war his planning paid off. TWA earned worldwide recognition as the most progressive airline in flying equipment, knowhow and procedures. The Civil Aeronautics Board, where route decisions were made, realized this too, and Hughes obtained almost 25,000 miles of new international routes including the "Rich Plum Run" across the North Atlantic from New York to London and Paris.

Hughes thus became the first proprietor of an American airline with both domestic routes and international routes. Pan-American, although well routed and scheduled internationally, had no runs inside the continental limits of the United States. This gave TWA the edge as the first national, as well as international, airline. TWA was completely prepared for around-the-world service when it obtained routes through Egypt and India to the Orient. The final link required a Pacific run and routing through China. The latter was barely defeated when the Chinese Communists took over Shanghai in 1948. Although he never got routing around the world, nevertheless Hughes did realize his goal of having the only American airline offering service both within and without the continental United States.

The American airlines tended, primarily as a result of the "grandfather routes" acquired with the establishment of the Civil Aeronautics Board in 1938, to run either in a north-south direction or in an east-west direction. Eastern and National are examples of primarily north-south runs whereas United and TWA cover basically east-west routes.

This is not, of course, an absolute because there are routes which move diagonally and other routes, basically east-west, which also travel north-south runs. However, a study of the routing of any domestic airline (excluding the regional airlines) will quickly indicate its major character to be either of the north-south variety or of the east-west variety.

Just as Hughes had broken the pattern of national vs. international lines he decided to break the pattern with respect to north-south vs. east-west carriers. The grant of a north-south run to an east-west airline would not be of any real significance unless that particular north-south route was equally significant. Probably the major north-south route in the United States in terms of lucrativeness of traffic is the Boston-New York-Philadelphia-Washington-Miami route.

From October to March this route is unquestionably one of the most profitable in the world and as Florida grows in importance as a summer vacation resort the route gradually assumes aspects of an all-year-around gold mine. The question thus becomes—how does an east-west airline like TWA with international commitments get in on an East Coast north-south run coveted by practically every airline in the United States?

The problem seems almost insoluble: A direct application by TWA for such a routing would have no chance of being granted. Despite the complexity and seeming impossibility of accomplishment, the determined Howard Hughes almost carried it off.

Northeast Airlines was born in 1931, controlled by, and as a complement to, two New England railroads. Its major purpose was to assist these railroads in handling passenger traffic throughout their area without necessitating the laying of additional track to handle some of the unprofitable longer hauls.

At the time of its establishment Northeast was a stepchild, suffering because it owed its birth to the needs of railroad men rather than the enthusiasms of air travel devotees. When new legislation forced the divorce of airline carriers from rail carriers, the control of Northeast passed into the hands of Atlas Corporation, a holding company controlled by Floyd Odlum. Odlum was not a flyer but his wife was the famous aviatrix, Jacqueline Cochran.

Up to this time Northeast Airlines had functioned as an adjunct to the railroad. Now it began to strike out on its own. In the late 1940's Northeast applied to the Civil Aeronautics Board for permission to fly between Boston and New York. This busy commuter route was then primarily the property of American Airlines. The CAB granted Northeast the route and thus set the stage for the next step.

In the 1950's Odlum was busy acquiring uranium mine holdings for Atlas. He believed that development of atomic energy was the coming field and therefore uranium had to become the most precious mineral. To acquire such holdings Odlum needed cash; he also anticipated great profits from them and wanted to find a tax loss corporation to offset this probability. He found both of these in a company owned by Howard Hughes—RKO Pictures Corporation. This was not the motion picture studio but just a corporate shell with $18 million in cash and a $30 million tax loss carry forward. Odlum made a deal whereby he acquired the corporation from Hughes in exchange for 10% of Atlas Common Stock.

Hughes now became the largest individual holder of Atlas Corporation. But Atlas controlled Northeast Airlines and Hughes controlled TWA. The Civil Aeronautics Act does not permit one man to control more than one airline without consent of the CAB. Therefore Hughes was forced to place his Atlas stock in a trust. Nevertheless, shortly after Hughes entered the Northeast picture that airline applied for a certificate to fly between New York and Miami, making convenient stops in both Philadelphia and Washington.

Northeast Airlines had been losing money and it desperately needed a profitable operation to keep it alive. There is little doubt that the decision to grant the certificate was based on sound economics rather than backstage influence by Hughes. Some airline economists believed that the grant of this temporary certificate in 1956 was made on the theory that traffic on the route in question was going to become heavy enough to outweigh the ability of the two existing airlines then servicing it to keep up.

Naturally, both Eastern and National argued long and vehemently that they would be glad to accommodate all passengers. But there were also cogent arguments based on the predicted increase in passenger traffic between Megalopolis, U.S.A., and Florida vacation lands. There were also other analysts of the situation who believed that the CAB granted the certification simply to help an obviously ailing airline.

Whatever intention CAB had, the fact that the grant was temporary helped to defeat the purpose. Because the new routing was temporary the airline could not arrange any permanent financing and it faced intervals when it could barely meet its bills for food and fuel. Each time this happened Hughes came to the rescue, making loans to keep the airline in operation.

Bad luck dogged the steps of Northeast Airlines. Just when the company received delivery on new equipment for the New York-Florida route, one of its planes crashed on Rikers Island where the survivors could be interviewed by television on the spot—a piece of negative publicity and unfortunate advertising that no other airline has had to face. In addition, in the first five years of flying the Golden Route there were two financial recessions which cut heavily into holiday and vacation traffic between New York and Miami.

Only Hughes proved willing to help Northeast financially. Many airlines tried to take over Northeast primarily for the purpose of acquiring the route but only Hughes actually put in dollars. Despite this the CAB continually rendered decisions adverse to Hughes and when the Eastern finance group forced his TWA stock into a voting trust in 1960 the CAB indicated that it would take a long, hard look at the situation before permitting Hughes to gain control of Northeast.

This was not the only time that the Board demonstrated hostility to Hughes. In 1958 a CAB examiner set up a plan which would permanently bar control by Hughes of Northeast Airlines. Even the first trusteeing of Hughes' stock became a fight between Hughes and CAB. Although Hughes had puchased his 10% control of Atlas Corporation in 1956 it was not until August of 1958 that word leaked out that the CAB was investigating the possible violation of law by Mr. Hughes in his endeavor to control two airlines.

On August 20, 1958 the CAB issued an official pronouncement that it would end its investigation if Hughes would agree to put his holdings of either TWA or NE into a trust. Hughes wrote a short note to CAB Chairman James Durfee that he would set up a trust within 20 days and report to CAB on its operation. Although Hughes accepted the Board ruling he wrote a sharp letter through his attorney, Raymond A. Cook, stating that he disputed the "fairness and necessity" of the divestiture of his stock. He also pointed out that in his opinion the system of ordering a settlement as a substitute for investigation was a dangerous precedent in the field of regulatory law.

Despite the opposition of CAB, in 1960 Northeast Airlines announced its intention to merge with TWA. The plan called for the exchange of 1 share of TWA stock for 3 shares of NE stock. Opposition to the merger became immediately manifest. Chairman Emanuel Celler of the House Judiciary Committee announced that he had requested CAB and the Justice Department to investigate possible violations of law inherent in the proposed merger.

The CAB challenged the merger and indicated that it might well resort to the cancellation of the certification for the Northeast Airline's New York-Florida route if the two companies persisted in the merger plans. Recognizing at last the utter futility of a frontal assault on the CAB, Hughes abandoned his merger plans.

Meanwhile NE continued to lose money, possibly a little faster than before. However, following the Hughesian tradition it was not only not economizing, it was in fact expanding. In 1961, at the height of its financial troubles, NE announced that it was going to build a new passenger terminal at Idlewild Airport (now JFK), in conjunction with Northwest and Braniff Airlines. Completion was scheduled for the spring of 1962 and the cost would be about $10 million.

CAB was experiencing a frantic reaction to its dealings with the determined and willful Hughes. It could visualize either the bankruptcy of NE on the one hand or complete control by Hughes on the other. Now the board was driven to take a most unusual step: behind the scenes the suggestion was made to other airlines that they might consider merging with NE.

By this time the five year temporary certificate authorizing the New York to Florida run was about to expire and although application for extension of the temporary certificate and also a request for permanent certification were pending, it was an open secret that the CAB was holding up approval, hoping for a merger to materialize.

Although CAB was working behind the scenes the airlines were out in the open. Pan American announced publicly that it would consider a merger provided that the New England local routes would be transferred to other carriers—this long-haul airline did not want to become involved with the interesting but short runs from Bangor to Barre or Boston to Burlington. It wanted it known, however, that it most assuredly would be interested in taking on the Boston-New York-Philadelphia-Washington-Miami route. In fact, Pan Am had been trying unsuccessfully for 15 years to get permission for a New York to Florida route. It had even tried to swap stock with National Airlines which did fly that run. However, CAB refused to sanction that maneuver.

A non-passenger carrier now evinced interest also. Riddle Airlines transported cargo over the same New York to Miami routing. Acquisition of Northeast Airlines would permit it to carry passengers along with its cargo. Riddle submitted a plan which offered a low fare air-bus service along the East Coast. However, it seemed highly doubtful that CAB would approve the idea of this cargo carrier entering the stiff competition for business on the coastal run.

Early in 1961 Hughes concluded a deal for Toolco to purchase the 56% of Northeast Airline's stock which Atlas owned. This transaction had to be approved by CAB and for a while it appeared that the Board would reject it out of hand. Meanwhile financial conditions at NE were going from bad to worse and Hughes was the only person in sight offering succor. With great reluctance on May 4, 1962, a CAB examiner made a halfhearted recommendation for approval of Toolco's plan to buy control from Atlas.

That summer CAB finally approved the plan but included some severe restrictions. There was to be no transaction between Northeast Airlines and Hughes Tool Company in excess of $100,000 in any single year without prior approval of the CAB. The major purpose of this ruling was to prevent implementation of Hughes' normal operation: Having Toolco buy planes and equipment and then either reselling them, or renting them, to Northeast at a profit for Toolco. This had been done with TWA and the CAB regarded the practice with sour disapproval.

Time, reporting on the CAB action, called it a "Pyrrhic Victory" for Hughes, who was paying $5 million for Northeast Airlines which in 1961 had lost almost $10 million and was running at a current balance sheet net worth deficiency of over $23 million.

Things did not work as well as they might have done. In February of 1963, one of Northeast's new jetliners crashed in the Everglades killing 43 people. The news made nation-wide headlines, and caused a particular stir in Florida. For the remainder of the season travelers requested, "Please book me on National or Eastern—I don't want to fly with NE."

In April, 1963, a CAB examiner who had been investigating the problem of whether the New York-Florida Certificate should be made permanent recommended not only that it not be made permanent but that the route be taken away from NE entirely.

In July CAB dealt what appeared to be the critical blow when it ordered NE to give up its New York to Florida route and on a Petition for Rehearing on August 16, 1963, reaffirmed its original decision that Northeast would lose all routings south of New York. This decision was greeted with wailing and gnashing of teeth in many places, particularly in New England. Even the conservative *Wall Street Journal* printed an article condemning the decision, under the title, *Expertise-Gone-Awry.* The United States Department of Justice, then under Attorney General Robert Kennedy (a New Englander), attacked the CAB decision and made application to intervene in the dispute. The CAB turned the Attorney General down cold. The Board's attitude was simple: "It's none of your business."

In September the announcement was made that nine Viscounts purchased by Northeast Airlines in 1958 from Vickers of England would be foreclosed and sold at public auction to pay off some of the debt owed by NE to Vickers. This was the death rattle.

Hughes did not take these developments quietly. With the order to cease the Florida run taking effect in October, time was running out for Northeast. At the last possible moment, attorneys for the troubled airline got a court order from the Circuit Court of Appeals superseding the CAB order and holding everything in status quo until further hearings could be arranged.

To bring greater pressure to bear on the Board Hughes caused TWA to resume merger negotiations, which put CAB on notice that any possible merger of TWA with NE would be contingent upon the grant of permanent certification for the New York-Florida run. At the November annual meeting of Northeast Airlines the number of Directors was increased from 9 to 16 and seven representatives of the Hughes Tool Company were elected to the Board.

In April of 1964 the Federal Court of Appeals in Boston handed down a decision ordering the Civil Aeronautics Board to reconsider its edict taking the Florida run away from Northeast Airlines. CAB began immediate hearings to examine the additional evidence which the Boston Court said should be investigated.

Believing that a good offense is also the best defense, while CAB was considering whether to permit NE to continue the southern run, the airline itself applied for routing certificates into the Caribbean to serve the Bahamas and also to extend its service in the north throughout Canada.

While these requests were pending the CAB launched another low blow at Hughes when, in response to his application to regain control of TWA, the Board ruled that it would not even examine the issue unless Toolco first gave up control of Northeast Airlines.

Hughes acted promptly. Within days after the order he named Louis J. Hector as trustee of all the NE stock owned by Hughes Tool Company. Hector was a Miami attorney who had been a member of the Civil Aeronautics Board and who had resigned with a blast at the Board. He and maverick Hughes were kindred spirits on the subject of CAB.

In October of 1964, NE Airlines and Toolco filed a proposed Trust Agreement with the CAB. As part of the plan for Hector's trusteeship a number of directors would resign from the Board of Northeast Airlines, including Chester C. Davis, who might be regarded as Hughes' General Counsel; Raymond A. Cook, a lawyer and partner in an Eastern law firm which had long served Hughes; Robert S. Montgomery, an official of Hughes Aircraft; Maynard Montrose, President of the Oil Division of Toolco; and Raymond M. Holliday, one of Hughes' General Managers.

The Trust Indenture filed with the CAB implied that the major purpose of the trusteeship was to liquidate Hughes' interest in Northeast Airlines. Thus, the trustee was granted unlimited powers to sell, initiate and complete mergers or consolidations, transfer property, and take any and all action necessary to liquidate the interest of Hughes and Toolco in Northeast Airlines. At the time Hughes' spokesmen made it clear that the filing of the indenture didn't mean they were giving up the fight to continue the Boston-Florida run.

The CAB maintained its unbroken record of ruling against Hughes when it announced in December that after reconsideration, as ordered by the court, the Board had again voted to confine Northeast Airlines to a role as a local New England carrier and therefore NE had to relinquish all its routes south of New York.

Through President James Austin of Northeast Airlines, Hughes immediately announced "We'll fight!" and all parties returned to the Federal Court of Appeals in Boston, which had been much more sympathetic to the cause of Northeast and Howard Hughes.

Immediately following the CAB decision with respect to Northeast Airlines, a Bill was introduced into Congress which would, in effect, overrule the decision. The legislation provided that any trunk line operating with temporary authority under any scheduled line since 1957 should become permanent. Although it sounded like legislation of broad scope, it was cleverly worded to affect only Northeast Airlines.

This would not be the first time that Congress had in effect overruled the CAB. It had last done so in 1955 when legislation gave a local service carrier permanent authorization despite the CAB.

As was to be expected the CAB protested angrily against the proposed legislation. Board Chairman Alan S. Boyd was particularly vehement about the Bill and continually stressed that Congress had set up the entire regulatory system under the jurisdiction of the Civil Aeronautics Board and if Congress didn't like the way the system operated it could change it but not by legislating against the Board's rulings.

Hastings Keith, a Massachusetts Republican, sponsored the new law. He said bluntly at one point, "If there are no Florida routes for Northeast Airlines there may well be no Northeast Airlines."

In another speech Keith announced, "I cannot believe that it was the intention of Congress to have an airline which has efficiently served New England and the East Coast . . . for more than seven years, denied this operation [the Miami run] by a Board it [Congress] created to promote the best possible air-passenger service."

Massachusetts Senator Edward M. Kennedy also supported Northeast and denounced the refusal of the Civil Aeronautics Board to extend the Florida-New York run of Northeast Airlines. He announced to the press that he believed the CAB action was a "shocking misjudgment on both regional and national transportation needs." He further stated that in his opinion the CAB acted "without hearing a word of evidence of the encouraging record made by Northeast during the past year-and-a-half."

Now a new problem arose—Eastern Airlines and National Airlines jointly went to the trustee, Attorney Hector, and offered him $15 million to give up the appeal relating to the Florida run and to commit Northeast Airlines to becoming a subsidized New England regional air carrier.

Before the offer could be considered, an airline pilot named Mudge filed suit in a Massachusetts County Court to get an injunction to restrain the directors from even acting on the offer.

Many observers thought they detected the fine hand of Howard Hughes in this suit. Cleverly it argued a basic theory of law: that any time a corporation changes its basic nature it must obtain the approval of stockholders. For example, if a publicly held department store wanted to go out of that business and become a movie theater it would have to obtain approval of the shareholders. Mudge's theory was that giving up the fight for the Florida route was the equivalent of a complete change in the basic nature of the corporation and required approval of the shareholders.

The County Court granted a Preliminary Injunction restraining all action on the offer and appointed a Master to take testimony on the merits to decide whether the Injunction should be granted. The case dragged on and neither the offer nor the case ever got anywhere.

In June, 1965, Hughes received an offer to sell his stock in Northeast Airlines to the Storer Broadcasting Company. He would get about $5 per share for his stock and the Company would repay much of the debt owed by Northeast to Toolco. Since the stock on the American Stock Exchange had been ranging between $2 and $4 a share, and the chances of getting the debts repaid were small, the offer was attractive. On June 3, 1965, Storer obtained an option to purchase Toolco's majority interest in the airline.

On July 30, 1965, the trustee conveyed all of the interest of Hughes Tool Company, consisting of 973,226 shares of common stock in Northeast Airlines. Thus ended Howard Hughes' effort to amalgamate a north-south airline with an east-west airline.

Shortly after the sale Northeast Airlines common stock, which had been hovering around $4 a share, skyrocketed to $39 per share! There was little logic to this rise and, in fact, it was so absurd that at the annual meeting, George Storer, Sr., Chairman of the Board, stated that he felt that Storer stock was a rather good investment but he was extremely skeptical about the high price of the common stock of NE Airlines.

"We paid about $5 per share and last night I read it was selling at $37 per share," he said. "This is a mystery to me. I don't think it's worth that much."

That day Northeast stock closed down $4. In spite of this drop, it did manage to maintain its inexplicably high price and went into 1967 selling in the 30's. This marks one time when Hughes failed to sell at the top. If he could have sold the stock at the $30 mark rather than the $5 mark he would have realized $25 million more on the transaction. One must conclude, however, that this is a comparatively small matter to a billionaire!

Howard Hughes and His Secret Headquarters

THE YEAR 1926

PLANS WERE announced for the construction of a bridge across the Hudson River from Fort Lee, N.J., to Fort Washington in Manhattan. Later the bridge was named the George Washington.

Congress created the Army Air Corps.

Airmail service between New York and Boston was inaugurated.

Gertrude Ederle, age nineteen, swam across the English Channel—the first woman to accomplish the feat. It took fourteen hours and thirty-one minutes.

Sinclair Lewis declined the Pulitzer Prize award for *Arrowsmith,* saying that prizes tended to make authors "safe, obedient and sterile."

Popular songs of the year: *I Found a Million Dollar Baby in a Five and Ten Cent Store, Bye Bye Blackbird, Desert Song,* and *Play Gypsy.*

The Warner Theater in New York introduced the first "talking movie" in the film *Don Juan* starring John Barrymore. The sound was produced by a compatible phonograph record.

Gene Tunney became Heavyweight Champion of the World when he defeated Jack Dempsey in a ten round fight at the Sesquicentennial Stadium in Philadelphia. A record crowd attended—118,736.

Brazil and Spain left the League of Nations. Germany joined the League. Russia and Germany signed a treaty of "reassurance." Hirohito became the Emperor of Japan as Yoshohito died.

Howard Hughes was twenty years old.

21

Shortly after arriving in California in 1926, Howard Hughes purchased 51 percent of the stock of Multi-Color, Inc. This corporation purportedly owned the patents and had the knowhow to make color movies. The far-seeing twenty-year-old believed that some day most, if not all, movies would be filmed in color.

Hughes was ahead of the times with Multi-Color. The idea was excellent in theory, but in practice it failed to work. He poured money into research, but the experimenters could not evolve a practical process for the development of motion picture color film. Ultimately, Multi-Color turned out to be one of Hughes' few financial flops.

Although the project itself failed, out of it Hughes acquired the building at 7000 Romaine Street in Los Angeles, which was used as his headquarters until 1953. At that time he sold the building to Eastman Kodak but apparently later regretted his action. In 1957 he repurchased it, and today it remains his major headquarters, message center, and general command post.

The structure is a two-story beige stucco building with no mark to identify it as a business property. Most of the time the doors are locked and no one gets in who is not expected.

The building is staffed primarily with Mormons. Hughes long ago learned that Mormons make excellent employees. They do not drink, smoke, or carouse, and they are noted for unswerving loyalty and integrity.

It is to this headquarters that Hughes generally relays his requests and commands, and it is through this same headquarters that his employees throughout the world communicate with him. As a message center, the Romaine Street headquarters operates with speed and efficiency.

An asphalt parking lot on one side of the building belongs to the headquarters. It is staffed with crew-cut young Mormon men who drive nondescript, usually older-model, battered Chevrolets. Any suspicious act in the general vicinity will cause one or more of the cars to emerge to investigate. Also, it is from this point that Hughes can dispatch a car to pick up and deliver someone to his home or other meeting place.

For many years Hughes made his home from time to time about ten minutes away from 7000 Romaine Street in either a house in Hollywood Hills or a bungalow on the grounds of the Beverly Hills Hotel. Despite his proximity he rarely went to the headquarters but preferred to communicate by telephone.

On those occasions when Hughes actually visited his Romaine Street office his primary purpose would be to dictate some specific business contract or letter that he wanted to do personally. This act was accompanied by an elaborate ritual. First, he insisted on having two different typists prepare the identical letter. Second he dictated directly to the typists, not trusting to the transcription skills of stenographers. When the typists were ready to start, he personally adjusted the typewriters so the margins of the letters would come out where he wanted them to be.

Hughes is a perfectionist who will not tolerate an erasure or even a smudge. He might dictate half a letter, then change his mind about a word and require the typist to start over on fresh stationery.

The selection of the secretaries who would work in the beige building perhaps involved more screening and more investigation than the CIA uses for its agents. The amount of intelligence material compiled on a secretary was unlimited, primarily because Hughes wanted to be absolutely certain there would be no leaks from his headquarters.

After they were selected, secretaries received unusual instructions. They were not permitted to wear nail polish or perfume. Make-up had to be kept to a minimum and, although lipstick was not prohibited, all other cosmetics were strongly discouraged.

Each girl worked alone in her private office so that no one could know what anyone else was doing. Great emphasis was placed on the following instructions to each employee: No one is permitted to receive personal phone calls at work. Away from the job it is strictly forbidden to talk to anyone about the work or about the employer or supervisor.

Hughes' personal typists led a fairly easy life. Primarily they were required to remain on call at any hour of the day or night. Other secretaries were available as substitutes if needed, but typists had to record in advance the fact that they were going to be out on any particular night. These special typists had few additional duties, but when they were actually called upon to work it was usually between midnight and morning. At those times they worked very hard. All night they typed—boring, tedious work because usually it was repetitious.

In addition to restrictions on the use of cosmetics, all typists were required to wear rubber gloves while typing or handling the paper. (This was probably because of Hughes' bacteriophobia.) When a page was scrapped a special attendant came with a container in which the paper was placed. The contents of this container were then taken to be burned. It is difficult to say whether this procedure was to maintain security for Hughes' confidential work or for the sake of sanitation—or both.

So much emphasis was placed on cleanliness to the point of anti-septic sterility that its occupants frequently called the building "the maternity ward."

Amid these sterile surroundings Howard Hughes paced up and down between the two desks where two secretaries typed as he dictated slowly and methodically an important letter or a paragraph of a contract. The girls who performed this job had to be prepared for long hours without eating. Even when there were breaks for food, no one left the premises. All food was brought in. Hughes would not trust any typist to leave the office to go out to a drugstore for food, where she might be tempted to gossip with others about the important work she was doing. Apparently he tried to ignore the awful fact that inevitably these same girls had to return to their respective homes.

The Romaine Street headquarters is a treasure house of the finest and most sophisticated forms of electronic gadgetry usable in the counter-espionage field. Various warning devices can be triggered by almost anything trespassing in the area under surveillance. There is a device which will sound an alarm if anyone tries to get information about documents inside the headquarters by use of X-ray outside the headquarters! There are lead-lined safes and burglar-proof vaults. There is electronic equipment to repel radio waves and to neutralize electronic snooping devices.

Such a mass of complex equipment carries with it the seeds of its own problems. This came to light when, during the litigation involving TWA, one of Hughes' attorneys astonished eminent opposing counsel, representing the leading banks and insurance companies of America, by accusing their forces of attempting to take illegal X-ray photographs of documents inside Hughes' Romaine Street office. It later developed that Hughes' battery-operated anti-X-ray warning system had sounded a false alarm when its battery ran down!

Publicity about the location of Hughes' secret headquarters and his inaccessibility has led to several attempts to enter the Romaine Street building illegally. No known attempt has ever succeeded.

In the 1960's some changes were made in the procedure at headquarters. Before this time, anyone who called OL 2-4500 would hear the operator reply simply by giving the phone number. Anyone asking for Hughes would be instructed to state his name, telephone number, and the nature of his business and would be informed that Mr. Hughes would be advised. A series of people then evaluated the message and made the decision about whether Hughes would be called.

In the early 1960's Hughes served notice that he was not to be called under any circumstances. His attitude, very simply, was, "Don't call me—I'll call you." Now from time to time Hughes or someone close to him does call the headquarters to check on messages. This is presently his sole contact with his empire on any formal basis.

Howard Hughes and
His Personal Life

MARCH 13, 1957

POPE PIUS XII celebrated his 18th anniversary and 81st birthday. The Soviet Union and East Germany signed treaties covering the stationing of Soviet troops in East Germany. The House Un-American Activities Committee opened four days of hearings into Communist infiltration in the publishing business in New York.

In the movies: *The Ten Commandments; Around The World In Eighty Days; Lust for Life* (Kirk Douglas); James Stewart in *The Spirit of St. Louis;* and Deborah Kerr and Robert Mitchum in *Heaven Knows, Mr. Allison.*

On stage: *Major Barbara* with Charles Laughton, Burgess Meredith, Eli Wallach and Cornelia Otis Skinner; Paul Douglas in *A Hole in the Head;* Cyril Ritchard in *A Visit to a Small Planet;* Rosalind Russell in *Auntie Mame;* Judy Holliday in *Bells Are Ringing;* Paul Muni and Ed Begley in *Inherit the Wind;* and Rex Harrison and Julie Andrews in *My Fair Lady.*

Howard Hughes was fifty-one. And on this day he married Jean Peters.

22

ANY ATTEMPT to study or analyze the personal life of Howard Hughes creates a confusing, chameleonic problem. Not only Hughes himself, but the very nature of his life, contributes to the difficulty. For example, Al Hirshberg and Joe Kenney in the 1947 edition of "Famous American Athletes of Today" devote a chapter to "Howard Hughes—Aviator and Sportsman." In describing his birthdate they said:

"This fabulous man was born Howard Robard Hughes . . . in Houston, Texas, on Christmas Eve in either 1904, 1905 or 1906. The mixup in dates is characteristic of the mystic qualities of the man involved. In 'Who's Who in America' the year of his birth is listed as 1904. In records in Houston, it is listed as 1905. But his late father, who should have known, always claimed that Howard was born in 1906 and that the Houston record of 1905 was a clerk's error."

In fact, the Texas Bureau of Vital Statistics did not have a birth certificate recorded for Hughes until the filing of an affidavit on January 5, 1942, executed by Annette Gano Lummis, of his mother's family, and Estelle Boughton Sharp of his father's partner's family. A careful examination of all records makes it appear reasonably likely that the affidavit was accurate and that he was indeed born December 24, 1905.

The Women in His Life

In his relationship with women Hughes followed a series of principles and systems. He rarely became emotionally involved with his female stars. Many people in Hollywood believed that Hughes chose Jean Harlow for stardom because he had fallen in love with her.

Jean Harlow herself said with respect to Howard Hughes, "He never mixes business with pleasure. As far as I'm concerned, I might be another airplane. He expects you to work the same way—never get tired, give your best performance at any hour of the day or night, and never think about anything else. . . . The nearest he ever came to making a pass at me was offering me a bite of a cookie!"

On another occasion Jean Harlow remarked that Howard Hughes was the only man she had ever been associated with who did not utilize the opportunity to try to become her lover.

The women in Hughes' life fell into three major categories. First came the group he designated the "crows," with whom he was never seen in public. His association with them remains his private affair.

A second class of women made up the group he rated "good properties" and subject to exploitation. They were moneymakers like a good script, an improved drilling bit, or a new idea for a jet motor. This category includes such actresses as Jean Harlow at an early stage of Hughes' life and Jane Russell at a later stage. Although Hollywood wags insinuated that Hughes' interest in Jane Russell's mammary equipment was not solely economic, facts indicate the contrary. There is not an iota of objective evidence to imply that Hughes' relationships with most of the movie stars he created went beyond the bounds of an employer-employee connection. However, there were exceptions.

The largest class of female relationships involving Hughes comprised those beautiful women of the world whom he escorted in public, wooed and courted, and might have married. During the period when he was emotionally involved with a particular female he lavished upon her the same degree of attention he would give, under other circumstances, to a faulty piston in a racing motor. He spent his time, attention and money as freely as an Arab potentate.

One of the first recipients of his devotion was the famed actress Billie Dove. Hughes first met Miss Dove when she was a Broadway showgirl noted for her shining blond hair and magnificent complexion. She and Hughes were guests at the same cocktail party. Hughes, untidily dressed and laconic of manner, failed to make any impression at all on the beautiful blond girl who so piqued his interest. Following the party, Howard bombarded her with phone calls, flowers, jewels, perfumes and other gifts he hoped would impress her and make her receptive to him.

Up to this point his attentions were not unusual for a love-stricken young man to pay to an attractive woman. However, Hughes went further. If she went out for an automobile ride with someone she might well be buzzed by an airplane flown by a hand-waving

Howard Hughes. If she stopped with her date to picnic there would be Hughes flying over them and even landing to join them if he could find a clear place on which to set down his plane.

In 1929 Hughes, aged 23, was tall, darkly handsome, with impeccable manners and Old World charm. He soon succeeded in making Billie Dove his number one female companion.

For a while Billie Dove felt like a queen with Hughes as her devoted Prince Charming. He honored her every command. Then, little by little, mysterious disappearances began. Suddenly Hughes would be off on some project of his own and would not see her again for a few days, a week, even months. Ultimately the Billie Dove phase of his life passed completely out of existence. During the early 1930's Hughes was seen with many women, including the ingenue June Collyer, and well-known actresses Lillian Bond and Ida Lupino.

Following the Billie Dove affair, Hughes' next widely publicized romance was with Katherine Hepburn. This well-educated socialite-turned-actress got along famously with Hughes. He taught her to fly and for some years they were seen everywhere together. During Hughes' famed flight around the world he kept in touch with just two people—first, Katherine Hepburn and, second, the man in charge of his airfield headquarters.

The avid reader of newspaper accounts, gossip columnists, and restaurant publicity squibs in the newspapers of the '30's could have easily concluded that Howard Hughes had affairs, platonic or otherwise, with almost every actress in Hollywood. An outstanding illustration of the absurdity of this conclusion can be found in a column by Louella Parsons, the leading Hollywood gossip columnist of the time, who declared that Howard Hughes and Olivia deHavilland were on their way to the altar.

Early in 1939 Hughes' affair with Katherine Hepburn was just coming to an end. He and Olivia deHavilland had not yet met. Shortly after the column appeared the actress received a phone call. The caller introduced himself, "This is Howard Hughes." The surprised young actress said nothing and Hughes continued, "I read in a newspaper that you and I are going to get married."

Miss deHavilland laughed.

Hughes added, "Since we have not met, I think we ought to get together before we do anything so permanent."

Olivia deHavilland, just twenty-one, was still asking her mother's permission to go out on dates. Her mother consented to this one.

After their first date, Hughes began to rush the young actress. At times his attentions would extend to phone calls several times a day and regular nightly visits. Then without a word he would disappear for a month. Suddenly she would be deluged with boxes of exotic orchids and Hughes would reappear. He taught her to fly a plane and took her to the finest restaurants in Hollywood.

However, in discussing love and marriage Hughes invariably said, "I have no intention of getting married until after I reach fifty. I have too many other things to do." His attitude always seemed to deny that he had ever been married.

Hughes did not see Olivia deHavilland for several months and as 1939 drew to a close she became certain that he had forgotten her. Then, at 10:00 o'clock on New Year's Eve, he phoned. Imperiously he informed her, "I'll be by for you in a few moments. We've been invited to Jack Warner's house for a New Year's Eve party."

Olivia had been dating Jimmy Stewart, who had invited her to the same party. A few days earlier she had fallen ill and had been forced to break her date. Lying in bed, weak and feverish, she tried to explain about Jimmy Stewart and the party. She reminded Howard that she hadn't heard from him for a long time. Did he think she was going to mope around the house all the time he was away? She went on to say all the other things a woman says to a man in such circumstances.

The words splashed over Hughes' head like water dripping from a tile roof. He reiterated, "I'll see you in a few minutes."

The actress could not resist. She felt almost well so she got up, dressed, and called Jimmy Stewart. That night the beautiful Olivia arrived at the party with Hughes on one arm and Jimmy Stewart on the other. At the party Errol Flynn gave her her first drink. In her own words, "I was twenty-two years old and had three of the most attractive men in the world around me. I don't know how my reputation survived. But by dawn my bronchitis was gone and my temperature was back to normal."

Olivia deHavilland says she recalls Howard Hughes with fondness and gratitude and adds, "I'm also grateful we did not marry."

In the early 1940's Hughes met a starlet with whom observers thought he had fallen in love. Her name was Faith Domergue. When she was in her middle teens a Warner Brothers talent scout discovered her and signed her to a contract. The studio changed

her name to Faith Dorn and she became an understudy and an acting student.

Hughes met Faith at a yachting party he was giving on a rented
yacht. A guest had invited Faith to go along. As soon as Hughes
saw her at the wharf he suggested that everyone board the motor
launch which would take them to the yacht. He himself would show
Faith how to sail the small sloop.

Hughes was completely charmed by the beautiful young girl.
During the trip on the sloop out to the yacht, throughout dinner,
and for the remainder of the evening, Hughes stared wide-eyed at
Faith Dorn.

A few days later Hughes bought her contract from Warner
Brothers—price unknown. He even bought a Lincoln car from Faith's
father, Leo Domergue, manager of a Lincoln agency. Then Hughes
had her resume her own name and start her studies under a drama
coach.

Years passed and, although the regular income from Hughes
supported her comfortably, Faith still wanted to become an actress.
From time to time she was seen with Hughes and on one occasion
she is said to have insisted, in a towering rage, that she would never
see him again or have anything to do with him unless he found her
a movie part. Hughes is reported to have conceded finally, "Okay,
pick the story you want to do."

Faith studied an assortment of scripts and decided on one called
Vendetta, which Hughes agreed to make. At that time Hughes had
an arrangement with Director Preston Sturges to make movies together, so he asked Sturges to produce *Vendetta* with Faith Domergue in the starring role. Sturges spent almost a million dollars
making the film and for once Hughes had nothing to do with one of
his movies. While it was being filmed Howard was in the hospital
recuperating from a crash, but when he saw it at last he concluded
it was no good. Max Oefuls, a European, was the director. When
Hughes' criticism became known Oefuls resigned but desultory
shooting continued almost ad infinitum.

George Dolenz, the leading man in *Vendetta*, told the story of
meeting Hughes in the men's room and referring to the picture,
which had been in the process of shooting for over two years.
Hughes told him, "Have faith, I am going to get a new director and
we will start over again."

Several years after shooting began, the film ground to conclusion and was released. It caused no excitement.

New actresses appeared on Hughes' arm in the night spots of New York, Las Vegas and Hollywood in the 1950's. Terry Moore, Mona Freeman, Jean Peters and Mitzi Gaynor all had their turn at having Howard for an escort.

To get publicity for themselves or for other personal reasons many of the young ladies babbled about potential marriages to Hughes. Terry Moore temporized, "I don't know whether I'll marry him or not—I have to wait until my own divorce from Glen Davis is final."

Mitzi Gaynor assured her friends that she was the one Howard would marry. Some of her friends even said that Miss Gaynor was breaking off her engagement to the attorney, Charles Coyle, because she was in love with Howard Hughes and intended to marry him.

The shapely Italian star, Gina Lollobrigida, was also part of Hughes' string of stars. In this case the Hughes tactic proved to be a mistake. Howard Hughes had selected her from a photograph, purchased her contract and brought her to Hollywood.

He installed her in a huge suite in the Towne House Hotel on Sunset Strip with instructions not to leave without permission from Mr. Hughes or one of his lieutenants. She was regarded as such a valuable property that, not trusting just to the instructions given her, a force of detectives also guarded her front door around the clock.

When the beautiful young actress tried to go out she encountered a variety of impediments in her way. Possessed of an artistic temperament and a true Latin temper, she tempestuously disregarded orders and left at will. Her life became even more aggravating when her husband, who was supposed to join her, learned that immigration authorities would not give him the necessary visa. He bombarded her with sorrowful telegrams from Italy and each time one arrived Gina would scream she was going back home.

All in all the guards experienced a violent time. The actress had a fully planned schedule including English lessons, drama lessons, reading scripts, and the myriad of activities that constitute the making of an actress. Once in a while Hughes put in an appearance, usually in the early hours of the morning, and then the orchestra in the Towne House dining room would be paid overtime to remain and play while Hughes danced and talked to the fiery actress. It was all to no avail, however, and at last Gina escaped and returned to her native Italy.

In the 1950's Hughes was seen frequently with Linda Darnell, Yvonne DeCarlo, Elizabeth Taylor, Ava Gardner and Jean Peters. The girls varied: Ava Gardner had been married a number of times before her association with Hughes began and she represented the essence of sophistication and chic—in sharp contrast with Jean Peters who was naive, would as soon wear blue jeans as an evening gown and preferred her own cooking to dining in a restaurant. The common denominator of all the women was their possession of the epitome of feminine Anglo-Saxon facial beauty.

From the moment Hughes began to make pictures he searched for the perfect starlet to turn into a great star. Talent scouts from all over the world sent him photographs of girls. Those he liked he would bring to Hollywood, house in the finest hotels all expenses paid, and promptly forget.

There are many stories about girls brought to Hollywood by Hughes only to languish forgotten and unknown in some hideaway. Typical of the tales was that of Gail Ganley, an 18-year-old student at UCLA. One day in 1958 she was contacted by telephone and told that a famous man was interested in having some photographs made of her with the possibility that she might become a movie star.

Miss Ganley, who had been seeking a career in Hollywood, referred the caller to her agent who later notified her of the arrangements which had been made. Following orders she went to a photographic studio in Hollywood where she posed for a number of pictures.

A few days later she received a check for the time she had spent being photographed. Some time later she received another phone call that her pictures were being studied and she would hear again. A few weeks later she was notified she would receive coaching to improve her acting ability and to prepare her for an important role in a forthcoming motion picture.

During all this time she repeatedly asked both her agent and the mysterious caller, "Who is it? Who is doing all this?" She had her suspicions but she wanted them confirmed. They were, when one day a chauffeur arrived at her home to take her to the studio of a famous Hollywood dramatic coach who revealed that he was working for Howard Hughes. The young lady grew quite excited and visualized her name in headlines as the star of a future *Hell's Angels* or *Outlaw*.

Her handling exhibited the quintessence of good taste. She followed a rigid routine. Every afternoon a chauffeur picked her up in a battered Chevrolet and drove her, accompanied by her mother, to the studio of the drama coach. She would work for two hours and then they would be taken to dinner at the Beverly Hills Hotel. They were authorized to order anything on the menu and charge it to Hughes. After dinner they returned to the drama coach's studio where Gail worked till 10:30. Then the chauffeur would drive them home.

This routine continued for a few weeks with no change in its conventionality. Reassured, Gail's mother dropped out of the picture and Gail carried on alone. After some time Gail grew bored. She called her agent, who communicated with his Hughes contact, Walter Kane, and they began to discuss contracts.

Kane told the agent, "We have a contract all drawn up but Hughes is not available to sign it."

However, Kane honestly and sincerely avers that Gail continued to study and to eat elaborate meals at the Beverly Hills Hotel, all on the Hughes expense account. At last Gail refused to continue playing what appeared to be an elaborate and expensive game. She believed if anything were to come of the arrangement, it would have to be at once. She dropped out of college, gave up her drama lessons and joined an orchestra. She was playing a date in San Diego approximately two years later when she received another phone call from the Hughes forces holding out the same promises. They insisted on new stills but this time they offered a contract and expense money. They even gave her a script, *A Pale Moon*, to study. She complained that it was poor but she was assured it had cost a lot of money and told, "Don't worry—we have expert writers doing it over."

The old familiar routine began again. This time, however, she was older and was trusted without a chauffeur. She was also permitted to eat in several other restaurants.

Gail was no retiring flower and every time she met someone from the Hughes organization her questions flowed freely and insistently. "When do I get a screen test? When do I meet Mr. Hughes? When do we start?"

Soothingly, the Hughes representatives kept promising that everything was imminent and to please be patient. And always every member of the Hughes team stressed, "Don't mention to anyone that you are connected with the Hughes organization or that you have anything to do with Mr. Hughes."

Gail ate at expensive restaurants and received a lot of attention but she was not happy. Most of all she wanted a contract and none was forthcoming. Her expenses, although minor, at last caused her to run low on funds. This was a serious problem that could not be glossed over with promises and she made it clear to the Hughes representative that either they provided her with expense money while all this nonsense was going on or she would have to go back to work.

An elaborate system was set up to furnish her with expense money. At a specific time she had to meet a Hughes man in front of 7000 Romaine Street. He would be in an automobile and, when she appeared, he signaled with his horn. Immediately a confederate waiting on the second floor of the building opened the window and lowered a white envelope on a long string. The driver of the car got out, took the envelope, signed the attached paper and clipped it back on the end of the string. The paper rose slowly and disappeared through the second floor window and Gail received the envelope containing her expense money.

This comedy continued for some time until finally she was authorized to drive to the building herself and do her own "beeping." Down would come the envelope. After receiving money in this way for many months, the desperately curious young girl walked around the place asking questions but never getting an answer. For about two years the farce played on while Gail learned the script of "Pale Moon" letter-perfect. One day she received a call to report to Walter Kane's office.

Kane told her sadly, "I am sorry to tell you that Mr. Hughes has decided not to do the picture."

Miss Ganley was forthwith released from her non-contract. She promptly brought suit in 1962 for $553,000 and like most other suits against Hughes, it was settled. The amount of money paid . . . undisclosed.

Marriage

From the time of his divorce in 1929 Howard Hughes was seen

publicly with almost every unmarried and unattached Hollywood beauty. With some the stories went further than with others. In the case of Katherine Hepburn in the late '30's Hughes' friends assured each other that he was going to marry the brilliant young society actress. The two individuals most concerned acted publicly as though there was little question but that their romance would culminate in marriage.

It did not.

In the middle 1940's it was Lana Turner whose name was linked with Hughes and, as the Hollywood columnists frequently reported, "a merger of Howard and Lana was imminent." However, the reports were that when Hughes insisted, against Lana's wishes, on personally piloting the test run of the photo-reconnaissance plane which subsequently involved him in his most serious crash, she was so torn with fear that it caused the romance to break off.

It was Miss Turner who haunted the Good Samaritan Hospital weeping and red-eyed, during Hughes' struggle for life after the accident. Lana Turner had received a forceful lesson in the psychology of Howard Hughes. No woman could come between Hughes and his love for his planes nor affect his unwavering determination to test-fly them himself.

Hughes once again began to be seen publicly with a variety of women who believed and told their friends that marriage was ahead.

All of this changed after Howard met Elizabeth Jean Peters. Her attractive face and figure gave this five-foot-five-and-a-half green-eyed, dark-haired beauty the physical qualities Howard valued highly. She possessed a flawless creamy skin, Grecian features, a figure designed for bathing suits and the carriage and posture of an empress. In addition, she had a tantalizing indefinable aura that intrigued and attracted Howard in a way none of the other women did. She was wholesome, unspoiled, and independent.

Jean Peters' father, an Ohio farmer, died when she was ten. Her mother managed to maintain the family home and provide enough money to educate Jean through her first year at the University of Michigan. Then she was forced to go to work for a time, after which she entered Ohio State University. In 1945 her roommate at Ohio State, convinced that Jean was one of the most beautiful women in the world, without Jean's knowledge entered her photograph in a beauty contest to select Miss Ohio State University. Out of 267 contenders for the title Jean Peters won the honor. (One of the judges was John Powers, famed for his pulchritudinous models.)

The prize included a train trip to Hollywood and a screen test. The impression Jean made on the viewers of her screen test at 20th Century Fox earned her a seven year contract. Her first role was as Tyrone Power's sweetheart in *The Captain From Castile*. She followed this with many other successful pictures including *Viva Zapata, Three Coins in the Fountain, It Happens Every Spring*, and *A Man Called Peter*.

Hollywood partying and night life failed to absorb Jean. Instead she pursued her interests in painting and music, sewed her own house dresses, and read Aristotle, Plato, and Nietsche.

She had already earned herself a name in the movie colony when she met Howard Hughes at a party. He made a date with her and thereafter she got the full Hughes treatment. He would call her personally, or have a call made for him, announcing his intention of honoring Jean with a date that evening or at some time the following evening. He rarely made calls far in advance. While most Hollywood actresses were ready to break a date at any time for the privilege of going out with Howard Hughes, Jean Peters was not. Because she refused to accord him special treatment, his interest was piqued.

When Jean did consent to go out with Howard she did not care to be seen at the popular Hollywood night spots. She was content to go for a ride and to eat at some out-of-the-way spot not patronized by the "in" crowd. Frequently she used no make-up and wore a plain dress which she had made herself. Howard Hughes was completely captivated, but he probably failed to realize that he was in love with the girl until 1956 when she married another Texan, Stuart W. Cramer, III, an oil man. Now he found how much he missed her. Jean's marriage was unsuccessful and a year later, on January 17, 1957, her divorce from Cramer became final.

Hughes was elated at the news. For a few months he saw no one else and on March 13, 1957, Howard R. Hughes and Elizabeth Jean Peters were married. Hughes, at fifty-one, had fulfilled his prediction that he would not remarry until after he was fifty. After the ceremony Hughes called Louella Parsons and announced, "I'm married to Jean."

The gossip columnist shouted with excitement. "What a story! It'll make page one in every newspaper in the United States!"

"I don't want it to make page one. Either handle it my way or there will be no story," Hughes told her curtly.

Louella protested, but Hughes remained adamant. He told the columnist, "Louella, I am making a bargain with you. If you put the story on the front page, I'll deny it. Write it the way I want it and you can have it, not otherwise."

Her efforts to elicit information met with no success. She tried: "Where were you married?"

No answer.

"How did Jean get you?"

"She doesn't care about my money," came back the reply. "She thinks the way I do. We are interested in the same things."

"Can I print that?"

Emphatically, "No."

"What can I write?"

"Only that we are married."

He not only insisted that she keep the story short, simple, and confined to her column but that she call him back and read it to him.

She wrote a simple announcement in a few paragraphs and checked it with him. His reply was typical, "That's no good. You have too much information."

It took five more efforts before he convinced her that he meant what he had said. He wanted the announcement confined to the few words that Howard Hughes had married Jean Peters.

Louella Parsons was thoroughly annoyed when she learned later that not only had Hughes continually checked on her story but even after they had agreed upon the wording of the announcement he called her publisher, William Randolph Hearst, Jr., in New York to tell him how he wanted the story handled and to ask him to supervise the matter personally so that there could be no possibility of a slip-up in carrying out Hughes' wishes. While these precautions were being taken, a Hollywood columnist, Florabel Muir, learned that the item would appear in Louella Parsons' column and she broke it as a Page One story in non-Hearst papers. Florabel Muir thus received credit for the story which Hughes had intended as a Louella Parsons exclusive.

After the story broke reporters searched the marriage license dockets in California, Nevada, and Mexico but found nothing. To this day the exact location where the marriage took place has never become public. In fact, no known person has been able to uncover evidence that the ceremony even took place. Nevertheless, shortly after the announcement, friends began to receive cards, such as "get well" cards when ill and Christmas cards, all signed "Jean and Howard Hughes."

The newlyweds settled down to quiet family living in their home in Hollywood Hills. Neither Howard Hughes nor the former Jean Peters has again been associated with motion pictures. Jean made records for the Braille Institute for the Blind, specializing in technical material for sightless college youth. She continued with her painting and sewing, and became a classical music buff. Occasionally she appeared at a Hollywood concert, frequently alone.

In the early 1960's Jean Hughes began to be seen more often in public. Previously when she wanted a new dress, exclusive shops sent garments for her inspection and she would make her selection without the attendance of sales persons. Then she began occasionally to appear in the shops to inspect the available models and purchase clothes. She was seen in a box at the Hollywood Bowl during a public concert. She stopped to chat with a reporter who caught up with her. When asked whether she had any intention of making another movie, she replied, "Not unless I'm offered a dream role— and those don't come along very often."

In 1965 Jean Hughes was discovered reading regularly to Sunday classes for blind children sponsored by the Braille Institute in Los Angeles. She was using the alias "Jane Smith."

About the Hughes Menage

Until recently, Mr. and Mrs. Hughes lived behind iron grilles in a two-story house surrounded by spacious grounds in Belair, a suburb of Los Angeles. However, one rarely saw Howard Hughes. Even the landlord to whom Hughes pays $50,000 a year rental never laid eyes on his tenant nor could he even be positive it was Hughes. The house resembles a French chateau and is patrolled around the clock by private guards.

Few people see Hughes. He has become a voice on the telephone. Even Chester C. Davis, Hughes' New York chief counsel and the man who masterminded the fight to retain control of TWA, did not see his elusive client for years after being retained by him.

A staff of loyal servants run the household. Elsa, the day cook, and Angela, the night cook, handle most of the cuisine. In addition Hughes employs a French chef named Robert. Harvey, the personal cook for Hughes, is always available for odd hour snacks. Mrs. Hughes employs a personal maid and Howard Hughes has a valet, Harris, who is reported by *Life* magazine to be "the only other person in the world besides Jean Hughes who has face-to-face meetings with him every day."

Even Eddie Alexander, Hughes' visiting barber, is gone. Eddie became a sometime member of the Hughes menage at the end of World War II when he ran a small barbershop in Hollywood. He numbered among his clientele many Hughes bodyguards. One day one of the bodyguards, while getting a haircut, asked Eddie if he would like to cut the boss's hair at the house. Eddie was assured that he would be well paid for doing the job. He acquiesced and a few days later a car picked him up at his shop and took him to a bungalow behind the Beverly Hills Hotel.

Eddie related of this experience, "I walked in and there in a chair was Howard Hughes, badly in need of a shave and a haircut, talking to a couple of generals."

Hughes motioned to Eddie that he should start his operation, but did not slacken his conversation or his negotiations with the generals. That first haircut took three hours because Hughes continually took, calls over a specially designed telephone equipped with an amplifier. The telephone voice came out so loud that Hughes, although hard-of-hearing, could hear it clearly. So could everyone else in the room.

Thereafter for more than fifteen years Eddie Alexander was Hughes' regular barber. Eddie was not exempt from the "standby" treatment accorded other Hughes retainers. And just as Hughes liked to check up on his other employees, he would sometimes call him at two o'clock in the morning after Eddie had been asked to remain on call, just to see if he was actually standing by.

The Hughes penchant for keeping people waiting was amply illustrated in the case of Eddie the Barber. Many people might find it understandable to ask a barber to stand by for a few hours or even a day or two. However, Eddie Alexander was once asked to close his shop and hold himself available when he was kept waiting for thirty days! That haircut cost Hughes $1,200.

Toward the end of Eddie's regime Hughes grew a full beard and it became Eddie's function to trim it when he cut his hair. When Hughes at last asked Eddie to close his shop permanently and become a personal standby barber, Eddie refused and their relationship ended.

Hughes rarely had personal guests. His wife from time to time invited a few old friends to the house for a drink or a swim in the outdoor swimming pool. All guests, even though invited, had to telephone ahead to register with the guard the make, model and license number of the car to be used.

When the car arrived at the iron gate a guard checked the identification with the painstaking attention given anyone seeking entrance to a top secret government installation. Even those favored guests who did get inside rarely if ever saw the master of the house. When they did, generally it was by accident.

Once a guest asked for a glass of milk and Jean told her to help herself from the refrigerator. She went to the kitchen, opened the door of the first refrigerator she saw, and was transfixed by the gasp of horror emitted by one of the cooks.

"That's Mr. Hughes' ice-box," screamed the upset guardian of the larder.

In this fashion the startled guest learned that Howard and Jean had separate refrigerators and no one was allowed in *his* refrigerator except *himself* and his personal cook.

Hughes used to be an expert golfer. As in all things, so, too, in golf, Howard was a perfectionist. To improve his form he hired a cameraman to take motion pictures of his strokes and then he pored over them with a golf pro who analyzed his faults. Hughes would then strive to correct them, after which he would take more pictures. As a result of the expenditure of large sums of money for motion pictures and large amounts of effort to correct his faults he became one of the best amateur golfers off the tournament circuit. In recent years he seems to have given up the game. Certainly he is never seen any more on the golf course nor even handling a golf club.

Although airplanes and flying were for him a consuming passion, he has given up flying. Correspondence with the Federal Aviation Agency revealed that Hughes has not taken a physical examination since January 17, 1955, and consequently has not been eligible to pilot a plane since 1957. He would be required to have a current physical examination and it is unlikely that he could pass one now.

He owns two planes—a DC-6 and an old Convair which stand lonely and unattended on a strip at the Santa Monica Airport. Neither one has been off the ground for a decade.

Hughes has always been one of the "night people." He appears to function best between the hours of midnight and 5:00 A.M. and frequently made appointments during those hours either to see people in person or to talk to them on the telephone.

Because he had lived this way for so long it never occurred to him that there was any imposition involved in informing some individual at one of the plants or a person with whom he was negotiating, "I'll call you about two o'clock the day after tomorrow." Most people would interpret this as referring to 2:00 P.M. but when Hughes said it, it usually could be understood to mean 2:00 A.M.

To accomplish results Hughes often worked around the clock. He carried no watch and had no interest in the passage of time. He could drive himself for as long as three days without sleep, and then, completely exhausted, he would drop on the nearest bed in the nearest room he could find and sleep for an extended period of time. When he awakened, he would go right back to the project which had absorbed him. Most of his sleeping would be during the day because he preferred to work at night.

Once he had been going over a problem with Greg Bautzer, his attorney. The latter, drugged with weariness, noticed it was three o'clock in the morning. He remarked to Hughes that he could hardly understand how Hughes could be so alert at that hour.

"Listen for a moment," Hughes said softly.

Bautzer and Hughes sat and listened. There was no sound.

Hughes continued, "You don't hear anything, do you? No car noises, no people noises, nothing to bother you."

This, indicated Hughes, was the perfect time to concentrate—completely free from outside distractions. Hughes called it "the clean time of the night."

In spite of the large number of typists and stenographers working at 7000 Romaine Street, Howard Hughes has no personal secretary to keep track of his affairs. The person closest to filling that position is an attractive 28-year-old brunette named Mrs. Betty Patrick, who works at the Hughes Tool Company in Houston, Texas. In reality she works directly for Raymond M. Holliday, Executive Vice-President of Toolco, but she also handles phone calls coming in for the unreachable Howard Hughes, and the rerouting of his mail. She receives many calls for him, most of them from crank inventors. Her standard reply is, "I'm sorry, Mr. Hughes is not here. I don't know where he is."

Questioned on the subject, Mrs. Patrick insists that she herself has never spoken to Hughes. However, she admits that she does regularly consult Holliday by telephone on problems relating to Hughes. All such calls are made on a private "hot line" that does not go through the company switchboard.

Hughes is a firm believer in the "hot line." Because he is such an inordinate user of telephones, he has learned a great deal about them and how they work. He is always careful of tapped wires, eavesdroppers, and listening devices which might create an intelligence leak by telephone. Consequently, for a long time all of his executives have had special telephones rigged in such fashion that they do not go through the switchboard. These phones are never used for outgoing calls so that the lines can be kept open for Hughes' use. These are the instruments generally known as the "hot line."

When Hughes operated Northeast Airlines he ordered a "hot line" installed in the office of President James Austin. Much time and effort went into the placing of the telephone, the way it would be connected, etc. Finally, the line was satisfactorily in operation. During the several years that Hughes was the *de facto* boss of Northeast Airlines he never called that "hot line" once.

From time to time rumors about Hughes crackle along the grapevine. Hughes has always been a natural target for rumors. He is a handy fantasy figure for big dreams. When there is a rumor that a wealthy man is buying a hotel chain, Hughes is the name bandied about. When there is a need for a second evening newspaper in New York City—a project that would require twenty-five to fifty million dollars—Dame Rumor reaches for H.H. When *Newsweek* reported that Douglas Aircraft's stock rise had no discernible cause, it was attributed to the rumor that Hughes was buying it up. (At the time in question Hughes was in Boston, ill and undergoing a thorough medical examination and numerous tests.)

When the word went out that Jack Warner preferred his lavish home on the Riviera to the hurly-burly of Hollywood and therefore Warner Brothers was up for grabs, the natural whisper was that Howard Hughes was dickering for the studio.

About a year ago, Hughes left Boston for the West by rail. Once again in the dark of night the train unloaded—this time its occupants took up residence in the five penthouse suites on the ninth floor of the Desert Inn in Las Vegas. He seems to have settled down at last in the Unreal City where there are no clocks and time never really passes. The Vegas way dovetails nicely with the Howard Hughes way. People are alert and active at 2 A.M. Money is the city's most respected commodity.

For a time, Hughes and his staff occupied the entire ninth floor of the hotel. The popular story is that at some point he was informed that the hotel wanted the room space for an expected seasonal influx of gamblers and that he would have to move. He thereupon bought the hotel and casino.

A more likely story is that members of the then-ownership of the operation were under severe pressure from a variety of Government agencies and decided that it would be healthy to show a capital gains transaction that netted them millions of legally earned dollars they could show and spend.

Buying the Desert Inn wasn't as simple as buying an ordinary hotel: The transfer of the casino required approval of the Nevada Gaming Commission. In mid-March, 1967, Hughes filed with the three-man Board his application to operate a gambling casino. The information in the application was typical Hughes—it listed his name, his age (sixty-one), and his address (Las Vegas—that's all), and his occupation as "self-employed." It also disclosed that he was investing $6,250,000 cash and assuming obligations of $7 million.

The Board scheduled a hurried hearing on the application for the last week in March. On Tuesday of that week Hughes announced his intention to contribute from $4 million to $6 million to fund the first medical school to be founded in the state of Nevada. The announcement was made to Governor Paul Laxalt, who promptly called a press conference to make the matter public. The money was apparently to be funneled from the Hughes Aircraft Company through the Howard Hughes Medical Institute to the medical school. This public-spirited generosity would cost Hughes nothing since the money involved was already committed to charitable causes.

Forty-eight hours after the school fund announcement, the Gaming Control Board recommended that Hughes be licensed to operate a gambling casino in Las Vegas. In answering questions Board Chairman Alan Abner said that none of Nevada's gambling authorities had met Hughes personally but, he added, "Hughes' life and background are well known to this Board and he is considered highly qualified."

It was also revealed that the F.B.I. had "investigated" Hughes for the Board. Nevada's Governor then announced that the Hughes donation for a medical school "had nothing to do with the application for a gambling license."

On Friday, the last day of March, the entire Nevada State Senate unanimously sponsored and enacted a resolution praising. Hughes for his generous offer to give the Silver State a medical school.

The State Gaming Commission granted the license that day. Hughes had bought himself a new plaything.

The famed Desert Inn includes a famous golf course, gourmet restaurants, gala nightclubs and, of course, round-the-clock casinos. Hughes himself does very little gambling but that is because of personal penchant, not from principle.

As soon as he became official owner of the Desert Inn, it was announced that the renowned annual Tournament of Champions wouldn't be held at his hotel. It was transferred across the highway to the Stardust Hotel.

There was a change of casino management and casino cashier cage money when Hughes took over at midnight. Hughes didn't come down from the ninth floor for the occasion. And months later, no casino employee could report with certainty ever having seen Hughes in the flesh.

A Desert Inn doorman "believes" he has seen him on occasion, just before sunrise, going out to play golf. But this report is not verified by others.

The only sure account of seeing the bashful billionaire came from Jack Walsh, genial manager of the Desert Inn. He saw Hughes when he arrived at the hotel in November, 1966. Walsh says that Hughes appeared to be in reasonably good health and was not bearded. Nor was he paralyzed or otherwise impaired.

Hughes sent word to the casino staff through his own people that the place had been showing a good profit and he would not change a good thing. The only changes made to date have been improvements in some of the services and an increase in the advertising budget. The hotel and casino staffs seem as content as Hughes seems to be about the lack of confrontation.

Hughes has a large personal staff to do his instant bidding. Although the vast Desert Inn kitchen serves many restaurants, including the posh Monte Carlo room, Hughes has never eaten of its offerings. Rather he has his own chef and kitchen on the ninth floor.

There are, in the city built by hope, superstition and rumor, many rumors about Hughes. Las Vegans by the dozen are willing to "swear" they saw Hughes driving (very doubtful: he probably doesn't even have a driver's license anymore); they "see" him landing or taking off in a jet plane (almost certainly impossible since he doesn't pilot a plane anymore); they "see" him dancing, gambling and golfing (he isn't known to do any of these today).

Actually, there is no evidence that he leaves the ninth floor. Nor can one visit the ninth floor to ask. The ninth floor button has been removed from every hotel elevator and replaced by a lock and key arrangement. Even the fire exits to the floor are securely fastened against entry from below.

Jean Peters has been seen by astute observers—though rarely. At the openings of some of the Desert Inn shows, she slips into a table at the back of the room after the lights go out and always leaves before the lights come up.

(When the movie version of *The Carpetbaggers* was ready for distribution, Hughes' lawyers insisted on a private preview showing. Rather than buck Hughes' power, the producer complied with the request. After the private screening, Hughes attorney and friend Greg Bautzer remarked: "Any day in the life of Howard Hughes is more exciting than that whole mucking film." It requires considerable imagination to understand how this can be so today.)

There is one belief that Howard Hughes has become such an expert in disguise that he wanders about Las Vegas completely unrecognized. This is probably as valid as Johnny Meyer's claim that he pays room rent in four different parts of the United States where, he claims, he is storing documents from which someday he will write *his* biography of Hughes.

In June, 1967, Hughes bought a 518-acre ranch about twenty-five miles west of Las Vegas. The previous owner, the Baroness Vera Krupp, wouldn't disclose her selling price but it is known to be in excess of one million dollars.

A spokesman for Hughes said that the industrialist wanted the ranch "to assure his privacy." It would seem that privacy was already assured for Hughes also owns a forty square mile plot of land not far from the ranch.

Hughes' living-room window in the Desert Inn penthouse suite he occupies with Jean Peters has a large window that faces on the shimmering world-famous "Strip"—a broad avenue of sparkling, neon-spangled gambling casinos, nightclubs, restaurants, and luxury hotels. Hughes has the window covered with a dark green canvas—shutting out one of the best-known views in the world. But, the ninth floor contains the only window that offers a direct view of The Sands hotel.

The Sands is the "in" spot in Las Vegas. It is easily the best run hotel and casino in the highly competitive hotel and casino-packed city. Four months after he took possession of the Desert Inn, Howard Hughes bought The Sands. Sands stockholders weren't aware Hughes' acquisitive eyes had fastened on their gambling gold mine until three days before the public was told. The purchase price was $14,600,000 and Hughes also assumed mortgages of about ten million dollars.

Immediately, it was announced that there would be no change in the successful management of The Sands.

Hughes continues to make other purchases in the area. Not all are publicized. For example, he bought the Alamo Airways Airport for one million dollars just a few days after the deal for The Sands was closed. The private airport is adjacent to the field which is used by millions of tourists each year. Hughes has become the largest single property owner in Clark County, the county which includes Las Vegas.

To this day, no one can quite understand why one of the wealthiest men in America wanted to own two casinos. Nevertheless, Las Vegas abounds with new rumors, almost daily. Hughes doesn't like the neon lights flashing at that club on the other side of the Strip so he's buying the place. Hughes is planning to buy this casino or that hotel. The rumors simmer and boil. But from the ninth floor of the Desert Inn: regal silence.

Howard Hughes and His Medical Foundation

DECEMBER 17, 1953

PRESIDENT EISENHOWER announced he believed the United States should exchange atomic information with the other countries of the world.

Premier Nguyen Van Tam of Vietnam and his cabinet resigned after months of pressure from anti-Communist forces. Tam wanted a United Front to negotiate with France to obtain greater internal freedom and better contacts with the Vietminh Reds.

An Air Force B-29 crashed through a housing area on Guam, killing sixteen, including six children.

The United Nations Security Council met to hear the complaint of Syria against Israel.

The French Parliament met in Versailles to elect a President. There was some talk of electing Charles de Gaulle but he declined to enter politics.

At the Roxy: *Beneath the 12-mile Reef* with Gilbert Roland; the Palace: George Raft in *The Man From Cairo;* Radio City: Esther Williams, Van Johnson and Tony Martin in *Easy to Love.*

The Illinois State Library banned distribution of all books "relating to sex" to protect teen-age readers.

Howard Hughes, who would be forty-eight years old in eight days, chose this day to incorporate his medical institute.

343

23

MANY WEALTHY PEOPLE, both individually and as families, have established tax-free foundations. According to Representative Wright Patman there are about 45,000 such foundations, including the Ford Foundation, the Rockefeller Foundation, the Carnegie Corporation, and the W. K. Kellogg Foundation. That number may be exaggerated but the total certainly exceeds 15,000. Inevitably Howard Hughes established his own foundation.

The H.H.M.I. Corporation was begun on December 17, 1953. A year later the name was changed to Howard Hughes Medical Institute.

The organization of this foundation, its establishment, its operation, and even its location are a testament to the Hughes style. In fact, the Medical Institute is probably the most characteristic of all the Hughes operations. Most of Hughes' enterprises, including Toolco, RKO, and TWA, already existed when Hughes took over, and it was necessary to superimpose the Hughes image upon a going enterprise. However the Medical Institute was his own creation, and he could do with it what he wished from its inception. This turned out to be a monument to his penchant for secrecy, intricacy of finance, and ability to suppress information.

From time to time the Foundation Library Center prepares a substantial encyclopedia entitled *The Foundation Directory*. The Russell Sage Foundation publishes it for the Center; and it appeared first in 1960, with a second edition in 1964. This directory reports information on 6,007 foundations.

The directory defines a foundation as a "non-governmental, non-profit organization having a principal fund of its own, managed by its own trustees or directors, and established to maintain or aid social, educational, charitable, religious or other activities serving the common welfare. Both charitable trusts and corporations are included."

The Howard Hughes Medical Institute appears to meet this requirement. It is certainly nongovernmental and nonprofit. It has assets approaching $100 million and had an income in excess of $25 million for the period 1953 to 1961.

Despite all this the directory does not contain a single word about the Howard Hughes Medical Institute. The directory states that "a substantial group" of foundations refused to furnish information or failed to reply to the questionnaire. The directory says, "Concerning these we have supplied such data as are publicly available." In short the data about the Howard Hughes Medical Institute are so sparse that *The Foundation Directory* was not able to furnish even skeletal information.

My personal efforts to obtain information from the Institute turned into a comic opera undertaking. The location of the Institute is listed as 4014 Chase Avenue, Miami Beach, but it moved from that address early in 1967 without leaving an announcement of its new location! Amateur detectives tracked it to 1550 N. W. 10th Avenue, Miami, Florida.

A barrage of letters to the Institute requesting information about the nature of its work, its personnel, and its accomplishments produced at last a two-line letter signed "Howard Hughes Medical Institute," not even bearing the initials of the dictator or the typist! It also enclosed a nine-page bibliography of articles which have appeared in various periodicals.

One of my more persistent emissaries finally reached a Mr. Wright in charge of Public Relations. I received the following report: "This man did everything to evade answers and double-talked me for one hour. He wanted a commitment that you would write nothing detrimental about Howard Hughes and wanted also to see the article. . . ."

In general, I can say this about the Institute. Dr. Verne Mason originally interested Hughes in its establishment. (Dr. Mason was the physician-in-charge for Hughes after the Beverly Hills crash in the summer of 1946. Hughes gave Mason full credit for saving his life and for preventing any crippling aftermath of the injuries.) Mason became a cardiologist, and initially the Institute was established to specialize in research on cardiovascular diseases. Dr. Mason died in November, 1965, and the present Director for Medical Research is Dr. George W. Thorne, Chairman of the Department of Medicine of Harvard Medical School.

The Institute maintains a committee which selects research men from all over the United States. The major function of the Institute is to engage in basic research. Universities recommend talented young men, who are investigated and accepted purely on their merits.

Each researcher is assigned a grade level not unlike the grade used by universities—professor, associate professor, department head, etc.—and the salary is based upon the assigned level. Researchers devote themselves completely to research; the Institute relieves them of all administrative details and paper work. The researchers are not necessarily limited to working within the physical confines of the Institute in Miami but may also work in laboratories, colleges, universities, or elsewhere throughout the world.

The charter of the Howard Hughes Medical Institute places the complete control of the Institute in a single trustee. The trustee has tenure for life and is specifically authorized to name his successor.

The current trustee is Howard Robard Hughes.

Howard Hughes and
His Biographers

JULY 2, 1965

THE FEDERAL Civil Rights Act became effective. President Lyndon B. Johnson ordered a speed-up in the development of a supersonic plane. Hanoi rejected an appeal from Prime Minister Wilson to receive a peace mission. Astronauts Frank Borman and James A. Lovell, Jr., were named to fly the Gemini 7 on a two week orbit next year.

In the movies: Jane Fonda and Lee Marvin in *Cat Ballou; Those Magnificent Men and Their Flying Machines; To the Moon and Beyond* in Cinerama at the World's Fair in New York.

Golden Boy at the Majestic suspended showings because Sammy Davis was injured during the performance. The Shubert sold standing room only tickets for *The Roar of the Grease Paint, the Smell of the Crowd* with Anthony Newley and Cyril Ritchard.

In the literary orbit, Henry Miller's classics *Sexus, Plexus, The World of Sex,* and *Quiet Days in Clichy* had become best-selling paperbacks.

Howard Hughes was fifty-nine and Rosemont Enterprises, Inc., was incorporated on this day.

24

A FAVORITE indoor sport among publishers is speculation on the topic, "I'd like to do a book about. . . ." Inevitably many publishers and quite a few writers would add as the object of the preposition, "Howard Hughes."

As a result, the rumor collector will find a plethora of indications that there are a myriad of people who have written or are writing biographies of the movie-cum-aviation tycoon. The rumors continue unabated.

In April, 1965, Louella Parsons announced, "Knowing Howard Hughes' dislike (terror is a better word) of publicity, he is sure to blow a fuse over learning that Leonard Slater is writing his biography. Slater has a current best-seller, *Aly* (Aly Khan), on the stands." The Hollywood gossipist went on to assure Howard that before he "blows his top" he should rest assured that the book will be flattering and picture him as a "bloomin' genius in the science of aeronautics and a brilliant industrialist."

In December of that same year another columnist reported that a former member of the Hughes staff, Bob Hall, was in Spain writing a biography of the billionaire. Hall had been a Hughes bodyguard.

In August, 1966, Florabel Muir, Hollywood columnist for the *New York Daily News*, the lady who wrote the front-page story concerning Hughes' marriage, reported that Russell Birdwell had just completed a biography of Hughes which covered primarily the decade 1940 to 1950, when Birdwell was Hughes' public relations "trumpet."

Again Miss Louella Parsons reported, "Last time Howard got wind that a magazine story was being planned on him he threatened to buy the publication to stop it."

There is little question that many biographies of Howard Hughes have been started but few are finished. *Newsweek* last year commented on this same topic, "It is difficult to write a biography of a ghost, particularly when the ghost is a misanthropic billionaire who doesn't want it written. For years, Howard Hughes, one of the nation's richest and most celebrated eccentrics, has successfully blocked any attempt to let the public in on his life. At least two prospective biographers have disappeared into the ranks of his amorphous organization, never to be heard from again."

That is one way in which the biographies are stopped. There are others. Perhaps the story of my encounter with Leo Guild best illustrates the machinations of the Hughes forces to stop material concerning the man from being written.

On my list of people in Hollywood who knew Hughes and could give inside information about him was a writer named Leo Guild. Guild, a Hollywood old-timer, had worked in various capacities associated with, or close to, Hughes for many years. He is now associated with Bentley Morriss of the All-American Distributors Corporation, a national distributor of paperback books and magazines, based in Hollywood.

Since many of the paperback books offered for sale by this organization touched the gray area of possible "obscenity" and because it was my function to approve or disapprove such books for distribution to a healthy slice of the population area of the country, I knew that I would be "persona grata" at AADC and believed that I might secure the wholehearted cooperation of Mr. Guild.

Consequently, in the spring of 1966 my wife and I took off for Hollywood. One of my first interviewees was Leo Guild. I told Mr. Guild my mission and what he said—practically verbatim—was this: "Mr. Gerber, I certainly wish I could help you. Unfortunately, I can't. You see, some time ago I started a biography of Hughes myself. Of course, when I began to interview people the word got back to the Hughes organization about what I was doing and the next thing you know I was visited by a member of the organization. He made me a very handsome offer. I signed a contract." He tapped the bottom drawer of his desk.

"The contract is right here in my desk."

I misinterpreted the remark as an invitation and asked, "Could I see the contract?"

Leo Guild smiled regretfully. "No, that's one of the provisions of the contract. I can't tell anybody its provisions and I can't show anybody the contract."

Wanting to be sure there was no misunderstanding, I repeated, "As I understand it, you are telling me that you received money in order to give up the writing of a biography of Hughes."

Perhaps the words were too bald. Guild squirmed before he answered lamely, "I guess you could say that. All I can say is I have a contract and in this contract I still get paid, but if I talk about Hughes I don't get paid. So I don't talk about Hughes."

When I left Mr. Guild's handsome new office in its new, modern office building in Hollywood, I was incredulous. Wouldn't it be the height of futility to engage in a project of dashing about the countryside busily buying off biographers? Obviously, it was simply not possible to pay off every would-be biographer. For one thing, how could the Hughes organization possibly know who was serious? But the more I probed the more I realized that the story was true.

Any remaining doubts concerning the Leo Guild story and many others like it were removed by a close study of the Ezra Goodman case.

Ezra Goodman is a veteran California movie critic. He is also known as a writer of articles and books. In December, 1964, Lyle Stuart, the New York publisher, discussed with Ezra Goodman the writing of a comprehensive biography of Howard Hughes.

Goodman said that other publishers he'd spoken with were very much afraid of the project. Stuart said that he wasn't very much afraid of anything. As a matter of fact, he had unsuccessfully approached Noah Dietrich some years before for his story. Later he had suggested to Hughes an autobiography. Here the response was a public relations man's friendly call saying that because of the court battles, Hughes was not quite ready for such a book.

On December 9, 1964, Stuart and Goodman signed a contract which provided that Goodman would receive $10,000 in advance on royalties and would deliver the Hughes manuscript to Stuart not later than December 31, 1965. Stuart gave Goodman a check for $10,000 and Goodman set out to research and write the book.

In the spring of 1965, Stuart received a call from Greg Bautzer inviting him to cocktails. Stuart accepted and a date was arranged.

Stuart visited Bautzer at Faye Emerson's brownstone home in the East Sixties. Bautzer was currently renting the place and using it as an office and occasional sleeping quarters.

Bautzer explained that he was a personal friend of Hughes. He said he thought he could be "helpful" to Stuart. He offered to keep the conversation "off the record."

Stuart said that insofar as he was concerned, everything said could be "on the record."

Bautzer had a variety of propositions—all predicated on Stuart's "delaying publication" of the Goodman book. The conversation was amiable but Stuart made his position quite clear:

"You're not going to buy me off. I know you aren't going to believe this, but I don't have a price. I didn't go into publishing just to make money in the first place but I've made my million. You're not going to threaten me off either. I know that Howard Hughes is a very powerful, very influential man who has lots of friends. I've got some friends too. If we have to fight, I'll fight."

Bautzer then came up with a startling offer. If Stuart would only delay publication until the TWA court decision came down, Hughes in return would cooperate on the book.

"I don't believe it," Stuart said flatly.

Bautzer said that Goodman could have access to never-before-made-public corporate records. He listed other material that would be made available.

"How about Hughes himself?"

"Nothing doing," said Bautzer.

Nevertheless, before the two men parted Bautzer agreed that he would relay to Hughes the proposition that Hughes answer, in writing, a variety of questions. There would be three sets of questions, and finally, a face to face confrontation for a one hour interview. Everything could be discussed "except the girls."

Bautzer was firm about the girls. He explained that Jean Peters got upset when she read about the girls. Howard simply didn't want to upset her.

Stuart agreed to consult with his author. "I'll give him the opportunity because he's the one who has to gather the material. But I might as well tell you now that I'm against the offer."

"Fire your best shot," Bautzer said. "Think about it and I'll be in touch with you."

Before the two men parted Stuart happened to mention that Goodman and he had labeled the book "project X." This brought a surprised laugh from Bautzer who said that quite coincidentally, he and Hughes had named the Stuart-Goodman book "project X" and referred to it that way in phone calls and memos!

Some weeks later there was a conference in the Emerson home. Goodman had been flown from California and was Bautzer's guest at the St. Regis hotel in Manhattan. He was accompanied by his attorney. Stuart's attorney, Martin J. Scheiman, was present. Also attending was Perry Lieber, a former Hughes press agent who was still linked to the Hughes organization though serving a major film company as his full-time job.

The conference was unsuccessful. Stuart wasn't buying.

As it later turned out, Goodman was very much of a mind to sell.

Next, either Hughes or his representatives concocted a unique device to block the biography. In September, 1965, a company known as Rosemont Enterprises, Inc., was formed. The officers and directors of the new corporation consisted of three people: Maynard E. Montrose, president and a director (he was also senior vice-president of the Hughes Tool Company); Chester S. Johnson, vice-president (also a retired officer of Toolco); and Chester C. Davis, secretary-treasurer and a director (long-time attorney for Hughes personally and for Hughes Tool Company). These three individuals owned all of the stock of Rosemont.

Why "Rosemont?" There was a Rosemont Enterprises doing business in New York. A fellow named Norman Rosemont managed theatrical people, including Robert Goulet. But when Hughes wanted something, nothing could stand in his way. Rosemont sold the right to his corporate name.

The new company qualified to do business in New York and in California. In New York its office was located at 120 Broadway, which just happened to be the office of Attorney Chester C. Davis. The address of the California office was 17000 Ventura Boulevard, Encino, California. All of the furniture in the latter office was the property of Hughes Productions—a division of Hughes Tool Company which just happened to occupy a neighboring suite in the same building. All of the employees in the California office, in fact, worked for Hughes Productions. There is no question that Rosemont Enterprises, Inc., was simply a corporate tool of the Hughes empire.

The incorporation, although purporting to be dated July 2, 1965, apparently really took place in September of that year, which presented something of a legal problem because they needed a contract to predate the incorporation.

Shortly thereafter Rosemont Enterprises, Inc., entered into a contract with Howard Hughes in which Hughes purportedly granted to Rosemont Enterprises the *exclusive* right to use, publish, write, etc., the name, personality, likeness, biography, life story, and incidents relating thereto of Howard R. Hughes. The contract is dated before the company was incorporated.

The formation of the corporation and the signing of the contract were bald-faced legal maneuvers designed to allow entry into court with the statement, "Here, your Honor, I have the exclusive rights to all of the information about Howard Hughes and anybody who writes a biography is violating my contract."

In addition, there is a significant subsidiary purpose. Hughes always tried to avoid bringing legal actions on his own, because as the plaintiff he would subject himself to examination in pretrial depositions, could be made to appear in court, leave himself open to cross-examination, and in general become liable to suffer all of the personal vicissitudes of litigation. Hughes never knowingly or wittingly permitted himself to be caught in such a trap. The invention of the corporate entity—Rosemont Enterprises, Inc.—would be a Hughes-type action to achieve his purpose without exposing his person. It is surprising that a trained lawyer would use such a device, knowing how regularly the courts "pierce the corporate veil" whenever anyone tries to use a corporation for a purpose other than that for which the corporation is explicitly intended.

It is obvious that Hughes formed Rosemont Enterprises, Inc., to try to stop the many biographies that were actually or theoretically being written about him.

The first effort was directed against Ezra Goodman and Lyle Stuart because Goodman was a seasoned writer who could unquestionably produce a competent biography of the reluctant Hughes and Lyle Stuart, widely known as a fearless publisher, couldn't be frightened off or bought off.

Efforts to stop publication produced the following results: Rosemont Enterprises, Inc., entered into a secret contract with Ezra Goodman on November 22, 1965, which provided that Goodman would submit his manuscript about Hughes to Rosemont before it could be published, and before it was submitted to Lyle Stuart. In addition, $38,250 was paid to Ezra Goodman for an outline of a biography of D. W. Griffith, and Goodman's lawyer, Lyman Garber, received a fee of $4,250. Thus, Hughes paid $42,500 to stop one biography.

Obviously there is not much purpose in writing a biography of Hughes if the Hughes organization reserves the right to censor it. In addition, submission to censorship would not earn the right to an "authorized" biography because Hughes' people would neither cooperate nor give any information.

The net result of the contract between Ezra Goodman and Rosemont Enterprises was a new number in the myriad legal actions involving Howard Hughes. Lyle Stuart, when he smoked out the secret deal, filed two immediate actions. In one he sued Ezra Goodman under their contract, which contained a clause for arbitration by the American Arbitration Association. This suit was started in an effort to recover the $10,000 advance plus such general damages as the arbitrator might award. In December, 1966, Stuart was granted an award of $10,000 plus costs and now it only remains for him to locate Goodman, who seems to have taken a lesson from Hughes in the fine art of dropping out of sight.

The action before the arbitrator was designed primarily to even the score between Goodman and Lyle Stuart. In addition, the facts in the case indicated a valid cause of action by Stuart against Hughes and his associates for inducing Goodman to breach his contract. Stuart therefore brought suit in the Supreme Court of the state of New York against Howard R. Hughes, Gregson Bautzer, Rosemont Industries, Inc., Chester C. Davis (Hughes' New York attorney), and Perry Lieber (Hughes' New York public relations man).

This case involved $500,000 for breach of contract (a form of action resembling a personal injury suit except that it relates to contractual rights), and requested an additional $500,000 for loss of profits.

There are other legal actions involved. Ezra Goodman apparently represented to the Hughes forces that he had a great deal of material completed which he would turn over to them promptly. When he did turn over something to Rosemont Enterprises, Inc., it was not satisfied with what was received and brought a California action against Goodman to recover the $38,250 paid to him.

In this small kettle there are enough worms in motion to keep legal luminaries fishing for years to come. But there is much more. The September 7, 1962, issue of *Life* published an article about Howard Hughes credited to Thomas Thompson, a reporter. Thompson immediately received a number of inquiries about whether he'd like to write a book about Hughes. The most serious offer came from Robert D. Loomis, a senior editor at Random House, Inc., and one of the most experienced book editors in the industry. Mr. Loomis had been the editor for many distinguished writers including Laura V. Hobson, Terry Southern, Mack Hyman, and others. He was the editor of many biographies, including one of President John F.

Kennedy (*A Day in the Life of President Kennedy*), Mrs. Lyndon B. Johnson (*The President's Lady*) and Jackie Robinson (*Wait Until Next Year*).

Loomis said, "For a number of years, I, in common with a great number of other editors, have been interested in publishing a biography of Howard Hughes. This long dormant project was activated when I read a story about Howard Hughes by Thomas Thompson appearing in . . . *Life* Magazine. . . . I believed that Mr. Thompson could use the material he had gathered for the *Life* article as the basis for a full-length biography about Mr. Hughes. I contacted Mr. Thompson to see whether he was interested in such a project. Mr. Thompson informed me that he was, but that a number of other distinguished book publishers including Harper & Row had also contacted him as a result of his article about Hughes."

In any case, Loomis was persuasive and after much negotiation Thompson entered into a contract to write a biography of Hughes for Random House. This would be Thompson's first book; he was a comparative unknown in the field of nonmagazine writing.

In the middle of 1963 Thompson submitted his first rough draft to Random House, and Loomis decided it was unpublishable without a major overhaul and a large number of "revisions." At this time Thompson became the Entertainment Editor of *Life,* and the press of his new duties prevented him from doing further work on the book. Thompson and Loomis agreed that the latter would try to get someone else to finish it, using the Thompson research and manuscript as the basis.

After searching for about a year, Loomis, through a literary agent, located John Keats, a professional writer of nonfiction books (*The Insolent Chariot, The Crack in the Picture Window* and *The Sheepskin Psychosis*). Random House signed a contract with John Keats and agreed to turn over to him all of Thompson's material. In return Keats would write a book about Hughes. Keats, as was natural in writing a biography, wanted to contact Hughes himself and try to check out a lot of the information.

Loomis, now editor for Keats, said, "I was continually aware of Mr. Hughes' reputation for spending large sums of money to suppress all articles and books about him." Therefore Loomis discouraged Keats from trying to see Hughes. He feared the possibility of triggering Hughes into an effort to stop the book.

At last Keats completed his first draft and Random House sent the book to the late Jacob S. Raskin, one of the leading copyright experts in the United States. Raskin made some suggestions for changes, all of which were carried out.

By this time it was common knowledge that Random House was readying a biography of Hughes. In June of 1965 Bennett A. Cerf, the distinguished man of letters, chairman of the board of directors and chief executive officer of Random House, Inc., received a telephone call from Attorney Gregson Bautzer who arranged a meeting with Cerf in the latter's offices at 457 Madison Avenue, New York City.

The purpose of the visit, Bautzer indicated, was to give Cerf some friendly advice. He, Bautzer, understood that Random House was preparing to publish a biography of Howard Hughes and he wanted Cerf to know that Mr. Hughes was strongly opposed to the publication of such a book. Furthermore, Mr. Cerf should realize that Hughes had unlimited funds and other resources at his disposal and if Random House actually published the book it would find itself in endless trouble.

Mr. Cerf, not easily intimidated, told Bautzer forthrightly that his threats were futile and that Random House fully intended to publish the book. The next step in the melodrama was a letter to Cerf from Chester C. Davis, the alternate Hughes legal luminary. This letter read as follows:

September 29, 1965

Mr. Bennett Cerf, Pres.
Random House, Inc.
457 Madison Avenue
New York 22, N. Y.

Dear Mr. Cerf:

I have been told that Random House may be contemplating the publication of a story relating to Howard Hughes and Mr. Bautzer suggested that I address this letter directly to you. I am informed, and you may be aware, that unauthorized persons have in the past sought and are now seeking to exploit commercially, the name, achievements and incidents in the life of Mr. Hughes, through the publication of works which may fictionalize and embellish events in a manner not conforming to what in fact occurred even though such publication would invade the rights of Mr. Hughes, including his right to privacy. Recognizing that the name and achievements of Mr. Hughes now have commercial value, being willing to make use thereof in a manner consistent with his interests, my client, Rosemont Enterprises, Inc., has obtained the sole and exclusive right to use or publish his name, likeness, personality, life story or incidents therein. The publication of any such story about Mr. Hughes would appear to invade such rights, even if the matters contained therein are assumed to be factually accurate.

I am confident that Random House has no desire to invade or interfere with the rights of others and, therefore, if in fact Random House is considering the publication of any story about Mr. Hughes, I would appreciate an early opportunity to discuss the matter with you and any would-be author.

Sincerely yours,

/s/ Chester C. Davis
CHESTER C. DAVIS

CCD:cb
cc: Gregson Bautzer, Esq.
Bautzer, Irwin & Schaab
190 N. Cannon Drive
Beverly Hills, California

The letter produced no more effect than had the original conversation. Hughes' men, however, are both determined and persistent. Not long thereafter Mr. Bautzer again called upon Mr. Cerf. This time the Hughes forces offered persuasion rather than threats. Bautzer advised Cerf that Howard Hughes was ready to make it very worthwhile financially if Random House and the author would refrain from publishing the biography. The Hughes people knew that the offer of money was unlikely to impress either Cerf or Random House, but then came the real inducement—if Random House would give up this book, Hughes—and not only Hughes but also his wife—would be willing to let Random House publish an "authorized biography" with the complete cooperation of Mr. and Mrs. Hughes. Bautzer assured Cerf that such a book would "raise the hair on your arm" and Mr. Bautzer, displaying the acting talent that every good attorney must have, proceeded to rub one of his arms to illustrate the point.

Cerf wanted to know how his publishing company could be assured of Hughes' cooperation, including interviews, and the delivery of the manuscript by a specific date.

Bautzer was prepared for this question. "If we don't perform we would be willing to agree to pay a penalty."

After brief reflection, Cerf rejected this interesting offer and stated that the projected biography would come out as scheduled.

Meanwhile the Hughes biography was moving quickly, but not smoothly, towards completion. Originally it had been intended that the book would carry the names of both Thomas Thompson and John Keats as co-authors. However, after seeing the almost completed manuscript, Thompson asked that his name be withdrawn. At the same time John Keats protested that he did not want to be the sole author. Keats also caused Random House much uneasiness because he wanted to obtain the permission of various magazines, columnists, and others whose materials were being used in the book. He could not rid himself, either, of concern because he had not contacted Hughes directly. Loomis wrote the following letter to Keats on the subject:

July 1, 1965

Mr. John Keats
Rockport
Ontario, Canada

Dear John:

I am glad you wrote a fairly lengthy letter about your concern that neither we nor you have contacted Hughes directly. I had no idea it was still bothering you. I believe I understand your feelings quite clearly now, although in all fairness I don't think you quite understand our objections about trying to go to Hughes and show him the manuscript. I think you are right in wanting to go to Hughes—in fact you are easily on the side of the angels. Under ordinary circumstances, this would not only be the proper thing to do, but could only help the book. I also appreciate the fact that as a responsible writer you feel that you should contact Hughes simply because it is the right thing to do, and would indicate your eagerness to be both accurate and fair.

This last reason I would consider important enough all by

itself to urge you to go ahead and try to make some arrangement—were it not for the fact that I believe there are extremely
good reasons why you should not.

In the first place, it is not only unlikely but almost a certainty
that Hughes would not see you or anyone else. At most your
contacting him would amount to nothing more than a gesture,
and at worst it would lead to a planned involvement which
would simply delay the book for as long as Hughes and his associates could drag it out. Surely you must agree that Hughes'
position is not that he wants a fair book or an honest book, but
no book at all, and anything that you or Random House does
could not help the project in any way, but might indeed hinder
it.

As for showing him or anyone on his staff the manuscript,
that would be suicide. Our lawyers have said flatly that if we
show any part of this manuscript to Hughes "we might as well
forget about the book." All he would have to do would be to
object that parts of the book are inaccurate or misleading or
libelous or whatever, and that would in effect prevent us from
ever publishing. We might ask them until we were blue in the
face just what was inaccurate or misleading, but I am sure they
would never tell us. If we then went ahead and published we
would be in a very bad position legally, because we would have
been warned and would have, therefore, been acting in the face
of that warning, and as such it would be extremely difficult to
defend any legal action brought against us.

I seem to get from your letter the impression that you think
there is a slight chance that Hughes might cooperate. I honestly
think you are mistaken here, and so does everyone else who has
known Hughes or had any dealings with him. I am not concerned that a request for cooperation would only further infuri-
ate him. I am concerned that once any attempted cooperation
is made, the Hughes people would then have a weapon they do
not now have to stop the book. It's even possible that they might
pretend to cooperate at first to see part of the manuscript, and
once that happens we would really have to consider scrapping
the book. Believe me, I do wish that there were some way that
we could follow your wishes, but I am absolutely certain that
this would lead to no book at all about Howard Hughes.

If you are still concerned about this I wish you would give
me a collect call so we can talk it over and perhaps come to a
better understanding.

I am delighted at the way the manuscript is coming in now.

I have most of it at home, and so far I have only glanced at it because I couldn't resist it. What I read was wonderful. By this week-end, I'll have read all of the new material carefully.

As ever,

/s/ Bob

RDL:hb
Air Mail

While Random House carried on its internal struggle with its authors and with other problems involved in the task of getting the book out on time, the Hughes forces were busily adding weapons to their arsenal in the fight to prevent its publication. By early 1966 it was obvious that the Hughes people had obtained a copy of the Random House manuscript. They concluded after careful study that a considerable portion of it paralleled a *Look* magazine series which had appeared in three installments in 1954.

Now someone conceived the brilliant idea of buying the *Look* copyright and thus gaining an additional ground for stopping Random House. At first Cowles Magazines, Inc., the owner of *Look*, was reluctant to cooperate but they finally did in exchange for a promise of future cooperation from Howard Hughes. *Look* assigned the copyright to Rosemont Enterprises, Inc.

In May of 1966 the Hughes forces recorded their assignment of copyright of the *Look* articles and in the same month Random House published and released its biography. The stage was now set for a new legal battle.

Rosemont Enterprises, Inc., started legal action in the Supreme Court of the state of New York in February, 1966. It brought a major action against Random House, Inc., and John Keats, in the New York Federal District Court. The Rosemont Enterprises suit was based upon two major grounds:

1. Rosemont Enterprises, Inc., had complete rights to the life of Hughes as though his life were a patent, trademark, or some other copyrighted process. They claimed that he had, in writing, and for a valid consideration, assigned all the rights to his life. Therefore, anyone else who wrote about his life interfered with the property right possessed by Rosemont Enterprises. It was a new concept in the law and, if upheld, would make interesting precedent.

2. Rosemont Enterprises contended that the bulk of the Keats book was based upon the three *Look* articles of 1954. Rosemont

now owned that copyright and therefore could stop Random House from infringement. In support of this theory the Hughes counsel produced pages and pages of copy from the *Look* articles on the left side of a printed exhibit, while on the right side was printed similar material from the Random House book. (This was the *exact* technique used against Hughes when Barry sued him for allegedly stealing his material to use in *Hell's Angels.*)

The case came up before Judge Bryan of the Federal District Court of New York amid a welter of affidavits, counter-affidavits, exhibits, and masses of material that would take weeks to digest. Rosemont remained adamant in its request for a preliminary injunction against the continued publication of the book. This was a harsh tactic, for in the United States a judge rarely enjoins the publication of a book. The basic American tenets regarding freedom of the press are just a little too strong for such an injunction, except on a rare occasion and under unusual circumstances. In spite of this, Judge Bryan did grant the injunction and Random House was forced to withdraw the book from sale.

Judge Bryan's decision was based primarily on the amount of copying in the Random House book from the *Look* articles. His opinion emphasized the number of words and lines which Author Keats lifted directly from *Look*—some with quotation marks and some without. The court recognized that some of the quotations and other statements were based upon fact, but the judge said, "They are no mere recitals of fact."

The judge believed that these statements were "an expression by White, the author of the 'Look' articles, of his own ideas and conclusions expressed in his own style and language and represent his own creative efforts." On the legal grounds, the court stated that it was indubitably true that any historical facts found in a biography are not copyrightable and go into the public domain for use by anyone; nevertheless, "The manner in which such facts are expressed by the author and his own thoughts, descriptions and conclusions are plainly entitled to copyright protection."

The judge cited many cases to support his point; he was particularly intrigued by similarity in phraseology. He pointed out, for example, that the *Look* articles, in discussing what happened after Hughes' father died and he took over the management of Hughes Tool Company, said that Toolco under Hughes' management "leaped ahead" and the Random House book, although paraphrasing the remainder of the paragraph, used the same language: "leaped ahead."

Judge Bryan commented, "It is highly unlikely that these and other instances of the use of identical or highly similar wording, phrasing and structure could be the result of mere coincidence, particularly in the light of facts regarding preparation and writing of the Random House biography which will be later discussed."

Random House argued that much of this material can be found in many other places. On this point the judge remarked, "It is not without significance that in these instances the Random House accounts bear a closer resemblance in terms of both style and content to the *Look* accounts than they do to the other available sources."

Judge Frederick vanPelt Bryan signed an injunction order in June, 1966, holding that Random House infringed on the copyright of the *Look* articles. The reason for the creation of Rosemont Enterprises—to prevent anyone else from writing a biography of Hughes—was not discussed by the judge.

Random House, of course, took immediate appeal to the next court, the United States Court of Appeals for the Second Circuit. Chief Judge Lumbard and Circuit Judges Moore and Hays heard the case. The appellate court limited itself to the discussion in consideration of whether the district court had erroneously issued the *preliminary* injunction.

Putting aside the permanent issues to be decided, the major initial complaint argued that the lower court had granted its injunction in error.

After hearing oral argument and studying the briefs, the Second Circuit Court of Appeals quite promptly (seventeen days after the argument) on August 17, 1966, reversed the trial court and vacated the preliminary injunction which had been granted two months before.

The basic ground for reversal by the appellate court was the doctrine of "fair use," which is the right of the public in general or anyone in particular to use copyrighted material in a reasonable manner notwithstanding the existence of a copyright. Whether someone is permitted to do this depends upon the public interest in the "free dissemination of information" and whether this is better served by making the particular material available for use or restricting it because of the copyright.

In discussing Hughes' passion for anonymity (what the court categorized as "almost an obsession as to his privacy and his rights thereto") and whether the publication of a biography is a denial of those rights, Judge Moore declared, "When one enters the public arena to the extent that he has, the right of privacy must be tempered by countervailing privilege that the public has some information concerning important public figures."

The above was the majority opinion of the Circuit Court but in addition Chief Judge Lumbard (with the concurrence of Judge Hays) wrote a separate opinion in which he said that since Rosemont Enterprises, Inc., was really a personal instrument of Howard Hughes created to suppress a biography it did not come into court "with clean hands." This ancient doctrine of the courts provides that a plaintiff who asks in court for relief in the form of such an extraordinary remedy as an injunction must be above reproach himself. Since Rosemont and Hughes were not really complaining about the violation of something which they had copyrighted but were trying to stop the biography at any cost, then the court would be lending itself to the nefarious scheme of a plaintiff who had dirtied his hands with a trick and this the court would not do.

Chief Judge Lumbard said: "It would be contrary to the public interest to permit any man to buy up the copyright to anything written about himself and to use his copyright ownership to restrain others from publishing biographical material concerning him."

The chief judge cut sharply through all of the cloaks and veils with which Hughes and his attorneys had surrounded Rosemont and arrived at the decision that this was nothing more than a Hughes instrument. He stated, "There is ample factual basis in the record to demonstrate that Rosemont was dominated by Hughes himself; employees of his wholly-owned Hughes Productions opened Rosemont's important mail, answered its telephone, and performed clerical and computer work for Rosemont, all without charge. In addition, Rosemont's part-time research man has testified that he takes his orders from the Hughes Tool Company executive."

The judge then reviewed all the other attempts to write a biography of Hughes, including L'Affaire Goodman with Lyle Stuart and the endeavor to bribe or threaten Bennett Cerf. He concluded, "The implications from all the above facts are obvious. Hughes wanted nothing written about himself, the publication of which he could not control. The Rosemont corporation was created to this end. The purchase of the 'Look' copyright was part of the Hughes plan to prevent the publication of his biography. It is inherent in the nature of a man's biography that the major events in his life must be treated, and some similarity with prior works is thus inevitable. As such, a claim of infringement may often be a colorable one."

Immediately upon receiving the decision of the Second Circuit Court of Appeals, Hughes and his attorneys applied to the United States Supreme Court for a Writ of Certiorari. In January of 1967 the High Court denied the writ.

Howard Hughes--
an Appraisal

THE TWENTIETH CENTURY

THE FIRST seven decades of the 20th century have probably changed the world more than any period of time even five or ten times greater. The only comparable period from the view point of the progress of mankind would be the Renaissance which ran from the 14th to the 16th centuries.

Some idea of the technological progress can be seen from the fact that in the first year of Howard Hughes' life, in 1906, inventor Lee De Forest gave the world the vacuum tube, which made possible radio, television, and in fact all electronics. From this humble beginning, in the short space of one man's life technology achieved giant computers, space vehicles, and soft landings on the moon.

In that same year in Brownsville, Texas, a few Negro soldiers shot up the town and in retribution President Theodore Roosevelt ordered the dishonorable discharge of three companies of Negro soldiers! An equivalent presidential act today could bring riots throughout the country.

At the beginning of the century, the United States Supreme Court was rendering the most repressive decisions imaginable. A law prohibiting discrimination against union labor was found to be in violation of the Fifth Amendment. Prohibition of Child Labor was regarded as unconstitutional.

However, despite the great progress in technology, in legislation, in judicial thinking, penology, civil rights, and humanity, the world still lags in the ability to abolish war. During the

365

seven decades the world fought four major and scores of minor wars. As the world nears the 21st century the ability to stop war appears no better today than it was when the century opened.

Man lags in many other spheres. He seems unable to gain for all people freedom, equality and elementary fairness. These are all problems of human relationship—man's ability to get along with his fellow men.

Probably no man epitomizes our neurotic century better than Howard Hughes.

25

A study of the events that shaped the life and character of Howard Hughes could lead the analyst in several directions. Thinly disguised films and books about him ranging from *The Carpetbaggers* to *Barefoot Contessa* don't begin to tell his story. When the film version of *The Carpetbaggers* was ready for screening, Hughes' attorneys insisted on previewing it. They walked out, agreeing to take no action. It is possible to evaluate the simple facts of the life of Howard Hughes and reach the conclusion that he was more a product of luck than of genius.

One may reason: Consider Hughes and his handling of the TWA situation. TWA as a profitable enterprise never really got off the ground until the Eastern capitalists forced Hughes out of control and replaced him with Tillinghast. Shortly after the Hughes people were superseded, TWA began to emerge as a valuable corporate property and the price of the stock began to soar. Therefore Hughes made a fortune *because he was forced out of control* of TWA.

This is, on the surface, a logical analysis. But the observer who probes beyond the elements of coincidence to uncover the basic causes of the rise in price of TWA stock will almost certainly come to another conclusion: that it was the flawless foundation so carefully laid by Howard Hughes which enabled the later management of the company to develop a smooth-running, profitable operation.

Re-examine the facts. Hughes set the stage for a world airline, for an all-jet airline, for profitable routes with good potential, for a personnel training system and a cadre of trained personnel second to none, and for a host of other improvements which pointed the way for Tillinghast and his cohorts to achieve a fine airline and an extremely lucrative one.

There is, of course, no gainsaying the fact that in various Hughes ventures—TWA, Hughes Aircraft Company, RKO, and others—it was not Hughes who *achieved* the success but it was certainly

Hughes who benefited from it. Hughes was the individual with the vision to see the future and the courage to accept the risks of involvement and it was always Hughes who set the stage for the final success.

While this book was in preparation the Number One question asked was, "Is Hughes really a genius?"

The legend told of Thalês by Plato, and recounted in Chaucer's *Miller's Tale*, relates how Common Sense and Genius once went out together for a moonlight stroll. Common Sense, carefully watching his way, returned home when the moon went behind the clouds and it grew too dark to see. Genius, trying to see the stars behind the clouds, stumbled into a river and drowned.

Hughes' genius frequently seems to dowse him in the river, but he has had too much common sense to drown. One aspect of his rare ability to see the stars is his talent for predicting important future technological requirements and developments. It was this foresight that led him, immediately after World War II, to diversify Hughes Aircraft Company into the field of electronic research and development. It was the same genius that caused him to experiment with Multi-Color.

In the same way, in 1944, he became involved with television. He foresaw its vast potential and tried to prevent premature standardization of technological development, as evidenced by his statement: "My company feels most strongly that no standards should be adopted and that the public should not be permitted to increase substantially its investment in television-receiving equipment until the results of all related research and development carried out during the war are made available and thoroughly analyzed."

Foresighted though he was, he could not always take proper advantage of his vision. The time to have developed a television enterprise either as a broadcaster or as a manufacturer was immediately after World War II ended. But at that time Hughes was absorbed in trying to get the "Spruce Goose" to fly, in feuding with Senator Brewster, in getting his motion picture *The Outlaw* distributed, and in a host of other things. Television was just another of his plans that never got off the ground.

That he did not execute every plan perfectly is no reflection on his "genius." The word itself presents a problem in semantics and its definition must affect any determination of Hughes' claim to it. The Carlyle-Buffon-Disraeli theory that genius is "the transcendent capacity for taking trouble first of all" or an "infinite capacity for taking pains" or "unlimited patience" apparently can be easily applied to Howard Hughes. On the other hand, acceptance of the edict of Lord Sydenham that a genius equals "a consummate sense of proportion," eliminates Hughes out of hand.

Amiel said, "Doing easily what others find difficult is talent; doing what is impossible for talent is genius." Again, Hughes becomes eligible. With painstaking effort he has accomplished prodigious tasks: Breaking speed records, making historic, precedent-shattering movies, and designing airplanes that contributed markedly to the progress of aviation. Going beyond these tangibles, Hughes' trip around the world, his construction of the "Spruce Goose" (which remains to this day [two decades later] the largest airplane in the world that has actually flown), and the more recent spectacular achievements of his electronic company, are all clear evidence of the accomplishment of the "impossible."

If Hughes enters the arena of genius, it then becomes necessary to examine the concomitant quality, described by Seneca quoting Aristotle, "There is no great genius without some touch of madness." On the possession of this ingredient unquestionably Hughes qualifies.

The individual Hughes has kept waiting for weeks, months and sometimes years, inevitably must conclude that he is dealing with a madman. To someone trying to do business with Hughes who is told to wait on some windy street corner where he is picked up in a battered old car, driven either by Hughes or a crewcut Mormon, and taken by a devious route to a midnight rendezvous—the frustration cannot help but be mixed with bewilderment.

Charles J. Kelly, Jr., an eminent Wall Street lawyer who at one time was assistant to the Secretary of Commerce, says in his book *The Sky's the Limit* of Howard Hughes:

"Over the years, almost everyone has tried to explain his behavior in complex psychiatric terms. My opinion is quite simple. I think Howard Hughes has grown old without changing his little boy's fascination for airplanes, movies and girls. To the tired, middle-aged ethos of our business world, Hughes' intrigues and eccentricities are an enigma—but any small boy would instantly understand or appreciate the secret night negotiations and delight in his complicated dealings. Unpressed, unshaven, tireless and in dirty sneakers, Howard Hughes is the Huck Finn of American Industry."

This is but one side of the diamond. There are others, as for example the Hughes whose knowledge of aircraft design so surprised engineers when he worked with them on the Convair 880.

The subscribers to the theory of Hughes' genius give him full credit for the development of the new plane. On the other hand the believers in the theory of "madness" offer other evidence to prove their point.

Hughes has many idiosyncrasies and presents a fertile field in which they can grow. Some are contradictory. He is an able Twentieth Century man of science, well-versed in electronics, aerodynamics, solid state microwave techniques, and other phases of modern technology ranging from submarines to satellites. At the same time Howard Hughes is a confirmed bacteriophobe. When someone comes to the door and Hughes already knows in advance who it is he will open the door a narrow crack and command, "Hurry up, step lively, then shut the door and keep the germs out."

It is difficult to determine whether or not he is jesting.

Hughes takes a very broad view of property rights. As one of the richest men in the world—if not actually the richest—it is only natural for him to respect money and property and to insist others do the same. Hughes goes beyond this concept to include not only respect for material wealth and protection for private rights but also unlimited protection for his ideas. Howard Hawks, the well-known Hollywood director, tells a revealing story.

Early one morning Hawks was wakened by the continued ringing of his front doorbell. Suffering from the overindulgence of the night before, he slowly and painfully forced himself to the door which he opened to reveal a tall, thin, angry young man who announced abruptly, "I'm Howard Hughes and I'm making an airplane picture. I understand you're making an airplane picture too."

The startled Hawks tried to say something but Hughes interrupted, "You have a scene in your picture where the pilot gets hit by a bullet and then vomits blood. That's my scene. I already have it in my picture and I insist you take it out of your picture."

Hawks could not decide whether to laugh, get angry, or simply close the door. Finally he sputtered, "Mr. Hughes, what you are saying is true. I am making an aviation picture and I have such a scene in my picture. But isn't that the normal thing that would happen to a pilot who was hit by a bullet in the stomach or throat? Won't he spit up blood?"

" patentability "

The answer was logical and should have turned away a reasonable man's wrath. But Hughes was far from a reasonable man where such incidents were concerned. He continued to protest, thoroughly convinced that he had a prior right amounting almost to a patent on the scene because he thought of it first and had used it before Hawks. Hawks could not change the mind of the irate young man who left, still unshaken in his belief that Hawks had stolen his idea.

Throughout Hughes' Hollywood career similar incidents occurred. Any time he thought of a clever idea he felt he was entitled to legal, moral and economic protection for it. He was blind to the doctrine that an idea of itself is not patentable. Patentability has many requirements; merely having an idea is not enough. This fact Hughes would never grasp.

As time went on, and he found that many of his ideas were used by others, he became obsessed with the need for secrecy. The world is replete with examples of simultaneous spontaneous cerebration but Hughes refused to accept the existence of such a phenomenon.

It was for this reason that he felt such bitterness against the Army Air Corps and its successor, the Air Force. He conceived of plans for a fighter-plane and the fact that someone else had the same idea earlier was unbelievable to him. He knows only one thing—he had had an idea and subsequently the Army produced a plane based on that idea. This was enough evidence to cause him to leap to the conclusion that his security had been breached and someone—some traitor—had stolen his idea and sold it to a competitor! His ego dictated that *his* ideas were bigger, better and first—sacred and inviolable.

All That Money

A question of major concern to those interested in Hughes is: "How much money does he really have?" This is a difficult question to answer. The bulk of Hughes' real wealth is buried in Toolco. Few rich people today keep their fortunes in their own names because of the heavy tax bite taken by the Federal Estate Tax and a variety of state inheritance taxes. Hughes, one of the sharpest of monied people, gets most of his fortune from Hughes Tool Company. Because Toolco is not a public corporation it neither prints nor publicizes its financial affairs. Hughes as the sole owner of the company is the only person entitled to this information, except for

Toolco
100%.

the United States Treasury Department's Bureau of Internal Revenue, which receives his income tax returns.

Many public records are available for examination so it was possible for purposes of this study to obtain a copy of Hughes' birth certificate, details about his driver's and pilot's licenses, and other types of public information. On the other hand the United States Congress wisely provided in the Internal Revenue Code of 1954 that it was a crime for any federal employee to reveal, or for any other person to obtain and/or reveal, the tax returns of any taxpayer in the United States. Therefore no effort was made to obtain the tax returns either of Howard R. Hughes or the Hughes Tool Company. Nevertheless, it is possible to piece together various segments of information and, by applying deductive reasoning, to arrive at a figure.

On May 3, 1966, the national underwriting investment banking house of Merrill Lynch, Pierce, Fenner & Smith, Inc., issued a check for $546,549,771 to Toolco. Hughes Tool Company, before the TWA transaction, had an estimated value of roughly a half-billion dollars. Very simple arithmetic now discloses that issuance of the check doubled Toolco's value to a figure of approximately $1 billion.

Hughes Aircraft Company, internationally known for its outstanding work in the electronics field, is easily worth several hundred million dollars. Although the Howard Hughes Medical Institute owns the assets of the aircraft company, Hughes as the sole trustee of the Institute retains control of them, so for all practical purposes the company can continue to be regarded as part of his financial empire. To all of the above must be added his personal wealth, extensive real estate holdings, and other miscellaneous assets.

In 1965 *Fortune* estimated his worth at $1,432,000,000. The following calculation produced that figure:

```
Hughes Tool Company ................... $500 million
Hughes Aircraft Company ................   300 million
TWA ....................................   365 million
Real estate (Culver City) .................   150 million
Real estate (Tucson and Phoenix) ..........   100 million
Northeast Airlines .......................    17 million
```

As it happened the TWA stock turned out to be worth much more than $365 million. In addition, this listing omits any mention of

Hughes' personal wealth or such considerations as the Texas brewery (recently sold), also a highly profitable enterprise, or the Desert Inn (recently purchased). My own conclusion is that if all of the assets which Hughes owns and controls could be compiled the total would surpass $2 billion.

What has all that money done to Hughes? Throughout his life, from childhood to the present, Hughes has been amply provided with money to cover his personal whims. When he required hundreds of millions of dollars *in cash* to buy jets for TWA he had to do a lot of scrounging to get it, but this is not the same situation. Putting together large sums of money for business purposes is really financial engineering. Spending many thousands of dollars to buy a private airplane or even as much as several hundred thousand dollars for a flight around the world—these are the real fruits of possession of practically unlimited funds. In the latter category Hughes could always indulge any of his desires. The real question is, what effect did this freedom from financial care have on him?

There is a general tendency to think of people as possessing monolithic characters and temperaments—to believe that they will always respond to a specific stimulus in a given way. But humans do not react like well-programmed robots. Their reactions are influenced by such apparently unrelated events as a poor breakfast or a random bit of news in the daily paper, or even a conversational interchange which may or may not have been pleasing.

The identical stimulus will produce a reaction totally different each time, depending on surrounding, although unrelated, circumstances. In just this way Hughes, only human, reacted to his background of financial security differently on each occasion.

Glen Odekirk reminisces about Hughes' plebeian characteristics and humble temperament. Hughes and his crew landed in Indianapolis once, and Hughes took the crew into town to check into a hotel while Odekirk remained at the airfield to supervise the bedding down of the plane. Hughes told Odekirk that he intended to check in at a specified hotel. When Odekirk at last arrived, he asked the hotel desk clerk, "What's the number of the Hughes suite?"

The clerk looked at Odekirk in bewilderment. "There is no Mr. Hughes registered here."

"That's funny," Odekirk replied. "Mr. Hughes said he was going to come in and register with the crew."

The clerk recoiled as he suddenly realized his error. "You mean that was Howard Hughes who came in here?" he gasped, appalled.

Odekirk nodded.

"I thought they were a bunch of bums," the clerk explained, "the way they were dressed and the way they looked and everybody needing a shave. I told them we were full."

Odekirk laughed and registered himself. Then he made some phone calls and finally located Hughes. Jokingly he asked, "Why didn't you come into this hotel?"

Hughes explained patiently, "The clerk told me they were full. How the hell did you get a room?"

Hughes had the reputation of being reluctant to identify himself as *the* Howard Hughes. Odekirk has a wealth of stories about the problems Hughes became involved in just because he would not identify himself. If he made an unscheduled stop in a small town he would generally go to the nearest grocery story to buy a bottle of milk and a sandwich or a box of crackers. His customary costume was sneakers (no socks), a tieless white shirt (not always clean), old nondescript trousers (frequently stained and always unpressed), and a battered felt hat. He would take his paper bag of food and eat seated on a park bench, or, if it were raining, standing under a store awning on the street. The appearance in town of a bearded stranger, poorly dressed, eating in a public place a meal typical of a flophouse bum, would result in questioning by the local police. More than once he would end up in a police station, where he would ultimately identify himself. This was not always easy for him because he might not be carrying a wallet or any other identification. Sometimes he even failed to carry any money.

When this unwashed, unpressed, and unprepossessing figure suddenly announced, "I am Howard Hughes," one policeman answered, "And I'm Joseph Stalin."

Fortunately for Hughes and the local guardians of the law there was always a local representative of a Hughes company or of TWA or of some other Hughes enterprise to dash in and identify him. Biographer John Keats cites this as evidence that "though Hughes was wealthy and famous he never threw his weight around."

In spite of this apparent humility, Hughes also has an imperious quality that approaches despotic arrogance.

During World War II he frequently flew his personal converted B-25 into the Air Transport Command's airfield at Long Beach, California. The normal, if not universal practice when approaching any airfield is to call the tower, identify the craft and request permission to land and landing instructions. But this was not the Hughes way. If visibility was good and he could see that there were no planes either landing or taking off, he totally disregarded the tower, selected his own runway and landed.

The first time this happened when a new operations officer was in charge, he gasped: "That's got to be either the President of the United States or the King of England!"

One attribute that Hughes' great wealth gives him is his fearlessness of authority. A story told and retold by any group discussing standing up to authority relates to Hughes' reaction before the Senate Committee when Senator Ferguson was badgering him concerning the whereabouts of John Meyer.

The Subcommittee Chairman asked Hughes directly, "Where is Johnny Meyer?"

Hughes replied laconically, "I don't know."

He was then advised that the committee wanted to see the man and that they had been looking for him to subpoena him. Hughes remarked simply that Meyer had gone off to Europe on business.

"He is your employee. You knew we hadn't finished with him," Ferguson complained.

Hughes answered, "I have 28,000 employees and I can't know where all of them are all of the time."

"The Chair feels that as president of the company you should know where Meyer is. I must warn you of possible contempt."

Again the question was repeated—Where is Meyer?

"I don't remember," Hughes replied, undisturbed.

The Chairman, losing all control, shouted, "Will you bring Mr. Meyer here at 2:00 P.M.?"

A blanket of silence enveloped the room. Then very calmly Hughes uttered his now famous reply, "No, I don't think I will."

In common with many other rich people, Hughes dislikes carrying money. He regards it as just one more bit of trivia with which to complicate one's life.

Because he carries little money he does not ordinarily leave tips. His bills are sent to either Hughes Tool Company in Houston or the headquarters at 7000 Romaine Street. Much to the chagrin and annoyance of a waiter or waitress unfamiliar with Hughes, he merely signs his check, "H. Hughes," but does not add an amount for the tip. Invariably, however, he will be followed by one of his bright young men who will give the waiter a $50 bill.

The bellboys, maitre d's, waiters, waitresses, doormen, and other service personnel, once they get to know Hughes, give him the fastest and best service that is humanly possible. Even the President of the United States probably does not regularly receive the kind of service that Hughes finds commonplace. In addition they won't talk about him. It is impossible to find out anything from a waiter who has served Hughes. Actually if he is asked the name of his patron, the stock reply is "I can't tell you." The word is around that Hughes employs special operatives who check up to learn who talks about him. Whether this is true or not the rumor effectively keeps mouths closed. It is not even possible to learn what he ordered for dinner!

Hughes' failure to carry money with him has given birth to many tales. One of the best of these is the story told by General Harold L. George, who became general manager of Hughes Aircraft Company. On one of Hughes' infrequent visits to the plant he had notified them of his expected time of arrival and General George was alongside the runway with a car. As they drove back to the Administration Building from the air strip they passed an outdoor phone booth and Hughes asked George to slow down so that he could make a phone call.

Hughes felt around in his pocket as he walked toward the phonebooth, then turned to General George and asked, "Will you please lend me a dime?"

The General dutifully pulled out a dime and handed it to his boss.

Hughes stepped into the booth, then suddenly returned to the car saying, "I don't have to spend a dime—I can make the call from the guard booth."

Hughes got back in the car and as they drove toward the plant entrance George asked humorously, "How about giving me my dime back?"

Whereupon General George reports that Hughes searched through his pockets, plucked out the dime and reluctantly returned it to the General.

On another occasion General George reports that they were in a Los Angeles hotel when Hughes asked the General for a nickel to make a phone call. Assuming that Hughes already had one nickel and needed a second to make up the required toll, General George handed him the coin.

In a few minutes Hughes returned and said sheepishly, "Damn it—phone calls are a dime. I forgot. Lend me another nickel, will you, Harold?"

To pay Hughes' bills, once a month Toolco transfers funds, charged to Howard Hughes' account, to Hughes Productions, Inc., a corporate shell which was once engaged in the making of motion pictures and which uses 7000 Romaine Street as its address. It puts funds at the disposal of L. M. Company, which is simply the name of an account at the Bank of America, and which gets its name from the first initials of Lee Merrin who at one time was the general manager of Hughes Productions. Merrin makes sure that the bills are paid.

The Penchant for Privacy

There is an ambivalence about Hughes' penchant for privacy. He very definitely wants to be left alone but at the same time he wants to be widely-known, respected and recognized—on his own terms. Some people desire privacy to such a degree that by preference they remain anonymous. Hughes does not possess this passion for anonymity.

Russell Birdwell, the Hughes publicist, relates that when Hughes approached Birdwell to become the press agent for *The Outlaw* and was asked why he was returning to the motion picture field, he replied, "The other day I wanted to speak to a man and I called him. His secretary said he was not in and asked me to leave my name. When I left my name it was obvious she had never heard of me. I decided it was time to do something about that."

This is certainly not the reaction of a man who wants to be a nonentity in public. Hughes seemingly doesn't like to be bothered. He doesn't welcome people besieging him for autographs. He doesn't enjoy being recognized and whispered about. He doesn't wish to have fingers pointed at him. But he *does* want to be known.

Some evidence of this paradox about public recognition was apparent early in his career. In his younger days he was much less of a recluse than he is at present. Those people who knew him best fix the turning point at the period immediately following the crash of the FX-11 in 1946. He emerged from this crash with a number of problems.

The accident left scars which annoyed him each time he looked in the mirror. His long-standing hearing problem became more pronounced after the injuries he suffered. For some time he had been the victim of either a prostate or bladder difficulty which necessitated frequent trips to the bathroom. The crash apparently aggravated this problem. Together these disabilities served to make him more withdrawn than ever before, caused him to eschew public appearances and to seek maximum personal privacy.

In my research for this book I endeavored by mail, phone, and personal visits to discover such facts as the contributions Howard Hughes made personally toward the electronic phenomena developed by Hughes Aircraft Company.

Certainly the development of the well-known Early Bird Satellite and of the Surveyor moon-landing craft are achievements people would like to know more about. The Hughes Aircraft Company would tell me absolutely nothing. They would not even answer my letters. All communications were referred to the public relations firm of Carl Byoir & Associates, and that firm would give me no information.

I learned during my research that Hughes Aircraft Company was regarded as one of the outstanding examples in the United States of an industrial enterprise that made a special effort to hire the handicapped. This must certainly stem from Howard Hughes' own belief that people should be employed for their ability and competence regardless of their handicaps. To some degree, of course, it emanates from Hughes' own handicaps. It would be natural for such a man to implement the "Hire-the-Handicapped" efforts.

Even this most praiseworthy and beneficent program is administered on an impersonal and practically anonymous basis. My first letters to the Hughes Aircraft Company on the subject of the handicapped were ignored. Then I received a little brochure which publicizes "The President's Committee on Employment of the Physically Handicapped." The folder also describes an interesting thirteen-and-a-half-minute sound film narrated by Bob Cummings which demonstrates that hiring the handicapped is beneficial both from the viewpoint of the employer and of society. There is absolutely no mention of the fact that the motion picture, quite expensive, and available both in 16 mm. and 35 mm. was produced by Hughes Aircraft Company as a public service.

With shrieking unobtrusiveness the folder mentions the fact that someone by the name of L. A. Hyland said, "Hiring the handicapped is good business." It doesn't mention that Hyland is the longtime General Manager of Hughes Aircraft Company.

The Personnel Department of the company finally and with great reluctance admitted to me in writing the following: "Hughes Aircraft Company's leadership in employment of the handicapped workers can be described more as an 'attitude' than as a program. That is, the company considers each handicapped applicant for employment on the basis of what he or she can accomplish in terms of productive work, rather than on the basis of quoted or planned programs. We make every effort to help the physically handicapped adjust themselves to their occupation. This is done through counselling service; by providing them some mechanical aids such as ramps, special parking space, and minor modification in some facilities."

It is a praiseworthy program, possibly one of the best ever inaugurated under Hughes' auspices. But the same heavy hand which prevents anyone from getting information about Hughes' private and personal life bars the researcher from information concerning this most salutary project.

This attitude has been typical of Hughes throughout his life. For example, someone once told Hughes that a daughter of an acquaintance of his had just been stricken with polio and required an iron lung. Unfortunately none was available in her area. Hughes immediately contacted one of his aircraft and dispatched it to the nearest medical center to pick up an iron lung and bring it forthwith to the child.

Hughes' public relations staff learned about this and essayed a timid effort to obtain permission to publicize it. Hughes, hearing of the plan, laid down an absolute prohibition, even threatening the caller that if the story got out he would be fired.

Any time that Hughes learned that one of his employees faced a problem he was always ready to help. He found out quite by accident that a child of one of his mechanics was desperately ill, but the doctors were unable to arrive at a diagnosis. Hughes stopped what he was doing, sat down at his favorite instrument— the telephone—reached a number of specialists, and had them flown in at his expense to consult and render opinions.

Almost everyone who has done research into the life of Hughes has stories to tell of his kindness. Louella Parsons related the story of the young RKO starlet, Mala Powers, who became critically ill with an incurable blood disease. Hughes heard about it and notified the hospital that he would accept all her bills. In addition he asked one of his own medical friends to look in on her and make sure that she was getting the best of care.

Some time later he learned that soldiers on their return from Korea had elected Mala Powers "Queen of the Fleet." Hughes decided that knowledge of this could give a wonderful boost to the young starlet's morale. So he equipped a plane with a hospital bed and arranged for the sick actress, a nurse, and Louella Parsons to be flown to San Diego to greet the returning servicemen.

When Hughes crashed the FX-11 into a Beverly Hills house he was helped out of the wrecked plane by a marine and a fireman to whom he quite possibly owes his life. A story circulated that he never even sent them a thank-you note. Louella Parsons says, "I know how generously rewarded the boy was but that was another story that Howard would never let me write." The late Dorothy Kilgallen said that he arranged a lifetime income for both of these men.

Hughes is in ways a very kind and gentle man. He has a broad sympathy for all living creatures. At one time he called his associates—Richard Palmer, an aeronautical engineer, and W. C. Rockefeller, a meteorologist—and asked them to drive with him to Santa Barbara where he had a date. They were at that time working on his first speed plane, the H-1, and he wanted to talk to them about it. In Hughes' mind the time to do this would be while driving to a date and during the date, too, if necessary. The two men picked him up and while riding along they hit a dog which had darted out in front of the car. The driver stopped the car while Hughes jumped out, picked up the wounded animal in his arms and insisted that they go to the nearest veterinarian to treat the animal. After the dog was in capable hands Hughes went on to his date. During dinner Hughes kept calling the vet to find out how the dog was doing.

On one occasion Hughes' prolific generosities let him become the butt of a joke. David Susskind tells this story: In May of 1948, immediately after the announcement that Hughes had purchased control of RKO, Alfred Levy, a partner in Susskind's production company, put a full page advertisement in the *Hollywood Reporter* saying simply, "Thank You, Howard Hughes." It was signed, "Alfred Levy." Mr. Levy began to receive calls from everyone in Hollywood who liked to be on the inside of things. There were calls from

Hedda Hopper, Louella Parsons, reporters, agents, writers, actors, and all the Hollywood hangers-on who could use an "in" at a major studio. To one and all Al Levy gave the same reply, "I promised not to discuss it." This was true but the promise was to David Susskind, who paid half the $600 cost of the ad, not to Hughes. Of course, everyone was sure that Al Levy was going to be the new head of RKO or, at least, be one of the top men.

In due time Levy received a call from Noah Dietrich, who said, "Mr. Levy, I'm Howard Hughes' right hand man and he has asked me to call you. You know in the course of any day Mr. Hughes performs a great many kind acts and he doesn't even try to keep track of them all. However, in your case he has forgotten what it is that he did for you, and I wonder if you could tell me?"

Levy replied, "Oh, he didn't do anything for me."

Dietrich was nonplussed, "But Mr. Levy, you have an ad in the *Hollywood Reporter* thanking Mr. Hughes—what's that for?"

"Oh, that," replied Al Levy, "I am thanking him for being an inspiration for me. You see, when I look at him I am heartened and encouraged. After all, here's a guy who goes around like a slob, wears dirty old sneakers, is hard of hearing, dresses like a bum and yet has accomplished so much. He became rich, is obviously great with the broads, and now even buys a big studio. This is inspiring to me—it gives me hope for what I can accomplish!"

Can such a man also be vindictive? Phil Santora, a newspaperman writing about Howard Hughes, said, "You are not dealing with an ordinary guy, you're dealing with a feudal baron, the kind of guy who can throw us tenant farmers into the discard."

Santora goes on to say that Hughes was "vindictive to an alarming degree, which is the reason that so many of his associates and employees firmly refused to discuss him—even to utter words of praise."

Another writer is quoted as saying, "Take a look at those blazing eyes and tell me honestly if you think you'd like to talk about a boss who looked at you like that. The guy scares me . . . count me out. Forget you ever met me. I have a growing family. And they are in the habit of eating."

On occasion Hughes' forgetfulness is pointed to as corroboration that the man is both cruel and unkind. Indubitably, one of Hughes' outstanding characteristics is his absentmindedness, but another interpretation of this same trait is that it results from over-concentration on the matter at hand to the exclusion of all other matters. Possibly the latter explanation is more relevant to Hughes.

Regardless of the reason, in point of fact Hughes gave up the ownership of automobiles because after he parked one he could never remember where he had left it. He would on occasion borrow a car from one of his employees and then forget that he had borrowed it, and consequently not return it. It is no easy matter for an employee to go up to him and say, "Mr. Hughes, could you tell me where the car is that you borrowed from me?"

In his intense concentration on the work in hand he could even forget people. On a flight from Los Angeles to New York he took a mechanic with him. He told the man to check into a hotel, tell the desk clerk his whereabouts, and carry on until Hughes was ready to return, at which time Hughes would pick him up. But Hughes forgot all about the man. Estimates as to the time the mechanic waited vary from one month to two years. The truth probably lies somewhere in between but the fact that Hughes could and did forget is unquestioned.

Hughes combines this characteristic with a tenacious memory for the things that he must remember. He does not forget legal decisions and cases or principles of physics, aerodynamics and electronics. This, of course, is completely in keeping with his practice of concentration on the problem at hand.

The Layman Lawyer

In the early 1950's before Hughes stopped granting interviews he picked up a Los Angeles newspaper reporter one day and drove around expounding his views. The reporter tells how Hughes at one point, while trying to date a specific event, said wistfully, "That was an unusual time when I was not involved in any litigation."

It was in truth most unusual because Hughes throughout his life has been engaged almost continuously in litigation. One could say that even his litigation bred litigation! For example, the court fight between Howard Hughes and Paul Jarrico came hard on the heels of a legal battle with Jean Simmons and Stewart Granger.

On the day Hughes walked into the courtroom of Superior Court Judge Orlando H. Rhodes to testify in the Jarrico case he received service of a federal court complaint in which Attorney Martin Gang sued him for $600,000 for libel. Gang alleged that Hughes had publicly made damaging and detrimental statements reflecting on the out-of-court settlement made between Hughes and Attorney Gang's clients, Simmons and Granger. Among other remarks Hughes is alleged to have said that Gang was unwilling to settle that case until his "fee was well taken care of."

The details on every significant court case in which Hughes was involved would fill a substantial volume. Almost every motion picture he made gave rise to some legal action. After he released *The Outlaw*, relatives of some of the descendants of the principals portrayed in the motion picture brought action on the ground that the characters of their ancestors had been impugned.

Part of Hughes' callous disregard for litigation probably stems from his broad knowledge of many facets of the law. Hughes is generally credited with having a keen understanding of corporate and tax law. Many who have been involved in negotiating with him leave their meetings convinced that he knows more about corporation and tax law than most lawyers who specialize in the field.

Evidence indicates that at least to some extent this is true. On the other hand, he uses the knowledge like an amateur, not a professional. A lawyer who finds a loophole in a statute will always evaluate not only whether the loophole exists but also whether the courts will give effect to it. Lawyers know too well that although the plain words of the statute or regulation leave a gaping opening the courts will interject "legislative intent" or "equity" or some other smothering doctrine in order to deny the discoverer the use or value of the loophole.

One of the weirdest manifestations of the species *Hughesus Litigationem* appears in Hughes' help to Richard Nixon during the Nixon-Kennedy presidential campaign of 1960. The facts of the case border on the fantastic and at some point reach breathtaking heights of absurdity. The reader may examine them with more than the proverbial grain of salt.

Hughes apparently extended help to Nixon to the tune of $200,000 to $250,000. The money was channeled to Nixon via his mother. An accountant was the innocent intermediary who at one time somehow had some money either left over and not transmitted or returned by Nixon and on the way back. The sum involved was substantial and unclaimed. Hughes commented on the subject in such fashion as to impugn the integrity of the accountant-stakeholder.

The latter promptly retained the internationally known lawyer,

Melvin H. Belli, to sue Hughes. Belli, one of the best trial lawyers in the United States, started a suit against Howard Hughes for defamation of the character of the accountant.

The suit came in the midst of the Nixon-Brown gubernatorial campaign. Hughes no longer cared about the money the accountant still held; he didn't care about the law suit, what did concern him was the timing of the suit. Newspapers would have learned of the Hughes contributions, the help Nixon had given Hughes on TWA routings, plus all the color and background imparted by the people involved which could have been most injurious to Nixon in the middle of an election contest for the governorship of California.

So, Hughes settled the case. The accountant (and, of course, his lawyer) received a very substantial sum of money under a secret agreement which provided that no further mention of the affair would be made during the gubernatorial campaign. The agreement was kept. If it were not for my methodical examination of dusty legal records, this case might never have come to light.

If Howard Hughes has something of the psychology of a small boy, he certainly has also strains of genius. Like many a genius he is peculiar in many ways. His absurd attitude of proprietorship over words and ideas, the bacteriophobia, the obsession with privacy —all these are the marks of idiosyncrasy that overshadows mere eccentricity.

In a sense, Howard Hughes, America's bashful billionaire, epitomizes the dilemma of twentieth-century America: inventive, brilliant, fantastic, overwhelming in technical precocity and accomplishment —suspicious, complex, contradictory, and sometimes downright antediluvian in social outlook.